Showing and Telling

Film heritage institutes and their performance of public accountability

Nico de Klerk

With an introduction by Professor William Uricchio, MIT

Vernon Series in Art

VERNON PRESS

www.vernonpress.com

In the Americas:
Vernon Press
1000 N West Street,
Suite 1200, Wilmington,
Delaware 19801
United States

In the rest of the world:
Vernon Press
C/Sancti Espiritu 17,
Malaga, 29006
Spain

Vernon Series in Art

Library of Congress Control Number: 2017932451

ISBN: 978-1-62273-240-1

Table of contents

Acknowledgements   1

Introduction   3

Preface   9

Chapter 1 Shared poverty   15

Chapter 2 Unstated understandings   35

A case of reframing   37

A hangover case   47

A paratextual case   59

A case of mythology   72

A case of appropriation   94

Conclusion: a case of looseness   105

Chapter 3 Showing and telling: an exploratory survey   115

Set   117

Mix   119

Formats   124

Survey   127

Evaluation   226

History   226

Technology   232

Aesthetics   236

Chapter 4 A programmatic conclusion   **243**

Safeguarding   247

Future scenarios   256

References   **269**

Index   **303**

Acknowledgements

Without the help, advice, and suggestions given by the following people this text would not have been the same:

Roland Cosandey (École cantonale d'art de Lausanne)

Scott Curtis (Nortwhestern University, Doha)

Tom Gunning (University of Chicago)

Daan Hertogs (archival consultant, Nijmegen)

Nicholas Hiley (University of Kent at Canterbury)

Ratana Lach (Bophana Centre de Ressources Audiovisuelles, Phnom Penh)

Sabine Lenk (Utrecht University)

Martin Loiperdinger (Trier University)

Diane McAllen (Ngā Taonga Sound & Vision, Wellington)

Diane Pivac (Ngā Taonga Sound & Vision, Wellington)

Dafna Ruppin (Utrecht University)

Sofia Sampaio (Universidade de Lisboa)

Bjørn Sørenson (Norwegian University of Science and Technology, Trondheim)

James Steffen (Emory University, Atlanta)

Dan Streible (New York University)

Lee Tsiantis (Turner Entertainment Group, Atlanta)

Klaas de Zwaan (Utrecht University)

and my former colleagues at Eye, Amsterdam: Rommy Albers, Anke Bel, Catherine Cormon, Simona Monizza, Leenke Ripmeester, Elif Rongen-Kaynakçi, Ton Söder

Special thanks I owe to William Uricchio (MIT, Boston/Utrecht University), who supervised the writing of the PhD, of which the present text is a revised version. His encouraging and perceptive comments, from the tiniest detail to the largest concept helped in shaping it in invaluable ways.

A special thanks as well goes to Frank Kessler (Utrecht University), who invited me to join two monthly postgraduate seminars during writing the PhD. As peer group contact opportunities they were extremely important and stimulating for me.

Introduction

Writing in the decade after the Second World War, French film critic and theorist Andre Bazin famously asked *Qu'est-ce que le cinéma?* It's something that people seriously concerned with film have been asking ever since. A broad question, it has taken stylistic, technological, industrial, historical, ontological, and epistemological turns in the hands of various thinkers. An urgent question, particularly at a moment when the photographic image and its celluloid base have given way to bits and bytes across a spectrum of media forms, it has reactivated interest in media specificity. A concretely situated question, it is enmeshed with Bazin's context at a moment of cultural redefinition in postwar France. That context included particular institutions (the Cinémathèque française, *Cahiers du Cinéma*), new circuits of film distribution (including a wave of US productions), and distinctly French dynamics (the cultural battles played out by the nation's political factions).

All of these–and myriad other framings–offer potentially productive ways to answer the question 'what is cinema?'. But they respond to completely different assumptions, and thus yield radically different insights. Context matters if we want to have any hope of untangling an utterance's many possible meanings. And it is essential if we want to share knowledge, to communicate. Context helps to elucidate the conditions for a text's existence, helps to make clear how it wound up in our hands, and if and why we should take it seriously. It offers vantage points, provides specificity, links the textual world to the experiential world, and gives a sense of implication and impact. And this is as true for Bazin's question as it is for the cultural artifact that ultimately provoked it: film.

Of course, we can shoot from the hip, making whatever spontaneous sense we can of a question or a cultural artifact, and offering up whatever insights come to mind. But sorting things out on the fly does not necessarily lead to knowledge, at least the kind of knowledge that we can share and build meanings upon. In fact, associations, however subjective and free-form they might seem, are themselves always already situated and encrusted with prior experience. That experience may not be articulate or systematic and may not even be shareable, but neither is it raw and untainted. Rather, it is mute. Free-form interpretation is an oxymoron, to echo Lisa Gitelman's description of raw data.[1] And although a commitment to carefully delineated context occasionally gets dismissed as dogmatically historicist, in fact it makes visible–and better, makes conscious use of–the framing strategies implicit in an any sense-making activity, even the most associational. The difference between the contextually grounded and the free-form associational boils down to the visibility of the meaning-making process. The more explicit the references and process, the more we can share, learn, and evaluate. Context, in other words, is a constant ... but it is not always visible or acknowledged.

In your hands is an eloquent, empirically grounded, and impassioned case for why context matters, what forms context can take, and ultimately, why heritage institutions have a cultural responsibility to make context publically available. Nico de Klerk's analysis of film heritage institutes (or what are commonly referred to as film archives, cinematheques, and film museums) offers an insider's look at the state of things together with a deeply informed set of cases that demonstrate both what is possible and why it matters. At the end of the day, culture, and in this case, film culture, binds us together. Culture deepens our relationships by providing a common history, informs our stance in the world by developing shared vantage points and values, and celebrates our plurality by giving us common sites for discussion and debate. Culture, to the extent that it is accessible and shared, is enabled by context. Indeed, one might go so far as to argue that culture *is* shared context.

De Klerk's case for film heritage institutes is a particularly timely one considering the ongoing and fundamental changes in the very ontology of the film medium (digitization), the transformed political climate inhabited by most western heritage institutions (neo-liberalism), and the distinctive media experiences and expectations of today's young audiences (including mobile, participatory, and on-demand access). Each of these developments has altered 'business as usual' regarding established work flows, resources, and institutional remits. Each has helped to disrupt established strategies for generating and affixing context to cultural artifacts. And as a result, each has challenged fundamentally the status of cultural legacy. Galleries, libraries, archives, and museums – not to mention universities– have all felt the impact of these changes. But

---

[1] Lisa Gitelman, *'Raw Data' is an Oxymoron* (Cambridge: MIT Press, 2013).

film heritage institutions offer a singularly vivid case for exploration, with particularly pointed insights of relevance for the entire cultural sector.

Digitization, while framed as a panacea for problems such as creation, storage, and access, has in fact proved to be something of a mixed blessing. Yes, digitization has broken distribution bottlenecks, routinized accessibility, and supported a widespread participatory culture; but it has also produced challenges. In the film archival sector ever-shifting software and digital formats have recast celluloid's slow decay as, by comparison, stable; the disjuncture between copyright laws designed for physical artifacts and the legal needs of digitized cultural forms has led to an impasse; and more. But of particular relevance to the cultural work of heritage institutes has been the ability of texts to slip their moorings and float freely in networked spaces. While often framed as a legal issue, of concern to rights holders, and an economic issue, of concern to those benefitting financially from control, this slippage, as De Klerk argues, also has profound implications for context. It has enabled films to become separated from their institutional settings, to become disaggregated from the contextual wraps that typically accompanied them.

Heritage institutes, it seems, have put a premium on digitization and access, but in many cases that has meant shifting budgetary and staff resources away from the work of contextualization (research, programming, public presentation). Yes, we have a growing mass of digitized 'assets', but from a cultural heritage perspective things such as provenance, print versions, and the many traces born by celluloid that combine to make them rich historical palimpsests and learning opportunities are too often absent, ignored, or beyond budgetary reach. Digitization has too often worked to flatten our film past, disambiguating text from context, and leaving great potential in its wake. And in the cases where this has happened, viewers are left simply to free-associate with the filmic shards they stumble across, rather than encountering them as portals to informed experience, cultural knowledge, and communication.

Of course, disambiguation is not a necessary condition of the digital. Indeed, well-curated DVDs and websites offer multiple versions and rich documentary contextualization of particular titles, and stand as strong counterexamples. And easy access to digital prints across multiple archives provides low-hanging fruit for researchers and those interested in the histories and comparative analysis of prints, while enhancing the opportunities for film identification in those cases where credits are unknown. But these endeavors require expertise, initiative, support, reference collections, and so on ... elements that have long taken institutional form in the film archives, cinematheques, and film museums at the core of De Klerk's argument. The digital has not magically taken up these tasks, nor ceded them to the wisdom of the crowd. But it has, potentially at any rate, enabled new partnerships and offered new tools to heritage institutes.

The near parallel turn towards what might, in shorthand terms, be labeled a neo-liberal agenda has exacerbated this disambiguation of text and context. Since the 1990s, governmental policies in many western nations have increasingly embraced deregulation, fiscal austerity, and reductions in government spending and simultaneous privatization of sectors once supported by the public. Cultural organizations that once enjoyed ample governmental support saw their budgets shrink and were forced to scramble in order to sustain themselves and build their audiences. Gift shops, restaurants, after-hour rentals of gallery space, 'blockbuster shows', and increased admission fees emerged as vital profit opportunities, while many formerly core activities such as research, educational outreach, collections, and programming lost their centrality and with it, budgets.

Film heritage institutions have not been spared these pressures. Initially, digitization seemed like a solution, offering a way to extend reach, expand audience, build DVD and web-portal revenues, and for a brief moment emerged as a rare growth area in a time of budgetary cutbacks. Alas, the hard work of research and context-building too often paid the price. And ironically, that bill was due just as freshly minted digital film formats offered new opportunities for heritage institutions to do what they have traditionally done best, and to do it in creative new ways: contextualize their holdings.

The twin dynamics of digitization and neo-liberal governmental policies are inexorably intertwined with a larger dynamic of cultural and social change that will continue to play out in the first few decades of the 21st century. Contemporary audiences enjoy unparalleled access to global cultural production; new distribution pathways including social media offer robust alternatives to the monopolies once enjoyed by centralized heritage institutions; and participation has displaced consumption as a dominant cultural modality. Rather than authorized cultural institutions 'pushing' a carefully curated cultural agenda, audiences are 'pulling' on-demand the pieces that they find interesting, remixing and sharing them with their circle of friends. They are using media where and when they want to.

These are powerful if not yet fully understood cultural logics. And while read by some as marginalizing the work of heritage institutions by circumventing their monopoly status, this by no means threatens these institutions' relevance. It simply repositions their work, which must now operate in tandem with new distribution systems and a more participatory public. De Klerk draws on scholars such as Anthony Giddens and Howard Becker to argue that heritage institutions should be defined less as cultural bottlenecks and more by such characteristics as expertise, public accountability, trust, and self-reflexivity–characteristics that can actually help to enable the cultural work of the new distribution systems. Film heritage institutions have long preserved, presented, interpreted, and contextualized their digitized works. But De Klerk argues that they do more, elucidating the connections between artifacts and their enabling technologies, going beyond the film text to the larger medium and the lived spaces it inhabits.

This is context that matters! No mere footnote to the text, context offers a working system of knowledge that connects text to medium to larger social developments. And while this context-creation process plays out differently in analogue and digital contexts, it remains the defining element of these institutions' public accountability. Film heritage institutes can embrace their contextual responsibilities as much by maintaining and deploying analogue film technologies and presenting historically responsible programs as by creating new ways to meaningfully present works and their histories in digital settings, all in the interest of a shared and, indeed, participatory culture.

In an era when we rightly celebrate the promise of a more dynamically connected and creatively engaged public for culture, we also need critically to assess that culture's enabling logics. The algorithmic layer behind many of today's digital cultural interactions is itself authored, and we are slowly learning that this authorship has both agency and an agenda, even if both are routinely masked. In this setting, the public accountability of (film) heritage institutes is more urgent than ever. Their expertise and trust is as relevant to the maintenance of a performative *dispositif*, in which the public can experience the analogue technological and textual composites that defined a century of cultural practice, as it is to the new contextualizing strategies designed for digital texts in today's networked and participatory world. Nico de Klerk maps multiple paths and illuminates various strategies towards embracing both goals in the pages ahead.

Culture binds us, is common to us, indeed, enables a lived sense of the first-person plural. Simply deferring to the logics of neo-liberalism will create markets with different buy-in points and cultural participants who shoot from the hip. But markets do not make a public any more than free association makes a culture. And this is where context matters, and why the public accountability of heritage institutes matters. So long as film heritage institutes continue to do the hard work of contextualization, of illuminating the relations among texts, media, and society, we have a hope of creating knowledge, of building shared frames, of finding common cause, even if for purposes of disagreement.

William Uricchio
Professor of Comparative Media Studies, MIT
Professor of Comparative Media History, Utrecht University

Preface

This work, a revised and updated version of my 2015 doctoral thesis of the same title, is rooted in my research and curatorial work in a film heritage institute, at the time known as the Nederlands Filmmuseum. During my tenure there my activities focused on film and film-related materials, their histories and contexts that were largely uncharted in both film archiving and film historiography. It was concerned with such topics as early nonfiction film, colonial cinema, the program format or advertising films. Although the original occasion for my employment there was research on early cinema, it soon became a voyage of discovery through the entire archive, a voyage fueled by ongoing surprise. Sheer surprise at the range of materials I had been unfamiliar with. Joyful surprise at the immense variety and wealth of these materials and the opportunities for research and presentation they offered. But an unsettling surprise, too, because I gradually learned that many film heritage institutes were—and are—not in the habit of fully acquainting their public with this variety and wealth of their collections. As my own experiences and ideas have traced a growing awareness of the importance of contexts of all kinds, matched by an increasing dissatisfaction with the almost exclusive approach—and restriction—within film heritage institutes to films as objects of art, I have never ceased wondering about this withholding of wealth. It is this unwillingness to share materials and information with the public that has prompted what follows.

Framed by an introductory and a conclusive chapter, this work's two central parts are complementary. The first argues a specific way of doing film heritage work that is based on the range of sources in the care of institutes dedicated to this heritage. Although in its most widely known form cinema was, and is, a theatrically presented, overwhelmingly popular entertainment, it also appeared, and appears, in various technological supports, for many other purposes besides entertainment or aesthetic enjoyment, in many performative configurations, in many different venues and for many different audience categories. This part, therefore, is structured according to a series of case studies, all based on my own archival work. Each case study explores the histories of an object commonly found in the archives of general (i.e. national or regional) film heritage institutes. But because these institutes do not commonly or consistently present these objects to the public in screenings or exhibitions nor promulgate their histories in visitor information media, my case studies are also meant as a more general investigation into the public role of heritage institutes.

In the second part I expand on these case studies by contextualizing my observations and experiences in one institute and enlarging this personal 'database' with an exploratory survey, and its evaluation, of the public activities of 24, mostly publicly funded film heritage institutes around the world. "Public activities" here refers to both public presentations and visitor information about those presentations. I call it exploratory, because there is no research of any substantial scope or longitude of such activities.[2] So this is a modest start, essentially based on data collected from these institutes' websites during the month of February 2014. These two central chapters, although they mark the difference between my work in one film heritage institute and the information culled from the other institutes, share the same concern: the institutes' performance of public accountability through the two abovementioned public activities.

To sum up this work: chapter 1 is an introductory chapter, titled 'Shared poverty', in which I present a general account of what I consider the deficient public role of film heritage institutes. Chapter 2, titled 'Unstated understandings', contains the abovementioned case studies of film archival objects and their historical contexts and resonances that are potentially relevant for the public activities these institutes undertake. This chapter concludes with a conceptual apparatus that captures the full range of objects in film heritage institutes' care in order to enable their meaningful presentation. Chapter 3 contains the survey followed by its evaluation. This evaluation zooms in on three aspects of the surveyed institutes' public activities that are emblematic of their poor public performance: the limited temporal range of materials presented to their home public; the lack of transparent and consistent screening policies in an era of technological flux; and the notion of film as a universal language that underlies a general focus on film as an aesthetic object. The survey's

---

[2] A recently completed PhD examines the policies and their changes of three film heritage institutes; see: Ramesh Kumar, National archives: policies, practices, and histories. A study of the National Film Archive of India, Eye Film Institute Netherlands, and the National Film and Sound Archive, Australia (2016).

database of web information about these public presentations and visitor information of the month in which it was conducted cannot be retrieved in its entirety anymore. Readers interested in this research source are advised to send a request to the author.[3] In the final chapter 4 I present my conclusions, the most general and critical of which is that the transfer of full, up-to-date knowledge to their publics is not film heritage institutes' major concern. And this, I argue, contributes in its turn to their marginal intellectual and moral position in the public sphere. However, as my conclusions are programmatic, I also present a number of suggestions to counteract this marginality and improve the performance of public accountability and meaningfulness, notably on the basis of digital technology.

Next, a brief word about the term *film heritage institutes*. I use this admittedly burdensome term to cover various types of institute dedicated to the custodianship of the film heritage of a given society. This role of the custodian can be seen as taking three functionally different forms: there are institutes that are solely devoted to collecting, researching, describing and/or preserving film and film-related materials; others necessarily restrict themselves to public presentations only, as they have no collections of their own; and then there are institutes whose presentations may draw on the archival collections they preserve, describe and/or research. One might distinguish these types by different terms: film archives, cinematheques, and film museums, respectively. However, the official names of my set of 24 institutes surveyed shows that this distinction in nomenclature is merely academic. Functionally, the institutes in my set would be museums, as they all have collections that are featured, to a lesser or greater degree, in their public presentations. But as most of them are called *cinematheque* or *archive*, I use *film heritage institute* instead as a catch-all term.

In writing this work two sociological works functioned as signposts: Howard Becker's *Art worlds* and Anthony Giddens's *The consequences of modernity*.[4] Becker, in his classic book, took a contrary approach to the

---

[3] This database is a Word file listing all 24 film heritage institutes' presentations and their visitor information about these presentations for the month of February 2014; the original designs and layouts as well as illustrations have been elided. Requests can be addressed to: nhdeklerk@gmail.com.

[4] Howard S. Becker, *Art worlds* (1984 [1982]); Anthony Giddens, The consequences of modernity (2013 [1990]).

mainstream sociology of art, which at the time—the early 1980s—customarily took "the artist and art work (...) as central to the analysis of art as a social phenomenon." He, however, defined his approach "in a more technical way, to denote the network of people whose cooperative activity, organized via their joint knowledge of conventional means of doing things, produces the kind of art works that art world is noted for."[5] It means, for instance, that artists who produce outsized work or have outrageous ideas relative to the conventions within specific art worlds will have more trouble finding outlets and co-workers to realize these works and ideas. (And if, in the end, they do, that doesn't necessarily mean that the artist is a genius and the rest of us are duffers; it may, for instance, have been the outcome of someone in that network who was willing, for whatever reason, to take a risk.) I found the idea of art worlds a sobering concept for its focus on how a work of art—or, more generally, a cultural product—is created and finds its way into the world; on its material and personal resources; and on the conventions (including aesthetics) that contribute to its acceptance by distributing organizations (archives, museums, galleries, concert halls, publishers, TV stations, etc.). Becker's work has been grouped under an approach called the production of culture, which studies the conditions that determine which products have a greater chance of becoming part of the culture by virtue of their being published, performed, broadcast or otherwise exposed to an audience.[6] A most important aspect that this approach brings sharply in the crosshairs is that of the gatekeeper: "a gatekeeper filters products (or people) as they enter or leave a system."[7] It is the gatekeeper function that captures the abovementioned public activities of film heritage institutes that I focus on in what follows.

Establishing what it is that these institutes allow to leave their gates is not merely a matter of what they put out. The very limits they set as gatekeepers also affect their publics' sense of their film heritage and its histories. That, however, is not easy to account for. In effect, Becker does not accommodate the public into his scheme of things, except in the shape of art criticism, and even then largely as input for those very

---

[5] Becker (1984), pp. xi; x.

[6] See for an overview: Victoria D. Alexander, Sociology of the arts: exploring fine and popular forms (2011 [2003]), pp. 65-172; see also: Diana Crane, The production of culture: media and the urban arts (1994 [1992]).

[7] Alexander (2011), p. 76.

producers' and distributors' considerations. Surely, it would take a completely different approach and a different type of research to get a sense of what publics take away from cultural artifacts, and their publicity, on offer. (For instance, a recent study on this topic was based on archival and ethnographic research and focused on one location, Nottingham, England; I suspect that the necessarily empirical aspect of such studies makes the local level the most feasible.[8]) But reception per se is not what I am actually after in this book, rather what it is that visitors are offered.

Here, then, Anthony Giddens takes over from Becker, particularly with his concept of *expert systems*, which he defines as impersonal "systems of technical accomplishment or professional expertise that organise large areas of the material and social environment in which we live today", and how they are accepted and feed into a society's members' concepts and practices.[9] This term allows one to evaluate the completeness and soundness of the film heritage institutes' professional expertise to which the public is exposed. In other words, the moment of publicizing their presentations provides heritage institutes not just with an opportunity, but also a responsibility to put reliable contextual and historical information forward for consideration and to potentially enrich visitors' encounters with their artifacts. "Potentially" means, of course, that the public does not have to like or believe what it is they offer. As a typical characteristic of modern life, according to Giddens, expert systems merely proffer *claims* to truth and expertise. Their success lies in the ways they are able to convince their publics of their authoritativeness. Of course, the word *convince* does not imply a mere capitulation to one or another current popular taste or ideological position. Quite on the contrary, at the very least it should be a function of the state-of-the-art knowledge that—in this particular case— film heritage institutes are mandated and expected to have. There, opportunities present themselves to harness that trust—another central term in Giddens's work—to other ends.

Unlike, say, a film studio or record company that markets the products it has selected and developed from a much larger range of works and proposals submitted (which for all practical purposes will remain forever unknown), film heritage institutes make public only a selection, predominantly in broad terms of a number of film genres or types, from

---

[8] Mark Jancovich, Lucy Faire with Sarah Stubbings, *The place of the audience: cultural geographies of film consumption* (2008 [2003]).

[9] Giddens (2013), p. 27.

the much larger range of artifacts they *have* accepted as belonging to that heritage—and which therefore need not remain forever unknown to the public. According to their mandates, film heritage institutes are about their collections and their histories—i.e. their films' and film-related objects' presence at certain places, at certain times—, and what they show and tell about them, whether they are about war or slapstick. In promotional terms, their expertise of cinema and its histories is their unique selling proposition. In professional terms, if a film heritage institute has no such expertise to offer, it threatens to drift from its public and societal underpinnings.

Much of my outlook on film heritage work was formed during the first decade of my tenure at the Nederlands Filmmuseum, where I enjoyed the intellectual stimulus of a number of colleagues. Prominent among them were Daan Hertogs, who was responsible for hiring me, and Hoos Blotkamp, who was the museum's director between 1987 and 2000. In fact, it was she who guided the transformation of the museum from a rather sleepy place into a leader in the field of both archival and public activities by 'collecting' a number of people whose ideas and vision led to an astonishingly rich and creative phase in the museum's existence. It was a time during which I was allowed to learn and then demonstrate how any type of material, film or film-related, canonical or totally unknown, could result in exciting work.

In recognition of the complete trust and the freedom bestowed on me during this significant time, I dedicate this work to Daan Hertogs and to the cherished memory of Hoos Blotkamp (1943-2014).

Chapter 1

Shared poverty

Allow me to start by stating the obvious. A traditional film element, that is to say any analogue type or generation of motion picture and/or audio carrier that is being accessioned to a film archive never comes alone. It arrives with a history, or rather: histories. Some of these histories have left traces on the element: accidentally through wear and tear (e.g. scratches, repair splices, torn perforation) and inevitably as a result of chemical reactions (e.g. shrinkage, color-fading, vinegar syndrome) or biological processes (the growth of fungi or bacteria). They all point to a small set of causes, mostly of interest to the restorer, at various points in the lifespan of an element during recording (in the equipment), processing (in the lab), screening (in the projector), and storage conditions. Other histories enter the archive in the shape of various elements of the same title (ranging from camera negatives to outtakes to any number of projection prints), on the basis of which the archivist can reconstruct its genealogy during production, distribution and/or exhibition. Besides incidental traces, such as carelessness or indifference, there are functional traces that point to a wide range of trade practices and interventions, from manufacturers' names and edge codes printed on virgin film stock to signals for projectionists (e.g. punch holes near the end of a reel). And then, of course, an element's stock, gauge, aspect ratio as well as the presence or absence of perforation, color or type of soundtrack are all indicative of technical, legal, financial, marketing, or stylistic histories and contexts (and helpful in determining the date of the element). Projection prints have particular histories in the shape of regular, invasive measures taken at various moments during its commercial life: additions (e.g. foreign distributors' logos, subtitles, extraneous footage), excisions (e.g. censorship cuts), or permutations (e.g. dubbing tracks, alternate colorings or endings).[10] Finally, there are traces that can only be found outside the

---

[10] Digital technologies as such allow chronologizing, too. But in contradistinction to analogue elements its histories only affect the carrier (if that word is still applicable), not the work. But that, of course, only applies to digitized works; decay of born-digital materials affects both as well; see: Teresa Soleau, 'Preventing digital decay', at: The Iris (October 20, 2014).

element, in sources that sometimes do, sometimes do not accompany its accessioning, or come without any trace of the film elements. Examples are business and personal papers, scripts, set photos and stills, censorship records, catalogues, posters, program bills, etc.[11] For some histories, moreover, one will need to inspect even more remote sources, some of which may be obvious (e.g. newspapers, biographies), others less (e.g. demographic data, tax laws); the range of potential "signifying contexts" is open-ended.[12] There is, then, a wealth of sources for a wealth of histories.

I have no illusions about how all this may strike the informed reader as unsurprising, if not indeed obvious and self-evident. But what strikes me as equally self-evident, obvious, yet astounding at the same time is how little of this wealth is shared by the film heritage world with their publics and how the knowledge to be gained from it mostly enriches those who deal professionally with and have privileged access to film archival materials: the archivist and the scholar. Shocking even is that in their public activities, as I will show, many film heritage institutes by all appearances have not allowed themselves to benefit from the knowledge scholars have thus been enabled to develop. Instead, they are inclined to confine themselves to the received wisdom of a professed aesthetic approach, at the expense of so many other aspects, and to a largely repertorial range of presentations, at the expense of so many other materials they administer in their collections. It is this incongruity that lies at the basis of my argument. I will comment on this incongruity by juxtaposition in chapters 2 and 3 of this work.

My general statements about this state of shared poverty summarize a tendency that I observed in a survey, performed during the month of February 2014, of the websites of 24 film heritage institutes worldwide. There are exceptions, on which I will duly report, too, but it is a tendency no less. These statements, however, may seem counterintuitive now that so many materials are being digitized (from both restored and unrestored sources) and made available through numerous and variously accessible

---

[11] These elements, which of course have their own histories and ways of decay, are called film-related, because they were generated by the production, distribution or exhibition of a particular film. Sequentiality, however, does not, in my view, imply a hierarchy of archival or historical importance, as will become clear in this text.

[12] I borrow the term *signifying context* from: Giorgio Bertellini, 'Shipwrecked spectators: Italy's immigrants at the movies in New York, 1906-1916', in: *The Velvet Light Trap* (1999), p. 47, although he used it specifically with regard to reception.

websites as well as through DVDs. Some of these are excellent, as they provide contextualizations that are instructive and productive. Still there is more than enough to give one pause.

For instance, in the same month of February 2014 an ambitious web portal was launched, European Film Gateway 1914,[13] to commemorate the 100th anniversary of the beginning of World War I. Twenty-one European film heritage institutes contributed materials digitized from their collections to this portal. EFG1914 is a so-called aggregator, representing the European film archival sector for the larger Europeana network that gives access to countless digitized museum, library, and archival materials.[14] Besides the films, magic lantern slides, posters, press articles, and stills uploaded since February 2014, Europeana features many more materials from or related to the war—e.g. official documents, postcards, letters, diaries—from sources both public and private. A wealth of sources, indeed. But is it a wealth of histories?

To gain prominence on the web is first of all a matter of the sheer bulk of digitized materials and (meta)data. This is a circumstance reinforced by funders who want to see their money's worth. But as funding, particularly for ad hoc inter-institutional, collaborative projects (not uncommon in the film heritage world, if only for getting money for digitization in the first place), often have a finite running time, two of the most distinctive advantages of digital databases, updating and maintenance, cannot usually be sustained. Furthermore, unless based on sound IT architecture and tools, the editorial requirements to make that bulk meaningful and meaningfully productive are commonly thwarted by a portal's very size. Hence the 'outsourcing' of editorial, determinative, and/or interpretative tasks to the user. Wikipedia, YouTube, and Internet Movie Database (IMDb) are among the most popular as well as more sustainable examples of this strategy. Because of their high participation rate, the latitude allowed in content input and, certainly in the case of Wikipedia, a capacity for quick self-correction, these sites' editorial control can remain relatively weak and is rather a matter of marginal review (all three have a set of 'soft' guidelines: IMDb, in the coverage section of its 'Contributor zone', admits being "historically" incomplete;[15] Wikipedia "does not employ hard-and-

---

13 http://www.europeanfilmgateway.eu/1914.

14 http://project.efg1914.eu/.

15 http://www.imdb.com/czone/?ref_=nv_cm_cz_2.

fast rules",[16] while those of YouTube are often simply disregarded). But when participation is less frequent, less widespread or limited in terms of time or personnel, this new editorial model, based on the expected aggregate wisdom of the crowd, can become problematic, all the more so where it concerns film materials, as in EFG1914.[17]

One problematic example I happened upon in the hundreds of hours of uploaded films to EFG1914 involves the partial overlap in two prints, one from the Deutsches Filminstitut Filmmuseum, Frankfurt, and one from Eye, Amsterdam, of scenes showing war-related destruction. The German print, titled KINO-KRIEGSSCHAU NO. 14, is an episode of a war newsreel series that shows, according to the accompanying synopsis, the aftermath of an attack by the Ottoman navy on ships, facilities, and infrastructure at the Russian commercial port of Novorossiysk and its environs, in late October 1914. It lists Germany as production country, Edmund Hubert as production company, 1914 as year of production, and has a running time of seven minutes. The footage suggests that all its action took place on the Russian Black Sea Coast. The Dutch print has an archive title, KOPICZINCE, and shows the ceremonies on the occasion of the retaking of the town by that name by German and Austro-Hungarian troops, followed by the scenes of the aforementioned destruction, now attributed to the Russians, sometime in 1916. It lists Austria as country of production, Sascha Film as production company, 1916 as year of production, and it has a running time of ten minutes. (The Dutch synopsis, incidentally, situates the events in Ukraine, without mentioning that at the time the town belonged to—and was apparently reclaimed by—what was then the Austro-Hungarian Empire.)

---

[16] http://en.wikipedia.org/wiki/Wikipedia:Policies_and_guidelines.
In his survey of Wikipedia's historical articles historian Roy Rosenzweig concluded, nevertheless, that both its open-source model and the quality of contributions cannot be dismissed out of hand; see: 'Wikipedia: can history be open source?', in: *Clio wired: the future of the past in the digital age* (2011), pp. 51-82 (orig. publ. in 2006).

[17] One way to counter this circumstance, albeit without solving all problems, is to form strategic alliances; see for instance the Library of Congress's Flickr pilot project to tag the Library's historic photographs; see:
https://www.flickr.com/photos/library_of_congress/collections/72157601355524315/. See for a skeptical account of current crowdsourcing: Tom Simonite, 'The decline of Wikipedia', in: *MIT Technology Review* (October 22, 2013).

As far as the destruction scenes are concerned, the German synopsis casts doubt upon this latter version of the events by telling us that the Edmund Hubert company marketed this newsreel by advertising it as being "sensational"; this would specifically apply to the scenes of burning naphtha and gasoline storage tanks. Indeed, one can infer from the Dutch print's title panels that Hubert's footage was bought at some point by the Austrian company Sascha Film (all panels bear the stamp of that company), which in its turn sold it to an unknown Dutch distributor. One may therefore surmise, furthermore, that the compilation of the Novorossiysk and Kopyczynce footage was done in Austria, where it obviously would have functioned as propaganda—even though it presupposed audiences' unfamiliarity with the geographical niceties—, rather than in neutral Holland. (Interestingly, no attempt was made to render these compiled scenes more similar by either coloring the black-and-white Kopyczynce material or by striking a black-and-white variants of the tinted Novorossiysk scenes.)

This is an example that one can *only* happen upon at this portal, because the two uploaded films have no search terms—such as production company, country and year of production, location, or even the word *fire*—in common. And although the lengthier and more thorough German synopsis seems more dependable than the Dutch one—after all, Kopyczynce, in today's western Ukraine, at the time was a trading center in an agricultural region, unlikely to have harbored huge storage facilities for industrial fuels[18]—, users may well remain unaware of the histories involved, in the theaters of war as well as in the contemporary film trade. The knowledge they might gain (assuming they find it satisfactory) depends on which of the two uploaded records, once again unrelated as far as the portal is concerned, they have consulted. The Dutch print's first shot, for instance, shows a sign on a station building saying "Kopiczince", thereby grounding subsequent scenes in that town by implication. With no contradictory information in its title panels—of which the last one merely

---

[18] And *if* it had harbored such facilities, they would have been located near a railway: in peacetime, fuels and similar cargo from the eastern hinterland had been transported by rail to Vienna's Nordbahnhof; see: Carina Lesky, '"Der Nordbahnhof in Wien ist seit 4 Uhr morgens ein Bild lebhafter Bewegung." Szenen und Gestalten des Alltäglichen am Wiener Nordbahnhof zwischen 1914 und 1918', paper presented at *Kriegsschauplatz Wien. Transit, Verwaltung, Konsum. Internationales Kolloquium des Clusters Geschichte der Ludwig Boltzmann Gesellschaft*, Vienna, April 21-22, 2016.

announces, "The gas tanks set afire by the Russians"—this may have
sufficed as persuasive arsenal to continue to lead spectators then, and
archivists and users now, to believe that the devastations shown took place
in this Ukranian town. The Dutch print, then, camouflages its history of
scenes compiled from various sources to suggest a series of connected
events in a circumscribed area. The German print, on the other hand,
establishes its veracity by an itemized sequence of destructions of objects
commonly found in a commercial port, the reason, perhaps, that its
intertitles omitted mentioning locations at all.

The EFG1914 portal is coordinated—by the Deutsches Filminstitut
Filmmuseum—, but has not been edited in any meaningful sense to point
to or weed out contradictory and incorrect information, mold it in a
uniform way, provide cross-references. Nor to relevantly *limit* the search
results: its connection to the wider Europeana network was apparently
conceived as an asset, but looking for World War I footage one also gets
World War II footage; using the search term Verdun one also hits a 1964
news item on the Christmas season in Austria; and one result of using the
search term Black Sea is a 1938 documentary on fishery off the coast of
Scotland... And neither editorial policies nor initiatives by the
participating institutes have led to the provision of information about the
uploaded *materials* and their histories: What sort of prints underlies the
digital semblances we are looking at? What are their characteristics, their
genealogies? What invasive measures do they reflect? What about their
completeness, their integrity, their restoration? And what about the
integrity, restoration, and formatting of the semblances themselves? The
missing answers to these questions are ever so many missed opportunities
to inform today's users and make them more savvy with respect to the
material, factual, and ideological aspects at a certain moment in (film)
history, albeit at a digital remove.

With respect to World War I specifically such information would throw
light on contemporary practices of the film trade, most particularly on
how propaganda was carried out. For instance, during the war the
compilation of disparate image sources seamed by leading intertitles
flourished as never before; based on my experience of watching thousands
of early nonfiction films, I would say that the war, particularly in European
film history, marked a rhetorical watershed. One reason, obviously, was
that a "considerable portion of filmic production was shaped, directly or
indirectly, by state organisations which produced and distributed their

own films, or cooperated with the film industry in these activities.".[19] And while, for instance, white, vertical scratches (so-called tram lines) in the uploaded German print as well as a narrow, visible segment of its perforation strip show that at least parts of it were copied at one time from another print, not much more than that can be concluded by watching the uploaded versions.

Such material aspects normally remain largely invisible, literally as well as conceptually—that is, unacknowledged and unexplained—, while information about them is usually more readily and dependably available than summaries of and comments on what images show or intertitles claim. In short, EFG1914 (and many other portals with it) does not adequately inform its users by telling them what it is they see (scratches, color fading, etc.) nor by showing the things cut off from sight, even though the entire film strip can be much more productively made inspectable in digitized versions than in theatrical projection. Portals and websites that claim to feature film materials not merely show their semblances—a circumstance of presumed similarity not elucidated either—, but also provide abstracted content. That is to say, by focusing on *what* is represented, at the expense of *how*, the user is provided with a false security. To put it informally, the material may have been messed with at one time and/or another (e.g. pirated, recombined, cut, intertitled), but that apparently is 'mere' context; the image—the 'text'—is considered to speak for itself. Most consequentially, the true potential of digital technology, the equivalence of text and context, has not been realized or comprehended.[20] And, finally, nowhere does a user get a sense of the major and inherent irony of film materials, long before the digital era: their perfect, mechanical reproducibility notwithstanding they have always been among the most vulnerable and changeable artifacts. The extent to which they got away with that is indicative of the level, or lack, of the public's knowledge.

---

[19] Ine van Dooren, Peter Krämer, 'The politics of direct address', in: Karel Dibbets, Bert Hogenkamp (eds.), *Film and the First World War* (1995), p. 98.

[20] Elke Bauer, 'Bildarchive im digitalen Wandel: Chancen und Herausforderungen', in: Irene Ziehe, Ulrich Hägele (eds.), *Fotografie und Film im Archive: sammeln, bewahren, erforschen* (2013), pp. 29-30, 37-38; Paolo Cherchi Usai, David Francis, Alexander Horwath, Michael Loebenstein (eds.), *Film curatorship: archives, museums, and the digital marketplace* (2008), p. 199.

Surely, content is what portals such as EFG1914, or its predecessor the EFG Project (2008-2011), are made for. EFG1914 promotes its "quick and easy access" and encourages users to "discover" and "explore". Portals and sites that feature archival collections typify a time when historians have long ceased to be archives' primary target group, yet such client-oriented, do-it-yourself language, reminiscent of advertising, masks a lack of coherence and connectivity that in reality shortchanges the interested lay user for which this architecture—and the money laid out for it—was ostensibly intended.[21]

Another important consequence of making content available online is that it reinforces a tendency to withdraw certain types of material from public screenings (if ever they were publicly projected) on site—signally all types of documentary genres, such as propaganda, industrials, travelogues or newsreels, but also musical shorts, animation or advertising films. This may be a matter of strict separation. A telling example comes from one of the permanent exhibitions at Cinematek, Brussels, titled *Moviola's*. It consists of four consoles that "unlock 60 hours of [digitized] moving image materials, exclusively from our own archives and organized thematically. *The films have hardly been screened.*" (my italics) These are all nonfiction films—documentaries, newsreels, etc.—made between 1900 and 1970. More commonly, this tendency may be observed in feature-length film screenings' exclusivity. For example, in 2014 a number of institutes showed programs of films commemorating—yet largely made after—World War I: retrospectives at the Cinemateca Boliviana, La Paz; Cinematek, Brussels; Deutsches Filminstitut Filmmuseum; Filmarchiv Austria, Vienna; Filmmuseum, Munich; Filmoteca de Catalunya, Barcelona; Filmoteca Española, Madrid; and Museum of Modern Art-Film Department, New York. As well there were rereleases of A FAREWELL TO ARMS (1932) and PATHS OF GLORY (1957) by the British Film Institute-National Film & Television Archive (BFI-NFTVA), London; the release of the two-part documentary TROIS JOURNÉES D'AOÛT 1914 (2013) at Cinematek; one-off

---

[21] The emergence of the so-called archival divide, the split between professional history and archives, is traced in: Francis X. Blouin, Jr., William G. Rosenberg, *Processing the past: contesting authority in history and the archives* (2013 [2011]), pp. 13-93; see also: Karel Dibbets, 'Op zoek naar een digitale conservator'*, in: Mieke Lauwers, Bert Hogenkamp (eds.), *Audiovisueel: van emancipatie tot professionalisering. Jaarboek 2005*** (2006), pp. 189-197.
*'Looking for a digital curator'; **Audiovisual: from emancipation to professionalization. Yearbook 2005*

screenings of VERDUN: VISIONS D'HISTOIRE (1928) at both the Cinémathèque de Toulouse and the Australian Cinematheque, Brisbane, and of WESTFRONT 1918: VIER VON DER INFANTERIE (1930), preceded by a lecture, at Eye, Amsterdam; a series of one-off screenings at the Österreichisches Filmmuseum, Vienna, featuring ALL QUIET ON THE WESTERN FRONT (1930), PATHS OF GLORY, OKRAINA (VORSTADT; 1933), and WESTFRONT 1918: VIER VON DER INFANTERIE. Most of these screenings were restricted to a few, partly identical, canonical, postwar feature fiction titles. Save the Cinémathèque de Toulouse and the Filmmuseum, Munich, visitor information was largely provided in the form of more or less perfunctory plot summaries.

The only institutes that put considerable effort into their commemorative programs and provided a broader (film) historical context for World War I were BFI-NFTVA (besides its abovementioned rereleases) and the Cinémathèque française-Musée du Cinéma, Paris. In the spring of 2014, BFI-NFTVA launched its three-part, four-year theatrical and online program to mark the centenary.[22] *Before the war*, the first part, consisted largely of programs devoted to the prewar years, e.g. MAUDITE SOIT LA GUERRE, a 1913 feature containing an uncanny portrayal of warfare that before long would become all too familiar, as exemplified by the 1918 documentary short that preceded its screening, EN DIRIGEABLE SUR LES CHAMPS DE BATAILLE. It also includes *Edwardian drama on the small screen*, TV adaptations of plays popular in those years, and two feature-length compilations, one of mostly prewar silent films, *On the eve of war: around the world in 80 films*, and *A night at the cinema in 1914*, which also containes titles screened during the first year of the war.

The first of the two-part program at the Cinémathèque française-Musée du Cinémaa, also screened in the spring of 2014, was, not unlike the abovementioned retrospectives, devoted to (mostly feature fiction) international cinema about and made after the war. But the second part, screened in the fall of 2014, continued with films made and exhibited during the war and consisted of features and war-related shorts (comedies, serial episodes, newsreels, industrials, propaganda, etc.) that made up the film programs at the time in France and other warring countries, but also films that were made for designated audiences, such as medical films. Besides plot summaries, the Cinémathèque provided, as it

---

22 'Major BFI projects announced to mark First World War centenary', at: http://www.bfi.org.uk/news-opinion/news-bfi/features/major-projects-announced-mark-first-world-war-centenary.

is wont to do for its larger retrospective programs, background information to this diptych in a 46' video interview with the curator on its website.[23]

The exceptionality of providing ample information and of recreating the flavor of contemporary cinema programs with materials that usually remain in the vaults brings out by contrast film heritage institutes' resemblance to modern day cinema theaters. The experience they offer is in many ways indistinguishable from commercial and arthouse cinema shows, not in the least since a sizeable number among them screen new or recent, mostly feature-length fiction films (see chapter 3). Mechanical projection technology as well as the range of materials that used to make up the cinema experience, the range, that is, of heritage materials stored in the institutes' vaults, seems to have a subordinate and decreasingly meaningful place in their on-site public presentations.

This shift traces an ambition to shed the accouterments of what sociologist Diana Crane has called the domain of an urban—or local—culture and take on the colors of wider cultural domains. Many film heritage institutes, until not too long ago, typically belonged to this *urban domain*, which is characterized by the production and/or distribution of less current, even offbeat cultural works which attract predominantly local (yet in terms of outlook often cosmopolitan) audiences; organizations in such a domain, rather than being amalgamated, commonly belong to voluntary networks (notably FIAF, the acronym of the Fédération Internationale des Archives du Film). This Crane contrasted with, first of all, the *peripheral domain* of culture, which "is dominated by organizations (...) that disseminate culture on a national basis but to distinct subgroups"—examples are record companies, publishers of magazines and books, public libraries; and, secondly, with the *core domain*, which "is dominated by conglomerates that disseminate culture to national and international audiences and to which all members of the population are exposed to some extent"—examples are TV, major newspapers, and film (the latter, of course, in its familiar manifestation of major corporations and conglomerations that control production, distribution, and exhibition).[24]

---

[23] '*Centenaire de la Grande Guerre au cinéma.* Présentation par Laurent Véray', at: http://www.dailymotion.com/video/x1ihbrg_centenaire-de-la-grande-guerre-au-cinema-presentation-par-laurent-veray_shortfilms.

[24] Crane (1994), pp. 5-6.

Crane's distinction between cultural domains dates from the pre-internet era, when television was the major player in the world of media culture in terms of corporate power, reach, and audience penetration. That doesn't mean, however, that her model, despite its American bias, has become obsolete; many of its distinctions are still valid. It allows one to see, for instance, how film heritage institutes nowadays tend to behave like publishers and distributors through their output of books and DVDs, film distribution labels, and traveling programs, while at the same time they strive for a bigger audience share by moving into multiplexes. And even though that in itself certainly hasn't turned all of them into major players, it did entail a shift to more mainstream and contemporary fare in their public activities.[25]

The film heritage world is an institution that is made up of a variety of members: film heritage institutes proper, such as archives, museums, cinematheques and their archivists and curators; but also film labs, their technicians and, recently, digital R&D specialists; academic film studies departments, archival training programs and their scholars and students; associations and other interest groups (e.g. FIAF, Domitor); festivals and their programmers; seminars, symposia and their organizers and participants; journals and their editors and contributors; collectors, etc. Members of this institution can be said to not only constitute, in the words of Howard Becker, a network, but also, in the words of literary scholar Stanley Fish, an *interpretive community*—or rather perhaps a number of interconnected interpretive communities (because the activities of some overlap more with one group than with another: lab technicians, say, tend to interact more closely with archivists about certain standards or procedures than with, say, scholars). On the whole, interpretive communities share "a public and conventional view" about values, goals, and interests, although different opinions and different institutional priorities about those values, goals, and interests cause these views to change, even split, over time. But, importantly, the conventions and

---

[25] Many of these changes have been enabled or reinforced by the internet: publicity for their books and releases, as well as their programs, even the possibility of virtual participation in some of their events that involve personal appearances, and access to digitized materials from their collections. In this respect Crane's model does need some modification, since the internet cuts through the domains she distinguished. It has changed the game to the extent that the easy access of the world wide web application allows even the smallest of organizations to potentially gain a measure of exposure undreamed of before.

competences developed within these communities allow their members to operate efficiently, because their communication presupposes, and proceeds on the basis of, a limited number of relevant perspectives and interpretations.[26] (Even my obvious-seeming first paragraph of this chapter is full of terms and phrases—e.g. *vinegar syndrome; edge code*— that are readily understandable within the film heritage community, but for most outsiders would need more clarification.)

Fish introduced the term *interpretive community* with reference to the literary institution, one that is blessed with the advantage of having its materials, the printed texts that play a central role within it, as a rule unproblematically available or accessible, except for reasons this community would accept as being normal (unique manuscripts or incunabula, for instance—although these are becoming increasingly available online[27]—, variant editions or the lack of translations). In the film heritage world a different situation prevails—and here is where Howard Becker's notion of *art world* intersects yet contrasts with Fish's term. Film heritage institutes that manage collections occupy an influential position, because of their control about and to their materials. They act as gatekeepers—Becker actually uses the term *distributors*.[28] Apart from regulating access to hands-on inspection of archival materials, which is as a rule restricted to professionals, what most crucially affects the academic and other pursuits of the film heritage world's interpretive communities is these institutes' power to decide what comes out in the shape of both presentations and information. Affects it more, that is, than their decisions about what goes in and gets preserved or not, because the latter decisions rightly belong to their discretion, based on internal considerations such as mandate and mission, collection policy, allocation of budgets, etc. But it is this gatekeeping function, or more to the point, the *withholding* of materials and their histories from public inspection, which impoverishes the know-how of all interconnected interpretive communities. And not just them: by restricting their know-how the institutes also default on their wider public obligations. This is a circumstance that potentially has serious consequences for their social

---

[26] Stanley Fish, 'Introduction, or How I learned to stop worrying and learned to love interpretation', in: *Is there a text in this class?: the authority of interpretive communities* (1980), pp. 14-17.

[27] Blouin, Jr., Rosenberg (2013), pp. 200-201.

[28] Becker (1984), pp. 93-130.

relevance. Because if they fail to update the public about new data, insights or developments, they impede their own functioning as institutes of expertise and risk losing the trust invested in that expertise by the public.[29]

This situation is compounded by what cannot be but a self-imposed knowledge gap that has opened up between these institutes and academic film history programs. While film archives were the source and catalyst of the so-called new film history that emerged in the late 1970s, subsequent research and development of ideas and theories has largely been the responsibility of film scholars (to which the flowering of early cinema studies in particular attests).[30] Why film heritage institutes have tended to hold on to yesterday's conventional wisdom is a question I cannot answer. But whatever it is, the result is that the information many of those institutes provide today is often glaringly out of step with state-of-the-art film historical research and knowledge. Take, for example, the online information of the Cinemateca Portuguesa-Museu do Cinema, Lisbon, about its permanent exhibitions of objects and equipment. It mentions late 19th-century research into the phenomenon of persistence of vision and the related optical instruments, yet fails to point out the disproval—as early as 1912, in fact—of this alleged phenomenon's relevance for the perception of motion, real or apparent.[31-32] Or take programs that have no film historical relevance to speak of, such as the retrospective *Fratelli nel*

---

[29] While describing the challenges of the archival profession as a whole, archivist Ian E. Wilson also provided, no doubt unwittingly, a rather helpless sketch of the current archival expert system—and of the problem central to my thesis: "The imperative to conserve, to protect, the fragile reminders of our past is at the heart of our profession and our mission. Yet this separates the people from their heritage. They have entrusted our profession with these treasures. Increasingly, we are the only ones who now can approach the originals. The 'gift of one generation to another' seems to be the gift to an obscure profession." See his: '"The gift of one generation to another": the real thing for the Pepsi generation', in: Francis X. Blouin, Jr., William G. Rosenberg (eds.), *Archives, documentation and institutions of social memory: essays from the Sawyer Seminar* (2009 [2006]), p. 339.

[30] Philippe Gauthier, *Histoire(s) et historiographie du cinéma en France: 1896-1953* (2013), pp. 158-164.

[31] http://www.cinemateca.pt/CinematecaSite/media/Documentos/Livro-carvalhos.pdf.

[32] Joseph Anderson, Barbara Anderson, 'The myth of persistence of vision revisited', in: *Journal of Film and Video* (Spring 1993), pp. 3-12.

cinema, at the Fondazione Centro Sperimentale di Cinematografia-Cineteca Nazionale, Rome, which is introduced as follows:

> *The invention of the cinema is linked to the names of two brothers,*
> *Auguste and Louis Lumière. Since then, in the history of cinema,*
> *there have been so many brothers who, in collaboration or in*
> *competition, have dedicated themselves to this métier. The cinema,*
> *as you know, is a contagious disease that often spreads within*
> *families.[33]*

With such inanities a film heritage institute not only makes a fool of itself, but, much more seriously, ignores and obstructs the transfer of state-of-the-art knowledge. And not just within their interpretive communities. Because it also damages the wider democratic notion of enabling its publics to acquaint itself and engage with a heritage that is in a fundamental sense theirs. This objection applies a fortiori to those institutes, such as the Centro Sperimentale, that are mandated and fully financed by public bodies.

Today's buzz of so-called pull models and other DIY-fantasies of unconstrained, non-contextualized digital archival access is simply unable to countervail these objections. For one thing, these models assume a type of informed lay user of which there still are but few, while the institutes' very—and very strict—gatekeeping is unlikely to significantly expand their numbers.[34] As a matter of fact, nowadays it seems rather that the academe is a catalyst to make film materials meaningfully productive by inserting them in a scholarly research context; a good example (although its project funding has ended, too) is the website 'Colonial film: moving images of the British Empire'.[35]

---

[33] 'Fratelli nel cinema', at:
http://www.fondazionecsc.it/events_detail.jsp?IDAREA=85&ID_EVENT=999&GTE MPLATE=newsletter_mailing_ctTrevi.jsp.

[34] Nico de Klerk, '100 years of image control: the case of J.C. Lamster's films for the Dutch Colonial Institute', in: *Early Popular Visual Culture* (November 2013), pp. 317-319.

[35] See: http://www.colonialfilm.org.uk/.

Another drawback of pull models is that film archival objects are only one among many other sources that film historical topics require for piecing together a decent account. A good and instructive counter-example is film historian Michael Hammond's approach to the difficult subject of cinema-going and what audiences saw, heard, did or thought while attending a show. This is a topic that is critically dependent on many disparate sources, some of which can be found in film archives (ephemera such as handbills, program booklets, besides film prints, photographs, cinema theaters' architectural plans, etc.), while others may be found in local and special-subject archives or in more remote places, including the memories of participants elicited in oral history projects, while again others are scattered randomly (in memoirs, diaries, letters, photo albums, and other so-called egodocuments) or must be traced in various forms of "intertextual evidence".[36] But most certainly not all of them will be found online. That hasn't stopped Hammond from undertaking a plausible and moving reconstruction—he uses the term *reception context*—of attending a screening of Thomas H. Ince's 1916 production of CIVILIZATION in a particular cinema in Southampton, England, during World War I, in order to provide a sense of how it might have affected the thoughts and feelings of audiences, represented by two particular (yet fictional) patrons.[37] By setting this visit in a framework of wider contemporary local and social significance he avoids the all too common substitution trick of having stylistic and other formal aspects implicitly stand in for spectators' responses (such scholarship, historian Charles Ambler aptly writes, "generally incorporates a textual determinism that effectively marginalises the audience."[38]). More even than its plausibility or veracity, what struck me about Hammond's brief case study is indeed the scope—the wealth—of sources and contexts that were input for this evocative reconstruction, a result of thinking what sources might be productive rather than easily available: newspapers, trade papers, and fan magazines; the 1916 Entertainment Tax; the ascent—thanks to the war—of American film

---

[36] William Uricchio, Roberta E. Pearson, *Reframing culture: the case of the Vitagraph quality films* (1993), pp. 10-15, where they describe their pioneering use of eclectic, period sources.

[37] Michael Hammond, '"A great American sensation": Thomas Ince's CIVILIZATION at the Palladium, Southampton, 1917', in: Melvyn Stokes, Richard Maltby (eds.), *Hollywood abroad: audiences and cultural exchange* (2004), pp. 35-50.

[38] Charles Ambler, 'Popular films and colonial audiences in Central Africa', in: Stokes, Maltby (2004), p. 135.

imports; booking strategies, advertising and publicity; the theater visited by his characters; the film they saw; as well as the city's transportation infrastructure; the suffragette movement; and, of course, the war, which constituted, besides Belgian refugees, a clear presence and source of anxiety in the form of wounded soldiers who were shipped to this port from the battlefields.

For the academy the perennial problem, insofar as it is perceived as one, is to reach a wider audience for its ideas or findings. With the way Hammond journalistically concretized his paper's argument he perhaps sought, certainly deserved, a wider readership than the collection of essays in which it was included, inspiring though it is, will have reached. This is the type of publication that is printed in limited editions and finds its way mostly to academic and specialist libraries. Such circulation of ideas and information within a specific niche, often using specialist terminology, is obviously an important reason why they do not easily percolate through more everyday, popularizing sources of information, such as newspapers, weeklies, even film magazines as well as radio and TV programs (which sociologist Paul Hirsch called "surrogate consumers"[39]). But the values, goals, and interests *they* share are largely determined by these media's commercial environments, which constitute another layer of gatekeeping.

Similar considerations may well have affected the implementation of certain mandated, public tasks of film heritage institutes, too. In recent decades, in a number of countries more or less comparable developments have obtained regarding the conceptualization of responsibilities in the cultural sector: decreased financing from public budgets has gone hand in hand with an increased reliance on private money, such as sponsorships, matching funds or self-earned income, and quantifiable elements, such as turnover or number of visitors. The tendency to shift from a nonprofit to a for-profit orientation, coinciding with an increase in size and/or responsibilities, seems to reflect the abovementioned move from one cultural domain to another—or in terms of position and repertoire:

---

[39] Paul M. Hirsch, 'Processing fads and fashions: an organization-set analysis of cultural industry systems', in: Simon Frith, Andrew Goodwin (eds.), *On record: rock, pop, and the written word,* (1990), p. 132 (orig. publ. in 1972).

towards a larger remit and attendance.[40] But, as noted, with no available research of any scope or longitude on the field of forces in which film heritage institutes operate, specifically with regard to their public activities, I can only formulate my conclusions in a programmatic way. "Programmatic" here means a way of doing theory:

> *It is normative and practical, not descriptive and predictive. It aims*
> *not so much to describe what we actually do as help us to decide*
> *what we ought to do. It is theory from the actor's, the agent's, the*
> *practitioner's perspective.*[41]

My programmatic approach is not meant to present a blueprint of ideal archival practices, if only for the simple reason that each institute also operates in a local context with its distinct forces and pressures; only a separate study based on longitudinal, wide-ranging source materials would be able to provide solid answers as to what these were.[42] Yet I do find it important to provide a perspective on what I find programmatically relevant. This is what I do in the following chapter, at the end of which I propose a conceptual apparatus that fits the specific expertise that one would reasonably expect from film heritage institutes. These considerations are tested in a subsequent chapter against a wider database in the form of a survey and evaluation of film heritage institutes'

---

[40] Crane (1994), pp. 131-132. A Dutch publication devoted to the business side of heritage institutes captured this mentality with its re-definition of a museum as "an enterprise aimed at realizing a goal, with products, projected results, target groups, limited means, and a relevant environment (users, funders, sponsors, etc.)."; see: C.F. Plaisier, C. van Katwijk, K. Schoenmaker (eds.), *Bedrijfsvoering in musea** (1992), p. 15.
**Museum management*

[41] Trevor Livelton, *Archival theory, records, and the public* (2003 [1996]), p. 11. However, I see the present work as being less about norms than about values. In other words, it is not so much about ways of doing, or implementation, but rather about ways of thinking, or principles. I see the work of heritage institutes essentially as commensurate with the disciplines of history and sociology, viz. as being concerned with 'knowing thyself'.

[42] How these forces and pressures, and the responses to them, actually differ is described in: Kumar (2016).

public activities. But in all chapters I give due importance to the one thing that remains constant throughout the set of institutes: the notion of public accountability. For this aspect, though, broader terms are required.

In my general conclusion, therefore, I will argue the relevance of archival science for film heritage work. In recent decades the notion of public accountability has been the focus of inspiring discussions within this discipline, particularly in its pleas for extending the base of archival representativeness.[43] Secondly, I will connect my conclusions with some of the ideas put forward by sociologist Anthony Giddens, specifically his linked concepts of *trust* and *reflexivity*.[44] Trust, in his view, is a fundamental term in the modern world, a result of the disembedding of social relations and interactions and "their restructuring across indefinite spans of time-space."[45] It is, therefore, inextricably bound up with the aforementioned *expert system*—of which I consider film heritage institutes an instance (albeit a minor one). As impersonal "systems of technical accomplishment or professional expertise that organise large areas of the material and social environment in which we live today" their emergence has made modern life possible and allowed members of societies to accomplish time-space detachments without constant verification. In fact, members unworriedly go through expert systems all day every day, knowing these systems have been assigned "abstract capacities"[46] as well as a legal responsibility and remit. An example Giddens provides is the amalgam of rules and regulations that govern the making and maintaining of the built environment in order to keep it, and us, safe and in one piece. And if not, we are handed over to, and put our trust in, the expert system of health care. But even if we may never experience the breakdown of the built environment or see the inside of a hospital, we are being made aware

---

[43] Hans Booms, 'Society and the formation of a documentary heritage: issues in the appraisal of archival sources', in: *Archivaria* (Summer 1987), pp. 69-107 (orig. publ. in 1972 as 'Gesellschaftsordnung und Überlieferungsbildung. Zur Problematik archivarischer Quellenbewertung'); Gerald F. Ham, 'The archival edge', in: *The American Archivist* (January 1975), pp. 5-13 (orig. presented in October 1974 at the 38th annual meeting of the Society of American Archivists [SAA]); Terry Cook, 'Mind over matter: towards a new theory of archival appraisal', in: Barbara L. Craig (ed.), *The archival imagination: essays in honour of Hugh A. Taylor* (1992), pp. 38-71.

[44] Giddens (2013), pp. 29-45.

[45] Giddens (2013), p. 21.

[46] Giddens (2013), pp. 27, 26.

of their impact through various channels and media reflecting their views on, for example, safety rules or unwholesome behavior. This is a condition for the phenomenon of reflexivity, which denotes a world where "social practices are constantly examined and reformed in light of incoming information about those very practices, thus constitutively altering their character."[47] As the production of information is not a unified activity, but a discordant, often competitive affair of "multiple expertise, with multiple claims to authority",[48] this way of knowledge acquisition and decision-making is a typically modern practice of comparing, or picking from, a multitude of sources, rather than relying on a single, received form of knowledge. Modern man is free to choose, but he may not always have an easy time of it.

Surely, like academic interpretive communities, film heritage institutes cannot claim to organize "large areas" of our lives nor do they commonly play a highly visible role in the public sphere as, say, opinion leaders or agenda-setters (the reason I called them "minor" expert systems). Nonetheless, because of their specific role as gatekeepers and their, to a certain extent, unique professional expertise, they are well-positioned to attempt and play an authoritative role in shaping the public's sense of its film heritage and history. On this, of course, rests their social significance, a responsibility *and* a task for which they surely have to work harder than the more societally vital expert systems of infrastructure, health care or the judiciary. Yet once the public does show an interest, film heritage institutes, like any other expert system, are bound by the same duty to make the public fully aware of their expertise for it to examine, reform its knowledge (and gain its trust).

---

[47] Giddens (2013), p. 38. This is an instance of what Giddens has called the double hermeneutic of the social sciences, "[t]he concepts and theories invented by social scientists circulate in and out of the social world they are coined to analyze". In other words, when members of society adopt them they thereby not only change their perception of social practices, but also change the practices themselves; see: Anthony Giddens, *The constitution of society: outline of the theory of structuration* (2014 [1984]), pp. xxxv; 3, 5-6; 25-28; 374.

[48] Anthony Giddens, Christopher Pierson, *Conversations with Anthony Giddens: making sense of modernity* (1998), p. 111.

Chapter 2
Unstated understandings

Each of the five case studies in this chapter deals with artifacts that represent categories of materials that do not feature regularly nor prominently in the public activities of film heritage institutes: a forty-five second political campaign film meant for a variety show's lineup of films; a handbill for a cinema theater's film program; the printed texts for lecturers in non-theatrical, colonial propaganda screenings; a Dutch-language version of an American B-picture from the Depression era; and a Dutch trailer for a French postwar feature set in resistance circles during World War II. I place these artifacts in less prevalent signifying contexts that can be summarized by the terms that play a central role in these studies: reframing; hangover effect; paratext; myth; and appropriation, respectively. Together they argue for a deeper and wider sense of cinema history as well as for a closer interrelationship with societal concerns. Basically they are meant to show that context matters in important ways and provides opportunities to enrich film heritage institutes' public activities and increase their relevance (without implying of course that these case studies, although brief, set a measure for the length of visitor information). Making these historical contexts matter, incidentally, also reflects how the (projected) film as an object of study has been decentered in the more comprehensive approaches that film historiography, early film historiography most emphatically, has undertaken over the past few decades.[49]

The case studies roughly cover c. 50 years of cinema history, from 1896 through 1948. I am fully aware, of course, that this selection, insofar as it is concerned with film materials, represents 'old' technology. They were eye-opening artifacts in my work as a collection researcher and curator in a film heritage institute, objects that I am most familiar with, having seen, held, and smelled them. During my tenure there 'new' technology simply

---

[49] Nico de Klerk, 'Das Programmformat. Bruchstücke einer Geschichte', in: *KINtop* (2002), pp. 16-17.

didn't play a significant role, because it was either a matter of research & development for restoration, storage, and access technologies or of specific acquisitions for the archive. My examples are rather intended to be, indeed, exemplary, that is to say applicable to related instances. Technology, after all, is not media-specific, let alone determinative.[50] What is of more consequence in the real world of film heritage responsibilities and tasks is in what ways these artifacts and materials, old and new, can be meaningfully presented and their histories meaningfully communicated to the public.

My selection should not be taken, then, as purposefully stopping short of the digital era. In fact, the massive switch to digital film production, distribution, projection or restoration should push film heritage institutes to unreservedly extend their remit. Accommodating these new technologies in their archival and museum tasks, both instrumentally (e.g. in restorations and reconstructions; cataloguing; publicity; and contextualization) and substantially (in collecting and presentation policies) strengthens their expertise and stresses the continuities between practices rather than the differences—the latter have long served a well-worn popular and sales rhetoric.[51-52] A museum, it has been argued, is not just about the preservation, presentation, and interpretation of an artifact, but about "a working system" through which it elucidates the connections

---

[50] William Uricchio, 'Media-specificity and its discontents: a televisual provocation', in: Nicolas Dulac, André Gaudreault (eds.), *From media to post-media: continuities and ruptures (forthcoming)*; see also: Wiebe E. Bijker, *Of bicycles, Bakelites, and bulbs: toward a theory of sociotechnical change* (2002 [1995]), pp. 1-17.

[51] Similar tactics of emphasizing difference were used by entrepreneurs in introducing film to new audiences in the mid-1890s; see e.g.: Nico de Klerk, 'A few remaining hours: news films and the interest in technology in Amsterdam film shows, 1896-1910' (1999), pp. 5-8 (orig. publ. in 1998 as 'Nur noch wenige Stunden: Nachrichtenfilm und Technikinteresse in Amsterdamer Filmvorführungen zwischen 1896 und 1910').

[52] Archivist Carolyn Heald writes: "That our documentary heritage increasingly resides in computer bits and bytes makes no difference. We still must strive to comprehend the nature of the medium. What do electronic records tell us about society? The fact that data are transitory, must be refreshed constantly, and will not be in the same format forever, says much about current social values and trends: the disposable, fragmented society, constantly in flux. What does it say about social and organizational hierarchies, for example, that the data entry clerk can communicate with the company president through e-mail?"; see her: 'Are we collecting the "right stuff"?', in: *Archivaria* (Fall 1995), p. 187.

between a variety of artifacts, enabling technologies, and the experiences they generate. Now that a growing number of countries have completed the transition to digital projection in commercial cinemas film heritage institutes may gain a new importance, as they will be the only places where the analogue working system can still be reproduced. At this point in time that may not excite a large number of people, but in the not too distant future it may well become an asset of their work.[53-54] The following string of brief studies, then, implicitly argues for a specific way of doing film heritage work for the public.

A case of reframing

In September 1896, the American Mutoscope & Biograph Company shot a view—in contemporary parlance—of presidential candidate Major William McKinley at his home in Canton, Ohio, as part of a series of Republican election campaign films.[55] Meant as an innovative way of electioneering the series blurred the "traditional distinctions between private and public, between personal presence and media representation". This so-called front porch campaign disseminated McKinley's living image while the candidate stayed at home, a strategy meant "to control access to the newspapers, whose reporters were invited to come to Canton", where they were received by McKinley at his house, the very site shown in the film.[56] There, according to a news report of the series' premiere attended by a delegation of Republican dignitaries, in October 1896 in one of New York's upmarket vaudeville theaters, the

---

[53] Cherchi Usai, Francis, Horwath, Loebenstein (2008), pp. 84-89.

[54] Cinematek, *Rapport annuel | Jaarverslag 2013* (n.d.), p. 55; Sabine Lenk, 'Archives and their film collection in a digital world, or: What futures for the analog print?', in: *The Moving Image* (Fall 2014), pp. 100-110; 'Digital cinemas lead to increased attendance', in: *DCinema Today* (June 27, 2011).

[55] McKINLEY AT HOME, CANTON, OHIO
USA (American Mutoscope & Biograph) 1896 | 68mm (nitrate), 35mm (safety print) | b&w | 0'45" | prints at Eye, Amsterdam, and British Film institute-National Film & Television Archive, London.

[56] The quotes come from: Jonathan Auerbach, 'McKinley at home: how early American cinema made news', in: *American Quarterly* (December 1999), pp. 803, 802.

Olympia, he could be seen on his front lawn while being handed "a paper". After this event, McKinley's living image went on a career of its own, gradually exceeding its original purpose.

A month later, after McKinley's electoral victory, one newspaper report immediately updated the scene by having him receive "congratulatory telegrams", instead of a mere paper.[57] Five months later, in March 1897, the view, now retitled THE PRESIDENT, WILLIAM MCKINLEY, AT HOME, CANTON, OHIO, U.S.A., appeared in Mutoscope & Biograph's film program at the Palace Theatre of Varieties in London, England, and was described as depicting "the president" at home shortly "after the inaugural ceremony".[58] A year later, from April through June 1898, the British Mutoscope & Biograph Company revived the film at the same venue on the occasion of, and subsequently amid views relating to, the Spanish-American War, a reminder perhaps of McKinley's campaign promise to liberate Cuba from Spanish misgovernment,[59] as well as an evocation of his presiding presence as Commander-in-Chief.[60] Again a year later, on

---

[57] The two quoted phrases come from the *New York Tribune* (October 13, 1896), and the *New Haven News* (November 23, 1896) respectively, reproduced in: Kemp R. Niver (ed.), *Biograph Bulletins 1896-1908* (1971), pp. 12; 18.

[58] *The Illustrated Sporting and Dramatic News* (March 27, 1897), quoted in: Richard Brown, Barry Anthony, *A Victorian enterprise: the history of the British Mutoscope and Biograph Company, 1897-1915* (1999), p. 45. The information in this report and the ones mentioned in the preceding note may or may not have been taken from descriptions in program bills or may or may not have been taken from projected 'intertitles' on lantern slides, which was customary during the Mutoscope and Biograph Company's screenings in America; see: Charles Musser, *The emergence of cinema: the American screen to 1907* (1990), pp. 180; 231; 342; 351-352.

[59] Stephen Bottomore, *Filming, faking and propaganda: the origins of the war film, 1897-1902* (2007), ch. V, p. 2.

[60] Surviving Palace Theatre program bills in the Archive Collections of the Museum of London show its screening for the weeks following April 25, 1898—the day America declared war on Spain—, May 9, May 16, and June 27, 1898, when the view of McKinley was joined by other war-related items. In terms of Stephen Bottomore's analysis of contemporary war footage, the McKinley view must have retained a sufficient "indexical connection" to the events to be considered "authentic"; see Bottomore (2007), ch. II, pp. 5-7. (At the Palace Theatre, British M&B continued to screen the other views related to the war until the end of July, while in October the program featured "Spanish-American war scenes", actually two other war-*related* films, one of Camp Wikoff, on Long Island, where returning troops were quarantined, and one of a regiment being dispatched to the Philippines.)

March 20, 1899, three months after the Treaty of Paris officially ended the war, a newspaper announcement for an "American Biograph" program in The Hague, the Netherlands, listed the view under the title PRESIDENT MCKINLEY AND HIS SECRETARY DISCUSSING TERMS OF PEACE (IN THE GARDEN OF HIS VILLA IN CANTON).[61] Finally, two and a half years later, the view returned on British M&B's Palace Theatre program for an altogether different reason: from the week of September 11, 1901, throughout the rest of that month, it was shown in honor of the President, who was shot on September 6 and died of his wounds on September 14; the latter event induced British M&B to also revive, from September 18 onwards, an older view related to the Spanish-American War, COLONEL ROOSEVELT'S ROUGH RIDERS, in honor of Theodore Roosevelt, who was sworn in as President on the day of McKinley's death.[62] This little honorific, twin revival remained on the program until early October, after which time the Roosevelt view was in a slot by itself for the rest of that month.

The instances of reframing in this little aggregate screening history exemplify a typically turn-of-the-20th-century exhibition practice. As such, it was a rather contingent affair, heavily dependent on the fact that film entertainment in this period consisted largely of views of real events (or their reconstructions), not seldom of great news value. But as the immediate newsworthiness faded after having shown it to sufficiently different audiences, or when new views took precedence, film businesses

---

[61] Dutch-language title: PRESIDENT MAC KINLEY [sic] MET ZIJN SECRETARIS DE VREDESVOORWAARDEN BESPREKENDE (IN DEN TUIN VAN ZIJN VILLA TE CANTON.); see: 'American Biograph', in: *Haagsche Courant** (March 20, 1899), p. 1. This newspaper had acquired the rights to show the M&B films at one of its properties in The Hague; see: Mark van den Tempel, 'Making them move again: preserving Mutoscope and Biograph', in: *Griffithiana* (1999-2000), p. 227.
**Hague Courant*

[62] Here, too, the "indexical connection" may have been felt as being sufficient, yet its screening was perhaps a mere expedient choice. The surviving program sheets of the Palace Theatre show that since late 1898 the British Mutoscope & Biograph Co., whose board was controlled by newspaper tycoons, focused its production heavily on news and actualities. Comic or trick films made by its international sister companies disappeared from its screens. Still one wonders why the company, given this focus, passed up an opportunity to show FUNERAL OF PRESIDENT MCKINLEY, an extremely topical view made by the American branch of M&B.
Comparable, though less protracted examples of reframing from this and other companies and/or exhibitors can be found in: Bottomore (2007), ch. III, pp. 16-17, ch. IV, pp.19-20, ch. VII, pp. 8-10.

looked for opportunities to extend the commercial lifespan of their properties beyond the event that had occasioned their filming. In other words, by shifting their signifying contexts. The McKinley view exemplifies how film companies and/or exhibitors—the latter usually bought and owned the prints[63]—welcomed and expediently utilized fresh motives to exploit their product. Had there been no Spanish-American War a year and a half after the view had been made, or had the President not been assassinated five years later, surely his living image wouldn't have been revived.

Expediency came in different ways. Sometimes a film's value, and meaning, could be stretched by including it in or, conversely, separating it from, a string of related films, or by changing its position in the line-up. M&B did that for years with its views of the Boer War, forced as it was by the long intervals between updates. By rearranging and recombining the order of the films that were at hand for weeks on end variation was created and meanings were suggested that were not apparent from the individual views.[64] And sometimes expediency itself was stretched, taking a film's meaning far beyond indexical connection. An example is the return on British M&B's Palace Theatre's film program, in March 1901, of the 1896 view SKIRT DANCE BY ANNABELLE, screened right after a section of views called *Funeral of the Queen*, in commemoration of Queen Victoria.[65] Its precise position and the function it thereby came to fulfill in M&B's usually

---

[63] Select, upmarket vaudeville or variety theaters were perhaps an exception. Rather than buying prints they contracted a film company for a season or more to make up programs from its own catalogue and screen its prints with the company's own equipment and projectionist. The Mutoscope & Biograph Company's preference for such an exclusive business model was no doubt a function of its unique recording and projection technology and the films' wide gauge, which gave it a competitive edge; see: Deac Rossell, *Living pictures: the origins of the movies* (1998), p. 160; Brown, Anthony (1999), pp. 44-45.

[64] Nico de Klerk, '"Pictures to be shewn": programming the American Biograph', in: Simon Popple, Vanessa Toulmin (eds.), *Visual delights: essays on the popular and projected image in the 19th century* (2000), pp. 214-215.

[65] The collection of the Palace Theatre's program sheets is not complete enough to establish precisely when this film had been shown prior to 1901. SKIRT DANCE BY ANNABELLE is an alternative title for BUTTERFLY DANCE, "[a] very graceful dance with voluminous draperies"; see: Elias Savada, *The American Film Institute catalogue of motion pictures produced in the United States: film beginnings 1893-1910* (1995), p. 140.

carefully made up programs at this venue suggest how its meaning and connotation were drastically changed: from a popular and spectacular entertainment (certainly not an actuality!) the filmed skirt dance's position not just cushioned the funerary section from the remainder of the program, but, as film historian Martin Loiperdinger has suggested, simultaneously 'borrowed' and continued its commemorative mood on a symbolic level by an angelic reading of the film, linking it to a familiar Victorian image; spectators' thoughts might have been even more nudged in that direction if the film's projection speed had been slowed down.[66]

Reframing, then, was a common tactic driven by commercial and practical considerations to update or change yet maintain a film's attraction. And, as the example of SKIRT DANCE BY ANNABELLE suggests, it could challenge or stimulate spectators' imaginations and interpretations by a programming style that at times was the equivalent of forms of editing traditionally associated with much later practices.[67] This tactic was a function of, on the one hand, the way commercial film companies operated around the turn of the 20th century, whether organized as what have been called "self-contained producers" (basically a matter of branding) and "exhibition services",[68] or as separate, specialized enterprises (for filmmaking or for exhibition). And, on the other, it was a

---

[66] Nico de Klerk, 'Programme of programmes: the Palace Theatre of Varieties', in *Griffithiana* (1999-2000), p. 243. M&B's projections allowed some latitude, as its films were usually recorded and projected at 30 frames per second (fps), at least twice as fast as was usual at the time.

[67] Yuri Tsivian, 'Notes historiques en marge de l'expérience de Koulechov', in: *Iris* (1986), pp. 49-59; Rick Altman, *Silent film sound* (2004), p. 71, although Altman doesn't acknowledge Tsivian's earlier description of reframing in Kuleshov's experiments; see also Charles Musser's comments in: Daan Hertogs, Nico de Klerk (eds.), *Nonfiction from the teens: the 1994 Amsterdam Workshop* (1994), p. 57.

[68] See respectively: Tom Gunning, *D.W. Griffith and the origins of American narrative film: the early years at Biograph* (1991), p. 58, and Charles Musser with Caroline Nelson, *High-class moving pictures: Lyman H. Howe and the forgotten era of traveling exhibition* (1991), p. 58. Gunning defines "self-contained producers" as "a self-contained (...) illusion-producing apparatus that included the camera that took the films, the films themselves, and (...) the projection machine" as well as a projectionist; this definition and his example of the American Mutoscope & Biograph Company suggest that this business practice included the manufacture of equipment. Musser and Nelson define "exhibition services" as providing "a projector, a projectionist, and a group of films"; here, the origin of the equipment and the films seems not to have been of overriding importance.

function of the entertainments in which films were predominantly exhibited, either in sedentary shows in variety or vaudeville theaters or in itinerant shows in opera houses, public halls, on fairgrounds, etc. In other words, the length of a film's commercial life was fundamentally a matter of scarcity: a limit on exploitable merchandise as well as on opportunities. In the theatrical setting of the variety or vaudeville programs, for example, with only a few shows a day and the exclusive engagement of the services—the films, their programming, and projection—of one company for a season or more, a film could be screened for months on end in programs that changed slowly and gradually. But insofar as film exhibitions traveled from one place to another, a film's commercial value depended rather on the number of locations it was taken to.[69]

Given the preponderance of actualities around this time, reframing also informed a proposal, published in 1898, in Paris, for the creation of "photo-mechanical departments" in museums. In a short treatise Polish photographer and film operator Bolesław Matuszewski advocated the collecting of both still and "animated" photography as a means of "investigating the past" by studying the images of persons and events of historical significance. Here, a photograph or a film was conceived as being a truthful record (such as Matuszewski's own views—he did not fail to remind his readers—of French president Faure's state visit to Russia, in September 1897, made for the Lumière company), stripped of its status as a commodity. Insofar as the proposal concerned existing films, rather than ones to be made expressly for the collections Matuszewski envisioned, it implied a redirection of purpose: from entertainment and business considerations to ones relating to history and heritage. A film's inclusion in a museum collection would separate the wheat from the chaff, the latter represented by an overwhelming number of what he dismissed as "trifles of life" and "entertaining and characteristic scenes".[70]

---

[69] For the economics of these practices, see: Richard Brown, 'New Century Pictures: regional enterprise in early British film exhibition', in: Vanessa Toulmin, Patrick Russell, Simon Popple (eds.), *The lost world of Mitchell and Kenyon: Edwardian Britain on film* (2004), pp. 69-72; see also: De Klerk (2000), pp. 211-216.

[70] Bolesław Matuszewski, *A new source of history* (1999), pp. 24-30 (orig. publ. in 1898 as *Une nouvelle source de l'histoire*). His inclusion, however, of what he called "the fleeting and moving aspect of cities" ("*la physionomie changeante et mobile des cités*") suggests that the intrinsic qualities of cinematography, its capability to record uncontrollable movements in particular, had nevertheless affected his criteria.

No records are known to survive that tell us why his proposal had no immediate, practical follow-up.[71] Apart from British cinema pioneer R. W. Paul's earlier offer of a small selection of his films to the British Museum, in 1896,[72] I am only familiar with one initiative that was reported to have been directly inspired by Matuszewski: Belgian alderman Huysmans's proposal, in 1899, to create an archive of filmed records of historical events in the city of Brussels. This information comes from a newspaper article published in 1911, in the Netherlands East-Indies; it omits the archive's early history—if any—and only mentions filmed records of then recent date, such as the funeral of King Leopold II, the Entry of his successor King Albert (both made in 1909) or the opening of the 1910 Brussels World's Fair. It also reflects practices current by that time when it states that, after being asked for advice about the conservation of the materials so far collected, "film companies (...) were unable to give definite answers; for them, a film merely has an immediate and practical use: it is not retained, but discarded as soon as its news value has passed."[73]

Nevertheless, for the lack of immediate response to Matuszewski's proposal a few considerations can be easily imagined. In very mundane terms, it would have meant additional expenditure to potentially relevant parties: to exhibitors or exhibition services in withdrawing a (well-worn) print from commercial circulation—at a time, remember, when they owned rather than rented the prints; to manufacturers in striking a new print, if they could find it in their hearts, as a donation; and if not, to museums on newfangled artifacts. None of this happened, at least not on a major scale—it would take at least a decade before the creation of

---

[71] Roland Cosandey, personal communication (December 1, 2012).

[72] Penelope Houston, *Keepers of the frame: the film archives* (1994), p. 9.

[73] 'Kinematografisch archief', in: *Sumatra Post* (September 20, 1911), p. 2 (my translation). I thank Dafna Ruppin and Klaas de Zwaan of Utrecht University for respectively finding and calling my attention to this news article.

"photo-mechanical" archives gained wider acceptance,[74] and another twenty years or so before the emergence of a more interconnected, international archival movement.

It was, furthermore, no coincidence that instances of a view's extended—and repeated—drawing power often involved those made of royalty, dignitaries, and celebrities; as long as their news value was easily renewable it never waned, regardless of the available images. This was reinforced by the fact that, unlike frequently recorded scenes of, say, animals, trains or sporting events (Matuszewski's trifles and entertainments), views of people of elevated status were generally much harder to make, given the restrictions on access they were able to enforce. Even the most photographed head of state in these and later years, German emperor Wilhelm II, was not wont to acknowledge the presence of film cameras or adapt the setting of and his behavior in the many public events he attended to allow them a better view.[75] As a result, such views were of vastly greater commercial value and would certainly not be disposed of. What is more, their initial runs often lasted longer than other views on the program, thanks in no small measure to the publicity their subjects generated. One example comes from a newspaper report about the series of views made on the occasion of the investiture of Dutch Queen Wilhelmina, in early September 1898, which were still being shown to

---

[74] The earliest, more systematic examples I know of are Albert Kahn's multimedia—photography, film, print—*Archives de la Planète*. It was set up on a professional basis in 1912 to sponsor and produce the artifacts it considered relevant for its archive, until the stock market crashes of 1929 forced its banker-founder to abandon his project in 1932; see: Paula Amad, *Counter-archive: film, the everyday, and Albert Kahn's Archives de la Planète* (2010); Jeanne Beausoleil, Pascal Ory (eds.), *Albert Kahn 1860-1940: réalités d'une utopie* (1995). And in 1913, the Danish National Archive for Historical Films and Voice was established to collect the moving image and speech of "famous Danes of our time". Insofar as film was concerned, the creation of the archive was short-lived; it consisted of purposeful recordings, made in 1912-1913, as well as gifts of mostly older, partly commercially released materials, made between 1899 and 1913; see: Esben Krohn, 'The first film archive', in: Thomas C. Christensen, Esben Krohn (eds.), *Det første filmarkiv/The first film archive* (2002), pp. 11-15, in the accompanying booklet to the DVD of the same title.

[75] Martin Loiperdinger, 'Kaiserbilder. Wilhelm II. als Filmstar', in: Uli Jung, Martin Loiperdinger (eds.), *Kaiserreich 1895-1918* (2005), pp. 253-268.

enthusiastic audiences almost five months after the event.[76] Another example, now from a production point of view, shows that such films boosted sales, too: British manufacturer of local films Mitchell & Kenyon's permission to record the funeral of Queen Victoria, in February 1901, and the coronation of her successor Edward VII, in August 1902, provided the company with its first opportunities to sell its actuality films on a national scale.[77] As well, with films made by arrangement *both* manufacturer and celebrity stood to gain, in terms of sales and publicity; examples are the appearances, coincident with matches, performances or book launches, of sportsmen and vaudeville stars before the Edison Company's cameras in its Black Maria studio.[78] In other words, the increasing commodification of persons and events of historical significance must have doomed Matuszewski's plan from the outset: he had singled out the very films that had the potential to make more money for a longer time.

After the turn of the 20th century, however, with the transformation and restructuring of the film business, this particular form of prolonged circulation was gradually curtailed and phased out. With it the possibilities of shifting signifying contexts were tightened. Over the course of the following decade a veritable industry emerged in the major production countries —notably the United States and France[79]—, which took the lead in cinema's institutionalization and commercial autonomy from other

---

[76] 'Is het Circus-Carré 's avonds de verzamelplaats...'*, in: *Het Nieuws van den Dag*** (January 27, 1899), 3rd section, p. 9. *'Is the Carré Circus the evening rendezvous...';
**News of the Day*

[77] Vanessa Toulmin, *Electric Edwardians: the story of the Mitchell & Kenyon collection* (2006), pp. 16; 30.

[78] Charles Musser, 'Early advertising and promotional films, 1893-1900: Edison Motion Pictures as a case study', in: Bo Florin, Nico de Klerk, Patrick Vonderau (eds.), *Films that sell: moving pictures and advertising* (2016), pp. 83-90.

[79] For the U.S. this process and the power struggles that determined its outcome are described in detail in: Musser (1990), pp. 297-495, and Eileen Bowser, *The transformation of cinema: 1907-1915* (1990), pp. 1-37. For France, see: Laurent Le Forestier, *Aux sources de l'industrie du cinéma: le modèle Pathé, 1905-1908* (2006); Jean-Jacques Meusy, 'La stratégie des sociétés concessionaires Pathé et la location des films en France (1907-1908)', in: Michel Marie, Laurent Le Forestier (eds.), *La firme Pathé Frères, 1896-1914* (2004), pp. 21-49. Richard Abel argues that this highly competitive process of restructuring the film business actually concerned the intertwinement of both countries' industries; see his: *The red rooster scare: making cinema American, 1900-1910* (1999), pp. 20-86.

entertainments and firmly established the interrelatedness of three distinct functions: production, distribution (or exchange), and exhibition. Aided by business expansion, a potent mainstream practice evolved in which films produced according to a schedule were distributed through a rental system for exhibition in cinema theaters. Heretofore a minority practice, these permanent, dedicated venues, whether storefront or purpose-built, became the linchpin of the industry: they were designed to increase demand through the renewal of film programs at regular and shorter intervals. This went hand in hand with a shift to systematic, studio-based fiction film production, thereby sidestepping the often irregular, unpredictable occurrence of reportable, newsworthy events.[80] This also boosted business by the requirement of striking film prints in greater numbers for widespread, simultaneous release and export.[81] Unlike the vaudeville program with its long engagements of acts, and unlike the traveling show with its schedule of venues called at, the frequency of quick—even daily—program changes at cinema theaters made reframing, at least of complete films, obsolete. Shortening the novelty value of individual titles and encouraging spectators to make frequent repeat visits contributed to the rise of the cinema habit, of the moviegoer. Within this configuration of abundance, reframing had to wait for World War I's film propaganda, particularly by means of intertitling and publicity, to play a role of significance again.

---

[80] To a certain extent nonfiction filmmaking became a less contingent affair, too, with such 'timeless' genres as the scenic (or travelogue) and the newsreel. The latter, a single-reel collection of news stories, became a regular number on the film program around 1910. It removed the difficulty of filming unpredictable events by focusing on ones that were known to occur well in advance, such as state visits, sports matches, aviation and fashion shows, and a host of annually recurring festivities and ceremonies on the social agenda. Unpredictable, dramatic incidents—state funerals, disasters, etc.—were commonly not included, as their popularity warranted a separate film.

[81] Not all these copies, however, were necessarily identical. A print's destination could affect its narrative or coloring; see, respectively: Corey Ross, *Media and the making of modern Germany: mass communications, society, and politics from the Empire to the Third Reich* (2008), p. 159; Elfriede Ledig (with Gerhard Ullmann), 'Rot wie Feuer, Leidenschaft, Genie und Wahnsinn. Zu einigen Aspekten der Farbe im Stummfilm', in: Elfriede Ledig (ed.), *Der Stummfilm. Konstruktion und Rekonstruktion* (1988), pp. 89-116.

A hangover case

A handbill for the program for the week of April 11-17, 1913, at Dutch exhibitor-cum-distributor Jean Desmet's Amsterdam cinema theater Parisien[82] listed as its last two "numbers"—to borrow contemporary parlance—the sad story of THE PASTOR'S DAUGHTER followed by the saucy tale of LEON'S FLIRT.[83]-[84] The two films differ in terms of mood and genre: a tragic German two-act drama followed by a mischievous comedy from France. This generic alternation was common and recommended. It just so happened, however, that both films were about the same subject, love betrayed, yet clashed in the way they presented it, not just in terms of register and genre, but also in terms of morals. The contrasts were even more pronounced as both films focused on their female lead, Henny Porten and Suzanne Grandais respectively, both of whom seemed tailor-made for their roles.[85] Together with the abovementioned differences, the distinctly dissimilar reputations of these actresses' portrayal of femininity—submissive and traditional v. restive and playful (particularly in Grandais' comic roles)—it is not at all unimaginable that the two films' contiguity undermined the effect that each was supposed to have. Here,

---

[82] Desmet Archief (DA) folder 317, at Eye, Amsterdam.
All handbills of Desmet's Parisien theaters are collected in one folder, with no further identification. Hence, all of the Parisien theater handbills mentioned in this paragraph should be implicitly understood as being included in DA 317, unless stated otherwise.

[83] original title DES PFARRERS TÖCHTERLEIN Dutch print title DE DOCHTER VAN DEN DOMINEE
Germany (Messter) 1913 | 35mm full frame (nitrate and safety) | b&w, tinting | 27' | Dutch titles | print at Eye, Amsterdam.

[84] original title LÉONCE FLIRTE Dutch print title LEON'S FLIRT
France (Gaumont) 1913 | 35mm full frame (nitrate and safety) | b&w, stencil coloring | 15' | Dutch titles | print at Eye, Amsterdam.

[85] As a matter of fact, the release of DES PFARRERS TÖCHTERLEIN marked the beginning of a consistent campaign to market Porten as a star after her production company, Messter, had been building up her image in various forms of publicity; see: Martin Loiperdinger, 'DES PFARRERS TÖCHTERLEIN: ein Schlüsselfilm für die Karriere von Henny Porten', in: *KINtop* (2006), pp. 210-212; Corinna Müller, *Frühe deutsche Kinematografie: formale, wirtschaftliche und kulturelle Entwicklungen* (1994), pp. 170-179.

then, we see how the program creates its own specific hangover—or 'contagion'—effect.

Did spectators actually experience a hangover effect? Did the comedy fall flat after the drama's heart-rendingly sad ending? Or was the drama dismissed as a lot of sluggishness when the merry comedy made light of similar problems of the heart? We don't really know for sure. One reason, of course, is that theatrically released silent films around this time were part of shows that varied according to type of venue, local or national customs, etc., and included, besides more films, musical accompaniment and, sometimes, lecturing, song slides or live stage acts, elements that affected reception in ways different from one performance to another. And for quite some time the practice of open admission allowed moviegoers to buy a ticket and enter the film show at any time they pleased, so that the printed program's final number could be a spectator's first. It was only three years after the opening of his first cinema theater, in early 1912, that Desmet removed the announcement that "patrons are allowed to enter the show at any moment" from the handbills of his Parisien theaters in Rotterdam and Amsterdam, a measure that may have strengthened the correspondence between a program's make-up and its audience's involvement.[86] But contingency remained. Because what we do know is that the dynamics that emerge from lining up a number of items is an inherent aspect of the program format. Undoubtedly, it made it more fluid than the contemporary design of boxed titles on posters or handbills suggested; in spectators' experience there were no outlines. On the contrary, sequent items tended to affect each other simply as a result of inevitable, cognitive processes, and not just with regard to subject matter. Spectators could pick up on any perceived similarity or dissimilarity and have their minds taken off what they were seeing to what they had seen before in the program. This effect could be purposely exploited, as the

---

[86] Film programs as closed viewings, however, apparently did not generally become the standard method for some time to come. For instance, in 1933 the Nazi regime's *Reichsfilmkammer* tried to end "the old convention of open admissions" in German cinema theaters; see: Ross (2008), p. 316. An even later example comes from a brief memoir of cinemagoing in 1950s Belfast, when "it wasn't common to arrive for the beginning of a film"; see: Ian Christie, '"Excuse me, this is where I came in..."', in: Maša Peče, Koen van Daele (eds.), *Films you wouldn't want to see anywhere else than in a movie theatre* (2014), pp. 63-65.

aforementioned SKIRT DANCE BY ANNABELLE illustrated, but it could also bring out unforeseen linkages.[87]

That does not necessarily mean, however, that these linkages were given free rein. Film historian Yuri Tsivian's recounting of how film audiences in early 1900s Russia created their own 'text' by misjudging the boundaries of (most often) single-shot films was an effect of unfamiliarity with the new entertainment compounded by the stunting of its structuring devices, a result of indifferent programming and projection.[88] But as this 'subversive' mode of reception was not something the business was prepared to tolerate, let alone encourage, it was a short-lived phenomenon. Handbills and their designs, their numbered listing, printed titles, all point to an officially sanctioned reception mode that framed the blurring and 'bleeding' of contiguous items as mistakes or misreadings. Parenthetically, it should go without saying that the effect discussed here is not meant to obscure that the same cognitive processes mentioned before would also have led spectators' minds to matters outside the screening and the venue (e.g. their memories of their favorite performers, of similar films, similar stories in other media or in real-life situations, their world knowledge, etc.). No theater manager would, or will, be able to prevent that; in fact, such associations and memories are conditional to making a film screening meaningful. So, from the industry's point of view the programming concern under discussion here was an act of containment, to stop the bleeding so to speak, and arrange materials in such a way that they suffered least from the workings of the mind.

---

[87] Robert C. Allen, *Vaudeville and film 1895-1915: a study in media interaction* (1980), pp. 47-50; Tsivian (1986), pp. 50-51; Nico de Klerk, 'Program formats', in: Richard Abel (ed.), *Encyclopaedia of early cinema* (2005), pp. 533-535.

[88] Yuri Tsivian, *Early cinema in Russia and its cultural reception* (1998 [1994]), pp. 125-129. And this recounting should be distinguished from descriptions that abstracted from the actual program for literary effect, as in: "I love the cinema. (...) It allows me to tour the world and stop, to my liking, in Tokyo and Singapore. I follow the craziest itineraries. I go to New York, which is far from beautiful, by way of the Suez, which is hardly more so; and during the same hour I travel through the Canadian forests and the Scottish highlands; I ascend the Nile as far as Khartoum and, a moment later, from the bridge of a transatlantic liner I contemplate the bleak expanse of the ocean."; see: Rémy de Gourmont, 'Epilogues: cinématographe', in: Richard Abel (ed.), *French film theory and criticism 1907-1939, vol. 1: 1907-1929* (1988), p. 48 (orig. publ. in 1907).
For the notion of "structuring devices" see: Erving Goffman, *Frame analysis: an essay on the organization of experience* (1986 [1974]), pp. 247-300.

That this concern was real is clear from contemporaneous comments, even though I have only come across a few reports on the vulnerability of cinema shows to the aleatory hangover effect. One instance is Tsivian's recounting of the measures the Russian court took to protect public screenings of filmed records of the czar and his family against potentially disrespectful   influences: besides being projected at the right (i.e. dignified) speed and screened without any musical accompaniment, they had to be clearly separated from all other films on the program by an intermission.[89] But an intermission, as we learn from an earlier example, may well have been insufficient to immunize a film from undesirable associations. A film show presented during Holy Week in a rented space in the Hall of Arts and Sciences in Utrecht, the Netherlands, elicited a disapproving editorial in a regional newspaper for screening a series of views of the festivities on the occasion of Dutch Queen Wilhelmina's wedding that followed the projection, after an intermission, of the Oberammergau PASSION PLAY: "Despite its charming variety, we nonetheless think it was inappropriate after the spiritually impressive representation of Christ's Passion."[90]

The sparseness of comments about this effect of the program format, therefore, does not warrant the conclusion that we can simply take it as a sign of its ubiquity or its acceptance. The aforementioned examples could equally plausibly suggest the opposite, or that exception was taken only when it concerned such lofty subjects as royalty and deity. Yet film historian Gregory Waller's reports of Passion Play screenings between 1899 and 1903, in Lexington, KY, mention no such complaints in the newspapers he researched. These screenings, though, appear to have varied in prominence in widely divergent, heterogeneous programs (i.e. combinations of film projections and other types of—mostly live— amusement), in the opera house as well in the church, ranging from the

---

[89] Tsivian (1986), p. 51. The protective, 'sanitary' measures he mentions probably reflected czar Nicholas II's opinion of cinema as "an empty, totally useless, and even harmful form of entertainment"—quoted in: Richard Taylor, Ian Christie (eds.), *The film factory: Russian and Soviet cinema in documents 1896-1939* (1988), p. 19. Nevertheless, the Romanovs did employ a court photographer who made films for propaganda purposes; see: Graham Roberts, *Forward Soviet: history and non-fiction film in the USSR* (1999), p. 10.

[90] *Utrechtsch Provinciaal en Stedelijk Dagblad** (April 1, 1901), quoted in: Herman de Wit, *Film in Utrecht van 1895-1915* (1986), p. 50 (my translation).
* *Utrecht Provincial and Municipal News*

serious to the entertaining. Examples Waller mentions are a stand-alone performance expanded with "illustrated songs, and a 'descriptive lecture', with Lexington's Central Christian Church choir on hand to provide 'sacred music'"; as a "prelude" to a stage show, *The South before the war*, which consisted of "old Southern plantation festivities"; or traveling exhibitor J.V. Snow's church screenings in combination with "comic motion pictures and newsreel-styled footage, with Snow himself providing vocal, cornet, and graphophone accompaniment."[91] Certainly from a musical point of view this "aesthetic of discontinuity" shouldn't surprise us: creating links in terms of subject matter or mood was not, according to film historian Rick Altman, an important consideration in, or expectation of, American 19th- and early 20th-century stage music.[92] Inappropriateness might only have been a concern in the first of these examples, which appears to have maintained a consistently religious tone and atmosphere. In the other two, decorum seems to have been less relevant; there, the Passion Play film may be more fruitfully understood as part of a miscellaneous collection of entertainments, not unlike the combination of instruction and amusement in magic lantern shows.[93]

But not quite like it either. In addition to its line-up of functionally related items—that is to say, not overlaid by a narrative or thematic meaning[94]—the magic lantern show as well as the exclusive film program and the vaudeville show (more particularly, its late 19th-century, cleaned-up version) emphasized their consistency rather in terms of tone and subject matter in order to make it inoffensive, if not respectable and fit for family entertainment. To be sure, these formats' line-ups were contrastive, but only in the sense that "the program progressed through a series of

---

[91] Gregory Waller, *Main Street amusements: movies and commercial entertainment in a southern city, 1896-1930* (1995), pp. 51-52.

[92] Altman (2004), pp. 32-36.

[93] The Spring 1898 *Sears Guide*, William Uricchio points out, actually suggested programmatic combinations of moving pictures, lantern slides, recorded music (all technologies that Sears offered for sale), and a lecturer's speech to make a spectacle out of popular and/or topical subjects; see his: 'Selling the motion picture to the *fin-de-siècle* American public', in: Florin, de Klerk, Vonderau (2016), pp. 71-82.

[94] Allen (1980), pp. 46-47.

recommencements, with each individual item ideally being different from its predecessor."[95]

Yet within the emerging cinema industry skepticism towards the realization of that ideal within the program may well have triggered concerns about the format's vulnerability and the way an individual film's intended reception was affected by its position. And not merely reception, of course. The financial stakes, given the trend towards incorporation and the investments in studios, theaters, creative personnel, and publicity; the scale—both nation-wide and international—of the industry; as well as the rise of a legal framework, initiated by the book trade, for copyright on motion pictures ever since the 1908 Berne Convention and its follow-ups,[96] were becoming vastly greater than those of magic lantern or vaudeville. Manuals produced by or for the film industry acknowledged the problem in various warnings, admonishments, and other advice with regard to the structure, mood, propriety or variation of the program. An influential German manual, for instance, dissuaded exhibitors from having a knee-slapping farce follow a deeply moving tragedy, as the program as a whole was meant to be balanced and harmonic (*"abgestimmt und harmonisch"*), while a British handbook recommended "making up" the arrangement of films "in such sequence that each one will, by contrast, help the next as much as possible."[97] Contrast, one may conclude, should be functional rather than demonstrative, tasteful rather than conspicuous.

Both manuals quoted were written or revised at a time when the program was still largely made up of quickly alternating, relatively short films whose lengths were not extremely different, a circumstance favorable to the hangover effect. This reflects the fact that when multiple-reel films began their ascent on the program, around 1910, they were not an immediate fixture. (A 1913 American manual's advice to theater managers implicitly describes short, small-time vaudeville programs—screenings alternating with a few songs or other brief, live

---

[95] De Klerk (2005), p. 534; see also De Klerk (2000), pp. 210, 220-221 n. 36 ; Allen (1980), pp. 48-50.

[96] Jasmin Lange, *Der deutsche Buchhandel und der Siegeszug der Kinematographie 1895-1933* (2010), pp. 63-73.

[97] See respectively: F. Paul Liesegang, *Handbuch der praktischen Kinematographie* (1911 [1907]), p. 247; Colin Bennett, *The handbook of kinematography: the history, theory, and practice of motion picture photography and projection* (1911), p. 203.

entertainments—of less than an hour that could be shown up to fifteen times a day; here, too, the longer "feature film" was still an exception.[98]) Nor did the longer film imply any sort of standard yet. On the contrary, what is striking was its enormous variation in length, its "*élasticité narrative*",[99] from two acts to what the Dutch trade—echoing its German counterpart—called *kilometerfilms*, while it also impacted program make-up in various ways. As a matter of fact, in our example of the Amsterdam program, THE PASTOR'S DAUGHTER, with its two acts clearly the centerpiece of the program, was just over ten minutes longer than LEON'S FLIRT—although for reasons unknown the surviving Dutch print in the Desmet collection is 200 meters shorter than the German release version (which equals about ten minutes when projected at its restored version of 18 frames per second [fps]). The multiple-reeler imposed itself gradually, since it was not the outcome of a unified campaign but came from various directions: new ways of production and distribution (e.g. the variously trendsetting initiatives of Pathé subsidiary SCAGL or those of Danish cinema owners in Europe[100]; Vitagraph's experiment with the release of its five-reeler LIFE OF MOSES [1909-1910] in the US[101]); of doing business (e.g. exclusivity, raising rentals and admission); and marketing (e.g. the star-system, upmarket or gentrified positioning through bigger and better venues). It took a number of years to develop, and reject, solutions to accommodate the feature and replace the variety-like way of lining up short films.

Judging from program handbills the rise of the longer film may well have mitigated the hangover effect by increasing differences in length between films and, eventually, by reducing the number of short films on the program. However, if the effect declined, it seemed to have been a side

---

[98] David S. Hulfish, *Motion-picture work: a general treatise on picture taking, picture making, photo plays, and theater management and operation* (1913), pp. 196-202; see also: Janet Staiger, 'Combination and litigation: structures of US film distribution, 1896-1917', in: Thomas Elsaesser with Adam Barker (eds.), *Early cinema: space, frame, narrative* (1992 [1990]), pp. 198-199.

[99] Eric de Kuyper, 'Le cinéma de la seconde époque: le muet des années dix (I)', in: *Cinémathèque* (May 1992), p. 31.

[100] See, respectively: Philippe Azoury, 'L'invitation à l'art', in: Marie, Le Forestier (2004), pp. 87-91; Müller (1994), pp. 124-125.

[101] Uricchio, Pearson (1993), pp. 170-172.

effect, welcomed perhaps, but not planned.[102] During a number of years, roughly between 1910 and 1914, the longer film posed problems for exhibitors in that they were faced with a fluctuating supply—one week a theater's program could be graced by a feature, while the next it resumed its line-up of short films—and with simultaneous yet contradictory demands, particularly with regard to maintaining balance and creating variety.

Coming back to the handbills for Desmet's Amsterdam Parisien theater, this collection, albeit lacunal, allows one to trace a number of measures, some impromptu, others eventually adopted, to meet the changing circumstances. The earliest available handbill, in fact the opening program of his Amsterdam Parisien theater for the week following March 26, 1910, stuck to the basic pattern of his first theater, the Parisien in Rotterdam, which had opened the year before.[103] It begins with a nonfiction item, a travel scene, and it ends on a comic note; in between, drama and comedy alternate and build up towards some sort of high spot right before the final comic number. Until c. mid-1911 the programs usually consisted of seven titles. The alternation of comedy and drama (the drama sometimes being a fairy tale, the comedy often being a farce) may have served another purpose besides balance: the comedies and farces, being shorter and lacking a complicated plot (not seldom a mere crescendo of destructions), may have allowed spectators who entered in midshow to settle in more easily. For those whose entry time did coincide with the program's starting time the comedy may have served to send

---

[102] Detailed accounts of this period, such as Müller (1994), Abel (2006), and Martin Loiperdinger, Uli Jung (eds.), *Importing Asta Nielsen: the international star in the making 1910-1914* (2013) do not mention or suggest this consideration. As a matter of fact, one example to the contrary comes from film historian Pierre-Emmanuel Jacques. He quotes a Swiss reviewer who was shocked by two *features*, a crime film starring Asta Nielsen and a temperance drama, screened back-to-back in a 1911 program that contained no short films at all; see his: 'Asta Nielsen in the cinema theatres of Lausanne, 1911-1913', in: Loiperdinger, Jung (2013), pp. 172-173, 175-176.

[103] Ivo Blom, *Jean Desmet and the early Dutch film trade* (2003), pp. 90; 110; 190-191.

them off with a smile on their face—obviously, this measure to secure customer loyalty was widespread.[104]

The handbill for the week following January 27, 1911, is the first with a real feature: WHITE SLAVERY, a Danish production (original title DEN HVIDE SLAVEHANDEL). No Dutch print has survived, so we don't know its precise length; in Denmark, it seems to have been released at a length of 45'.[105] But since it lists this film as being shown in two parts, the print must have been appreciably longer than the customary fare at the time. Undeniably it required adaptations to the program's template. First of all, the feature's two parts disturbed the strict alternation of drama and comedy. Having maintained the usual amount of three comic numbers, the first one separated the shorter drama ROSE O'SALEM-TOWN from the feature, while the program ended on the two remaining comedies screened consecutively. Alternatively, though, Desmet could have retained the alternation of genres more consistently by having one of the two final comedies follow the opening actuality, instead of ROSE O'SALEM-TOWN. In that case this short drama would still have been alternated with another of the program's three comedies to separate it from the feature (until then, as the handbills show, the *order* of alternating dramas and comedies had been largely immaterial). But this seems to have been no consideration. Why two of the three comedies were shown back-to-back remains a matter of speculation. Perhaps it was an attempt to pile up a certain mass of laughing material after an unusually long melodrama. Secondly, while the feature's announced two parts may reflect the separate reels on which it was threaded, this handbill—the first in this collection with a numbered program—also cosmetically maintained the notion of a full, seven-item line-up by assigning each part a separate number. In addition, the subdivision in parts may well have alerted those patrons who wanted to

---

[104] The printed line-ups of the aforementioned Palace Theatre of Varieties of a decade earlier, as well as a few U.S. Keith's theaters' handbills reproduced in Altman (2004; pp. 94, 100), clearly show that comedy also clearly functioned to create an audience out of a crowd of ticket buyers, as the line-up of stage numbers always opened with one or more comic acts. Of course, this arrangement also set the tone for an entertainment that was lighter than the average cinema theater show, as it hardly included acts that required what philosopher Martha Nussbaum calls "positional thinking", that is "the ability to see the world from another creature's viewpoint."; see her: *Not for profit: why democracy needs the humanities* (2012 [2010]), p. 36.

[105] http://www.imdb.com/title/tt0001258/?ref_=fn_tt_tt_1.

enter the cinema in mid-program. Conjecture aside, what is clear is that a feature complicated both program structure and open admission.

While the next handbill in the collection, that of May 2-4, 1911, reverts to Desmet's normal program make-up, it is the one for September 22 of that year that shows a drastic, albeit short-lived change. With only three titles on the program, it dispenses with actualities or other documentary genres and merely opens and ends on a comedy, with the three-part THE AVIATOR AND THE JOURNALIST'S WIFE as its centerpiece. No attempt was made to even cosmetically suggest there was a full and varied line-up, as the featured drama, again a Danish production (original title AVIATIKEREN OG JOURNALISTENS HUSTRU), was a *kilometerfilm* of 1,160 meters—at 18fps that meant a running time of almost an hour—listed as a single number. However, this measure did not herald a lasting practice. Two weeks later, the handbill for October 6-9, 1911, featured another one-hour drama, THE DEFECT (original title LA TARE) amid a much more, or rather more seemingly varied line-up. First of all, even as it retained the merest shadow of the Parisien program's template—opening with a nonfiction item and ending with two comedies—all items as well as each act of the featured drama (acts two and three called 'Continuation' and 'Conclusion') were numbered, adding up to six in all. Furthermore, one of the comedies as well as the opening newsreel were given rather extensive summaries. The newsreel in particular was exploited to suggest maximum variety by providing a summary for each of its nine individual stories, while its variation was reinforced, of course, by jumping to a number of locations.

Parenthetically, as Desmet was also a distributor who provided his clients with ample publicity material, we can see that the uncertainty of reconciling contradictory programming demands was spread to other theaters around the country. For instance, on its handbill for October 28-30, 1911, the Electro Bioscope, in the town of Middelburg, the feature THE AVIATOR AND THE JOURNALIST'S WIFE was listed, like Desmet's handbill, as one number, while THE DEFECT, on its handbill for November 15-17, 1911, was, again like Desmet's, numbered through from 2 to 6.[106] I give this example not to suggest an increasing conformity in the make-up of film programs: the Electro had a distinct (albeit inconsistent) way of arranging its programs, as had many other theaters in their competition for the patron's money. Rather, I think, it was a conformity of confusion.

---

[106] Both handbills of the Electro Bioscope can be found in DA 191-1.

Only months later, in the next surviving handbill for March 8-11, 1912, can one see how the feature film began to slowly tighten its grip on Parisien's program make-up. Being the earliest surviving handbill to drop the announcement regarding open admission it can be taken, moreover, as pointing in the direction of the feature's future impact. Instead of alternating genres, the program now clustered them: after opening with two documentary items—a newsreel and a travel scene—comes a three-part drama, followed by two comedies to round off the program. Although it would only gradually become more prominent, one specific impact of clustering is already evident from this specimen: it spelled the doom of the short, one-reel drama. In fact, by 1915 the short drama had practically disappeared from the surviving handbills of a number of Dutch cinemas I have inspected. With the feature providing about an hour's worth or more of drama—comedies did not attain this length for some years to come—, this element of the program simply had become superfluous.

Another consequence of the rise of the feature was its modification of the function of concentrating comedies at the end of the lineup: they now evidenced a uniform starting time that obviated the need to integrate the 'stray' spectator among those more or less settled in. And it also signaled a tendency to affect the mood of the film show, making it more consistently serious by linking documentary and (melo)drama without a comic break. And while screening features was still not a regular affair, as handbills of the next few months show (in those for March 22-25, April 9-12, May 24-27, and June 25-27, 1912, the original template is restored with six or seven short films in an alternating order), later on, when features did become a more regular part of the program, its template gradually and definitively turned away from alternating genres. And while it happened that a long film changed location, mood, and even, so it suggested, genre with each new act, as in the featured crime story THE DEVIL'S EYE in a 1914 Parisien program,[107] most film stories would not have lent themselves so easily to such mimicry of the 'old' program format. In any event, by that time Desmet's publicity already focused largely on the feature.[108]

---

[107] original title TEUFELSAUGE Dutch print title DUIVELSOOG
Germany (Vay & Hubert) 1914 | 35mm full frame (nitrate and safety) | b&w, tinting | Dutch titles | 888m | 44' | print at Eye, Amsterdam.
The handbill for the program featuring this film can be found in DA 232-c.

[108] Blom (2003), p. 278.

The clustering of films of similar genres produced one other effect: it restrained variation. With the gradual disappearance of the short drama and the reduction of comedies to a single, final number, variation around this time was largely a primacy effect of opening with two short documentary films. The handbill for October 31-November 6, 1913, for instance, opens with a (usually black-and-white) newsreel, followed by the colored nature film MAYFLOWERS, while the one for December 12-18, 1913, has its newsreel ("interesting actualities") followed by PICTURESQUE JAPAN ("beautifully colored scenic"). So, although as a rule the hangover effect remains difficult to control—it is, after all, largely in the mind of the beholder—, the strategy of clustering reduced the risk of its occurrence at the most obvious places in the program. The "programme proximity"[109] of THE PASTOR'S DAUGHTER and LEON'S FLIRT was perhaps a location-specific, collateral accident, as it happened at a particular moment in the adapted program's line-up that should have warranted a theater manager's utmost alertness: the fault line between drama and comedy.

Obviously the collection of handbills of Desmet's Parisien theaters offers just one instance of the program format as a site of competing measures, which included arranging a cinema theater show's elements in the most favorable way, counteracting unwelcome aspects of that very arrangement, and accommodating changes originating elsewhere in the film industry, all in the service of offering patrons an entertaining show. Certainly in the first decade after the emergence of the cinema theater, programs will have differed in the arrangement of items and in their adaptation to longer films, depending on local circumstances and traditions, and in the shifting ways films functioned within the format. Here, in fact, we witness a gradual, but fundamental transformation of cinema as an entertainment: the modular program format, whose elements had a functional (or positional) significance, was being made to accommodate a narratively integrated element that would go on to dominate the format—and publicity—while crowding out its shorter elements to the extent that these would merely fill out the show and keep up the appearance of variety.

---

[109] Tsivian (1998), pp. 129.

A paratextual case

On April 21, 1915, a selection of information films about the colony of the Netherlands East-Indies (today's Republic of Indonesia) had its premiere in the presence of Queen Wilhelmina and other members of the Dutch royal family, along with cabinet members and assorted dignitaries. The films, commissioned by the association 'Koloniaal Instituut', were made in the colony between March 1912 and March 1913 under the supervision of and partly shot by J.C. Lamster, a captain in the colonial army's Topographical Department (he was stationed in the Netherlands East-Indies, but was approached for the job while on leave in Holland in 1911). Various circumstances within and beyond the control of the association had contributed to the films' delayed premiere. Beyond its control, of course, was the outbreak of war, in August 1914. A scheduled royal screening for September of that year had to be cancelled in those uncertain times (the Netherlands had declared itself neutral. But so had Belgium...). Very much within its control was its intended distribution policy for the materials that had been shipped to Amsterdam. This policy was characterized by a rather stubbornly hostile attitude vis-à-vis cinema theaters and their perceived gaudy mix of comedy, melodrama, and exoticism—the almost proverbial cheap amusements. The association's board of directors had stated this position in a letter to the Secretary of Colonial Affairs, in which it presented its plans to propagate the East-Indies by means of cinematography: besides asking for financial support, more particularly to relieve Lamster of his army duties and pick up his salary for the year the assignment was estimated to last, it pointed out that the films were meant for the "instruction" of audiences, particularly students and pupils in all age categories.[110] Therefore, as the minutes of a later board meeting specified, the way the films were to be presented "must avoid the character of cinema screenings".[111] Accordingly the board had passed up a number of opportunities to make the collection of films known to the public. Requests by cinema owners to premiere the films had all been turned down for being too expensive, which was rather

---

[110] Letter of board of directors Vereeniging Koloniaal Instituut to Secretary of Colonial Affairs, November 7, 1911 (NA [National Archives], file no. 2.20.36.04 inv. 878).

[111] Minutes of meeting board of directors Vereeniging Koloniaal Instituut, January 15, 1912, p. 8 (KIT [Royal Tropical Institute], file no. 219).

disingenuous, since an offer to host the premiere free of charge was rejected as well.[112]

It is not clear from the institute's archives, by the way, to what extent its board was aware of the uniqueness of this collection of films. Having all of a sudden over fifty titles at its disposal was a major achievement. No Dutch production company, let alone an institute with research and museum ambitions, had made colonial propaganda films before, while screenings of foreign-made films of the Dutch colonies were few and far between. Most of the latter came from French multinational Pathé Frères, which was wont to send film crews to Asia and other colonial and non-Western territories every few years or so to shoot footage from which exotic touches for the commercial cinema program were cut. Its series of films shot in the Netherlands East-Indies in 1909, for example, had been released in cinemas at intervals of months.[113] And because after the outbreak of the war it was well-nigh impossible, for French as well as other European companies, to send crews abroad, the Colonial Institute, until the late 1910s, had a monopoly on moving images of Dutch colonial territories. But it seemed in no hurry to capitalize on that position.

What *is* clear is that the institute had painted itself in a corner with its anti-cinema policy. In Amsterdam, where the Colonial Institute was headquartered, there were no safe venues that met its criteria, because "only projection booths in cinema theaters complied with police regulations".[114] The premiere, therefore, had to be moved to another venue, in another town, that was properly equipped: a secondary school in The Hague. The event, in fact, had to be spread over two nights, since the school auditorium's limited capacity of 120 seats necessitated a second

---

[112] Minutes of meeting board of directors Vereeniging Koloniaal Instituut, March 9, 1914, pp. 2-3 (NA, file no. 2.21.043).

[113] Henri Bousquet, *Catalogue Pathé des années 1896 à 1914: 1907-1908-1909* (1993), p. 158.

[114] Minutes of meeting of the executive of Vereeniging Koloniaal Instituut, April 6, 1914, p. 3 (KIT, file no. 215). What is meant, of course, are regulations concerning fire safety.

'premiere' for parliamentarians.[115] The venue and the way the selection of films was introduced must nonetheless have satisfied the association's board members as a model of how it imagined future presentations of its films. Not only would they be screened in educational, non-theatrical settings—besides schools also universities, museums, etc.—, but, as they had detailed in the abovementioned letter to the Department of Colonial Affairs, "the films would be subordinate to, yet no less serious than accompanying lectures". In fact, its presentations were announced as being, indeed, "lectures" rather than screenings, in keeping with the grand tradition of magic lantern shows.[116]

For the royal premiere, the first of such lectures was delivered by the Department of Colonial Affairs' representative on the association's board of directors. A newspaper report gives a brief impression of his presentation of one of the films on the program, NATIVE VILLAGE LIFE:[117] "First Mr. Bakhuis showed us the bathing and the splashing of the natives, their children, horses, oxen, etc.", while he explained "that all this bathing cannot be entirely attributed to a sense of cleanliness, but rather to a desire for coolness; soap is not commonly used."[118] The summary clearly echoed, in fact, the films's intertitles and predated the text of what would become a standard procedure of the institute's screenings: lectures given on the basis of accompanying printed booklets, the so-called *Illustrations*.

---

[115] Janneke van Dijk, Jaap de Jonge, 'Johann Christian Lamster (1872-1954)'; Nico de Klerk, 'Een onmogelijke opdracht: J.C. Lamsters filmopnamen voor het Koloniaal Instituut'*, in: Janneke van Dijk, Jaap de Jonge, Nico de Klerk, *J.C. Lamster, een vroege filmmaker in Nederlands-Indië** (2010), pp. 32-35; p. 102, respectively. According to a news report of the royal premiere, the school must have been more than properly equipped, since one of its teachers, who doubled as projectionist, was credited with an invention that could safely arrest a film in projection; see: 'Films over Oost-Indië'***, in: *Nieuwe Rotterdamsche Courant**** (April 22, 1915), morning edn. B, p. 2. In fact, this school continued to be used as a venue for non-theatrical screenings in the 1920s.
*'Commission impossible: J.C. Lamster's film records for the Colonial Institute'; **'J.C. Lamster: early filmmaker in the Netherlands East-Indies; ***'Films about the East-Indies'; ****New Rotterdam Courant

[116] NA, file no. 2.20.36.04 inv. 878.

[117] original title HET LEVEN VAN DEN INLANDER IN DE DESA
The Netherlands (Koloniaal Instituut) [1912/3] | 35mm full frame (safety) | b&w, tinting | Dutch titles | 8' | print at Eye, Amsterdam.

[118] 'Films over Oost-Indië' (April 22, 1915), p. 2.

These Illustrations constitute a unique film heritage collection. Some forty-five of their printed texts, varying in length from three to ten pages, have survived. They were sent along with the film prints wherever they were screened (at least in the Netherlands, as there is no evidence of translated versions to date, even though a number of titles were available for screening abroad) and read aloud by the obligatory lecturer—not the kind that entertained in cinema theaters, but an expert on topics regarding the colony. There is a number of reasons that makes these sources unique. First of all, of course, unlike most cinema theater lecturers' expositions these texts *have* come down to us. The 1918 and 1923 editions of the institute's film catalogue mention that "speakers are expected to illustrate the films while running". As a matter of fact, various phrases in their texts suggest a direct connection between the Illustrations and what was screened, as in "Here you see...", "the next scene shows...", "In the foreground..."; and at times the texts attempted to direct spectators to a particular element, even sequence their eyes and attention, as in the Illustration to the film BATIK[119]: "On the right, large cloths (*sarungs* and *kains*) are being dipped in a large, shallow tub (the *sogan* tub), and on the left smaller cloths are being dyed in round tubs."

Secondly, these texts have been preserved in a fairly reliable form. Not so much because of their being 'frozen' in print; they were probably not quite that, as one would expect lecturers to have embellished on what the booklets contained, perhaps skipped a paragraph now and then, or provided updates. No, what makes them reliable is precisely the evidence they contain of such modifications. Written on the copy of the Illustration to NATIVE VILLAGE LIFE, for instance, are numerous red-inked suggestions for corrections.[120] And a hand-written comment in the margin of a copy of the Illustration to CAR RIDE THROUGH BANDUNG is even more explicit by calling the film "obsolete", since the town, as a revised version states, "was in the grip of a veritable building fever, changing the city day by day. The film, which was shot in 1913, certainly doesn't show present-day Bandung."[121]

---

[119] original title HET BATIK
The Netherlands (Koloniaal Instituut) [1912/3] | 35mm full frame (safety) | b&w, tinting | Dutch titles | 15'35" | print at Eye, Amsterdam.

[120] See the reproduction in: Van Dijk, De Jonge, de Klerk (2010), pp. 121-125.

[121] original title AUTOTOCHT DOOR BANDOENG.

Such comments, incidentally, also must have been one of the reasons for the changes made in the prints made of Lamster's footage. Each of the three successive editions of the institute's film catalogue—the first one was published in 1915—show that no title had escaped such changes. Prints of NATIVE VILLAGE LIFE, for instance, fluctuated from 200m to 244m to 165m, while CAR RIDE IN BANDUNG went from 150m to 125m to 220m. The films were re-cut, re-arranged, and/or re-titled: some titles were dropped, scenes of one film were included in another or, conversely, were separated and listed under a title of their own. Inspection of the prints also led to the insertion of filmed photographs, maps or drawings from the institute's collections to highlight details or show aspects that had not been recorded satisfyingly or at all. As well c. 1,000m of (probably unreleased) footage was bought from Pathé Frères, parts of which were inserted in a number of films.[122] Still, updating was largely—and because of the war, necessarily— a textual matter, in print (intertitles and Illustrations) and in speech.

Thirdly, on a conceptual level these booklets are examples of what literary scholar Gérard Genette, in his classic study *Seuils*, has termed *paratextes*.[123] He defined paratexts as "products" that belong to the text by "surrounding and extending it" in order to present it, in the usual sense of this term, as well as in a more emphatic sense: to "ensure [its] presence in the world, its 'reception' and its 'consumption'". Paratexts mediate between a text and its prospective buyers and readers: they announce, advertise, publicize, recommend, seduce, position, mark, inform, clarify, steer, interpret, deepen, but also mystify or mislead. In other words, they do anything to serve the text, and, by implication, its authors', editors' or publishers' considerations, intentions or interests. Conceived of as liminal, pragmatic elements, Genette has subdivided paratexts into those that are connected to—either around or within—the text, which he called

---

The Netherlands (Koloniaal Instituut) [1912/3] | 35mm full frame (safety) | tinting, b&w | Dutch titles | 11' | print at Eye, Amsterdam. The third edition of the Colonial Institute's catalogue of films was published in 1923, so the films must have been been available for more than a decade after their recording. CAR RIDE IN BANDUNG is, in fact, one of three titles of which different versions of their Illustration have survived.

[122] Suzanne Crommelin, 'Filmografie', in: Van Dijk, de Jonge, de Klerk (2010), pp. 118-121; De Klerk (2010), pp. 83-86, 94-99.
Films containing Pathé footage were marked in the catalogues of 1918 and 1923 to signal that copyright issues precluded their screening outside the Netherlands.

[123] Gérard Genette, *Seuils* (2002 [1987]).

péritextes; and those found anywhere outside the text, which he called *épitextes*. In his study, examples of peritexts are: dust jackets, covers, title pages, blurbs, dedications, forewords, chapter titles, etc. Examples of epitexts are: advertisements, interviews, reviews, etc., as well as more private sources such as relevant individuals' diaries or letters. Paratextual elements are to be understood, however, less as objects than as practices, or functions. Thus, the distinctions that result from their spatial definition are not fixed, but relative to the text, since the one can become the other. For example, a newspaper interview with a writer about his new book is an epitext; but when later appended in a scholarly edition or a volume of complete works, it has become part of that publication itself, i.e. a peritext.

Genette developed his terminology with reference to literary books, yet it is sufficiently non-specific to apply to other cultural objects, as he himself cautiously suggested.[124] When transposed to film 'texts', we may think of peritexts as additions to release prints, such as production and distribution companies' logos, translated titles, intertitles or subtitles, credit rolls, or "The end", while trailers, teasers, and publicity in other media (e.g. posters, catalogues, interviews), as well as those film elements that were never meant for public viewing (e.g. negatives, outtakes) can be considered as epitexts. And this type of film-related paratexts, too, can change function; just think of the currently popular bonus titles on DVD editions, such as trailers, bloopers or interviews. (As a matter of fact, over the years bloopers have been transformed into staged versions of themselves to enhance a DVD edition or even a theatrical release— features starring Jackie Chan are a well-known instance—, but also for 'reality' TV productions of the funny-video kind.)

In the specific case of the Colonial Institute's film collection, though, market forces affected the institute's decisions only minimally. Still, the publication of one of the films' epitexts, the first edition of its film catalogue, certainly was the result of external pressure. We learn from the minutes of a board meeting in May 1915 that the same Mr. Bakhuis who had lectured during the royal premiere expressed, on behalf of the Department of Colonial Affairs, its discontent with the institute's restrictive screening policy and lack of initiative in disseminating the films on a wider scale.[125] Despite the chairman of the board's protestations, this

---

[124] Genette (2002), p. 410.

[125] Minutes of meeting board of directors Vereeniging Koloniaal Instituut, May 17, 1915 (NA, file no. 2.21.043).

criticism by the project's major sponsor a mere month after the royal premiere—which, moreover, had been widely ignored in Dutch newspapers—was unmistakable. So, in its *Fourth annual report: 1914*, published in 1915, the institute dutifully appended its film catalogue as 'Annex XI'. And it was only during the course of that year that requests for the films, domestically and from abroad, began to trickle in. No departmental disgruntlements were recorded since.

The application of paratextual terms to the Illustrations, however, introduces a change of focus: as printed booklets they seem to be obvious epitexts, elements external to the films. Yet in a very real sense they had no readers or listeners, because there simply were neither texts nor paratexts until the moment a film's Illustration was *spoken* parallel to its projection; only then can we say that their intended functions were realized. But what are the consequences of this transformation—from print to speech, from reel to projection—for the structure of these performances? How do we conceive of their textual and paratextual elements? The question, incidentally, is not so much about the combination of different media per se. Such combinations were and are commonplace and have merely enlarged the arsenal of paratexts (e.g. today's combined book-DVD publications). But performances are different in the sense that they allow various channels to occur together in time, simultaneously, sequentially, or both. And this forces us think about their constituent elements and their cohesion, whether an element's status is intrinsic or incidental, and how these configurations differ from one type of performance to another. Clearly, the Colonial Institute's presentations, while concerned with moving images, had been modeled after the magic lantern show. So, in order to get a sense of their structure one has to look at the constituent elements of both contemporary magic lantern and cinema shows. For consistency's sake, though, one thing should be clear at the outset: if epitexts are by definition elements outside the text, they are perforce outside the performance, i.e. as not occurring sequentially and/or simultaneously within a specified time frame and a specified space.

While the magic that gives the magic lantern show its name firmly resided in its projected images, multiple channels were employed to accomplish its performance. Music and/or song may have framed the show and provided intermezzi to enliven the event as a whole, while they also served the projections by accompanying the visuals and bringing audiences in a mood appropriate with what was thrown on the screen. Their function, along with sound effects (if any), was to a large extent peritextual. That must also have applied to the very—and very visibly present—apparatus, the imposing triunials in particular, that produced the magic-like effects. But the role of the lecturer and his assistant(s), if any, was more ambiguous. First of all, in one or more numbers on the program lecturing could have been delivered *as* music and song, with either adapted existing texts set to music or purposely written material.[126] But ambiguity was also a direct consequence of the type of image material featured. Because apart from the brief, stand-alone entertainments of transformation slides—e.g. dissolving views or chromatropes—the available slide stories were lacunal by definition. Whether about travel, history, religion or countless other subjects, and irrespective of the number of slides a set consisted of, their immobility and narrative indeterminacy made it, if not impossible, then certainly cumbersome for them to be sufficiently meaningful or entertaining by themselves.[127] Pre-existing intertexts, notably biblical stories, notwithstanding, projection and lecturing were inseparable, as the lecturer's performance served two distinct functions. Not only did he string the slides together by providing what wasn't there to see (yet might be known), but these very gaps reinforced his peritextual role in creating a rapport with his audience through his storytelling talents and style of presentation—his diction and eloquence, knowledgeability or humor—that were crucial for the success of an evening's entertainment and instruction (even though he may now and then have recited a preexisting text, e.g. from the Scriptures or a poem). The lecturer, one might say, both embodied the text *and* mediated between it and the audience at the same time.

Here, parenthetically, I disagree with film historian André Gaudreault's argument that it is "more accurate to regard magic lantern shows as oral narratives supplemented by illustrations on screen" as a result of "the

---

[126] See for a reconstruction of such a performance *Ora pro nobis*, a partly photographed, partly drawn glass slide story manufactured by the British company Bamforth, in 1897, with authored text and music on: LICHTSPIELE UND SOZIALFRAGE/SCREENING THE POOR 1888-1914 (Germany: DIF, Medienwissenschaft Universität Trier, Filmmuseum München, 2011), | DVD | b&w, color | sound | 6' | *Edition Filmmuseum* no. 64.

[127] Lecture sets varied enormously in terms of their number, as examples of the abovementioned subjects show: "*Guernsey...* 11 slides" or "*Our Indian and colonial empire...* 73 slides"; "*John Wycliffe...* 12 slides" or "*English history...* 109 slides"; "*Life of Moses...* 23 slides" or "*The Old Testament....* 154 slides". These examples are taken from a list of lecture sets in: Walter D. Welford, Henry Sturmey (comps. & eds.), *The indispensable handbook to the optical lantern: a complete cyclopaedia on the subject of optical lanterns, slides and accessory apparatus* (1888), pp. 234-323.

short succession of the slides" and their "relatively small number." These two quoted phrases raise a specific circumstance to a general conclusion. His argument seems to be more accurate as a characterization of John L. Stoddard's late 19th-century travel lectures.[128] But in many other magic lantern shows of that time there seems to have been no reason for projected images to be subordinate to the lecture. As the referenced handbook shows, the number of slides a set might contain was variable (while a lecturer was of course free to 'edit' any set he had purchased), yet by the late 19th-century, "owing to the vast number of [photographically reproduced] slides now commercially available", larger sets were certainly no exception.[129] Their succession will have varied, too, partly as a function of the storyline a lecturer created by his arrangement of the slides, and partly of the variable gaps between successive slides.

Now let us turn to the period's cinema screenings. It has been said that silent films are semi-finished products, only completed by the accompaniment of live or gramophone-reproduced music, speech, and/or other sounds. The trouble with this viewpoint is that it silently postulates the film performance as an indivisible object. But one thing that is clear is that the cohesion of its constituent elements was weak at best. This situation was compounded by, if not a direct result of, film's multiple identities. Until industrially produced film screenings crystallized into a mainstream theatrical practice, alongside an already strong and prolonged non-theatrical tradition, they were included in and adapted to a variety of entertainments of which they were not seldom a mere element, as in such distinct presentations as travelogue lectures, vaudeville/variety shows or fairgrounds. But throughout the silent era— and clearly more evident than in magic lantern shows—paratextual and other regulating elements surrounding film screenings were replaceable, even detachable. A brief aggregate is all I can present within the space of this brief case study.

---

[128] André Gaudreault: 'Showing and telling: image and word in early cinema', in: Elseasser with Barker (1992), p. 276.
Film historian Rick Altman's characterization of Stoddard's lectures as being "only by chance an audiovisual medium" and an adaptation "to the fashion of his age" is mere circumstantial evidence that doesn't in any way address their structural aspects; see Altman (2004), p. 58.

[129] Welford, Sturmey (1888), p. 233.

Lecturing, for one thing, was only a constant element in travelogues and other documentary topics (e.g. wildlife, religion) in itinerant shows—these, too, had been modeled after the magic lantern show. In vaudeville, however, it seems to have been virtually absent, while in commercial cinema shows, it has been argued, its need varied in terms of what it was meant to accomplish. As an aid in comprehension, for instance, its presence was essential only at specific junctures in the history of film storytelling, at least in the West.[130] The extent to which it affected a theater's profit margin will have been no less an important consideration.

Music and sound effects, too, were detachable. For instance, until well into the 1900s film programs in American vaudeville were largely screened over an empty orchestra pit.[131] Moreover, wherever there was music, it did double duty for other pragmatic but noncoincident functions. It was not just, or always, meant to accompany the film. It could serve as entr'acte, with or without a singing voice; in nickelodeons music was known to be piped into the street to attract customers[132]—where live barkers did the same, probably distributing handbills while they were at it; it could function as marking the boundaries of and/or accomplishing the transitions to and from the film projections—what sociologist Erving Goffman called episoding conventions.[133] Simultaneously of course, music could serve to drown out noise or, indeed, silence.[134] And insofar as music *was* meant to accompany a film program, it was a highly variable and unstable element, ranging from picture songs to commissioned, artistically ambitious scores that were conceived as an integral part of the film show (or rather, of a single prestigious feature film) as well as to loosely connected scamping and tweedling—what philosopher Ernst

---

[130] Gaudreault (1992), pp. 276-279.

[131] Altman (2004), pp. 102-106; 113-115.

[132] Altman (2004)., pp. 128-130.

[133] Goffman (1986), pp. 251-269.

[134] "[I]t should not be forgotten that the Lumière Cinematograph was accompanied by piano music from the very first showings. It was probably felt from the beginning that the screen's uneasy, flickering silence represented a *lack*." See: Gaudreault (1992), p. 275.
Altman concludes from the lack of references to music in reviews that pre-release or press screenings were silent. But couldn't such screenings have countered the silence by, say, a house pianist's accompaniment that merited no mention? See: Altman (2004), p. 8.

Bloch called *"festliche Narkose"*.[135] Of course, the commissioned score proved to be as loosely connected as any other musical accompaniment when the film moved from its premiere in a metropolitan theater to more modestly endowed provincial and neighborhood cinemas.

Back to the Illustrations and the Colonial Institute's position that the screenings were "subordinate" to its lectures. It is clear that these performances resembled magic lantern shows inasmuch as the institute insisted on lecturers. And they performed a double role, too: besides providing substantive information in a narrative that often digressed from what was shown on the screen, they also had other paratextual functions. For instance, they evoked *couleur locale* through the scripted interspersion of Malay terms, besides the "here you sees" already mentioned.[136] The rigorous way in which the lectures had been prescribed by their printed versions may well have reinforced a similarity with magic lantern shows. But while this reflected a wish to control the reception of the films, at the same time it may have been an acknowledgment of the loose connection between film screenings and their paratextual elements. All in all, the performative simultaneity of lectures and moving images was seized as a powerful editorial opportunity.

This editorial strategy seems to have been designed to counteract spectators' cinemagoing experiences by highlighting those aspects the institute considered relevant for its own purposes: increasing knowledge about the East-Indies and encouraging spectators to emigrate to the colony and fill the jobs in its booming economy—while obscuring those associated with theatrical shows.[137] First of all, the absence of music of any kind may have announced a negative paratext, positioning these presentations as being quite different from a cinema screening, or even from the mixed educational and entertaining magic lantern show. And as far as the projected films were concerned, their stylistic and aesthetic aspects were subdued, not only in the disregard shown for Lamster's specific ways of recording by the cuts and other changes the Colonial

---

[135] Ernst Bloch, 'Die Melodie im Kino oder immanente und transzendentale Musik', in: Fritz Güttinger (ed.), *Kein Tag ohne Kino. Schriftsteller über den Stummfilm* (1984), p. 314 (orig. publ. in 1914).

[136] De Klerk (2010), p. 107; Nico de Klerk, 'The transport of audiences: making cinema national', in: Richard Abel, Giorgio Bertellini, Rob King (eds.), *Early cinema and the 'national'* (2008), p. 105

[137] De Klerk (2010), pp. 104-105.

Institute made over the years, but also by the discrepancy between text and image. The clearest example comes from the Illustration to JOURNEY WILLIAM I-YOGYAKARTA. This film follows the route of a then fairly recently completed railway line through a series of shots predominantly taken from the front of a moving train.[138] This particular style of filming, known as phantom ride, was familiar at the time from the popular genre of the travelogue, or scenic. In its commercially released versions this style allowed spectators to travel vicariously and, as if staring out of the window of a moving vehicle, dream away while being seemingly transported through a faraway landscape.[139] But the largely technical and factual Illustration to this film may well have served to frustrate that experience. While the stylistic option of the phantom ride was appropriate and potentially effective in showing what the film was about—the railway, various points of interest along the way—and carrying the spectator into another world, the lecture reframed it so as not to confuse entertainment with propaganda: instead of dreaming, spectators were adverted to more practical matters, ranging from information about the locomotives' capacity, the railway's construction and its adaptation to the hilly landscape, to the reassuring presence of the nearby garrison, and to advice about how to dress in the colony's tropical climate.

However, it is debatable that the lectures would have been able to restrain the films to a merely subordinate position. For one thing, the Colonial Institute appeared to conceive of moving images *as if* they were slides: by amplifying the films with information about factual, often unrecorded—or rather: unrecordable—matters such as historical events and future perspectives, economy, demographics, etc., it treated them like

---

[138] original title REIS WILLEM I-DJOCJA
The Netherlands (Koloniaal Instituut) 1912 | 35mm full frame (safety) | b&w, tinting | Dutch titles | 13' | print at Eye, Amsterdam.
"Willem I" was the name of the train station of the town of Ambarawa, in central Java; it was named for a nearby military garrison, which, in its turn, was named for the first head of state of the post-Napoleonic Kingdom of the Netherlands.

[139] A contemporary description stated that "[p]articularly railway scenes demonstrate the analogy with dream images. Dreams, too, have uninterrupted sequences, yet unmotivated changes of scenery—no dream ends in the place where it began". See: Theodor Heinrich Mayer, 'Lebende Photographien', in: Güttinger (1984), p. 121 (orig. publ. in 1914); see for reflections on this state of "reverie": Jennifer Lynn Peterson, *Education in the school of dreams: travelogues and early nonfiction film* (2013), pp. 230-233.

artifacts as lacunal and as indeterminate as their magic lantern counterparts. Which, of course, they were not. In fact, unlike magic lantern shows, in film screenings it is the lecture that is more likely to be subordinate to, or a paratext of, what happens on the big screen, as images show so much more than words can ever tell (or, put differently, trying to put into words all that is on the screen, let alone additional information, will inevitably cause a verbal jam). What is more, the very descriptions that were meant to steer reception may have provided spectators with an escape route from the institute's editorial efforts: the overly instructive, not seldom anaemically unimaginative Illustrations, in a contemporary context of a scarcity of moving pictures—or even of published photographs[140]—of the colonies, may have encouraged spectators to focus their attention on the screen rather than on the man next to it.

Whether successful or not, the editorial strategy pursued with the Illustrations in performance differs in another fundamental sense from Genette's formulation. His concern with literature understandably leads him to conclude that the main paratextual function is "to ensure that [a text's] fate conforms to the author's intentions."[141] On the basis of a wide range of examples—the bulk of which begins in the 18th century and continues through the post-World War II era—, he has unearthed an astonishingly prolonged, pragmatic tradition. Cinema's paratextual devices, however, mediate much less exclusively between spectator (or prospective ticket buyer) and 'author'. Surely, the Illustrations served the intentions of the commissioning institute rather than the actual maker of the films. Partly this was to be expected around the mid-1910s. Makers of theatrically screened documentary films were as a rule not identified in catalogues or on film prints. And while so-called non-theatrical screenings of documentary programs, specifically those consisting of travel, expedition, wildlife or missionary films, were often highly personalized, this was *only* because the showman—who was often but not always the filmmaker—traveled with and presented the films in person (the names of these ambulant paratexts, e.g. E. Burton Holmes, Lyman H. Howe, Cherry Kearton, Herbert Ponting or Colin Ross, could fill the house). J.C. Lamster's name appeared nowhere. The reason is evident: as the abovementioned, constant changes of the films showed, the institute had seized control of their authorship (affirmed by intertitles marked

---

[140] De Klerk (2010), p. 113.

[141] Genette (2002), p. 411 (my translation).

"Koloniaal Instituut", or merely "K.I.", or by the end logo that was later attached to its prints showing the institute's new headquarters that was completed in 1926). As sponsor and owner it could do with the footage as it saw fit. Lamster had been a mere hired hand, selected for his knowledge of the colony and its peoples rather than for his filmmaking expertise—of which he had none (in fact, shortly before he left for his assignment he was sent to Paris for a crash course at Pathé Frères, while he was accompanied by a professional cameraman during the first six months of the project).[142] After the mission was accomplished, he reported for work again at the Topographical Department.[143]

A case of mythology

On October 14, 1938, American major RKO released a feature fiction film titled A MAN TO REMEMBER. Shot in fifteen days at a budget of $84,000 it was obviously a B-picture.[144] But as B-pictures of the major studios were certainly not without merit and as a rule quite distinct from what the so-called Poverty Row studios turned out during that decade, it could happen that distributors or exhibitors raised them to A-status. That is what happened to A MAN TO REMEMBER.[145] It received, furthermore, the "ungrudgingly complete" admiration of *New York Times* reviewer Frank Nugent, who found the film "distinguished and unusual" and singled it

---

[142] De Klerk (2010), pp. 79-80.

[143] Van Dijk, de Jonge (2010), p. 41.

[144] Allen Eyles, 'Goldwyn, RKO, and the war: Garson Kanin', in: *Focus on film* (1974), pp. 40-41; the film was the directorial debut of stage director and screenwriter Garson Kanin, the article's interviewee.

[145] Brian Taves, 'The B-film: Hollywood's other half', in: Tino Balio, *Grand design: Hollywood as a modern business enterprise, 1930-1939* (1993), p. 315. Taves distinguishes four categories of B-films, that differed among each other as much as, if not more than, the A-films did. Specifically about the category of the majors' B-films he writes, "B films from the larger studios (...) aimed at filling the exhibition needs of their theater chains and lowering overhead by keeping facilities and contract talent constantly busy." (p. 318). Moreover, in the late 1930s the management of RKO, always the poorest of the Hollywood majors during the era of the studio system, emphasized the production of B-films; see: Douglas Gomery, *The Hollywood studio system* (1986), p. 138.

out for the *Times* list of ten best films of the year.[146] That was the film's first and last claim to fame. After its run it was not heard of again. That in itself was not unusual; in the heyday of Hollywood's studio system dozens, if not hundreds of features sunk without leaving a ripple in the ocean of films the voracious cinema entertainment created. B-films and programmers ran that risk even more, as they did not command sufficient interest from the film archival and scholarly worlds to be revived and remembered.

A MAN TO REMEMBER, however, not only happened to have disappeared, it had not even been missed. Until 2006, that is, when the current licensor of the RKO film library, Turner Classic Movies (TCM), received a query about why a certain title had never been aired. Research by Turner Entertainment Group legal manager Lee Tsiantis and TCM's then senior program manager Dennis Millay turned up that not only that one film, but five more had actually long before been sold out of the RKO library. The sale was part of a settlement negotiated in 1946, after more than a decade of legal disputes between RKO and Merian C. Cooper, of KING KONG fame, over revenue owed the latter from the films he had worked on during his short tenure as the studio's head of production, in 1933-1934. The settlement was for four films that Cooper had executive produced. But as two of these films had been remade—RAFTER ROMANCE (1933) into LIVING ON LOVE (1937), and ONE MAN'S JOURNEY (1933) into A MAN TO REMEMBER—the remakes were also included in the deal. A MAN TO REMEMBER, one might say, was a collateral catch. Cooper was allowed to purchase the rights of these six films and received 35mm fine-grain master prints, while RKO retained the camera negatives; all other elements were to be destroyed.

Next, the research led to the mid-1950s, a time when American television began taking an interest in broadcasting feature films. Through a business associate, Ernest L. Scanlon, Cooper had five of the six films licensed for TV release. Why did he leave one film—A MAN TO REMEMBER— out of this deal? The most plausible guess of Turner's researchers was that Cooper, who was known for his very conservative political opinions, must have felt no need to promote a film whose screenwriter was Dalton Trumbo, of Hollywood Ten notoriety, who was blacklisted at the time. Then, in 1959, after the disappointingly meager financial returns of the

---

[146] Frank S. Nugent, 'A memorable film is A MAN TO REMEMBER, now at the Rivoli', in: *New York Times* (November 7, 1938), p. 23; 'Turner Classic Movies plays sleuth, discovers six previously lost RKO classics', TCM press release (February 2007).

(mostly local) TV releases, Cooper, according to a letter in his papers deposited at Brigham Young University, sold the rights of the films to the same Scanlon as a tax shelter. Later, in 1965, he tried to buy them back, but to no avail. So, until Cooper's death, in 1973, nothing much could be done with the films, as the prints and the rights were now divided over two parties who had apparently fallen out. But everybody seemed to have lost interest by that time and RKO's prints, the researchers had to conclude, had disappeared. They did track down Scanlon's son and heir, from whom TCM bought the rights to the six titles. But obtaining the prints for its library was a more cumbersome matter of retrieving elements from various archives—mostly 35mm duplicate negatives made for TV broadcasts—and copying them. Except, A MAN TO REMEMBER, which was still nowhere to be found.[147]

On April 5, 1995, at the Nederlands Filmmuseum, I opened the first of eight cans of a nitrate release print of an American feature. For the next two hours I watched a 2,167m (79') Dutch subtitled print, with Dutch-language inserts, titled DE PLATTELANDSDOKTER on my viewing table. I liked the film instantly. For one thing, veteran actor Edward Ellis brought a wearied yet tenacious humanity to the title role. It was easy to imagine how his performance must have struck a chord in a country that was then in its tenth year into the Great Depression, in fact a year—1938—when it felt the full force of another stock market crash, the so-called Roosevelt recession, in August 1937, that raised the number of unemployed people with millions again.[148] Striking, too, was that the film, its mild tone notwithstanding, painted an unusually critical picture of America's laissez-faire mentality. I included these observations in a brief comment, recommended the film for preservation, and went on with the day's work through the archive's backlog of nitrate materials as part of the project 'Nitrate can't wait'. This was, note, before the museum had e-mail, which meant that it was not practicable to quickly exchange information with

---

[147] This summary is based on: 'How the "RKO: lost and found" films came to be lost—and found', TCM press release (October 18, 2006), with additional information provided by its uncredited author, Lee Tsiantis.

[148] Estimates vary: Robert S. McElvaine mentions a number of four million by March 1938, raising unemployment to 20% of the workforce; see his: *The Great Depression: America, 1929-1941* (1993 [1984]), pp. 297-301; a more conservative number of over 2.5 million—jumping from 7.7 million in 1937 to 10.4 the next year—is offered in: *A people and a nation: a history of the United States, vol. 2: since 1865* (2001 [1982]), pp. 713-714.

other archives about the materials each had. However, not knowing whether there were any other prints elsewhere was not essential insofar as the Filmmuseum's policy centered on Dutch film *culture*. That is to say, what Dutch audiences saw on the screens (which has always been of overwhelmingly foreign origin) was as important as the films produced domestically. I only learned that the museum had a unique print on its hands when, in 2006, Turner's researchers made an inquiry through the ListServ of the Association of Moving Image Archivists (AMIA). To cut to the chase: after a single-week's theatrical screenings of A MAN TO REMEMBER,[149] along with the other five lost and found RKO-titles, at the Film Forum in New York, TCM aired all six retrieved and preserved films on April 4 and 11, 2007.[150]

The publicity for these events naturally focused on these six films' being lost—or rather, forgotten—and their return to the market place,[151] while mentioning, besides Cooper and Trumbo, directors and performers that were still considered sufficiently familiar—e.g. Lionel Barrymore, Irene Dunne, Garson Kanin, Joel McCrea, William Powell, William Wellman.[152] But A MAN TO REMEMBER's resonance with contemporary circumstances and highly ideological issues, notably the controversy over the role of the federal government in economic affairs, suggests that its significance, besides the artistry of its script or performances, could have been enhanced by conceiving of it as a modern myth. A myth, however, that engaged with these circumstances in a rather uncommon and penetrating way.

---

[149] original title A MAN TO REMEMBER   Dutch print title DE PLATTELANDSDOKTER translated Dutch print title THE COUNTRY DOCTOR
USA (RKO) 1938 | 35mm (nitrate and safety) | b&w | sound | 79' | prints at Eye, Amsterdam (nitrate and safety), and Library of Congress, Washington, D.C. (safety).

[150] 'A matter of rights: a talk with Lee Tsiantis' (February 18, 2010).

[151] And *not*, as one newspaper article had it, "[b]ack in the RKO fold" (see: Susan King, 'Back in the RKO fold', in: *Los Angeles Times* [April 1, 2007], p. E24), which simplified the proprietary situation. The fact of the matter is that the six retrieved films are owned outright by TCM and, as it paid Scanlon, Jr. for the rights, it is also the successor-in-interest to their worldwide rights. A sister entity, Turner Entertainment Company (TEC), has a perpetual license to distribute all the other titles in the RKO library, while the library is owned by Warner Bros. See also: 'A matter of rights: a talk with Lee Tsiantis' (February 18, 2010).

[152] 'Turner Classic Movies plays sleuth, discovers six previously lost RKO classics' (October 18, 2006).

In pursuing this line of thinking I follow cultural historian Richard Slotkin's concept of myth as being intimately related to ideology. Whereas ideology is a basic system of concepts, viewpoints, and values typical for the way a society sees itself, myths are narratives rooted in a society's history in which its ideology and morality are exemplified. These narratives' significance is accentuated by their repeated, media-unspecific retellings, through which they are gradually both stereotyped and abstracted to such an extent that they become collective schemata of cultural ideals. As such, myths are invoked to understand events as providing reassuring historical continuity, including their adaptation to new technologies of production and distribution. In myths, Slotkin writes, "[t]he past is made metaphorically equivalent to the present and the present appears simply as a repetition of persistently recurring structures identified with the past."[153]

American mythology is remarkably rich and robust, a result, I assume, of the country's dynamic history. Not only have its myths absorbed the massive changes that took place within a relatively short time—e.g. from a number of settlements confined to the Atlantic seaboard to its western expansion; from colony to independence; from agricultural to industrial society; from isolationist country to world power. As well the United States, according to historian Gordon S. Wood, is a fundamentally ideological country, created on the basis of ideas and values (particularly as expressed in the *Declaration of Independence* and the Constitution) rather than on a shared history of its inhabitants. It was, says Wood, a state before becoming a nation. The nation "had to be invented or contrived."[154]

Mythology has contributed significantly to the invention of America as shared history. The importance attached to narrative in Slotkin's definition makes his approach appropriate for dealing with mainstream feature films, as his triple study on the myth of the frontier demonstrates:

---

[153] Richard Slotkin, *The fatal environment: the myth of the frontier in the age of industrialization, 1800-1890* (1998a [1985]), p. 24.

[154] Gordon S. Wood, 'The American revolutionary tradition, or Why America wants to spread democracy around the world', in: *The idea of America: reflections on the birth of the United States* (2011), pp. 320-322; see also: Sacvan Bercovitch, *The American jeremiad* (1978), p. 140: "Surely a major reason for the triumph of the republic was that the need for a social ideal was filled by the typology of America's mission."

after two volumes of tracing this myth in print—captivity narratives, sermons, biographies, memoirs, histories, novels, dime novels, travel accounts, etc.—, halfway through the third tome he switches to Hollywood genre films (westerns and war films particularly); in the period under consideration these films were, in his view, the most ubiquitous expressions of the myth of the frontier.[155] Moreover, the technology, economy, and business structure of the film industry made it possible for this and other American myths, ever since the early 20th century, to reach a nation-wide audience, if not virtually simultaneously, then certainly in a saturated way.

In fact, from early on American cinema has eagerly adapted the time-honored material of the country's mythology, either as a story's topic or as the canvas against which it was set. A perceived need to shore up American society and preserve the texture of American life may well have reinforced this focus, since at the time of cinema's early years the country had been facing a large influx of immigrants that it beckoned from places it had not traditionally received new arrivals from. Here, myths were invoked to accommodate new circumstances. And when such circumstances are seen as a threat or crisis, myths are challenged and put to the test. Crises can affect and adjust their retellings, their interpretations or, in the final instance, render them meaningless: "[m]yth may clothe history in fiction, but it persuades in proportion to its capacity to help people act in history."[156]

Besides the mass immigration of the late nineteenth and early twentieth centuries, American society experienced another crisis of unprecedented impact during the 1930s: the Great Depression. Although its effects had a huge international dimension, its origins were largely domestic. There had been severe depressions before, notably the Panic of 1893, but the cascade of events the stock market crashes of October 1929 set in motion led to an economic slump the financial and social

---

[155] The first volume appeared in 1973 and was titled *Regeneration through violence: the mythology of the American frontier, 1600-1860*. It was followed by Slotkin (1998a) and *Gunfighter nation: the myth of the American frontier in twentieth-century America* (1998b [1992]), specifically pp. 1-26; 231-660.

In a similar vein—and overlapping with the myth of the frontier—Bercovitch (1978) traces the changes the Puritan jeremiad underwent from colonial times through the mid-19th century.

[156] Bercovitch (1978), p. xi.

consequences of which were widely perceived as a direct challenge to the American way of life, a "watershed", a sign that "an era was ending", particularly as it affected "the enormous American middle class". [157-158] The lives of millions of Americans were upset as they lost their savings, their jobs, their businesses, their homes, their farms. In 1933, at the Depression's rock bottom, 13 million people, a massive 25% of the workforce, were unemployed.[159] And although the election of Franklin Delano Roosevelt as president, in November 1932, marked the beginning of change; and although his New Deal included legislation and measures to put a stop to some of the worst sufferings through public assistance and public works programs, it never ended the Depression. Mass unemployment only disappeared with the economic jumpstarts of the defense industry in the years leading up to and during World War II.

This, then, was a time of widespread insecurity,[160] a time when America's traditional myths were seriously under pressure and the myth-making film industry was hard put to provide adequate signifying contexts through its outturn. Warner Bros. exceptionally and aptly captured the hopes and fears of those days in the opening of its backstage musical GOLD DIGGERS OF 1933 (released in May 1933, only two months after FDR's inauguration), when a dress rehearsal of the upbeat song 'We're in the money' is rudely interrupted by the sheriff's office which, acting on behalf of the producer's creditors, closes down the show. On a narrative level this crushed the hopes of its production team and cast. But read allegorically, folding a show that opens with a singer and chorus clad in dollar coins singing "*The silver dollar has returned to fold/With silver you can turn your dreams to gold*" and "*Let's spend it, lend it/Send it rolling right along*" could actually be felt as justified for its suggested return to the heady days

---

[157] John A. Garraty, 'The Great Depression and the New Deal', in: William E. Leuchtenburg, *The FDR years: on Roosevelt and his legacy* (1995), p. 211 (orig. publ. in 1970); see also: McElvaine (1993), pp. 25-50.

[158] Warren I. Susman, 'Culture and commitment', in: *Culture as history: the transformation of American society in the twentieth century* (1985), p. 192 (orig. publ. in 1973).

[159] *A people and a nation* (2001), p. 696. Savings evaporated with the insolvency and closing of c. 5,000 banks, since there was no deposit insurance until new legislation in 1933. It has been estimated, furthermore, that between 1929 and 1933 over 100,000 businesses shut their doors.

[160] Susman (1985), pp. 192-197.

of the 1920s New Era. Such a message, of course, was quite out of tune with the country's changed mood, which Roosevelt articulated in his inaugural address when he condemned "a generation of self-seekers" and "unscrupulous money changers", warned that "[o]nly a foolish optimist can deny the dark realities of the moment", and stressed "interdependence on each other" in facing "our common difficulties".[161] So, while GOLD DIGGERS OF 1933 acknowledged the Depression, it didn't address the issue on the level of mythology. Among the films that did, A MAN TO REMEMBER, in its own modest way, not only diverged from most other such films, it actually revealed some of the traditional myths' flaws. To put this in perspective, we need to know what Hollywood, besides coping with its own economic setbacks (coming right after its costly transition to sound),[162] provided in terms of mythological reassurance.

Unsurprisingly, first of all, Hollywood did nothing of the kind and continued to do what it was expected to: provide entertainment. More or less throughout the decade its popular Astaire-Rogers or Shirley Temple vehicles, preceded by, say, a B-picture featuring singing cowboys and assorted short subjects, sometimes enhanced by lotteries, giveaway nights, and other attractions, would have importantly served to make people forget their troubles for a couple of hours. Indeed, film historian Tino Balio stated aphoristically that "[m]otion pictures might allude to the Depression or even exploit an issue, but the goal was always profits, not social justice".[163] Balio's focus on Hollywood's business practices remains largely confined to the major studios' production planning and the resulting films (mostly in terms of genre, or "production trends"), and largely ignores their distribution, exhibition or reception (the latter is represented by reviews quoted from *Variety* or the *New York Times*). This viewpoint tends to have a leveling effect (an impression reinforced by the jaded tone of the *Variety* quotes). But insofar as Hollywood *was* able to come up with appropriate stories that placed contemporary circumstances within a meaningful frame to understand or cope with the economic, social, and human disaster of the Depression—compounded,

---

[161] Franklin D. Roosevelt, 'Inaugural address, March 4, 1933'; McElvaine (1993), pp. 139-140.

[162] See for an overview: Tino Balio, 'Surviving the Great Depression', in: Balio (1993), pp. 13-36; see also: Scott Eyman, *The speed of sound: Hollywood and the talkie revolution 1926-1930* (1999 [1997]), pp. 241-252

[163] Tino Balio, 'Production trends', in: Balio (1993), p. 281.

furthermore, by an ecological catastrophe, the so-called Dust Bowl, that added its own specific repercussions, we need to look beyond mere corporate business considerations to account for these attempts.

Most crucially, any film that was set in a more or less realistic, contemporary setting was almost bound to fail in addressing structural issues, simply because the existing economic organization and ideology, fears to the contrary notwithstanding, remained in place and implicitly unquestioned: "[U]nder the New Deal (...) the economy itself continued to be capitalistic. The profit motive and private property remained fundamental to the system", while the distribution of income, the most fundamental cause of the Depression, was left virtually untouched.[164] Hollywood being Hollywood, any unconventional presentation that managed to come out of or was distributed by its majors during those years was wrapped in camouflage.

One accomplished mainstream feature that was squarely set in the everyday experience of the Depression was OUR DAILY BREAD (1934), produced independently but released via one of the major studios, United Artists. Announcing itself as being "inspired by headlines of today" the film engaged with, yet simultaneously retreated from, the contemporary economic situation. A combination of Depression and Dust Bowl story, it portrays a group of jobless people staking out a new life and livelihood for themselves in the countryside, near a town called Arcadia. Once there, and explicitly inspired by both Captain John Smith's and the Pilgrims' colonizing efforts, America's history is summarily reenacted on an unused 160 acre plot—the size of the sections allotted under the 1862 Homestead Act—with a small-scale repeat of an Oklahoma Land Run, but now in a communal rather than competitive spirit.

The film's storyline follows a pioneering, self-governing community whose franchised, self-employed farmers and craftsmen—indeed, all men—create an economy rooted in the notions of land and exchange, rather than industry and money. This reflected a specific, Depression-era instance of the back-to-the-land movement. But while its alternate concept of the exploration of America could have looked attractive, it may well have been too far-fetched and impractical for most middle-class citizens. The film echoed an outmoded, Jeffersonian and Crevecoeurian view of America's economy and governance, expressions of the myth of the garden of the world almost a century after the country's rapid

[164] *A people and a nation* (2001), pp. 725-726; McElvaine (1993), pp. 49-50.

industrialization. (This myth actually had to be reinvented and clad in more [sub]urban garb to survive the twentieth century.) Nevertheless, the film's gender-based economic arrangement may have constituted a point of entry, of identification, for 1930s audiences, a time when (middle-class) men were unquestionably seen as being the ones bringing in the money. In that sense, it addressed a then obvious but perhaps today underestimated tragedy: the psychological burden of not just being unemployed, but also of having the responsibility of supporting a family.[165] So when the film's farming and trading community's crops are threatened by drought the men are roused to overcome their differences and organize themselves into an army of workers that collectively builds an irrigation system to water the land with its promise of making them breadwinners again. This vicarious culmination of the American entrepreneurial spirit into, and reconciliation with, such New Deal programs as the Public Works Administration (PWA; 1933-1935) or Civil Works Administration (CWA; 1933-1934)[166] was hard to miss and made the film into a barely disguised albeit attenuated political statement. In mythical terms, then, the film explicitly upheld the equivalence of past and present.

The social problem film, the industry term for gangster and other crime stories, gave a twist to another myth, that of rags-to-riches, particularly its secularized version made popular by, if not canonized in, Horatio Alger, Jr. 's novels of the 1860s and 1870s. The selfmade success of Alger's heroes, who came up from a position of "honest poverty", both signals and confirms their character, a central concern in these tales. Conceived of as integrity, initiative, and compassion, and thus "deserving of good fortune", character was of critically moral importance.[167] However, the shift the social problem films exhibited by depicting the careers of their criminal protagonists actually brought to view what character, as a moral concept, had camouflaged already in Alger's own

---

[165] See e.g., Robert S. Lynd, Helen M. Lynd, *Middletown in transition: a study in cultural conflict* (n.d. [orig. publ. in 1937]), pp. 176-179. In fact, the film may have had even greater resonance in addressing the widely felt sense of shame and the associated, perceived lack of character that came up in many interviews in: Studs Terkel, *Hard times: an oral history of the Great Depression* (1986 [1970]).

[166] Robert D. Leighninger, Jr., *Long-range public investment: the forgotten legacy of the New Deal* (2007), pp. 35-54.

[167] Rychard Fink, 'Introduction: Horatio Alger as a social philosopher', in: Horatio Alger, Jr., *Ragged Dick* and *Mark, the match boy* (1962), p. 20.

time: the contradiction posed by the corporate, industrial world created by such entrepreneurial 'role models' as Andrew Carnegie, J.P. Morgan, John D. Rockefeller, and others. The paradox of the careers of these selfmade captains of industry was that, while conforming to the (secular, capitalist) rags-to-riches myth, the mastery of their own destiny entailed the ruin of the hopes and dreams, if not the very lives, of countless others—largely non-'Nordic', lower-class immigrants and their children—who worked in their factories and were not expected or allowed to take destiny into their own hands. In retrospect, Alger's heroes, rather than selfmade, were merely allowed to slip through the cracks in this capitalist universe.

Rooted in contemporary biography (e.g. Al Capone) and journalistic "reporting (...) which transcended mere fact",[168] some of the iconic social problem films—LITTLE CAESAR (1931), THE PUBLIC ENEMY (1931), and SCARFACE (1932)—focused emphatically on similarly rapacious, selfmade young men who managed to rise from an underprivileged, not seldom immigrant background to a position of wealth and power.[169] But, quite unlike Alger's heroes, their subsequent ruination marked not only the punishment for having used illegal and immoral means in reaching for the top or amassing their wealth, but also their lack of character—in the sense of a moral deficiency. And while audiences flocked to a number of these films to enjoy their car chases and machine-gun shootings and other setpieces of the recent sound film, at the same time their denouements may well have aroused feelings of vicarious justice, reinforced perhaps by seeing these heroes' downfall "as an implicit condemnation of the amoral marketplace values" that had caused the Depression.[170] In staying clear of

---

[168] Richard Maltby, 'Why boys go wrong: gangsters, hoodlums, and the natural history of delinquent careers', in: Lee Grieveson, Esther Sonnet, Peter Stanfield (eds.), *Mob culture: hidden histories of the American gangster film* (2005), p. 46. In the 1932 film SCARFACE, in a scene that feels like an afterthought, this yellow journalism was depicted as a serious concern of both authorities and civic organizations.

[169] This milieu, however, was soon largely abandoned with Hollywood's self-imposed enforcement of the Production Code, in June 1934, and an increasingly intolerant press. Meanwhile President Roosevelt's revoking of Prohibition, in 1933, made these films' topics, bootlegging in particular, instantly outmoded; see: Balio (1993), pp. 284-285.

[170] McElvaine (1993), p. 210.

the tribulations of millions of Americans this adjusted version of the myth focused less on the achievement of upward social mobility per se than on the ambiguities it entailed.

Focusing on character only, director-producer Frank Capra's social comedies of the decade (e.g. LADY FOR A DAY [1933], MR. DEEDS GOES TO TOWN [1936], YOU CAN'T TAKE IT WITH YOU [1938], MR. SMITH GOES TO WASHINGTON [1939]) may be taken as the counterpart of the social problem films. Set in contemporary environments, yet retaining a nostalgically safe feel of smalltown communities and of grassroots democracy, the films emphatically spotlighted the "little people", the John and Jane Does who merely claimed their place in the American sun and who resigned to their fate or hung on to what they had: they didn't go under, but they didn't make (or keep) "good fortune" either. What linked them to Horatio Alger's stories was the moral compass of their indestructible righteousness and integrity with which they resisted and overcame the corrupting effects of business or government. But it usually led them to a station not far from where they had started out. Character was its own reward.[171]

Those Hollywood features that somehow explicitly referenced the Depression didn't much "exploit", let alone explain, its dour economic and human costs. If there was any sort of direct engagement with the current problems beyond a dash of slumming, it was concerned with the policies that were meant to tackle them. The New Deal introduced not only something that was undeniably new, but also to take issue with both politically and ideologically, as it "radically altered the character of the State in America. As late as Hoover's presidency, policy-makers believed that government activity should be minimal; economic decisions should be determined in the market place, and the government should confine its function to that of neutral referee."[172] The controversies generated by the

---

Not in all films of the so-called pre-Code era behaviors that could easily be perceived as immoral or even unlawful were punished or neutralized (see e.g. OTHER MEN'S WOMEN (1931), I WAS A FUGITIVE FROM A CHAIN GANG [1932], THREE ON A MATCH [1932] as well as GOLD DIGGERS OF 1933). But in the abovementioned flagrant, organized crime stories murder set the limit.

[171] Even in some 1930s social problem films the good guy gets the short end of the stick, but is redeemed by his character; an extreme example is HEROES FOR SALE (1933), in which the preservation of the protagonist's integrity is stretched to the point of martyrdom.

[172] William E. Leuchtenburg, 'The achievement of the New Deal', in: *The FDR years: on Roosevelt and his legacy* (1995), pp. 242-243 (orig. publ. in 1985).

unprecedented role—so-called big government—FDR's administration assumed in public life and in the economy (e.g. control of financial institutes, deficit spending to finance relief, public works, and social security), were the topic of a small number of films that attempted to deal with these debates more or less directly.

Controversial itself was GABRIEL OVER THE WHITE HOUSE, released mere weeks after FDR's inauguration, in March 1933. Its direct engagement with current issues may well explain its brief success at the box office.[173] Still, it addressed these issues in an incoherent, fantastic way. The political about-face of its newly-elected president protagonist that leads to seemingly revolutionary measures (some of which foreshadowed those initiated by FDR) is scripted as the result of heavenly intervention. The actual implementation of these measures, however, is set in a state of national emergency overseen by an all-powerful executive—and God, apparently, on his side. In dealing with crime, for instance, this dictatorship for an alleged good cause substitutes courts for court martials, the Constitution for the biblical "an eye for an eye, a tooth for a tooth, a life for a life", after which judgment bootleggers and murderers are summarily executed by a fire squad. All in all, its story was simply too far-fetched to connect with any mythologically reassuring tradition.

Much closer to the harshness of early-Depression everyday life was WILD BOYS OF THE ROAD (1933), about two teenaged schoolboys who leave home to be less of a burden to their families and laid-off fathers. While hoboing across the country to find work they are constantly chased by train detectives and their clubs, while the camps they and their comrades occupy are brutally demolished (a certain reminder of the way the U.S. army, only a year before the film's release, mercilessly razed the Washington, D.C. campsite of the Bonus Army of jobless World War I veterans). However, after being tricked into a robbery the boys are saved from desperation and a possible life of crime by an understanding, fatherly judge. As if spliced with another film this rather saccharine ending may perhaps have given spectators a momentary gleam of hope, but not much more. What both this film and GABRIEL OVER THE WHITE HOUSE reveal, however, provides another reason to look beyond the business considerations of the film industry: the political or ideological ambitions of its producers, directors, and screenwriters in particular. After all, Warner Bros., the production company of WILD BOYS OF THE ROAD, staunchly

---

[173] McElvaine (1993), p. 166.

supported Roosevelt (the judge sits in front of a poster advertising the NRA, one of the early New Deal measures), while GABRIEL OVER THE WHITE HOUSE, was timely—and expediently—made by liberal producer Walter Wanger for populist newspaper tycoon William Hearst's Cosmopolitan Studios, when Hearst still supported FDR.

Dalton Trumbo's script for A MAN TO REMEMBER is similarly ambitious, though vastly different in tone and expressiveness. Structurally inventive, it tells its story of a country doctor in a series of flashbacks, after opening on the GP protagonist's funeral. This funeral's almost presidential grandeur—flags at half-mast, a motorcade of limousines, people lining the streets to pay their respect—may have wrong-footed the spectator, if only for a minute. But a connotation of achievement, of something "to remember", may have clung to the character of the doctor from the moment his story unfolds.

That story begins when he sets up a new practice in a niche 'market' readily granted by his fellow GPs. Soon his indignation is roused when he finds out why: most of his patients never received decent medical care simply because they live on the wrong side of the tracks. Stubbornly and, when opportunity presents itself, cunningly he campaigns in their behalf for an adequately equipped, modern hospital for the entire town community, regardless of a patient's income. The script captures the New Deal, if not contemporary American society tout court, in a medical metaphor: what the country needs is a good doctor.

Compared to contemporary films that nominally dealt with socially relevant themes, there is a subtle shift of emphasis: much as the story is about the ups and downs of the doctor, the sustained allegorical dimension—the doctor representing the President, the town the entire country—is unmistakable. This is signaled by the first scene—the first flashback—in which the doctor returns to the town of his youth to start a new life and a new practice. Although penniless the first thing he does is borrow money, persuading a former schoolmate-turned-banker into laying out money for what seems a hopeless cause. The scene must have resonated strongly with contemporary circumstances, since this was precisely the type of measure that was considered anathema until

Roosevelt's administration moved in.[174] The story, in other words, is not so much about the development of an individual; the protagonist is in a sense complete the moment he enters the story (rather than having a whole life before him, the doctor, a few hints suggest, has been through a thing or two). More importantly, from the very opening scene a mentality is depicted, exemplified by the doctor's three creditors who politely observe the funerary procession from the window of the notary public's office while anxiously awaiting the contents of the deceased's estate.[175] The creditors represent the business world that measures everything in terms of profit and loss (reminiscent of what sociologists Robert and Helen Lynd called the "commercial culture"[176]), in short, the ultimate belief in laissez-faire.[177] It is this mentality that the doctor will fight throughout the film's flashbacks. For such a story the rags-to-riches myth and its focus on the enterprising individual, rather than the socio-political context, is inadequate. A MAN TO REMEMBER connects with another

---

[174] Actually, borrowing money, as well as deficit spending, were anathema to Roosevelt, too, yet the crisis required unconventional measures. Nevertheless, what had compounded the depression of 1937-1938 was his decision to *return* to the gospel of a balanced budget, slashing government spending on public works in an economy too weak to absorb these cutbacks; see: Leighninger, Jr. (2007), pp. 23-24, 175-176; McElvaine (1993), pp. 298-299.

[175] Hence the abovementioned Dutch-language inserts: each flashback is triggered by a bill or IOU, for all of which substitutions were made for the Dutch release print at the time.

[176] The Lynds' two studies of Middletown (an anonymizing name for a representative American small town—actually Muncie, IN) appear to have left their mark on the film. With regard to health care, they observed in their 1924-1925 study that "public control of health has met with some opposition and is unevenly diffused throughout the city", while in their follow-up study of 1935 they reported that "if one takes a longer view of the correlation between available money and access to adequate health services (...), one receives a disconcerting reminder of the chronic burden of avoidable health disabilities which is 'normal' under our culture, particularly in cities like Middletown where the hospital conducts no outpatient clinic and free services are available through public and private charity only for the most desperately ill and indigent." See resp.: Robert S. Lynd, Helen M. Lynd, *Middletown: a study in American culture* (1929), p. 446, and Lynd, Lynd ([1937]), p. 391.

[177] With this the 'presidential' connotation of the doctor's character may well have been reinforced, since for decades it had been FDR's opinion that "business must get out of politics"; see: McElvaine (1993), p. 96.

American myth. But in order for it to provide "reassuring continuity" in ideologically confusing times, the film first had to expose a weakness of this myth, a contradiction contained within it. This is the myth of manifest destiny.

The term *manifest destiny*, coined in 1845 by politician and newspaper editor John L. O'Sullivan, referred to the country's annexation of and expansion to the west and southwest, roughly the area between the Mississippi and the Pacific Ocean. An area of supposedly limitless opportunities, it stimulated the imagination. In fact, it was not merely a real space, but also a mythical one in which the "destined progress" of America could be realized on an unprecedented scale.[178] It acquired, moreover, a social darwinist, if not altogether racist connotation: only the fittest were able to expand and build up the country, while the weak would fall by the way—with Native Americans, as was made manifestly clear, being considered the weakest of all.[179] Therefore, as Slotkin suggests, it makes sense to see the myth of the frontier as underlying manifest destiny.[180] As a 'sub-myth', manifest destiny addressed an important change in America's westward movement: the large-scale, industrial technology and power employed to explore the country. The myth adapted—"continued"—the image of the pioneering individual to the corporate agenda of economic exploitation (of mining, lumbering, railroading or meatpacking) by replacing the trail-blazing, heroic "man who knows Indians" with the captain of industry. Yet the contradiction this myth smoothed over in its adaptation was that the notion of private enterprise was compromised from the outset by the legislative and financial support of successive federal administrations that were anything but disinterested. For instance, the two railroad companies that were to connect America's coasts received very favorable terms for acquiring the

---

[178] Bercovich (1978), p. 164.

[179] See e.g.: John Fiske, 'Manifest destiny', in: *Harper's New Monthly Magazine* (March 1885), pp. 578-590. There are many versions of this text before it was published in *Harper's*, since Fiske had delivered it as a lecture for many years, within and without the U.S..

[180] Slotkin (1998a), p. 212.

land to lay their tracks, while individual settlers were given the go-by.[181] So much for laissez faire.

It is ironic, to put it gently, that a prominent and active role of the federal government in both public life and the economy, despite a long history of shared interests between government and business, was such a contentiously ideological issue in the 1930s.[182] Although this attests to the success of the myth of manifest destiny, A MAN TO REMEMBER punctured it by pointing out its self-serving nature. By the same token it is ironic, too, that big business itself had never been adverse to govern. Prominent businessmen had served on subsequent administrations in the late 19th century and during the 1920s.[183] On a local scale, the film is clearly reminiscent of this unsung tradition by showing how the film's setting, the fictive town of Westport (a sort of Middletown), is effectively ruled by a board of supervisors composed of a handful of local businessmen. In other words, rather than let public life and the economy take care of themselves—the professed ideal of small government—, business intensely regulates the town's affairs according to its own standards and on its own terms. This contradiction is the film's main target and provides it with its mythological task: to expose business's role in governance while at the same time redirecting and hitching it to the public cause—and make America better. Like the New Deal, there is revolution nor nostalgic withdrawal. Each of the flashbacks through which the story progresses sets up the opposition between a business mentality in which "people, resources and wealth [are] treated essentially as commodities"[184] and the

---

[181] Robert V. Hine, John Mack Faragher, *The American West: a new interpretive history* (2000), pp. 281-283; Slotkin (1998a), pp. 214-215; *A people and a nation* (2001), pp. 476-477. The American film industry was no stranger to this mentality either, as film historian Donald Crafton comments with as much comic understatement as lethality: "Like many good businessmen, movie leaders looked to Washington for aid in improving profits."; see his: *The talkies: American cinema's transition to sound 1926-1931* (1997 [1999]), p. 181.

[182] Leighninger, Jr. (2007), pp. 197-201.

[183] Most notoriously, Andrew Mellon, who served as Secretary of the Treasury under all that decade's three presidents, was reported to have welcomed the Depression as a "blessing" that "will purge the rottenness out of the system." See: McElvaine (1993), p. 30.

[184] Economist Daniel R. Fusfeld quoted in: Leuchtenburg (1995), p. 243.

idea of a moral economy that emphasizes cooperation and justice,[185] thereby gradually exemplifying the need for a change of course. All the while, as in so many Hollywood films, it maintains a mild, conciliatory note, summarized in the doctor's dictum phrased in his opponents' language, *"Keeping my patients alive, that's my business."*

A final point. Having found a surviving print of this particular film in a Dutch archive, one may wonder to what extent the relevance of mythology as a film's signifying context will be retained in a foreign setting. In the case of American cinema generally, one hardly needs to argue that its myths have been continually and massively circulated ever since World War I, when its film industry—although initially not yet the 'Hollywood' of the studio era—ascended to a dominant position worldwide. In archives around the world American films and their related materials reflect national cinema cultures that have been exposed to American images, ideas, icons, and language for decades. This, incidentally, points up the most significant characteristic of national film cultures: their audiences' *international* viewing experience.[186] Because of the strength of its (audio)visual industries throughout the 20th century, its mythical representations, whether pictured as fiction or fact, have fed the imaginations of political and business leaders as well as populations worldwide. Hollywood's products have given audiences a view of America and its history that can be called mythical in more than one sense. Firstly, many of its films are codified into generic forms, the western, musical, sci-fi, and social problem film most particularly, to deal with mythological content. And, secondly, since the feature film is not a strict history-telling medium, it could simultaneously pose as pure, 'value-free' entertainment, with any resemblance to real events and persons being purely coincidental—i.e. myth as invention. Indeed, the films often refer only implicitly or indirectly to historical events and persons, while time has often erased the references that once resonated with audiences. Moreover, such topical and historical references were often simply downplayed or obscured *before* reaching foreign audiences as a result of translation,

---

[185] McElvaine argues, however, that this was in itself a uniquely regressive aspect of the time, a mere delay in the development towards increased individualism; see McElvaine (1993), pp. 6; 198-202.

[186] Nico de Klerk, '"Volgt het voorbeeld van John Wayne": over onze grenzeloze nationale cinema'*, in: Rommy Albers, Jan Baeke, Rob Zeeman (eds.), *Film in Nederland* (2004b), pp. 415-416.
*'Follow the example of John Wayne: on our borderless national cinema'

censorship, publicity, marketing or programming (measures that together I call *appropriation*, the subject of the next case study). For instance, the domestic release title A MAN TO REMEMBER is much more evocative of the specific times in which the film was made, particularly through the presidential connotation of its protagonist, than its Dutch release title, DE PLATTELANDSDOKTER (while the latter's correct English equivalent, THE COUNTRY DOCTOR actually suggests a misleadingly meaningful reading, its literal—but improper—translation, THE COUNTRY*SIDE* DOCTOR, better conveys its lack of topical, political overtones).

Non-American audiences, then, are usually presented with artifacts that are different in ways material and nonmaterial from domestic release prints and their accompanying publicity or ways of screening. This as well as these audiences' own frames of reference and customs have led to ways of reception that are differently 'inflected'. Or, in Richard Maltby's words, "[W]hat circulates beyond the boundaries of the United States is not a full-blown mythology but rather its icons, its random fragments which (...) may take on meanings only tangentially related to those recognised at its points of origin."[187] Still, the same author's claim that "[c]lassical Hollywood cinema created an intensely self-referential world, much of the attraction of which lay precisely in its difference and distance from the world outside the cinema", distancing its foreign spectators "from any potentially troubling relation to the 'real'", is more difficult to swallow, because self-referentiality comes in different shapes.[188] Interestingly in this context is the Deutsches Filminstitut Filmmuseum screening, in January 2015, of a German-dubbed, 1952 release print of CASABLANCA, which was evocative of the specific time and place in which the film was shown, as all spoken references to the real world, notably Nazis and World War II, had been replaced.[189] Obviously, the American domestic release had not shied away from the real. Moreover, this specific case of imposed

---

[187] Richard Maltby, 'Introduction: "the Americanisation of the world"', in: Stokes, Maltby (2004), p. 2. All subsequent chapters in this book are case studies of the exhibition and reception of Hollywood's films at a number of non-American locations across the globe throughout the 20th century.

[188] Maltby (2004), p. 15.

[189] See: http://deutsches-filminstitut.de/blog/casablanca-in-massakrierter-fassung/. See also: Carla Mereu Keating, '"As time goes by". You must *not* remember this', in: Johannes Roschlau (ed.), *Kunst unter Kontrolle. Filmzensur in Europa* (2014), pp. 109-121, about similar measures taken for the 1947 Italian release of CASABLANCA.

and retrospective self-referentiality needs to be conceptually separated from the fact that feature films are inherently character-based narratives that work toward closure, whether or not they deal with recognizably real-life, historical topics. But when they do, they are perforce bound to deviate from received historical fact.[190]

Hollywood's alleged self-referentiality and distance from reality have also been argued from a more straightforwardly production-oriented approach by film theorists Vincent Amiel and Pascal Couté. Their point of view is largely informed by the type of blockbuster Hollywood has consistently focused on making since over half a century. They claim that these films, particularly since the 1980s, have become mere products advertising other products (tie-ins with or product placement for other companies; video and DVD editions, CDs, theme parks, and merchandise of all sorts for Hollywood itself) rather than being cinema "*par essence*".[191] This has led them to the more dismissively formulated conclusion that American mainstream cinema has simply lost (rather than imaginatively camouflaged) its connection to the real world in that it does not engage with the country's everyday reality, but has merely fabricated "an easily exportable" America of metonymical and stereotypical images.[192]

This argument suffers from an underestimation of foreign audiences' world knowledge and sophistication, while the authors' aesthetic approach is here and there as far removed from reality as they claim their subject is. Essentially, blockbusters characterize a period in American film production when moviegoing ceased being the habit that allowed flops to be compensated by hits. In other words, blockbusters typify a system of reduced, time-tested output. The contrasts that the authors set up with the studio era are only of secondary importance. Meanwhile they ignore, for instance, the stereotypes Hollywood was quite capable of producing then as well: countless are the "easily exportable" comedies, musicals or thrillers that it disseminated through its many-branched, worldwide

---

[190] This has also been reported by historians Roy Rosenzweig and David Thelen, albeit with regard to American audiences only, noting that insofar Hollywood, as well as television, are considered as sources of historical information and inspiration they are generally held in low esteem; see their: *The presence of the past: popular uses of history in American life* (1998), pp. 97-101; 235.

[191] Vincent Amiel, Pascal Couté, *Formes et obsessions du cinéma américain contemporain (1980-2002)* (2003), pp. 16-18.

[192] Amiel, Couté (2003), pp. 149-153.

network. As a matter of fact, by taking the blockbuster as the basis of their argument Amiel and Couté actually reiterate an old, European-centered, critical discussion of Hollywood's alleged uncultured, assembly-line way of filmmaking, articulated, for example, by Béla Balász: "Was wir bisher an 'Kunst' von drüben genossen haben, waren Reitereien, Revolverkämpfe, Boxduellen und dazu eine Sentimentalität flachster und primitivster Art" (a statement that was rather short on historical sense itself).[193] As well they omit to mention Hollywood majors' ownership of publishing houses, radio stations or recording studios at various times, or Disney's pioneering of merchandising in the late 1920s, through which the industry would reap the profits from the sales of sheet music, records, fan magazines, and other ancillary products.[194] All this is not fundamentally different from current practices, except that the ancillary products now bring in more money than the films. For in order to make a film's spin-offs attractive today, a unique selling point has to be decided, whether star, story or stunts, each of which will affect the production differently—Warner Bros. may profitably adapt BATMAN or SUPERMAN to its Movie World theme park, the adult theme of its MYSTIC RIVER would benefit more from a DVD release.

Because the authors ground their critique of contemporary American cinema predominantly, albeit it loosely, in business economics, they make too little of societal and political developments. They deplore the disappearance of stories that are rooted in an everyday America, stories that appealed to a notion of American community and identity, a mythological, shared history—and, incidentally, quite easily exportable, too (particularly in the films of John Ford and Frank Capra). Instead, they write, there is a trend in current filmmaking that concentrates on an ethnic, regional or demographic segment of America and its society.[195] What they have failed to note, though, is that the fragmented prospects such films provide may well be an effect of the legal and political watershed the Civil Rights movement has created, continued real-life setbacks notwithstanding. Ever since then it may have been felt more opportune to reflect on and address the foundations of the whitewashed myths of pre-1960s American cinema, screened until that time, moreover, in formally or informally segregated theaters. And whereas the so-called

---

[193] Quoted in: Verena Moritz, 'Amerika', in: Verena Moritz, Karin Moser, Hannes Leidinger, *Kampfzone Kino. Film in Österreich 1918-1938* (2008), p. 110.

[194] For an overview, see the chapters on the individual majors in: Gomery (1986).

[195] Amiel, Couté, pp. 153-156.

countercultural films of the late 1960s and 1970s that criticized or undercut traditional mythology nevertheless perpetuated it as a reference, these recent 'small', mostly independently made films may signal the emergence of an 'unshared' history, mythological or not.[196]

All in all, then, as many things American continue to affect non-American audiences it is imperative to critically explicate what in fact *is* mainstream American cinema's relation to the "real", perhaps more than ever before. Because contrary to what the quoted authors claim, much of contemporary American cinema, other than the bestselling blockbusters, is not explicitly addressed to the rest of the world. Certainly the abovementioned 'smaller' films and their more specific topics are no doubt less of an obvious export product: inward-looking or limiting their perspective—which is not necessarily self-referential—, their significance is perhaps more vulnerable to getting lost in transition. In fact, proportionally more of these films only get festival screenings abroad, with no follow-up release. (For example, two of the recent titles mentioned in the last footnote were not released in the Netherlands.)

Another factor is that the traditional focus of the press on name directors and star performers or on style continues to miss societal, historical, and mythical aspects, even of mainstream films. For instance, while reviews generally vilified the 2013 (very mainstream) feature THE GANGSTER SQUAD for its lack of stylistic and acting qualities, they widely and consistently failed to comment on its resonance with the zeitgeist, more specifically the increasing acceptance of the suspension of law in order to protect the United States against terrorist attacks. Precisely because screening off the real, wholly or partly, is what constitutes mainstream cinema's myth-making power—signalled by setting THE GANGSTER SQUAD's story in the world of organized crime in 1949—, it is important to uncover films' historical backgrounds and circumstances, the mythical discourses that did, and do, inform them and their "capacity to help people act in history". Such elucidation, incidentally, would not just be required for non-American audiences. Essayist Michael Ventura's statement that "Americans are less unified as a people than as an audience" suggests that domestically, too, American myths are often accepted at face value,

---

[196] A few interesting examples are: POWWOW HIGHWAY (1989); LONE STAR (1996); ULEE'S GOLD (1997); or WINTER'S BONE (2010), as well as the much earlier NOTHING BUT A MAN (1964).

despite their stark contrast with many people's lives and histories.[197] To the extent that his suggestion is correct, it is essential to explicate the filtering, myth-making process itself in these deceptively transparent artifacts.

A case of appropriation

On October 7, 1947, the Dutch Central Committee for Film Censorship approved the French feature film LES CLANDESTINS, a story about a resistance group during the German occupation of France, for audiences of 18 years and above.[198] As it was not unusual for a film to be released a week or so after the censor's decision, LES CLANDESTINS could have been premiered by mid-October. But it was not. Its Dutch distributor, City Film of The Hague, withheld release until May 1948, which was unusually late by any standard in the immediate postwar years. There were reasons for this delay.

Not specifically but nonetheless relevantly, the Dutch film business, like everything and everybody else of course, faced the destitution caused by the war. The German occupation had left the Netherlands a thoroughly ravaged country. The slow, piecemeal liberation—the south and the east, from the late summer of 1944 through the spring of 1945, the north and the west, in April and early May 1945—impeded the resumption of a more or less regular daily life almost everywhere. Not only had the Netherlands been one of the pivot points for the Allied march on Germany, as well the German leadership had designated the country as a 'shock absorber' for its own protection as well as a 'depot' to supply itself. During the protracted final stages of the war, from the failed operation Market Garden in September 1944 until German capitulation on May 5, 1945, all over Dutch occupied territory infrastructure (rail, water, air transportation and industry in particular), buildings, equipment, livestock, and materials of all sorts were largely either destroyed, dismantled, requisitioned or plundered by the German army. In the south, i.e. beneath the great rivers that cut through the country, various towns and cities, notably Arnhem,

---

[197] Michael Ventura, 'The Great Wall of Hollywood', in: *Shadow dancing in the USA* (1985), p. 173.

[198]   http://www.gahetna.nl/collectie/index/nt00402/0cdc18ac-7cc1-102d-a57f-005056a23d00.

Breskens, Nijmegen, and Venlo, were all but destroyed or severely damaged by bombing or shelling from both Allied and German sides; Arnhem and many other towns and villages, moreover, were forcibly evacuated (and then plundered). And agricultural as well as built-up areas were inundated for tactical reasons by friend and foe. The western part fared no better: already in the early days of the war, in May 1940, bombing had destroyed the city center of Rotterdam. In the final stages, both the Allied frontline and German reprisals for the railway strike of September 1944 cut off this most densely populated part of the country from significant food transports as well as from fuel and electricity. This situation was compounded by the famine of 1944-1945, a combination of continued German reprisals and a long, harsh winter.[199]

As far as film screenings were concerned, cinema theaters that opened in those parts of the country liberated before German capitulation were supplied with predominantly British and American films by the Supreme Headquarters Allied Expeditionary Forces' (SHAEF) Psychological War Division.[200] Some of the more explicitly propagandistic of these films, according to the website Cinema Context, had found their way to the rest of the country shortly after German capitulation (in fact, this is the earliest available documentation of these films, as data of their screening from before May 1945 are unfortunately lacking[201]). Furthermore, as far as feature fiction was concerned, Cinema Context also suggests that from late 1945, early 1946 onwards Dutch cinemas, such as there were, showed predominantly British and French fiction films; American features only began to arrive in substantial numbers by late 1946, early 1947. Theoretically LES CLANDESTINS could have been released sometime in 1946. However, with fewer venues to show films and a backlog of prewar films

---

[199] Loe de Jong, *Het Koninkrijk der Nederlanden in de Tweede Wereldoorlog**: 10a: Het laatste jaar I, eerste helft*** (1980), pp. 305-514); *10b: Het laatste jaar II, eerste helft****, 1981), pp. 1-43; 68-82; 153-266; *10b: Het laatste jaar II, tweede helft***** (1982), pp. 1081-1115; 1330-1394.
**The Kingdom of the Netherlands during World War II; **10a: The final year I, first part; ***10b: The final year II, first part; ****10b: The final year II, second part*

[200] Bert Hogenkamp, *De documentaire film 1945-1965: de bloei van een filmgenre in Nederland** (2003), p. 41
**Documentary film 1945-1965: the florescence of a film genre in the Netherlands*

[201] Such propaganda documentaries as TUNISIAN VICTORY (US, 1944), ATTACK! THE BATTLE OF NEW BRITAIN (US, 1944) or FROM D-DAY TO PARIS (UK, 1945) could be seen in the north and west from late May 1945 onwards.

from Allied and former occupied countries (either these had already been passed for exhibition before German occupation began, on May 10, 1940, and gradually banned thereafter, or they were released only when all of Holland was liberated), what becomes apparent is a tendency to release films according to 'seniority'.

There were also considerations of a more specific nature. Although it is unknown whether City Film actually had the rights to and copies of LES CLANDESTINS for some time already (in France the film had been released in April 1946), what is intriguing is that the date of the censorship board's approval more or less coincided with the day, September 29, 1947, on which the Special State Pension Act became effective. This act stipulated that members of the resistance or their surviving next of kin were eligible for a state pension if there was "a causal link between their acts of resistance or their stance (...) and a physical or mental misfortune."[202] With LES CLANDESTINS the distributor may have wanted to seize on an opportunity to promote its property by taking advantage of a popular piece of legislation (that heralded a social safety system of various collective insurances in the decades to come[203]) and a popular topic (the heroism of resistance fighters). One of the changes the company made to the French trailer of LES CLANDESTINS shows not only how it meant to exploit that opportunity, but also how it adapted its publicity, after the censorship board's decision, to the rapidly changing circumstances of the immediate postwar era.[204]

Initially, this trailer appears to be in no way different from the classical format common in the 1930s and 1940s that has as one of its most distinctive characteristics the purposeful withholding of storyline

---

[202] 'Rijkspensioen voor verzetsslachtoffers'*, in: *Medisch Contact*** (May 26, 1948), pp. 478-479. The official Dutch name of this act was Wet Buitengewoon Rijkspensioen***.
*'State pension for resistance victims'; **Medical Contact*; ***Special State Pension Act

[203] Kees Schuyt, Ed Taverne, *1950: prosperity and welfare* (2004), pp. 262-275 (orig. publ. in 2000 as *1950: welvaart in zwart-wit*)
*1950: prosperity in black-and-white

[204] archive title TRAILER LES CLANDESTINS translated archive title TRAILER IN HIDING The Netherlands (SCN-Profilti) 1948 | 35mm (nitrate and safety) | b&w | French titles, French spoken, Dutch titles, Dutch spoken | 7'50" | print at Eye, Amsterdam.

information.[205] It shows a number of dramatic, romantic, and action-packed clips while superimposed texts briefly wrong-foot the spectator: "Is this a gangster film? An adventure film?", etc., each question answered with a large "No", only to heighten the mystery by subsequently flashing a series of story ingredients—"Love–Courage–Heroism–Loyalty", etc.[206] But the plot cannot be reconstructed from these clips. Equally traditionally, two stock text panels, one drawing attention to the distributor's name, the other promising that the film will be "Coming soon to this theater!", seem to spell the trailer's ending.

But there the spectator was really wrong-footed, since the trailer continues with another text panel: "Now you will see and hear what some figures of the resistance, among whom His Exc. Secretary W. Drees, have to say about this film." What follows is a four-minute, staged scene in which Willem Drees, Deputy Prime Minister-cum-Secretary of Social Affairs, and H.M. van Randwijk, editor-in-chief of the weekly news magazine *Vrij Nederland* (which began as an underground publication during German occupation), are discovered behind a desk poring over papers when a City Film representative walks in and inquires about their thoughts on the film. In the ensuing conversation the distributor pledges that half of the release's earnings will be donated to the Foundation 1940-1945, an organization committed to the moral, spiritual, and financial support of war victims and resistance fighters. The two former resistance men welcome this gesture: *"Handouts are not accepted by the underground, but friendship is and so is friendly support"*, says Van Randwijk, and the Secretary reminds spectators of his recently enacted Special Pension Act, the implementation of which had in fact been outsourced to said foundation. The trailer, even though the Dutch addition is somewhat stiffly shot and edited, is a smart and unconventional combination of publicity, goodwill, and tie-in, endorsed, moreover, by two public figures, prominent in the resistance during the war and in postwar-Holland's public life.

---

[205] Vinzenz Hediger, *Verführung zum Film: der amerikanische Kinotrailer seit 1912* (2001), pp. 16; 121-127.

[206] The clips *and* the superimposed phrases make this into an example par excellence of the 'something-for-everyone-approach'—i.e. aimed at interesting a large public in a specific genre film—that Lisa Kernan defined as characteristic of one of trailers' rhetorical strategies, the "vaudeville mode"; see her: *Coming attractions: reading American movie trailers* (2004), pp. 18-20.

City Films's trailer for LES CLANDESTINS is an instance of what I have called *appropriation.*[207] Appropriation occurs whenever a film or other (commercial) cultural product is distributed outside its country or territory of origin. It consists of a set of measures that are applied, obligatory but also voluntarily, to adapt that product in such a way that it complies with local circumstances—particularly laws, language, markets, manners, and tastes—and thereby make it legal, apprehensible, acceptable, and/or attractive. These locally made alterations cover such matters as (self-)censorship, translation, marketing, publicity, programming, *dispositif* as well as traditions or customs. The alterations to the trailer of LES CLANDESTINS, moreover, show that the degree of appropriation may well depend on margins of autonomy—City Film's unusual measure was not hindered by a Dutch office of the film's production company, Essor Cinématographique Française (unlike, say, the American majors, most of whom had representatives in Holland). It is, by the way, important to stress the local aspect of appropriation in order to distinguish it from multiple language or montage versions made by one and the same production company before export and distribution.

The measures that constitute appropriation are made by various parties (e.g. administrations at various levels, censorship boards, distributors, exhibitors, as well as film heritage institutes[208]) and can be subdivided into invasive and contextual. Invasive are those that alter the product physically: additions such as subtitles, logos of local distributors, exhibitors or archives, panels showing censorship board's ratings, intermission announcements, notes on restoration or, indeed, new material; replacements such as dubbing tracks, altered endings, montage or coloring; or the excision of shots or scenes, etc. Examples of contextual measures include: selection of venue and target audience; type of campaign, tie-ins; booking strategies; musical and/or verbal

---

[207] De Klerk (2004), pp. 416-418; De Klerk (2008), p. 107.

[208] This happens, for instance, when it is felt that a preserved film's ideology needs to be cushioned against later sensibilities. For instance, when the Nederlands Filmmuseum preserved the American expedition film BY AEROPLANE TO PYGMYLAND (1927), largely set in Dutch New Guinea, it made a version for public screenings in which the many intertitles were not only reduced and condensed, also their often racist content was toned down.

accompaniment; adjustment to specific programming customs.[209] Appropriation, in other words, crucially affects local appreciation and reception.[210] My definition of appropriation as a limited set of institutional measures is particularly apt for countries, such as the Netherlands, where production is less important for filling national screens and seats than distribution, while it also allows one to distinguish between those measures that were and are employed commonly, if not as a matter of course, such as the subtitling of the snippets of French dialogue and French-language texts in City Film's trailer, and those occasioned by special circumstances, such as splicing it with newly made footage.

Indeed, as the combination of announcement, tie-in, and goodwill mentioned above points up Genette's observation that epitexts—of which trailers are an instance—are more free-floating, their paratextual function can as a result easily become overlaid with considerations that do not necessarily and exclusively serve the text (here, the announced feature).[211] Epitexts, moreover, easily allow allographic elements, i.e. elements made by or for others than the parties directly responsible for the text's production and presentation. The obvious stylistic and rhetorical break created by City Film suggests, therefore, that other than immediately self-serving motives might have come into play, too, in enlisting the help of the two former resistance men. In terms of territorial rights distributor City

---

[209] Inserting intermissions where there had been none, as was customary in Dutch commercial cinemas through the 1990s, was both contextual and invasive. Most frustratingly, particularly in converted multiplex cinemas where the capacity of the café determined the timing of an intermission in any of its auditoria, screenings were interrupted at callously arbitrary moments; consequently, cuts in the middle of a scene were not unusual.

[210] Most of the papers collected in Stokes, Maltby (2004) deal with the business side of appropriation, while only two focus entirely on popular ways of appropriation; see: Nancy Huggett, Kate Bowles, 'Cowboys, Jaffas and pies: researching cinemagoing in the Illawarra' and Charles Ambler, 'Popular films and colonial audiences in Central Africa', on pp. 64-77 and 133-157, respectively. Information about popular audience appropriation is scattered in published (auto)biographies, memoirs, letters and other, so-called ego documents, while another rich lode—people's memories—are mined in oral history projects (of which the abovementioned article by Huggett and Bowles is an example). A more concentrated source is the study of fans and their behaviors—see: Janet Staiger, *Media reception studies* (2005), pp. 95-114.

[211] Genette (2002), pp. 346-348, 350-353.

Film was, of course, legitimately self-serving. But specific circumstances, as I will argue, pulled the publicity of the trailer in another direction. In fact, the time lag that arose between the French and Dutch releases of LES CLANDESTINS may well have been critical in deciding on this appropriative measure.

City Film did not resubmit the feature to secure a less strict rating. The unanimous decision of October 7, 1947, was apparently felt as being beyond appeal, as it designated for removal too many scenes deemed important (e.g. "the burning of a village and the hanging of hostages" in retaliation for dynamiting a German train; a "realistic" Gestapo 'interrogation' of a Jewish physician). So, when the film was released, in May 1948, cinema listings still rated LES CLANDESTINS for 18 years and above.[212] There must have been, then, a more practical reason for the premiere's delay.

Assuming that the distributor meant to offset the loss of income resulting from the film's rating by repositioning it as a promotion for a good cause (to which, nonetheless, half its earnings were to be committed), it was all the more important to get the two popular, former resistance leaders before the camera. But the very fact of getting them to appear together proved to be time-consuming. To begin with, both had busy agendas. Van Randwijk was often abroad between August and October 1947, while during much of that and the following year his attention was in large part occupied by the very survival of his magazine.[213] As a cabinet member, Drees, besides being much absorbed with the reconstruction of postwar Holland, also became actively involved with the festering issue of the complicated political, military, and international law situation caused by the proclamation of the independent Republic of Indonesia, on August 17, 1945 (although not the entire archipelago had followed suit). Between mid-December 1947 and early January 1948 he was in Batavia (today's Jakarta) as part of a

---

[212] See for instance: 'Agenda', in: *Haagsche Courant* (May 21, 1948), p. 2.

[213] Gerard Mulder, Paul Koedijk, *H.M. van Randwijk: een biografie* (1988), pp. 598; 604-608; 614-624.

government delegation on an official visit that was meant to plumb how the conflict might be muted.[214]

As a matter of fact, the Indonesian question itself may well have contributed to delaying the two men's joint appearance during this period. In July 1947, the Dutch government had decided to send troops to what, under the 1922 Constitution,[215] it still considered its rightful, albeit de facto reduced and politically controversial colonial territory in order to quell the violence that had erupted after the proclamation of independence. The following week, Van Randwijk sharply criticized the government's—and thus Deputy Prime Minister Drees's—decision in an emotional editorial.[216] In it he pointedly avoided the colonial designation "Netherlands East-Indies" and instead spoke of "the young state of Indonesia", echoing and acknowledging the name the controversial leaders of the Republican independence movement had used. More shocking to a segment of contemporary readers was his equation of the moral right of the Indonesian Republicans to that of the Dutch resistance under German occupation. The editorial, finally, was also astounding for breaking ranks with one of the government coalition partners, Drees's social democratic party, to which the magazine was most akin in both ideological and personal terms. With such a principled difference of opinion the two men may not have relished each other's company, let

---

[214] Jan A. Somers, *Nederlandsch-Indië: staatkundige ontwikkelingen binnen een koloniale relatie** (2005), pp. 235-254; Hans Daalder, *Vier jaar nachtmerrie: de Indonesische kwestie. Willem Drees 1886-1988*** (2004), pp. 164-177; Willem Drees, *Zestig jaar levenservaring**** (1962), pp. 231-232.
* *The Netherlands East-Indies: political developments within a colonial relationship;* ***A four-year nightmare: the Indonesian question. Willem Drees 1886-1988;* *** *Sixty years of life experience*

[215] Somers (2005), pp. 135-136.

[216] H.M. van Randwijk, 'Omdat ik Nederlander ben'*, in: *Vrij Nederland*** (July 26, 1947), pp. 1, 5. The decision for a military intervention was euphemistically called "police action", because it was presented as a measure to restore order; see also: Mulder, Koedijk (1988), pp. 584-592.
*'Because I am Dutch'; ** *The Free Netherlands*

alone acted in a spirit of harmony.[217] So, as Van Randwijk can be heard saying in the trailer that *"in the world of 1948 we should not forget about the resistance during the years of occupation"*, the shooting of this additional scene must plausibly have taken place quite some time after the censorship committee's decision of October 1947, probably in the spring of 1948. The trailer was approved for screening in May 1948, coinciding with the film's Amsterdam premiere.[218-219]

Whatever the two men's personal feelings regarding each other, their authority and eventual cooperation may have served to support and accept the changing role and perception of the resistance as the war—at home—slowly slid into history. The immediate postwar years were a period during which the ideas and ideals of resistance movements all over Europe had been gradually neutralized. As well, resistance fighters had been swiftly disarmed in order to re-establish governments' monopoly on armed force. A much discussed issue in these circles during wartime had been the possibility of a new order, a "breakthrough" in the political and ideological arena. With so much of the war's burden falling on civilians this idea seemed to have catalysed a wider sense of solidarity: not just a blurring of class distinctions, but also a shared resentment against the traditional ruling elite. The most resounding expression of this sentiment was Winston Churchill's surprising defeat in the general elections of July

---

[217] All too commonly still in biographical and historical publications on late-19th century and later topics, moving images, let alone a humble trailer, are not considered as sources of any value, if at all. As architectural historian Edward A. Chappell writes, historians do not acknowledge "[f]ilm and history museums (...) because they represent media in which writing is not the distinguishing mode of communication." See his: 'Social responsibility and the American history museum', in: *Winterthur Portfolio* (Winter 1989), p. 247. No comments on both men's cooperation in this trailer are therefore available in the works cited. One intriguing detail, though, is that in Drees's memoirs Van Randwijk's name is never mentioned in any connection whatsoever (Drees, 1962). His biographer doesn't make much of this issue in terms of personal relationships either (Daalder, 2004).

[218] *Nieuw Weekblad voor de Cinematografie** (July 30, 1948), p. 6.
**New Cinematography Weekly*

[219] According to an advertisement the film was released on May 7, 1948 in Amsterdam; the Hague premiere followed two weeks later; see resp.: *Nieuw Weekblad voor de Cinematografie* (May 7, 1948), unpaginated; 'Agenda' (May 21, 1948) and 'Films van deze week'*, in *Haagsche Courant* (May 22, 1948), p. 6.
*'This week's films'

1945, shortly after war's ending in Europe.[220] But while elections in some western European countries resulted in a hesitant swing to the left—i.e. mostly social democratic—side of the political spectrum and an extension of the foundations of the welfare state, much of the period of reconstruction was defined by the American-financed European Recovery Program (1947-1952; popularly known as the Marshall Plan).

ERP was a logical result of the Truman administration's vision of a postwar world in which "economic growth was presented as the material condition for military security and political stability."[221] With the material reconstruction of Europe's war-torn societies often came a semblance, if not an actual restoration of prewar political power relations (involving government officials that had continued to rule and make plans in exile). For many the return to some sort of regularity was too familiar for comfort. As historian Tony Judt writes, for former resistance members, opponents to interwar fascist ideology, as well as the young, "politics was (...) *about* resistance". Their optimism, however, was short-lived, either because, as in Eastern Europe, new, dictatorial puppet regimes were brought in or, as in Western Europe, the resistance movement lacked the experience and acumen to have a lasting effect in the political arena.[222] (In Holland, film censorship was symptomatic of restoration. The censorship board, which was up and running again in August 1945 after its denazification, proceeded in the same spirit as before the war, blithely oblivious to what people had experienced and been exposed to over the five previous years. Remarkably, any more or less realistic portrayal of acts of war, whether in fiction or documentary, ran the risk of restricted screenings, or none at all. And so it could happen that not only LES CLANDESTINS was approved for restricted audiences, but also that the anti-German, pro-resistance feature ROMA, CITTÀ APERTA [1945], was initially rejected for general release in 1947, as it was deemed a mere "series of harsh and vulgar scenes". Yet in the latter case the moral confusion

---

[220] Ian Buruma, *Year zero: a history of 1945* (2013), pp. 243-251; Tony Judt, *Postwar: a history of Europe since 1945* (2010 [2005]), p. 69.

[221] Schuyt, Taverne (2004), p. 57.

[222] Judt (2010), pp. 63-67.

became apparent on appeal, when it was rated for audiences of 18 years and above after only two excisions.[223])

So, "in the world of 1948" the resistance was something to be remembered and admired within the safe frame of past heroics in the struggle against fascist enemies, if it hadn't already acquired a nostalgic ring. Writer and scholar Ian Buruma writes about the "flurry of war monuments in the Netherlands (...) to resistance fighters, fallen soldiers, to national suffering, to the sacrifice of brave individuals."[224] But it had no obvious place in the postwar parliamentary democracies. In other words, by this time the theme of LES CLANDESTINS may well have been felt in need of updating and reframing, which is precisely what Drees and Van Randwijk's appearance was meant to accomplish. Their reputations, secure as a result of their wartime exploits and their current positions, were now employed to safeguard the support of former resistance members within the new, consolidative welfare state that was under construction. A review in the *Hague Gazette* perfectly illustrated this state of affairs saying, "[f]or a few hours one is transported back to the days when the Germans terrorized Europe, hung hostages or burnt entire villages in retaliation, counteracted by the resistance of the heroic French underground that led—albeit at the cost of many lives—to liberation", while in the next sentence it informed its readers about the good cause to which their money would contribute.[225]

---

[223] http://www.cinemacontext.nl/cgi/b/bib/bib-idx?q1=rome%20open%20stad;c= cccfilm;type=simple;rgn1=simple%20fields;tpl=details.tpl;sid=f2966db3241c26714d b83068a5489539;lang=nl;sort=titel%20oplopend;cc=cccfilm;view=reslist;fmt=long;p age=reslist;start=1;size=1.
In 1948, the same director's PAISÀ (1946), about the liberation of Italy by the Allieds and the Italian resistance, was approved only for audiences of 18 years and above because of its scenes containing "fights with partisans", "the hanging of POWs" as well as a "seduction scene"; see: http://www.cinemacontext.nl/cgi/b/bib/bib-idx?q1=paisa;c=cccfilm;type=simple;rgn1=simple%20fields;tpl=details.tpl;lang=nl;si d=68556dc5de4a2abd68e873941a48ec12;sort=titel%20oplopend;cc=cccfilm;view=r eslist;fmt=long;page=reslist;start=1;size=1.

[224] Buruma (2013), p. 136. These monuments to Dutch heroics and suffering, Buruma points out, also camouflaged the embarrassment of allowing most of the country's 150,000 Jewish citizens to be taken to concentration and death camps.

[225] 'Films van deze week' (May 22, 1948), p. 6.

Conclusion: a case of looseness

Film curatorship, according to a recent, well-advised definition, is "[t]he art of interpreting the aesthetics, history, and technology of cinema through the selective collection, preservation, and documentation of films and their exhibition in archival presentations."[226] Although I agree, clearly my focus in this chapter was less on technological and aesthetic than on historical aspects. Yet it wasn't necessarily restricted to cinema history proper. In varying proportions these five, brief case studies are situated at the interfaces between cinema and societal, political or economic circumstances and considerations. They describe how these contexts affected cinema's manifestation, particularly through the ways in which film businesses and other interested parties made, organized, structured, and/or publicized their products and policies, and attracted or informed audiences in a specific setting with a specific promise, goal or recommendation.

These practices and their histories are not explicitly covered by the definition quoted above. Nor are they discussed in the authors' reproduced e-mail exchanges that led up to the definition's final formulation; at one point the term "historical traditions" was advanced, but it drew no comment and was tacitly dropped.[227] While in a book on film curatorship it is inevitable that its domain is delimited, the definition nevertheless remains loose. I use that word in the sense logician Olaf Helmer and philosopher Nicholas Rescher used it in their paper on explanatory statements in the "inexact sciences", their umbrella term for applied physical sciences, history, and the social sciences. In these disciplines specifically, they wrote, law-like formulations are "not unrestricted or universal", but "conditional in their logical form". That is to say, the looseness of definitions, predictions, etc. is a function of conditions of time, place, and circumstances "which may only be indicated in a general way and are not necessarily, (indeed in most cases cannot expected to be) exhaustively articulated." Sociologist Harold

---

[226] Cherchi Usai, Francis, Horwath, Loebenstein (2008), p. 231.

[227] Cherchi Usai, Francis, Horwath, Loebenstein (2008), pp. 222-230. Nonetheless, another reason for selecting this definition, besides its compact comprehensiveness, is that it is based on the four editors'—film curators of different generations—fully reproduced, lengthy and thorough discussions that are unrivalled in the film heritage world.

Garfinkel referred to and rephrased these conditions as the *et cetera rule*, by which he meant to cover—and in his experiments, to uncover—"unstated understandings".[228]

Take, for example, the statement that during the so-called Hollywood studio era eight film companies together controlled all aspects—production, distribution, and exhibition—of the American film industry between the mid-1920s and late 1940s. Besides the explicitly mentioned temporal and spatial limits, it was also conditional on a number of significant circumstances, such as the companies' vertical integration, their structure as stockholding companies with credit lines to Wall Street, their exemption from anti-trust laws, or their production modes of labor specialization and standardized product differentiation.[229] Looseness, furthermore, also implies that counterfactual examples can be explained, or absorbed, by the law-like statement.[230] For instance, Hollywood films did get produced independently, but to recoup costs and make a profit its

---

[228] Olaf Helmer, Nicholas Rescher, *On the epistemology of the inexact sciences* (October 13, 1958), pp. 8-13; Harold Garfinkel, 'What is ethnomethodology?', in: *Studies in ethnomethodology* (1984 [1967]), p. 3. Anthony Giddens completes the objections against the notion of universal laws in the social sciences particularly, stating that not only "methods of empirical testing and validation are (...) inadequate", but more importantly that "the causal conditions in generelizations about human social conduct are inherently unstable in respect of the very knowledge (or beliefs) that actors have about the circumstances of their own action. (...) This is a mutual interpretative interplay between social science and those whose activities compose its subject matter—a 'double hermeneutic'. The theories and findings of the social sciences cannot be kept wholly separate from the universe of meaning and action which they are about. But for their part, lay actors are social theorists, whose theories help to constitute the activities and institutions that are the object of study of specialized social observers or social scientists."; see: Giddens (2014), pp. xxxii-xxxiii.

[229] Gomery (1986), pp. 3-25; Janet Staiger, 'The Hollywood mode of production, 1930-1960', in: David Bordwell, Janet Staiger, Kristin Thompson, *The classical Hollywood cinema: film style & mode of production to 1960* (1985), pp. 311-319.

[230] Helmer, Rescher (1958), pp. 12-13.

producers needed to make sure they were going to be distributed through one of the eight companies.[231]

Here, I take looseness as an opportunity to *extend* (i.e. not replace) the notion of film curatorship by appealing to extra-filmic signifying contexts of film heritage artifacts and records. This is not a mere matter of opinion, because a stricter, 'textual' approach is in fact an obstacle to understanding those artifacts for which aspects of form and style are subordinate. What is more, their aesthetic 'bareness' merely exposes the conditions of time, place, and circumstance that operate on all of them.

Take the example, once more, of the film materials to which the Colonial Institute in Amsterdam supplemented its *Illustrations* in the 1910s and 1920s. As noted, the institute's disregard for what the filmmakers had recorded, as attested by the cuts, inserts, and other changes made over the years, rules out their textual integrity or any unequivocal attribution of authorship. Furthermore, from a traditionally aesthetic point of view these films are 'uninteresting', certainly not innovative: their long takes are typical of contemporary nonfiction filmmaking (the equivalent of fiction films' tableau style), where shots lasted as long as an action took to complete, e.g. each leg of an itinerary or each of the successive phases of a production process. But whenever it was considered expedient the Colonial Institute scissored such takes or their sequence. For instance, those shots for which the camera had been positioned so as to follow a vehicle's complete course from one point to another were apparently too long or lacking any 'hook' to attach a lecturer's text on. The Colonial Institute had no patience with filmically conceived sequences.

One intriguing sequence in this collection is specifically instructive in this regard. In the film COWPOX VACCINATION IN THE VILLAGE the assembled local population has been positioned on either side of a road to allow the camera to record the vaccinator's arrival in and subsequent walk through the village. This action is distributed over two shots connected by what looks like a then modern way of continuity editing: in the first the camera pans to follow the vaccinator until he disappears off-screen right, and in

---

[231] In fact, only through five of them, as during most of the studio era the so-called Little Three—Universal, Columbia, and United Artists—had no theaters of their own and distributed their films, too, through the so-called Big Five—Paramount, MGM, 20th Century-Fox, Warner Bros., and RKO. This is the reason for using the rather loose phrase "eight film companies *together*".

the next he is picked up again when he enters screen left from behind a building. The sequence might make one wonder whether there had been similar instances of joining shots before the Colonial Institute imposed its own editorial decisions on this print. This option assumes that the sequence happened to survive the film's curtailment over the years to less than a third of its length listed in the first catalogue, from 150m to 45m. It is likelier, however, that the sequence was accidentally *created* by the Colonial Institute's invasive measures, viz. the removal of one or more intermediate shots. Support for this explanation comes from a splice between the two described shots in the only surviving negative, a duplicate partly made on stock from the year of the third and last catalogue, 1923, as well as from two tinted nitrate positive prints that bear the marks of a copied splice between these two shots.[232-233]

Not to point out this physical aspect is an instance of obstructing the film's appreciation, understanding, and film historical significance; while to state that this and other films made under Lamster's supervision lack any formal or narrative distinction, let alone innovation, is simply beside the point. What the prints that have come down to us do reflect, of course, are deliberate decisions to realize the Colonial Institute's aims of education and propaganda. Their length testifies to the delivery of the spoken texts during projection, their changes to lecturers' adaptations. Length also points to their exhibition venues, or rather the cinema theaters where they were *not* shown: nonfiction films in commercial programs, in the early and mid-1910s, commonly lasted no more than five minutes or so, while the Institute's films are on average longer—the longest has a running time of twenty minutes. In the cinema theater, moreover, the organization of material in a program was a matter of diversity and rhythm as well of each individual film's contribution: to secure their entertainment value shots had better not outlast their visual

---

[232] I consider this an improvement over my earlier interpretation in: De Klerk (2010), pp. 90-91. Although it is common to say "between two shots", a splice was actually made by overlapping one image partially with the next one: after removal of one or more images, the two ends of a film strip were thus glued together. When copied, a splice can be seen in a positive print as a white, horizontal line, a result of the light deflected by the overlap during the duplication process.

[233] original title KOEPOK-INENTING IN DE DESA translated title COWPOX VACCINATION IN THE VILLAGE
The Netherlands (Koloniaal Instituut) 1912 | 35mm full frame (safety) | b&w, tinting | Dutch titles | 2'40" | print at Eye, Amsterdam.

and storytelling interest. So, whereas lecturers in cinema theaters, if and when their services were required, had to comply with the demands of the entertainments screened, in the Colonial Institute's non-theatrical screenings the spoken texts' information determined to a significant extent the length of the films and of the entire event.

The specific way the Colonial Institute's films were exhibited is just one instance of the many materials and practices that existed before and concurrently with what became cinema's mainstream theatrical exhibitions, their *dispositifs*, and technologies. In my view, it is the task of film heritage institutes not only to bring out the full range of materials and practices, but also to bring a wider array of signifying contexts to bear on them than the usual aesthetic categories. Surely, the very notion of looseness is a warning that any attempt at comprehensiveness is futile. Yet the inclusion of those materials and practices, conditions and conventions the interpretive communities of the film heritage world do know have existed, or still exist, will at least ensure that a definition of curatorship (if not of the task of film heritage institutes tout court) accounts for both majority and minority practices and do justice to cinema as a highly diversified phenomenon. So, as a legend to the definition's subdivision in technology, aesthetics, and history, I propose a conceptual apparatus that agrees with Howard Becker's delineation of networked, interdependent cultural worlds in that they cover the histories that have allowed the accomplishment of cinema, then and now, along or against the grain. Others may want to subdivide or supplement this apparatus, but for now I have settled on a minimal number of coherent, general concepts.

• *Continuity*, first of all, emphasizes the parallels and contact points between the histories of cinema and other (performing) arts and media, in terms of technologies, business models, personnel (ownership and management structure as well as crew or cast), narrative and presentational formats, venues, and audience composition. This concept is important, for instance, for understanding the acceptance of cinema by virtue of its introduction into established entertainments, for the rapid transition from silent to sound film, the importance of television as both an outlet and resource for cinema's products, or the current transition to and proliferation of digitally-based practices.

• *Manifestation* refers to cinema's manifold, multifaceted appearances and practices: its ways of organizing production, distribution, marketing, and exhibition: its purposes (e.g. propaganda, campaigning, instruction, research and documentation, education, advertising, recruitment, discovery or entertainment); target groups (e.g. family and friends, children, young adults, shoppers, students and trainees, the military, foreign audiences); presentation formats (e.g. mixed-media formats— ranging from variety shows to tie-in publicity campaigns—, multiple-channeled shows, framing events—such as Q&As or lectures—, programs, serials, festivals, playback systems); and venues (e.g. fairgrounds, variety theaters, department stores, coffee houses, cinemas and arthouses, schools, museums and cinematheques, world and trade fairs, drive-ins, as well as various home cinema systems and web applications).

• *Identity* pertains to the negotiation between local and international aspects. In the realm of distribution, screening, and reception the abovementioned practices of appropriation—measures to adapt foreign cultural objects to local legal, linguistic or market conditions as wel as all sorts of customs and traditions—, are the clearest and most ubiquitous examples. In the realm of production think, for instance, of multiple language versions or international co-productions.

• *Experience*, finally, refers to the ways cinema appeals to spectators' imagination, world knowledge, emotions, and involvement (including social and political commitment). Besides genre, narrative forms, rhetoric or style, they include the contexts that are most proximate to the film screening: the specific location and architectural properties of a venue as well as their social meaning;[234] the state of projection and display technologies; announcements of all kinds—e.g. posters, trailers and other forms of publicity, program formats, program booklets and info sheets as well as reviews produced elsewhere; live elements during a performance; souvenir program bills and memorabilia as reminders—I cluster fanzines and fan clubs in this category, too.

These concepts are not merely meant to flesh out the abovementioned definition of curatorship, they also propose signposts to the contexts of the film heritage in a given geographic region and historical era. In fact, they are meant to align with the notion of what archivist Hans Booms has called *functional context*, i.e. all those contexts that contribute to forming "a conception of a certain period in the development of the entire section

---

[234] A circumstance pointed out as early as 1914 when sociologist Emilie Altenloh commented on the difference in viewing experiences between neighborhood cinemas with their simple wooden folding seats and the picture palaces with their lobbies, refreshment rooms, and upholstered seating; see her: *Zur Soziologie des Kino, die Kino-Unternehmung und die sozialen Schichten Ihrer Besucher* (1914), p. 19.

of society".[235] This concept was developed to both broaden the remit of archives, firstly from the records generated by administrative bodies to those generated by all parties involved in a specific area of activity in a given society (e.g. by pressure groups, NGOs, media, relevant individuals, etc.). And, secondly, to cope with the overwhelming accrual of the record production by these parties, postwar administrative bodies specifically. A focus on functional contexts implies a different approach to research: instead of the custodial description of *documents* transferred and accessioned it calls for establishing the (hierarchized) functions and activities of record creators (also called macroappraisal) in order to prioritize *documentation*. While Booms's article was written in the context of a national archive (he worked at the German Federal Archives), it would already be quite an accomplishment to form some sort of complete conception of cinema in a certain place and period alone (although research in recent decades on Pathé Frères during the years leading up to World War I or Hollywood's studio era may come close).

My concepts are meant to create a fuller understanding of the institutions, in the sense of both organizations and practices, that affected cinema at certain places and at certain times. There is, however, a major difference with the way non-specialist, or general national/regional film heritage institutes conceive of their task. The time, money, and manpower the film world has invested and the practices and conventions it developed were all meant to create very concrete products—films and a number of ancillary products—that are no documents or records in the sense archival science commonly understands these terms.[236] They are

---

[235] Booms (Summer 1987), p. 103. For the focus on functional contexts, rather than on records and documents per se, see also: Terry Cook, 'Remembering the future: appraisal of records and the role of archives in constructing social memory', in: Blouin, Jr., Rosenberg (2009), pp. 169-181; Cook (1992); David Bearman, 'Archival methods: Archives and Museum Informatics technical report #9', in: *Archives & Museum Informatics* (1989); Philip N. Alexander, Helen W. Samuels, 'The roots of 128: a hypothetical documentation strategy', in: *The American Archivist* (Fall 1987), pp. 526-529.

[236] Margaret Proctor, Michael Cook, *Manual of archival description* (2012 [2000]), define record(s) as "[d]ocument(s) created or received and maintained by an agency, organization or individual in pursuance of legal obligations or in the transaction of business" (p. 254). Richard Pearce-Moses, *A glossary of archival and records terminology* (2005), allows wider meanings in terms of both purpose and medium ("Information or data fixed in some media" is one of his definitions), yet comments that "document is used synonymously with record" (pp. 126-127).

unlike, say, a production or distribution company's correspondence, which are records generated precisely in the service of making or distributing these products. Films, then, are artifacts. Film heritage institutes collect them less for their evidentiary value (i.e. "the quality of records that provides information about the origins, functions, and activities of their creator") than for their informational value (i.e. "the usefulness or significance of materials based on their content");[237] this, of course, is the distinction that allowed Tino Balio's comment on the output of Depression-era Hollywood: the "content" may at times have been socially uplifting, but the "creator" was profit-seeking. As artifacts, then, films invite all sorts of aesthetic judgments considered valuable in and of themselves; hence their selection usually goes beyond accessioning only a few items that are exemplary for various formal, stylistic or narrative aspects. As a matter of fact, even in dedicated institutes for useful film artifacts, 'functional' collecting of a limited number of representative items "documenting a design or function" is not common either.[238]

Films have always been the primary target of collection activities. This artifactual, and often aesthetic, bias will therefore doubtlessly have contributed to film heritage institutes' textually oriented conception of their mission. And because this conception largely favors questions of form and style and artistic meaning, film heritage presentations have often imposed *new* contexts on these artifacts that can be potentially enlightening—obvious examples are the output of one director, performer or studio. Yet they can also be potentially dubious, as when works unrelated in time, place or agency are hitched together under a collective title, often without overmuch consideration for the different conditions and signifying contexts in which they were made, let alone exhibited or received—"influence" commonly is the tenuous explanatory term here. Seldom do film heritage institutes in their presentations respect the archival principle of provenance, the entity "that created or received the

---

[237] Pearce-Moses (2005), pp. 152, 206. However, the distinction between artifacts and records is not all that rigorous, as "[a]rtifacts may be preserved as records, documenting a design or function" (p. 36). The latter notion, however, is not emphasized in the institutes' public information.

[238] E.g. Établissement de Communication et de Production Audiovisuelle de la Défense (ECPAD), Ivry-sur-Seine, for still and moving images of the French army, many of which had an instrumental function and were not meant for public screenings; or the Archivio Nazionale del Cinema d'Impresa (ANCI), Ivrea, for Italian-made industrial and advertising films.

items in a collection", or "the organizational, functional, and operational circumstances surrounding materials' creation, receipt, storage, or use, and its relations to other materials."[239] As archivist Lori Podolsky Nordland writes: "A document is more than its subject content and the context of its original creation. Throughout its life cycle, it continually evolves, acquiring additional meanings and layers, even after crossing the archival threshold. As such, archivists need to read documents against the grain to search for the deeper contexts of their meaning." She has termed these "additional layers of context" *secondary provenance.*[240]

The aesthetic bias, finally, may also explain why screening is such a prominent activity. Most consequentially, as the vast majority of in-house presentations of film heritage materials takes place in a theatrical setting, the artifacts that were screened in other types of venue and/or for other purposes than entertainment or aesthetic enjoyment have therefore become hard to account for in public activities. It is this circumstance that makes such artifacts into collection items and outcasts at the same time. Of course, it also impedes the presentation of the "working system" of various alternative settings.

So, to repeat my question at the beginning of this chapter, In what ways can these materials be meaningfully presented and their histories meaningfully communicated to the public? The mainstream, theatrical model that film heritage institutes have copied, with its regular daily programs, at regular times, in conventional screenings, seems to have directly affected the ways they have shaped and defined their gatekeeper function.[241] In such circumstances a program about the films

---

[239] Pearce-Moses (2005), pp. 317-318; 90.

[240] Lori Podolsky Nordland, 'The concept of "secondary provenance": re-interpreting Ac co mok ki's map as evolving text', in: *Archivaria* (2004), pp. 147, 149. The abovementioned measures of appropriation, as well as reframing, can be seen as specific instances of this broader concept of secondary provenance.

[241] Philippe Gauthier has developed a similar argument why Hale's Tours, a non-theatrical cinema illusion ride that was popular between 1905 and c. 1915, has received relatively little attention in general film histories. This, he claims, is because these histories conceive of the cinema theater as the central location, if not locus, of cinema; see: Gauthier (2013), pp. 194-207. Obviously, film heritage institutes would be hard put to reconstruct Hale's Tours without significant alterations to their own premises—and that, in fact, is a clear example of the obstructive effect of "conventional means of doing things"; see Becker (1984), p. x.

commissioned by the Dutch Colonial Institute, for example, would only become meaningfully enhanced, if not meaningful tout court, when spectators are informed about any or more of such contextual matters as the ideology and purposes of the Colonial Institute, the particular ways it attempted to control the screening of its films (venue and presentation format, its indebtedness to magic lantern shows), their distinction from commercially released exotica, etc., as well as matters—and myths— implied in the prints' "intellectual content"[242] (e.g. the colonial economy, demographics, or politics; information pertinent to specific items—e.g. vaccination as part of the colonial administration's early 20th-century policy of improving medical conditions), their extrinsic aspects, such as the prints' histories (e.g. splices, inserts, coloring, the additional Pathé footage, and other changes the institute subjected its films to—not to mention the invasive measures taken by the films' current repository) or contemporary camera and lens technology.

This is not a plea to reenact the original shows and their contemporary, illustrative texts (although the original presentation formats might be invoked for conveying precisely the categories of information mentioned above). What I do want to stress is that film heritage institutes need, first of all, a way of doing curatorship that activates—that is to say select and lift from the darkness of the vaults into the public light—all types of objects. Secondly, they need to develop different presentation formats. Particularly for screenings, such formats need to be more flexible and more imaginative than most film heritage institutes are accustomed to mount (see also the 'Evaluation' section in chapter 3). Obviously, this would allow them to accommodate a larger set of materials and their contextualizing information. More thoroughly contextualized presentations, moreover, may also play up the histories hidden, as we have seen, behind all those deceptively 'transparent' feature fiction materials.

If and when all this happens cannot, I suppose, be "exhaustively articulated".

---

[242] Bearman (1989), chapter III: 'Arrangement and description' [the PDF of the text is unpaginated].

Chapter 3

Showing and telling: an exploratory survey

In this chapter I present a survey and evaluation of two activities of film heritage institutes: public presentations and visitor information about these presentations. One might counter that this is only one task, a task that has been called (but does not necessarily exhaust) curatorship. And even though I am of the opinion that curating presentations implies the obligation to communicate the ideas and considerations that underlay them, I prefer to separate them here for reasons I will explain below. As noted, my survey is based on data culled from the websites of 24 film heritage institutes across the world during the month of February 2014. I am aware, of course, that websites may not always give a full account of what it is film heritage institutes provide in terms of public activities, visitor information most particularly. For instance, only one institute in my survey, Cinemateca Portuguesa-Museu do Cinema, explicitly mentioned the distribution of leaflets before film shows,[243] while a number of institutes listed introductions by staff, guest curators or invited experts, albeit not for all their presentations.[244] I think it is safe to state, nevertheless, that the various media in which presentations are publicized and introduced overlap rather than differ. For one thing, the sheer volume of activities many institutes present would seem to preclude a costly and time-consuming, multi-pronged publicity approach (and if a particular activity called for addressing additional, specific target groups, direct mailing would be the preferable method anyway). For another, insofar as institutes publish printed program bulletins (which are, moreover, also

---

[243] 'Lisbon annual report 2013', at: *FIAF rapports annuels 2013* (2014), p. 3.

[244] Cinemateca Boliviana; Cinémathèque française-Musée du Cinéma; Cinémathèque suisse, Lausanne; Cinémathèque québécoise, Montreal; Deutsches Filminstitut Filmmuseum; Filmoteca de Catalunya; Fondazione Centro Sperimentale di Cinematografia-Cineteca Nazionale; Irish Film Institute, Dublin; Jerusalem Cinematheque-Israel Film Archive; UCLA Film & Television Archive, Los Angeles.

available as PDFs on their sites) there are no major differences to be detected. As a matter of fact, the printed program overview of one institute, the Cinémathèque québécoise, contains less information than its digital counterpart. Finally, these days it seems safe to assume that film heritage institutes' potential visitors are expected to inform themselves of their activities through internet, an expectation confirmed (and, I trust, a trend reinforced) by the possibility of online ticket reservation and purchase.[245]

My inventory of presentations includes film screenings and exhibitions, both linear and online, that are meant to familiarize general audiences and users with the film heritage, although not necessarily of their own country or region, and the histories and interpretations thereof. The term "general audiences" implies that I have excluded activities of restricted access, such as those for professional peer groups as well as educational programs, either on-site or on location. It also means that I have left out children's shows, because insofar as they were part of an institute's presentations the works screened in these shows are to a large extent similar to children's shows in regular cinemas; as a rule their main point is to cultivate a next generation of visitors, yet they are not promoted as being about the film heritage.[246] Finally, I have also omitted consideration of the DVDs, books, and other products that some of these institutes have published on the basis of their collections, restorations or presentations, that is to say, other than those DVDs, books, and other products (e.g. Coppola's wine) unrelated to an institute's activities, for which its museum store is often just another sales outlet and a way to stack its shelves. Whether the publications initiated by an institute are targeted at an audience segment that is already motivated, if not specialist, or that it might hope to reach a larger public, they are usually not advertised as being uniquely available at the institute's premises, as

---

[245] The Cinémathèque québécoise has in fact decided to reduce the edition of its printed brochure and discontinue its mailing, its stated reason being "le désir de laisser de plus en plus de visibilité à la version numérique du dépliant."; see: *Rapport annuel 2013-2014* (2014), p. 35.

[246] But rules have exceptions: the Cinemateca Portuguesa-Museu do Cinema has an ongoing project aimed at schoolchildren, *Cinemateca Júnior*, which includes series of special screenings as well as activities in its permanent, interactive exhibition of 18th and 19th-century equipment for mechanically recording and reproducing images before the advent of film technology. For consistency's sake, though, I will not further discuss it.

institutes tend to sell each other's products[247]; and then, of course, there are regular (shops) and irregular (festivals) opportunities to increase sales. In other words, as more randomly distributed products they are quite different from an institute's concentrated efforts, such as screenings or exhibitions. But practical considerations of time, availability, and language barriers have, of course, also contributed to this restriction.

Set

The list of film heritage institutes included in the survey is the outcome of a number of criteria and circumstances. The latter largely comprise incidental matters of restricted acces or none at all, incomplete or meaningless information as well as linguistic issues. Until the moment data for evaluation were collected, in February 2014, the websites of a number of institutes could not be accessed, in spite of repeated efforts over the space of several months (e.g. Fundacion Cinemateca Argentina, Buenos Aires; Armenian National Cinematheque, Yerevan). Quite a few others either listed no regular public presentations (e.g. Bangladesh Film Archive, Dhaka; Sinematek Indonesia, Jakarta; South African National Film, Video, and Sound Archives, Pretoria; Swedish Film Institute, Stockholm) or, when they did, presented outdated announcements (e.g. Bulgarian National Film Archive, Sofia; Cultural Center of the Philippines, Manila; National Film Archive of India, Pune). Furthermore, the websites of two institutes didn't allow retrieval of full information of earlier date, not even a day after a public presentation (Centre National de l'Audiovisuel, Dudelange; Eye, Amsterdam). And in a number of cases language barriers, more specifically those languages the mistakes of which inevitably made in Google Translate were beyond my powers of correction—e.g. Danish, Georgian, Polish, Slovak, Thai—, discouraged the creation of a more extensive database. (Although the websites of a number of institutes were bilingual, this service was commonly restricted to their homepage, while visitor information, such as the PDFs of their program bulletins, was left untranslated.)

---

[247] Other exceptions are the Österreichisches Filmmuseum and Filmarchiv Austria (although the latter is not included in my survey), Vienna, both of which as a rule predominantly sell books and DVDs they have (co-)produced.

As a result, the database was necessarily limited to those sites whose information was provided in a number of West Germanic and Romance languages. The institutes evaluated in this study, therefore, reflect a heavier Western bias than desired. To compensate for the loss of geographical spread as well as for the fact that the month of February meant that institutes in the southern hemisphere might close or reduce their activities for the summer holidays (which was indeed the case in some institutes, but certainly not in all), I have included two privately funded film heritage institutes in South America: Cinemateca Boliviana, La Paz, and Cinemateca Uruguaya, Montevideo. They were selected, not so much to allow comparison with their publicly funded counterparts, but actually because they see themselves, and are being seen, as repositories and guardians of their respective national cinema heritage, despite the lack of government support. In the case of Australia, I selected an institute of regional status, whose program didn't seem reduced for the summer months. Finally, as I have tried to keep their number within limits of manageableness, I have selected only one institute per country.

I have therefore deliberately called mine a "set" of film heritage institutes for the simple reason that technically it is not a sample: as pointed out above, a statistically representative portion of a whole could not be made. Nor can it be called a selection: even though my interest was led by qualitative considerations, viz. public status, practical circumstances determined the set's makeup more heavily. Given this lack of statistical representativeness, my evaluation is foremost an exploratory endeavor.[248]

The makeup of this set was based on the directories of the Fédération Internationale des Archives du Film (FIAF) and the National Film Preservation Board. That in itself constituted an important limitation, as these sites largely contain links to institutes with either a national or regional remit. This restriction was meant to realize my most important criterion, which was that these institutes receive structural funding, wholly or partly, from public budgets at non-local levels and are mandated to assume responsibility for the film heritage of the society and territory

---

[248] I take the definitions of "sample" and "selection" from: Terry Cook, 'Many are called but few are chosen: appraisal guidelines for sampling and selecting case files', in: *Archivaria* (Summer 1991), pp. 26-28.

their governments administrate.[249] This implied, secondly, that these institutes operate within a legal framework that requires them to be publicly accountable for the way they allocate their subsidy and implement their missions. Thirdly, such institutes are likelier to attract adequate, at least sustained financial support. As a result of both their size and means, fourthly, they commonly provide public presentations on a regular and frequent basis. Moreover, as most film heritage institutes of such stature boast the facilities to be eligible as members of FIAF, they have access to each other's collections for their presentations.

The reasons, then, that in my survey I conceive of the presentations and visitor information of (predominantly) publicly funded institutes as discrete activities is that they are the most widely visible aspects of their accountability; as such they require, I think, separate inspection and evaluation. Hence I take the performance of accountability as visible evidence of these institutes' mandate vis-à-vis the public at large. It is there, moreover, that other publicly funded yet 'backstage' activities, such as preservation and restoration, can be showcased and accounted for.

Mix

Besides government funding, either direct or indirect (i.e. through an arts council or other publicly funded endowments), the increase in and structuring of private or corporate funding over the past few decades surely have demanded equally formalized and rationalized

---

[249] Three institutes, one private—Cinemateca Boliviana—and two public ones— Bophana Centre de Ressources Audiovisuelles, Phnom Penh, and Cinemateca Dominicana, Santo Domingo—mention in their mission or funding statements that they receive additional financial support, either generally or for a specific purpose, from *foreign* public budgets. This, however, should not surprise us in a post-colonial, globalized, and multinodal world, where the museum has become a sign of nationality and modernity, which in former colonies is largely a legacy of a former colonizing state but, apparently, has remained a continuing concern. See: Arjun Appadurai, Carol A. Breckenridge, 'Museums are good to think: heritage on view in India', in: Ivan Karp, Christine Mullen Kreamer, Steven D. Lavine (eds.), *Museums and communities: the politics of public culture* (1992), pp. 34-55; see also: John M. MacKenzie, *Museums and empire: natural history, human cultures and colonial identities* (2010 [2009]).

accountability.[250] In fact, the mission and funding statements of my set of institutes show that the mingling of public and private interests with respect to the public heritage is rule rather than exception today. Indeed, few film heritage institutes are wholly subsidized from public budgets (and those that are often seek additional funding from third parties for non-mandated, costly, and/or high-profile activities). Private sponsorship, either on an incidental (or "project") basis or as a long-term partnership, has become a fixture of the way cultural institutes, certainly those that are perceived as having prestige, operate nowadays. Moreover, mixed financial sources constitute a major element in the dynamics of the cultural field as a whole, compounded in more recent times by retreating government funding and/or making subsidies conditional on revenue from other sources, such as matching funds by sponsors, grantors, donors, endowments, etc. or a certain percentage of earned income (hence the ubiquitous museum store and cafe as well as archival sales departments, membership programs, and facilities rental).[251]

One example of this dynamics is described in sociologist Victoria Alexander's survey of American art museums between 1960 and 1986, in which she argues that the change of funding (in this particular case, from private—or philanthropic—to corporate and institutional) went hand in hand with a shift in museum policies and power: from a curatorial, internally oriented model in which a museum's public activities were based on scholarship, to a managerial model and its more external orientation to both funders and audiences. However, this shift did not imply that museums always simply marched to their new sponsors' drums. She observed rather that museum managements were often able

---

[250] Richard A. Peterson, 'From impresario to arts administrator: formal accountability in nonprofit cultural organizations', in: Paul J. DiMaggio (ed.), *Nonprofit enterprise in the arts: studies in mission and constraint* (1986), p. 170; Victoria D. Alexander, *Museums and money: the impact of funding on exhibitions, scholarship, and management* (1996), pp. 87-92.

[251] The funding statement of the Queensland Art Gallery | Gallery of Modern Art, which houses the Australian Cinematheque, lists a wide but nowadays common range of income sources: "The income of the Gallery comes mainly from the Queensland Government annual grant ($28.8m in 2014-15). Other major sources of income were donations ($9.2m, both cash and artwork); sponsorship ($1.5m, both cash and contra); exhibition admission revenues ($1.2m); and retail and food and beverage revenues ($2.1m and $4.3m respectively)"; see: *Queensland Art Gallery Board of Trustees annual report 2014-2015* (September 18, 2015), Part A, p. 64. A more detailed overview can be found in the report's Part B, p. 16.

to retain a high degree of autonomy by reshaping funders' demands or wishes in accordance with a museum's "portfolio", i.e. its own proposals for future exhibitions. So while popularly positioned shows often got the publicity sponsors were seeking in order to increase name recognition, museums were able, by public money thus saved or by door money earned, to continue mounting more traditionally curatorial exhibitions, albeit perhaps with a smaller splash. Alexander concluded that in art museums these developments have led, besides a conflictual relation between curatorial staff and management, to a "broadening of art", a trend exemplified by more, and often more popular, exhibitions and a break with the traditional high art canon.[252] As noted, film heritage institutes, judging from the 'symptoms' mentioned in chapter 1, have broadened their presentations, too, yet at the same time they have *narrowed* the range of materials presented from their (and sister institutes') collections.

Even though in actual practice the contrast between public and private pursuits has become increasingly blurred,[253] as a category publicly funded institutes can be contrasted with two other ones. On one hand, there are institutes, often similar in mode of operation, that are wholly or predominantly supported with private money. Apart from complying to laws and regulations that apply generally to the operations of privately funded organizations and enterprises—either nonprofit or for-profit—, these institutes are not obliged to act according to specific requirements by a legislator, only to the wishes and specifications, if any, of owners, donors, legators or grantmakers. Unless stipulated otherwise, they are under no obligation to account for any of their activities or even open up

---

[252] Alexander (1996), pp. 122-135.
Alexander's institutional approach, particularly the consequences of the emergence of the managerial model, mirrors sociologist Eliot Freidson's study of established, professional institutes (e.g. in the field of education or health care), particularly in his detailed analysis of the dynamics of power relations between rank-and-file and management; see his: *Professional powers: a study of the institutionalization of formal knowledge* (1988 [1986]), pp. 209-230.

[253] This is not a matter of funding nor of cultural institutes alone. On a more general level, too, the public impact of private institutes or the transfer of once public tasks to private parties have affected society as a whole, administratively, legally, and morally; see: Tom Nesmith, 'Still fuzzy, but more accurate: some thoughts on the "ghosts" of archival theory' [review article], in: *Archivaria* (Spring 1999), pp. 147-148.

their holdings to third parties, whether visitors or researchers. But that, I assume, is not a widespread practice. In fact, there are private organizations for whom public presentations are their express purpose; one example, as we have seen in chapter 2, is American TV corporations' acquisition of Hollywood studio film libraries as relatively cheap and attractive product for profitable broadcasting and DVD release; major global corporations, such as Sony, have done the same.

On the other hand, there is a recent category of privately owned repositories, the web-based platform or provider, that allows both individuals and juridical persons to create, store, and share born- or made-digital moving image materials; well-known examples are YouTube and Vimeo. They differ in terms of the functions distinguished earlier in that their emphasis is predominantly on access. But rather than resembling moving image repositories—albeit barely, given how unstable they are in terms of their 'catalogue', and their lack of source information—, what matters more is that their very ease of both uploading and downloading has created a new, certainly more pronounced participatory form of moving image culture. As the word "create" comprises materials homemade, appropriated (or pirated), and modified, content of these platforms may push the envelope of laws and regulations, those regarding obscenity and copyright most particularly. Access being their most distinctive characteristic, these platforms do not merely contrast with the more traditional privately and publicly funded institutes, they also significantly affect the dynamism of the entire film heritage field.

Of course, categorical and institutional distinctions do not make all the film heritage institutes in my set identical. Besides stature, they also differ in a number of other important respects. Some are stand-alone institutes (e.g. Cinemateca Brasileira, São Paulo; Cinémathèque québécoise; Irish Film Institute), while others are part of a larger cultural, administrative, archival or educational institute (e.g. Filmoteca de Catalunya, which is part of a public body for the commercial development of the Catalan cultural sector created by the Catalan Department of Culture; Hong Kong Film Archive, which is one of a number of heritage institutes managed directly by a government department; National Film Center at the National Museum for Modern Art, Tokyo). Again others have a remit that transcends cinema and its related collections (UCLA Film & Television Archive; Bophana Centre de Ressources Audiovisuelles, Phnom Penh, which collects sound recordings, still and moving images; or, since August

2014, Ngā Taonga Sound & Vision, which now unites New Zealand's radio, film, and TV collections[254]).

Furthermore, while the institutes surveyed perform one or more of the abovementioned tasks with regard to the film heritage, some have been given responsibilities, such as funding, production, distribution, promotion, licensing, authorization and/or training, that rather concern the film business or industry (e.g. BFI-NFTVA; Centre cinématographique marocain, Rabat; Fondazione Centro Sperimentale di Cinematografia— Cineteca Nazionale).[255] And finally, these institutes vastly differ in a number of, often interrelated, quantifiable aspects that may well have an effect upon the tasks prioritized and performed: the amount of funding they receive and/or raise; number of employees; capacity of the premises as well as the availability of other venues (Bophana Centre de Ressources Audiovisuelles, Cinemateca Dominicana, Santo Domingo, Filmoteca de Catalunya, and Ngā Taonga Sound & Vision make it a point to show all or part their presentations at venues and events over the entire territory they service); other facilities to realize their public presentations and disseminate their information (e.g. exhibition space; digital infrastructure—Cinémathèque française-Musée du Cinéma, Cinémathèque québécoise, Cinémathèque suisse, and Fondazione Centro Sperimentale-Cineteca Nazionale have uploaded selective recordings of their public activities on their websites or a separate web channel); or the number and frequency of their public presentations (for instance, in February 2014, the Centre cinématographique marocain showed a single public program, a combined feature and short film, in its one auditorium, while BFI-NFTVA offered a plethora of presentations, ranging from an exhibition, retrospectives, releases, a festival, a masterclass, and various other events in its four auditoria, exhibition space, and nearby concessioned IMAX theater all through that month; for both institutes

---

[254] In September 2014, an e-mail was sent through AMIA's ListServe, which announced the name change of the institute that was initially included in my set as the New Zealand Film Archive into Ngā Taonga Sound & Vision, the outcome of a merger with Sound Archives Ngā Taonga Kōrero and the Television New Zealand Archive. I will use the new institute's name retroactively. See also: Ngā Taonga Sound & Vision, 'Corporate information', at: http://www.ngataonga.org.nz/about/corporate-information.

[255] It is through such measures, too, that some of these institutes have transcended the abovementioned urban domain of culture and gained influence, cultural or even political, on a national level.

these presentations were not out of the ordinary). So, in order to make comparisons on the basis of criteria that apply throughout the set, I have disregarded quantitative aspects and focused on the qualitative aspects of their public activities and visitor information. And although I will mention conditions that may have impinged on the institutes' presentations, I concern myself largely with the content that is realized within their variously enabling and disabling circumstances.

Formats

Public presentations come in a small number of formats that are used by all of the 24 institutes in my set. Most of these formats are tried-and-true arrangements, largely developed in museums, cinema theaters or festivals before the emergence of the modern film archival movement in the early 1930s. In the following I make a distinction between only a handful of format terms, both to avoid the confusion that arises from the use of different terms for the same phenomenon (for instance, in English *series* and *retrospective* are sometimes used interchangeably, as are *hommage*, *rétrospective* or *cycle* in French) as well as to make comparison feasible.

Of the terms I will use, *virtual exhibition, (permanent/temporary) exhibition*, and *festival* are the only consistently continuous presentation formats (except at Ngā Taonga Sound & Vision, which interrupted its exhibitions when the institute closed a few weeks for the summer holidays; elsewhere the summer closure customarily sets a temporary presentation's term). With respect to film screenings I distinguish between the following formats.

• *one-off*, by which I mean an autonomous, single screening of a film or compilation of films (although I have allowed for the odd repeat screening)

• *release*, which I define as an autonomous, repeatedly screened film or compilation, either continuously or continually. A release can be a title from an institute's own label (which may include re-releases of preserved or restored films), from an outside distributor, a temporarily imported film or compilation, or simply a string of repeated screenings of the same film or compilation (the latter is not strictly a release in the trade's sense of the term, but as in many cases rights have to be cleared for a specified period and place, too, I see no urgent reason to make a distinction).

• *retrospective*, by which I mean a program of related screenings, shown either continuously or continually, of a number of films and/or compilations arranged under a collective title.

• *series* is a program of related screenings of films and/or compilations arranged under a collective title and shown periodically; in some cases a series comes in the shape of a film course.

• *event*, finally, is a usually one-off occurrence that involves a substantial personal appearance for a lecture, interview, panel discussion, Q&A, book or DVD launch, etc., by personalities that have sufficient audience appeal of themselves, i.e. no screening needs to take place. (I distinguish events from brief introductions by management, programmers or curators, etc., which are usually not considered to contribute to a show's drawing power, a reason why they may not always be listed. I also distinguish them from series, particularly courses, whose scheduled screenings are preceded by introductions. Admittedly, these distinctions cannot always be unequivocally made, as the respective 'weight' of screening and personal appearance can also be a matter of publicity.) Events are autonomous or part of either of the abovementioned formats—in which case it is organized on the occasion of whatever that format contained at a particular moment. Moreover, both events and festivals are formats for which a film heritage institute, because of its specific facilities, is not infrequently the host to other organizations.

Apart from the distinction between on-site and online exhibitions, which is principally a matter of access, the only parameters on which one format differs from another are frequency and duration. With regard to exhibitions—both on-site or online—, this parameter obviously defines the (semi-)permanent from the temporary ones. With regard to programs of screenings it defines the one-off from various forms of repeated and/or multiple screenings. The latter merely differ among themselves in terms of compression and continuity: either they are relatively brief—commonly measured in terms of weeks or months—and repeated and/or combined (e.g. release or retrospective), or they are prolonged—commonly measured in terms of seasons—and periodical (a series). In terms of content, however, these formats are mutable.

A few comments are in order here. First of all, strictly one-off screenings were rare; only two institutes in my set employed this format in a significant measure relative to their other presentations: the Jerusalem Cinematheque-Israel Film Archive and, most abundantly, the Cinemateca Portuguesa-Museu do Cinema. Elsewhere screenings were largely made part of some form of serial format. This is a sign of the role film heritage institutes are expected to assume by contextualizing their presentations in various ways, but also of their economics, since serial screenings, because of their prolonged, planned nature, conveniently allow preselling (e.g. season tickets) and the building of a subscription base. Also, formatted programming allows concentrated and cost-saving publicity (even the layout of the institutes' program bulletins—online or takeaway—reflect a compartmentalized arrangement of presentations with barely a loose end). Nevertheless, the tendency to show films in one context or another can become habitual to the point of compulsion. For instance, the screening at the Cinemateca Uruguaya, on consecutive Saturdays in February and March 2014, of four feature fiction films in its series *Trasnoches* can hardly be said to be meaningfully connected when its program bulletin states: "The late night shows (...) have returned with four films that share some (...) stylistic features, or at least whose directors were listed as being the coolest of the end of the millennium. (...) Anyway, four good excuses to stay up late."[256]

Secondly, the mutability of formats shows that these arrangements have no intrinsic value. Naturally, one-off screenings in themselves do not easily allow programmatic contextualization. Most formats, however, can shade into each other or be used expediently, if not arbitrarily. Cinematek, Brussels, for instance, mounted a *retrospective* of Bosnian filmmaker Danis Tanovic, during which it *released* his temporarily imported, latest film, which was shown under the label of its *series* of previously undistributed films in Belgium. More frequently and systematically, the Centro Sperimentale di Cinematografia-Cineteca Nazionale fuses various formats into one in presentations that seem to be one-off programs raised to the status of event by complementary personal appearances, yet which could just as well be seen as compact, one-day retrospectives, since they consist of the screening of a number of films collected under an umbrella title and connected to the occasion's topic (here, inversely, the film program is organized on the occasion of the event). To mention just one example: on February 4, 2014, the institute hosted a meeting with invited guest Italian actor Toni Bertorelli on the occasion of the launch of his book *L'effeto del jazz*, whose story was set in the Turin jazz scene in the 1960s. This event was surrounded by the screening of three feature fiction films that were related in one way or another to jazz in Italy; I use the phrase

---

[256] 'Trasnoches', in: *Boletín Cinemateca Uruguaya* (February-March 2014), p. 22.

"one way or another" by design to suggest that the book launch was given more substance by adding film screenings.[257]

Formats, then, do not determine content. Rather, they are ways of securing audience interest, which benefit from brevity in some cases, from length in others, from comprehensiveness in some, from selectiveness in others. But these considerations, too, depend on practical decisions and circumstances, such as the logistics of program planning, (inter-archival) print traffic, rights clearance, limits on screening, capacity of the venue, specific occasions, preferred programming style, etc.

Survey

In the following I will provide in alphabetical order vignettes of the institutes in my set and summarize and comment on their screenings and, if any, exhibitions or events, as well as on visitor information about these presentations. This will be followed by an evaluation of the survey as a whole. For my data I have relied, in addition to the institutes' websites, on notes made while consulting their websites on both previous and later occasions (particularly to get a sense of whether the public activities in February 2014 were representative of an institute's established procedures), their funding and mission statements,[258] e-newsletters, press releases, and older program bulletins (particularly to complement sparse visitor information about programs that had begun before and continued through February 2014), as well as occasional other web-based sources.

In evaluating the survey I have not used the equivalent of a questionnaire or other standardized form. As there is no prescribed range

---

[257] 'L'effetto del jazz. Lo Swing Club di Torino' (February 4, 2014); at: http://www.fondazionecsc.it/events_detail.jsp?IDAREA=16&ID_EVENT=991&GTE MPLATE=ct_home.jsp.

[258] I am aware that mission statements need to be taken at face value, as they are often a mere field in the paperwork required by governments, grantmakers, and other bodies vital to the operation of film heritage institutes. Usually boilerplate, as in "to collect, protect, preserve, and disseminate the moving image heritage" or variants thereof, some institutes' statements nevertheless transcend the formulaic and seem to seriously attempt to position themselves in a distinctive way. Indifferent funders notwithstanding, I consider film heritage institutes accountable to the statements they make.

or mixture of presentations, the survey is not meant to check off boxes. The fact that in a given case many boxes would have been left unchecked reveals no more than the observation that some formats were absent from the palette of presentations during a particular month. However, in some cases a preference, even a typical programming style could be identified, which I will duly mention.

With regard to visitor information I do have a number of criteria; these are largely related to the ways the institutes enable their users and visitors to learn more about the presented materials and their histories. The central considerations here are: informativeness, expertise, and relevance. Informativeness refers to the quantity of visitor information provided. Expertise, on the other hand, refers to its qualitative aspects, for instance the considerations—technology, aesthetics, history—listed in the definition of curatorship quoted in chapter 2, even though it depends on the specific presentation which of these three—or other ones—are appropriate. By relevance I mean here more specific considerations underlying a presentation. Furthermore, I compare introductions, plot summaries, contextual and other information with mission statements. Finally, I will not evaluate each explanatory text to each presentation exhaustively, but identify those aspects that I think are characteristic of or important to an institute.[259]

Australian Cinematheque, Brisbane

The Australian Cinematheque is part of the Queensland Art Gallery | Gallery of Modern Art (QAGOMA), a complex of two visual arts institutions in separate buildings 150 meters apart. The Gallery of Modern Art houses the Cinematheque's two auditoria (aggregate capacity 300), the smallest of which has retractable seating that allows multimedia performances and other, less conventionally theatrical presentations. Its screenings are partly based on the Gallery's moving-image collection in which Asian, Pacific, and Australian works are heavily represented. But while drawing on (and adding to) these collections, the Cinematheque clearly evinces a wider international outlook that features both recent as well as historical trends.

---

[259] I want to remind readers that the survey's database of web information about these public presentations and visitor information cannot be retrieved in its entirety. Readers interested in this research source are advised to send a request for a Word file of the databasee to the author at: nhdeklerk@gmail.com.

The Cinematheque's preference for programs of certain duration is plausibly a function of its immediate museum environment, which allows it to have some of its presentations coincide with activities, notably exhibitions, organized at QAGOMA's two galleries. From late June through September 2014, for instance, the Cinematheque's retrospective *Food on film* ran parallel with the Gallery of Modern Art's exhibition *Harvest*, "a celebration of food in art [w]ith over 150 works from the Gallery's Collection." Judging from its programming style, its preference for the retrospective format in particular, the Cinematheque has over the last few years favored programs in which connections and coherence were created between the works selected other than based on the most common, such as a filmmaker or genre (organizing principles that it features as well); a fairly large number of its retrospectives were thematic. Finally, its programming style is also a way of giving form to its mission: "retrospective and thematic film programs and exhibitions showcasing the work of influential filmmakers and artists". Besides retrospectives, its one-off screenings usually feature recently restored modern classics of international art cinema.

See also: http://www.qagoma.qld.gov.au/cinematheque/current

Summary of presentations:

• 1 one-off screening

MANILA IN THE CLAWS OF LIGHT (February 2015), screening of the 2013 digital restoration by the World Cinema Foundation (founded by filmmaker Martin Scorsese, in 2007) of this 1975 Filippino feature film.

• 1 retrospective

Fairytales and fables (January 10-March 30), a genre-based program that consisted of a large number of thematically arranged feature fiction and animation films covering a wide range in terms of both year of production and country of origin.

Summary of information:

MANILA IN THE CLAWS OF LIGHT received a one-paragraph description, preceded by fairly complete credits and some technical information. The paragraph deals succinctly with a number of aspects: its style ("slice of life", "true representation") as a corollary of Filippino director Lino Brocka's political engagement and critical stance against notorious, former president Marcos; a brief story summary of the trials and tribulations of its working class protagonist; the film's troubles with censorship; and information about the state of and the work done on the elements used for its 4K restoration and its premiere at the 2013 Cannes Festival.

Although relatively informative in the sense that the film's description was not limited to a plot summary, its succinctness could not but lead, one suspects, to unsubstantiated statements. With the phrase that MANILA IN THE CLAWS OF LIGHT is "considered to be the most significant film in Filipino cinema history" the Cinematheque relied on received knowledge, freeing itself from providing background or even an opinion. Furthermore, one wonders whether young visitors, in 2014, could be expected to know about "the corrupt and oppressive political regime of President Ferdinand Marcos" (unless that statement was considered sufficiently instructive), which ended almost thirty years before. On the technical side, while the film's credits mentioned "35mm", the screening format was DCP. This explicit discrepancy would benefit from further comment, as comparable screenings of recently restored films at this venue did not mention digital screening formats; the retrospective, too, contained a number of unelucidated instances where negative or printed format differed from screening format.

Fairytales and fables was introduced in a sweeping but brief overview of the program's range, in terms of time span: from turn-of-the-20th century trick films through early 21st-century works; genre: from various animation techniques to witty comedies, bleak political allegory, and experimental film; as well as production country. The retrospective was subdivided into six thematic sections: 'Coming of age' ("the trope of a child abandoned—emotionally or physically—in an uncertain world"); 'Classic tales and twists' ("cinematic renditions and reinterpretations of classic tales, as well as original stories that draw on the structural elements of both literary and oral fairytale and fable traditions"); 'Animals and shapeshifting' ("anthropomorphic animals with human character traits and protagonists who have been physically transformed, voluntarily or not, into animal form through magical intervention"); 'Through the looking glass' ("classic European fairytales [...] through another cultural lens"); 'Catch a fairy by the tale' ("the films [...] sidestep the retelling of any single tale and instead interweave fairytale fragments with elements of other genres. While not true fairytales, their use of fairytale archetypes and tropes compliments and renews the genre"); and the one exception to this motif-based division, 'Silent cinema'.

This retrospective was typical for the way the Cinematheque makes a large number of disparate films cohere within a broadly defined type of story, bringing out fairytale elements in a few films not immediately associated with it (e.g. GASLIGHT). The effort of mounting a program of some originality notwithstanding, it was unfortunate that the Cinematheque's visitor information for this program came largely from quoted newspaper and magazine reviews, distributors' catalogues, and program descriptions of art houses, festivals, and other film heritage institutes. Thus, by relying on outside sources for its visitor information it denied itself the opportunity to amplify its own considerations and vision and to strengthen its particular approach to film history. Not only did these copied texts frequently consist of mere storyline summaries, they were, of course, written for other purposes, within other contexts. In fact, the Cinematheque even quoted itself: the brief description one film included in the program, NIGHT OF THE HUNTER, was copied from another of its retrospectives, titled *Caligari and his sideshows: mental and representational instability*, in 2008. This apparently all-purpose summary undercut the retrospective's ambition to take a different look at films that "investigate and reinvigorate" the fairytale. Nor did it reflect its ambition, standardly formulated in QAGOMA's annual reports until recently, to "[m]aximise access to the Collection and to temporary exhibitions through display, information, educational and *interpretive services of the highest standard*" (my italics).

As a rule the Cinematheque's credits were fairly complete; and it is one of very few institutes that systematically mentioned both the source of the print it showed as its screening format. A missed opportunity, though, is that it refrained from explaining what circumstances led it to show prints on 16mm or DCP of films that were shot and restored on 35mm (after all, it has the facilities to show all these formats), or why it showed black-and-white rather than color prints of the retrospective's silent films.

Bophana Centre de Ressources Audiovisuelles, Phnom Penh

Founded in 2006, the Centre is the youngest institute in the set. An initiative of two filmmakers, Rithy Panh and Ieu Pannakar—the latter was at the time in charge of the Cinematic Division within the Cambodian Ministry of Culture and Fine Arts—, it is aimed at the retrieval, collection, presentation, valorization, and research of Cambodia's memories in moving images (film, TV), photographs, and sound recordings. The stand-alone Centre is not only of signal importance in the efforts to reverse the devastation of the country's cultural memory caused by three decades of war, most perniciously the Khmer Rouge's savagely thoroughgoing, genocidal regime (1975-1979; the Centre has actually been named after one of the regime's victims, Bophana, a young woman killed after months of torture). It is also meant to hand back the memories retrieved to both victims and those born after these war years, enable them to engage with these memories, and restore the broken bridge with the past.[260]

As mentioned above, the Centre is committed to showing its presentations all over the country, although the frequency of these presentations has stabilized while their geographical spread has diminished over the past few years;[261] its website does not provide specific data about what these projections showed. As for presentations at the Phnom Penh-based Centre itself (besides access to hundreds of hours of materials on video copies), they consist mostly of weekend screenings in two series called *Ciné samedi* and *Ciné Club*. In the month of February 2014, an exhibition, held over from January, brought together artists and "members of the Cambodian community" to engage with their family photographs. The relative sparseness of its public screenings may well be related to the weight the Centre attaches to other tasks and objectives, viz. its research and documentation center (which, judging from its website, reaches a far greater number of people than its screenings ever could), its training of a new generation of filmmakers and technicians, and stimulating discussion.

In its combination of societal, (film) historical, and, I daresay, healing approach the Centre is unique.

See also: http://bophana.org

Summary of presentations:

• 1 temporary exhibition

Jorng Nam (January 25-February 8), which "brings together artists and members of the Cambodian community to reclaim, reinvent and remember their family photographs and stories from Cambodia's vibrant past."

---

[260] The foundation of the Centre, then, appears to have been no small feat, given that it occurred during the increasingly corrupt and dictatorial reign of Hun Sen, a former Khmer Rouge military commander, prime-minister since 1985. However, its many foreign donors give the institute a certain degree of independence.

[261] 'Projections itinérantes', at: http://bophana.org/event/mobile-screenings/.

• 2 series

Ciné samedi (February 1, 8, 15), featuring historical and contemporary propaganda (e.g. SAINT-VALENTIN, a 2011 TV production warning against unprotected sex) and documentary films (e.g. Norodom Sihanouk's KAMPUCHEA 1965), as well as recent fiction in weekly screenings.

Ciné Club (February 9, 23), where international repertoire as well as new, national productions are screened and discussed—sometimes only discussed—every other Saturday (although this month on Sundays).

Summary of information:

The temporary exhibition *Jorng Nam* clearly fitted the general exhibition policy of the Centre by valorizing its collections and enabling artists to reflect on the country's history. Specific visitor information about *Jorng Nam* contained no more essential information than what was quoted above.

The two film series that make up the Centre's screenings, *Ciné Samedi* and *Ciné Club*, are to a certain extent each other's complement. The former is meant to familiarize audiences with the Centre's collections as well as with films from private collections in weekly screenings; print sources, however, were left unmentioned in the program notes. Summaries of individual programs predominantly emphasized their historical content, albeit in a superficially enumerative way. On a more general level, one would have expected that the presentations by an institute committed to "master, understand, and accept" Cambodia's history merited fuller background information in a country where c. 70% of the population is under thirty.

Ciné Club's bi-weekly programs cater more to film enthusiasts. Although it aims to show "a vast repertoire of films from all over the world", the two February programs happened to be exclusively domestic. In fact, as other instances of this series show, the types of films screened partly overlap with those of *Ciné samedi*, their complementariness notwithstanding. The main difference is that *Ciné Club* sessions are often followed by talks or Q&As with visiting filmmakers or experts—in fact, some are workshops rather than full-blown screenings. Discussion was likely to have followed at least one of the February programs, a compilation program of films made by young Cambodian filmmakers under the collective title 'Short film critics', although this was not explicitly announced.

Overall, information of the Centre's public activities is minimal, mostly restricted to insubstantial summaries (and, insofar as film screenings were concerned, short on film credits and technical details). However, the lack of contextualization may be only apparent as, according to its mission statement, its archives are brought to life by the conferences, debates, exhibitions, and workshops the Centre organizes so as to share the documents with different audiences and promote dialogue and reflection.

British Film Institute-National Film & Television Archive, London

The BFI-NFTVA, founded in 1933, is one of the oldest institutes of the modern archival movement.[262] It is also one of the biggest, not just in terms of the size of its collections, but also in terms of the responsibilities it has assumed in recent decades, such as distribution and the funding of film productions. As a film heritage institute, then, it does not concern itself merely with the past, it also stimulates current initiatives (thereby creating, of course, a future heritage to manage).

The institute's public venues are distributed over two locations, the Southbank (four auditoria, with capacities ranging from 38 to 450 seats, and gallery space) and the BFI IMAX theater, a 500-capacity auditorium at nearby Waterloo; the latter is operated by Odeon, an international cinema group.[263] The variety of presentations at these venues reflects one of the institute's strategic priorities: "to help build audiences for a broader range of films across all platforms". Its current, five-year digitization project, which will provide geo-filtered access to 10,000 digitized films for theatrical screening as well as for education and research through digital platforms (such as BFI Player), underscores enlarged visibility as a key element of the institute's policies.

The two-month exhibition *Derek Jarman: strange magick* (accompanied by events that valorized various aspects of the Jarman archives) at its Southbank venue, on one hand, and the *Lord of the Rings* trilogy all-nighter ("by popular demand") at its IMAX theater, on the other, marked the extent of the range of works BFI-NFTVA presents and the associated range of audiences it targets. As well its February 2014 previews of upcoming releases, under its own label (of new and restored films) as

[262] Houston (1994), pp. 23-37.

[263] 'BFI IMAX faq', at: http://www.bfi.org.uk/about-bfi/help-faq/bfi-imax.

well as by other distributors, ran the gamut from art cinema to Hollywood blockbuster. With this 'department-store approach' of a large assortment of simultaneously presented programs BFI-NFTVA projects itself as a place that promises to always have something for everyone. The size and variation of its collections (film, TV as well as related materials) and the responsibilities it assumes within the British audiovisual field make the institute a major player.

See also: http://www.bfi.org.uk/

Summary of presentations:

• 1 temporary exhibition

Derek Jarman: strange magick (January 23–March 30) marked the twentieth anniversary of the artists's death. The exhibition, from the institute's collections, featured a "selection of Jarman's famous notebooks alongside photographs and designs that showcase the filmmaker's long-standing fascination with magic, myth and religion".

• 7 one-off screenings

previews of feature fiction releases, either new titles (e.g. ONLY LOVERS LEFT ALIVE [2013]; THE GRAND BUDAPEST HOTEL [2014]; COMMON [2014]) or vintage (a new print of the MGM musical FUNNY FACE [1957]—screened as part of a Valentine's Day special compilation program) as well as *Lord of the rings* trilogy-all nighter and *BUG 41*, an evening on "the evolution of music video".

• 10 releases

A mix of recent (e.g. GRAVITY; JACK RYAN: SHADOW RECRUIT) and vintage feature fiction titles (e.g. NIGHT OF THE HUNTER [1955]; LIFT TO THE SCAFFOLD [ASCENSEUR POUR L'ÉCHAFAUD; 1958]), and one recent nonfiction production (JERUSALEM). Moreover, the films that were collected in a retrospective called *In the studio*—a title which merely referred to its Southbank location's smallest "boutique cinema space"—were essentially a number of then recent, mostly commercially released feature fiction films (TEENAGE; PHILOMENA; BLUE IS THE WARMEST COLOUR [LA VIE D'ADÈLE]; NEBRASKA).

• 5 retrospectives

A serious man, a modern world: Buster Keaton and the cinema of today, part 2 (February 1-26; follow-up of part 1, shown in January 2014) on the occasion of the theatrical release of the 4K digital restoration of Keaton's best known feature, THE GENERAL (1926). This, one of four personality-based retrospectives, mixed Keaton's films with contemporary works that shared one or more characteristics to argue and accentuate Keaton's modernity.

Al Pacino, part 1 (February 1–March 20), a chronological overview of the actor's career.

Feng Xiaogang: spectacular China (February 3-22), an overview of China's currently most successful feature fiction director.

Queer pagan punk: Derek Jarman part 1: Jarman and the occult (February 5–April 7), a selection of Jarman's work and other films variously related to it, screened parallel to the abovementioned exhibition.

Discover Arab cinema (February 4-22), a geography-based program that was part of a year-long "introduction to Arab cinema in 12 easy steps", showing recent and older features and shorts.

• 11 events (nine of which were organized on the occasion of some of the abovementioned programs)

Q&A with writer, producer, director, and cast following the preview of TV movie COMMON.

A conversation with Feng Xiaogang on the occasion of the retrospective of this Chinese filmmaker.

The Jarman season was strewn with Q&As—performers Jenny Runacre (JUBILEE), Toyah Willcox (THE TEMPEST), Dexter Fletcher (CARAVAGGIO), and producer Don Boyd (ARIA)—and lectures: *In the tradition of magick: the cinema of Derek Jarman*, lecture by season curator William Fowler, *Jarman on the Thames*, and *The Derek Jarman archives*, lecture by BFI Special Collections senior curator Nathalie Morris and a discussion of the editing of the book *Derek Jarman's sketchbooks*. *The centenary of The little tramp*, on the occasion of Chaplin biographer David Robinson's new book *The world of limelight*

BAFTA masterclass: cinematography with Anthony Dod Mantle, featuring this acclaimed director of photography.

• 1 festival

7th BFI Future Film festival (February 21-23), a brief, three-day festival, in which each day was dedicated to a specific type of film (documentary, fiction, animation) for young filmmakers (15 to 25-year olds) to show, watch, discuss, and network.

Summary of information:

Given its variety of presentations it was not surprising that BFI-NFTVA's visitor information distinguished between types of program and, implicitly, target audiences. For instance, all of its one-off screenings and releases usually received not much more than plot summaries or synopses. These screenings comprised mostly films that could also be seen in commercial theaters at the time, except those shown at BFI's IMAX theater. Clearly, descriptions functioned as publicity rather than information, ostensibly made to help casual filmgoers decide what to choose from London's volume of entertainments, while downplaying the archival or museum context (or, put differently, accentuating its social rather than its intellectual or sacred connotations.[264]). The films in the retrospective *In the studio* received similar summaries, but as pointed out above, this was a barely camouflaged string of releases (that also played in commercial venues), and a retrospective in name only. Apparently meant to strengthen the promotional character of these summaries, the brief artistic eulogies, mostly about performers, ("McConaughy is astounding"; "flawless performances"; "spectacular cast"; "Judi Dench and Steve Coogan give nuanced performances"; "Skillfully constructed from stunning footage") were not enlightening.

New, digital prints were screened of three classic films: FUNNY FACE; NIGHT OF THE HUNTER; LIFT TO THE SCAFFOLD. These films' cult status and/or star appeal will have had greater commercial potential than other films revived from history. But at the same time it can be taken as an attempt to add an archival touch and build "audiences for a broader range of films". While they received a somewhat more rounded treatment by expanding their summaries with statements about style or film historical significance, these additions leave one wondering even more whether their superlatives and throwaway phrases actually functioned as aids to

---

[264] Anthropologist Robert Kelly originally and specifically used the triplet intellectual – sacred – social to identify museum visitors' needs; see: George F. MacDonald, 'Change and challenge: museums in the information society', in: Ivan Karp, Christine Mullen Kreamer, Steven D. Lavine (eds.) (1992), p. 165. As "[t]he museum context, almost by definition, presents audiences with artifacts and information that fall outside of the demands of their daily routines and relationships", it seems that BFI-NFTVA's publicity likely serves to just get people in and loosen up their notions of the archive and the museum; the quote is from: Constance Perin, 'The communicative circle: museums as communities', in the same volume, p. 191.

understanding, particularly with regard to NIGHT OF THE HUNTER ("Charles Laughton's sole outing as director is a towering achievement, marvellously [sic] expressive in its highly imaginative use of cinematic poetry") and LIFT TO THE SCAFFOLD ("for the high contrast black-and-white look [director Louis] Malle engaged the brilliant cinematographer Henri Decaë" or that its "co-screenwriter was a leading rightwing literary novelist"). Slipping in FUNNY FACE amid recent features in a special Valentine's Day program may well have been more successful to realize the institute's strategic priority, what with the film summary's reference to recent mainstream productions—feature film THE DEVIL WEARS PRADA and TV series UGLY BETTY— that were also set in the world of fashion.

There was a change of approach with the five retrospectives, all exclusive and curated presentations, shown at BFI-NFTVA's premises. While plot summaries were provided for the titles included in this format, too, they were all introduced by more or less extensive, more or less informative texts that implicitly addressed another audience segment. This was best exemplified by *A serious man, a modern world: Buster Keaton and the cinema of today. Part 2*—incidentally, one of the few of the survey's retrospectives in the month of February 2014 that contained silent films shown with live musical accompaniment (but because they were all screened in digital formats, some apparently were shown with soundtracks). As its title indicates, it argued the continuing relevance of Keaton's oeuvre, accentuated by showing it alongside "a few recent films which (...) may help to shed light on the enduring modernity of Keaton's work", according to the curator. "Deadpan humour", "eloquent use of composition", "meticulous framing", "laconic performances", "inspired gags", among others, are identified as elements reminiscent of Keaton's films—though not necessarily, I would say, of "enduring modernity". Not exempt from hyperbole either, the program's introductory text and summaries relied heavily on film critical jargon. Because its target audience was assumed to understand this type of discourse and its references, the program's central argument was less explained than implied. Still, one wonders what even the cinephiles might have taken away from such copy as "[t]he spirit of Keaton is present, especially in the laconic performances of the lead couple (...), though Welles, Tati, Tashlin and Chuck Jones are hovering about, too."

The information for the retrospective of Derek Jarman's and related films, *Queer pagan punk: Derek Jarman part 1: Jarman and the occult*, suffered from the same throwaway phrases, as in: "his eclectic work is inspirational in its fearlessness yet remains touchingly personal"—where it remained unclear what the connector "yet" was actually meant to connect. Dropping the not exactly household names of artists John Piper and Paul Nash and its sometimes highbrowish summaries clearly signaled a different audience segment expected, and targeted, for this program.

The introduction to the retrospective of popular American actor Al Pacino failed to say much about the actor, a lack of precision that is characteristic of portraits of actors and what it is precisely what they do. What Pacino's talent consists of was not defined; this was epitomized in a quote from critic Robin Wood, "always, indissolubly Pacino". In the brief text the curator got a shot at it by mentioning two disparate things: that his acting is "predicated on the expression or repression of energy" and something about the perceived discrepancy between Pacino's star status and the type of "controversial" roles he played, particularly his bisexual bank robber, in DOG DAY AFTERNOON, and a serial-killing, undercover policeman, in CRUISING. One would think, however, that Pacino's very star status may well have insulated him from controversy (another film star, Richard Gere, was not only the first choice for the lead in CRUISING, but had in fact shown a keen interest in playing it). In a way it is funny, parenthetically, that the word "controversial" never comes up when someone plays, say, the head of a criminal organization... Moreover, these two roles are not linked to the types of stories, and the characters that people them, which were quite common in American cinema throughout the 1970s in otherwise fairly conventional, mainstream films.

Finally and briefly, the February leg of *Discover Arab cinema*, besides containing a number of films of highly topical interest (e.g. terrorism, of which London had had its share, too), was perhaps meant to lure a large audience by announcing its February lineup as 'Thrillers'. Because this was factually misleading, the introductory text immediately watered it down to "thrilling plots".

With its *7th BFI Future Film festival*, however, the institute's information may well have hit the right note. Aimed at a niche public of young filmmakers—15 to 25 year olds—, the upbeat text was direct and dialogic ("you" and "we"), reminiscent of TV advertising or radio deejays. It was clearly meant to enthuse, while at the same time it managed to enumerate the events lined up (workshops, guest speakers, screenings, awards, etc.) and the possibilities provided for networking, advice, etc. This event typified BFI-NFTVA's efforts in promoting and stimulating British moving image culture, an elaboration of its second strategic priority "to support the future success of British film by placing a strong emphasis on new voices and fresh ideas".

BFI-NFTVA is generous in its provision of general information for visitors and other users. Its lengthy policy strategy or the reasons for its decision to outsource the running of its IMAX theater, for instance, are all a click away from its homepage. As far as its presentations are concerned it certainly invests in attracting as wide and varied an audience as possible. Ironically, however, its double-barreled program information may either estrange casual filmgoers by clouding plot summaries with unenlightening comments or failing to address them at all, thereby either overshooting or undershooting one of its main strategic targets.

Centre cinématographique marocain, Rabat

Morocco's national cinematographic center, founded in its original form in 1944, is since its reorganization in 1977 first and foremost an institute for "the organization and promotion" of the country's film industry, ranging from production, distribution, and screening to securing professionalism. In practice this means, among other things, that CCM issues film permits, professional and operating licenses, and certifications; as well, it oversees compliance with the laws and regulations underlying these activities. Its facilities include a laboratory, a studio for sound recording, mixing, synchronization, etc., and other post-production facilities, and an auditorium for public screenings. CCM was also made responsible for the creation of "a cinematheque", although it actually boasts a film archive that comprises works ranging from the colonial era (e.g. French Pathé and Gaumont productions going back to 1905) up to current national productions (including CCM co-productions). Incidentally, the quoted charter in its mission statement does not mention legal deposit. As a member of INNA-News, which in its turn founded Paxos, a society for the commercial exploitation of documentary and journalistic moving image materials, CCM's archive probably constitutes an additional funding source with sales of copied materials to film and TV productions.

In its one auditorium, the Centre shows single programs of recent national productions, a combination of a feature fiction and a short film, in monthly changing programs. It is likely, however, that the features will have had a domestic, commercial release, as well as perhaps festival screenings or releases abroad, before being shown at its premises, because the Centre is not in the business of film distribution. The feature in its February program, for instance, was released in December 2013.[265]

See also: http://www.ccm.ma/

Summary of presentations:

• 2 releases

SARA (2013), a Moroccan feature fiction, preceded by the short film COLLISION (2011), co-produced by CCM; screenings twice daily.

Summary of information:

Both films received the shortest of summaries—in fact, they might better be called teasers, since they merely set up expectations—, preceded by a few credits and technical details. Such skimpy visitor information seems to support the notion that presentations are a mere afterthought for CCM; its auditorium is also used for audio processing and, perhaps, for (restricted) industry screenings. The institute is also uninterested in providing contextual information, of whatever kind, perhaps because the films screened are recent and information about them can easily be found at the usual sources. Less recent productions from its archive are not being shown at all; in accordance with its mission, they are only preserved.

Cinemateca Boliviana, La Paz

Founded in 1976, the Cinemateca Boliviana's mission is to "recover, conserve, and preserve the Bolivian moving image heritage". It also collects cinema's classics and distributes "the best of world cinema of yesterday and today." Besides it has set itself the educational task of servicing academic institutes by providing "critical tools" and audiovisual materials for the benefit of both teachers and students.

The importance of the national cinema patrimony is underscored by the project *Imágenes de Bolivia: propuesta de catastro, rescate y conservación de la memoria histórica del audiovisual, FASE 1*. Its aim is to build a database of Bolivian cinema based on the following criteria: "filmed in Bolivia for Bolivians; filmed abroad for Bolivians; filmed in Bolivia by foreigners; filmed abroad by foreigners, but about Bolivia and

---

[265] 'SARA de Saïd Naciri', at: http://www.yallacine.com/sara-de-said-naciri/.

Bolivians."[266] The project is supported by the Spanish embassy and by the Agencia Española de Cooperación Internacional para el Desarrollo (AECID), a fund of the Spanish Ministry of Foreign Affairs. But while the recently founded Bolivian Ministry of Culture has created a legal framework for the protection of cultural heritage, within which the Cinemateca functions as the repository of the country's audiovisual heritage, structural funding from its own government for all its activities does not seem imminent.

The Cinemateca recently moved into a new building that boasts a library, documentation center, and three auditoria (aggregate capacity 339). Funded privately, the Cinemateca's screenings are a crucial way to generate its much-needed income. Hence, one suspects, the emphasis on international releases, particularly new or recent Hollywood feature fiction, with occasional presentations of Bolivian films. These releases make its programming quite similar to commercial chain cinemas (Cinépolis and Multicine) in La Paz; it only distinguishes itself from these venues with its retrospectives and events. Every July however, on the occasion of the Cinemateca's anniversary, a generous selection of its archival holdings is digitally screened in one of its auditoria.

See also: http://www.cinematecaboliviana.org/

Summary of presentations:

• 1 one-off screening

CIRCLE OF IRON, a 1978 US feature fiction film. Its screening was occasioned by plans of a remake of this Bruce Lee cult film, shooting of which was scheduled to start in early 2014.

• 8 releases

Largely of then recent American feature fiction productions (e.g. THE HOBBIT: THE DESOLATION OF SMAUG; THE SECRET LIFE OF WALTER MITTY; WALKING WITH DINOSAURS; BLUE JASMINE), one Paraguayan (7 CAJAS) and one Bolivian feature film (YVY MARAEY-TIERRA SIN MAL).

• 3 retrospectives

Grandes directores y Shakespeare (February 13-26), featured the works of a number of internationally renowned filmmakers (in February 2014:

---

[266] Fundación Cinemateca Boliviana, 'Convocatoria al primer censo nacional de cineastas, videastas y productores', *Bolpress* (May 29, 2012).

Franco Zeffirelli, Kenneth Branagh, Akira Kurosawa, Roman Polanski, Peter Greenaway).

Ciclo 100 años Primera Guerra Mundial (February 20–March 12), a thematic program that showcased a small set of renowned feature fiction films (in February 2014: ALL QUIET ON THE WESTERN FRONT; PATHS OF GLORY; GALLIPOLI).

Ciclo Historias compartidas: raices comunes. Mes de la herencia afroamericana (February 25-27), a brief, three-day retrospective featuring a mix of two recent documentaries (DARK GIRLS and THE LOVING STORY) and one recent feature fiction film (THE HELP), all US productions.

• 2 events

Both were panel discussions with local representatives on the occasion of the retrospective *Ciclo Historias compartidas: raices comunes.*

Summary of information:

Visitor information of most of the Cinemateca's screenings, whether a one-off screening, release or part of a retrospective, consisted of brief plot summaries that were copied from the popular website FilmAffinity, followed by copious production credits copied from the same source. Or, to be more precise, FilmAffinity was the only credited source, because in a number of cases the equally widely used website IMDb carried the exact same information. Confusingly, when summaries were copied from IMDb only, they were uncredited. And both websites were left uncredited when, in a few cases, the institute expanded the copied summaries with a little comment of its own.

The introductory text to its retrospective program *Grandes directores y Shakespeare* merely reported on the number of adaptations, with a breakdown of the most popular titles (*Hamlet, Romeo and Juliet, Macbeth*), and concluded that Shakespeare is the most adapted author of all time. Obviously, what counted in this, as well as in the retrospective *Ciclo 100 años Primera Guerra Mundial*, was the reputation and drawing power of the canonical feature fiction films they largely contained (e.g. MACBETH; RAN; ALL QUIET ON THE WESTERN FRONT; PATHS OF GLORY). Both the program on World War I and the three-day retrospective *Ciclo Historias compartidas: raices comunes. Mes de la herencia afroamericana* had no general introduction at all. The latter had two of its screenings followed by discussion.

The Cinemateca's public presentations and provision of information leave much to be desired when measured against its mission, in particular the aim to meaningfully inform its public. As noted, much of its educational efforts are aimed at training and supporting teachers and students within the academy. For its activities aimed at the general public, however, the unsubsidized institute is understandably compelled to operate in a commercial environment and consequently behaves rather like a cinema theater. Nevertheless, it omits to give itself an edge over the competition, or indeed its visitors, by not providing more illuminating, distinctive information, apart from the events it occasionally organizes.

Cinemateca Brasileira, São Paolo

According to Brazilian federal law the Cinemateca Brasileira, the follow-up organization of the Cinema Club of São Paolo (founded in 1940), is the designated depository of all audiovisual materials produced under the Promotion of Audiovisual Culture Act. Films and TV productions as well as a great variety of related materials make up its collections. The stand-alone Cinemateca has two auditoria (108 and 210 seats), for screenings in which it shows a significant amount of films from its collections.

For its presentations it has developed the notion of "core programming", subdivided in the following categories: regular events; permanent series; and exhibitions and festivals. The first category, regular events, refers to recurring programs, of all types of format, realized by the Cinemateca Brasileira, usually in cooperation with other institutes and organizations, that have become regular features on its annual program schedule. Examples are the various editions of its human rights film festival *Mostra Cinema e direitos humanos na América do Sul*, silent film festival *Jornada Brasileiro de cinema silencioso*, and the series *Verão de clássicos*, the latest edition of which was programmed in February 2014 (the latter retrospective has become a fixture of the Cinemateca's programming schedule since its first edition in 2009[267]). Permanent series, secondly, are programs that are scheduled either weekly or monthly. These programs distinguish themselves by their Brazilian character, not just in terms of production, but also in terms of the organizations participating in their screenings, such as the Universidade Federal de São Paulo (Unifesp), Hospital Premier (in the context of which such topics as euthanasia and palliative care were being discussed), and Associação Brasileira de Cinematografia. Exhibitions and festivals, finally, concern formats that are

---

[267] Cinemateca Brasileira, *Relatório anual 2009* (2010), p. 55.

organized annually or bi-annually (e.g. *Mostra Mundo Árabe de Cinema*).[268] In all these manifestations the Cinemateca clearly shows an engagement with social causes and organizations besides film aesthetic or historical interests. Outside the holidays, one-off programs, new releases, retrospectives, etc. are weaved around these core programs throughout the season.

See also: http://www.cinemateca.gov.br/

Summary of presentations:

• 1 retrospective

Verão de clássicos (February 13–March 16), which collected a number of feature fiction films from the distribution collection of the Cinemateca that vary in terms of country and year of production (albeit predominantly from the postwar era) as well as genre. The entire program, it emphatically added, consisted of analogue prints. It ran during the summer holidays, when schools and universities are closed.

Summary of information:

Apart from the unique warning that the archival prints shown in this retrospective may wear the marks of use, its introductory text merely illustrated the variety mentioned above. The brief plot summaries of all the films screened were supplemented with a few technical details and credits for director and main cast, while the odd title received a commonplace editorial comment (e.g. "directed by the Italian master of low budget cinema"; "one of the highest grossing Korean films"; "one of the most important films of the Nouvelle Vague"), besides the mention of literary sources or awards. Such comments did not differ from the program's general introduction (in which the last example was described as "one of François Truffaut's masterpieces, with a great performance by Jeanne Moreau") and merely added more of the same.

Even though this is a 'holiday program', such visitor information was not different from regular programs at the Cinemateca. Coming from an institute that shows an interest in wider, social concerns and which, moreover, rather explicitly targets an educated audience segment in some of its programs, this rather perfunctory visitor information was surprising, as it contained nothing that its spectators couldn't have found or known themselves.

---

[268] Cinemateca Brasileira, *Relatório anual 2012* (2013), pp. 64-65.

Cinemateca Dominicana, Santo Domingo

As part of the Directorate-General of Film the Cinemateca Dominicana is wholly supported by its national government. And besides earned income from revenues generated by its activities it also receives funds from donations. Additional funding, moreover, mixed with other forms of support—technical, practical or otherwise—comes from embassies and diplomatic missions residing in the Dominican Republic as well as from various cooperative agreements.

Safeguarding, preserving, researching, accessing, and screening the country's cinema heritage are the tasks mandated to the Cinemateca since 1978. Moreover, the stand-alone institute is expected to provide outreach services by organizing screenings throughout the country. The national audiovisual works deposited at the Cinemateca are consistently contextualized, in its documentation center and mediatheque as well as in its film programs, by international cinema productions both old and new. This reflects its mission to "disseminate national and international film values". Personality- and geography-based programs feature prominently, as well as documentary film. In fact, the Cinemateca's February 2014 screenings happened to be exclusively—and, in the survey, uniquely—devoted to documentary. A retrospective of largely domestic, documentary productions on national themes was followed by the first edition of the *Festival internacional de documental de República Dominicana y el Caribe*, of which the institute was one of the host venues (making the institute's February program the least regular in the survey). The Cineteca boasts one auditorium (450 capacity) and a conference room for workshops, discussions, etc. for a maximum of 60 people.

See also:
http://www.dgcine.gob.do/esp/index.php?option=com_content&view=article&id=111&Itemid=271

Summary of presentations:

• 1 retrospective

Dominica en documental (January 30–February 12), an overview of recent and slightly less recent, mostly domestically produced documentary films devoted to the political, social, and cultural history of the Dominican Republic.

• 1 festival

The first edition of the *Festival internacional de documental de República Dominicana y el Caribe* (February 13-21) of which the Cinemateca was one of the host venues (besides the Santo Domingo-based Centro de la Imagen, other venues were the Centro Cultural de España, Centro Cultural Banreservas, and La Alpargatería). The festival collected works from the Caribbean and Latin America. The festival's competition awarded prizes in four categories: best short documentary; best Latin American documentary; best Central American and Caribbean documentary; and best Dominican Republic documentary.

Summary of information:

Information about the retrospective *Dominica en documental* was exclusively a matter of brief synopses of the films screened, with no general introduction. Because the retrospective collected films about the Dominican Republic made between 1991 (this oldest one was actually screened in January) and 2013, one may conclude that this was not a mere overview of recent works, but a curated program that covered topics from the political, social, and cultural history of the country since the early twentieth century. Nevertheless, an account of its selection was apparently deemed superfluous. Its mission to "promote a critical interest in the seventh art", however, as the Cinemateca is mandated to do, would have merited more extensive contextualization. With 47% of the population under 25 years of age, not every visitor could be assumed to be knowledgeable about topics ranging from the country's dramatic political history during the twentieth century (notably tyrannical dictator Rafael Trujillo, the subject of the trilogy featured in *Dominica en documental*, EL PODER DEL JEFE), to the Dominican community in New York, drug addiction, Dominican hiphop or baseball. But perhaps it was merely conceived, even though this was mentioned nowhere, as a showcase in the run-up to the first edition of the *Festival internacional de documental de República Dominicana y el Caribe*, which opened at the Cinemateca's premises with a Dominican production. Credits and print information are minimal or even absent.

Public information about the festival's films was its organizers' responsibility, so I will not discuss it within the framework of this study.

Cinemateca Portuguesa-Museu do Cinema, Lisbon

This stand-alone, national film heritage institute, founded in 1948, is a public institute under the responsibility of the Secretary of Culture. According to its annual FIAF report, the Cinemateca goes through a period of transition in terms of its legal status and its funding base (which has decreased, particularly as a result of reduced income from the television advertisement tax). At the time of writing (September 2014) nothing more definite could be said about the near future other than a few temporary measures to see the institute through the "legal void" created by government bureaucracy through the withdrawal of an earlier plan that had not even been implemented.[269]

Meanwhile the institute assiduously continued its public presentations in its three auditoria and its exhibition spaces. Three permanent exhibitions prominently feature the history and so-called pre-history of cinema, on the basis of recording, projection, and other equipment, either original or replica. Objects include various magic lanterns, a phenakistoscope, zootrope, and Praxinoscope as well as small gauge equipment, some of which is used for occasional demonstrations and shows. This consistent focus clearly reflects an element explicitly mentioned in its mission statement, namely to advance "knowledge of film history and the development of cinematographic and audiovisual culture."

In quite a different way its attention to film history is reflected in the large number of one-off screenings, sometimes up to five a day (with the odd repeat screening), of mostly feature fiction made worldwide between the 1920s and the 2010s. The collective title *Ciclo Outras sessões* (Other sessions) suggests a residual category, rather than a retrospective whose presentations are held together in a more emphatically meaningful way. In fact, their sheer variety seems to be the point of these screenings.

While these one-off screenings clearly dominate its film presentations, in February there was one, brief retrospective (although the Cinemateca has regularly mounted lengthier retrospectives devoted to important personalities of film history and, more uncommonly, to the work of other film heritage institutes). Finally, the Cinemateca keeps an eye on national productions with its previews of new or recent Portuguese documentary films.

See also: http://www.cinemateca.pt/

Summary of presentations:

• 3 permanent, linear exhibitions; the one that focuses on the pre-cinematic era has interactive elements. They are all based on

---

[269] 'Lisbon annual report 2013' (2014), pp. 1-2.

technological artifacts, largely equipment, from the Museu's own collections.

• 92 one-off screenings (a small number of which was repeated the next or a few days later). The films screened range from Hollywood (e.g. THE GHOST AND MRS. MUIR; THE ROBE; SWEET CHARITY) to European art cinema (OTTO E MEZZO; HOTEL DES AMÉRIQUES; DIE STAND DER DINGE), from classics (GONE WITH THE WIND; À BOUT DE SOUFFLE; THE WILD BUNCH) to recent hit or cult filmmakers (EVERYONE SAYS I LOVE YOU; YI YI; HOLY MOTORS), late silent classics (EROTIKON; GENERALYA LINNIA; LA PASSION DE JEANNE D'ARC), as well as, not unsurprisingly, a relatively substantial number of Portuguese-language films from both Portugal and Brazil. This variety was not just characteristic of this program as a whole, but of each day's line-up of screenings, too. It was reminiscent of what is now often called the old-fashioned cinematheque way of programming, in which a repertoire of international cinema was cyclically screened. Despite its collective title, *Other sessions* was no retrospective, as there was no text or other attempt to give explicit coherence to these screenings.

• 1 retrospective/event

Jon Jost (February 10-15), a selection of this American independent director's recent works, made between 1997 and 2012, in a five-day overview, with all screenings introduced by the filmmaker.

• 1 series/2 events

Ante-estreias (February 13; 28) featured two previews of new Portuguese documentaries, screened in the presence of their directors (which— again—made these presentations simultaneously into events).

Summary of information:

The Museu do Cinema's permanent exhibitions receive extensive, online background information. Texts about the objects and equipment in these exhibitions are of a predominantly technical nature. However, they do not seem to explain much about mechanical principles and their (dis)continuity, let alone their social construction or the physiology of perceiving images moving (in chapter 1, I already mentioned its failure to correct the false suggestion of the continuing relevance of persistence of vision). The exhibition in the Museu's Sala dos Carvalhos covers the period of so-called pre-cinema and of early cinema—although the latter era is allowed to last until the early 1930s by including small-gauge equipment, surprisingly yet misleadingly inserting private filmmaking into mainstream film history's timeline. The spotlight is understandably directed to the Museu's rare and original late nineteenth-century Praxinoscope, the machine French showman-cum-inventor Emile Reynaud used to show animated stories in his Théâtre Optique during the 1890s. Also its small-gauge recording and projection equipment (8mm, 9.5mm, and 16mm) receives ample attention. The permanent exhibition about the magic lantern is described more extensively and consistently in a short history of its technique and its uses, followed by a compact history of the magic lantern in Portugal, although it is in fact an excerpt of a Portugese-language, book-length history published in 1988. The efforts invested in promoting these exhibitions notwithstanding, the Cinemateca's visitor information would greatly benefit from an update based on state-of-the-art research.

The publicity for its film screenings, on the other hand, was dealt with much more perfunctorily. The bulk of it, the 92 one-off screenings, received brief descriptions: besides the barest credits, there were two- or three-sentence plot summaries—or not even that (as in "One of cinema's most romantic love stories", about AN AFFAIR TO REMEMBER). A small number of titles got additional, one-line comments, such as the odd quote by a filmmaker, a technical or stylistic pointer (e.g. "Pialat takes his 'brutalist' technique to a higher plane, with large ellipses and a certain amount of improvisation by the actors"; about À NOS AMOURS) or film historical tidbits ("three hours and forty minutes in color"; about GONE WITH THE WIND). Although the Cinemateca hands out in-house produced information sheets for all its screenings, those who consulted its website may have felt that such comments addressed the cinephile or the well-informed only, as the quoted comments implicitly assumed knowledge of Maurice Pialat's oeuvre or the fact that full-color films emerged only in the late 1930s. The institute's appeal to a target audience of connoisseurs of international art cinema became explicit when it introduced (and personalized) the screening of the commercial feature AIRPORT by way of an apology for its guilty pleasure: "a genuine bad movie we love." The selection of films featured what it called "the best" (a very frequently used word) of international art and studio cinema, but its efforts to interest a broader audience may well fall short. As many titles had Portuguese subtitles (as opposed to a few electronically Portuguese subtitled films), I assume that most of these films were programmed from the Cinemateca's collection.

The program of American independent filmmaker and artist Jon Jost focused on the digital technology he has been experimenting with since the late 1990s; it featured some of his most recent works, alongside a few earlier DV efforts. The retrospective was a continuation of a program of four of his "unpublished" digital works that the Cinemetaca showed in

2010 (a retrospective of his analogue films was screened in 1996). Being almost a regular of the Cinemateca perhaps explains why the program notes provided only minimal background information about Jost's work. But the filmmaker's presence at each show to introduce his work would have provided ample compensation—I remember from Jost's appearances at the Rotterdam Film Festival's screenings of the same and similar works that he is a profuse talker. The individual works were briefly synopsized, often including quotes by Jost and other filmmakers.

The two screenings in the series *Ante-estreias* (Previews) featured recent Portuguese documentaries, which appears to be common in this series. Synopses focused on the topics of the films screened—in both cases matters of domestic moment, viz. whaling in the Azores and the Portuguese architect Manuel Tainha (the latter's synopsis actually reproduced a relatively long text written by the filmmaker).

The distinct contrast between the Museu's information about its exhibitions and the Cinemateca's about its screenings revealed, more clearly than in any of the other surveyed institutes, a general trend: the separation of films from their enabling technologies. While the cameras, lanterns, and projectors on display are clearly conceived as technical artifacts, films constitute an oxymoronic category of disembodied objects, as any trace or history related to their material aspects was left unacknowledged and uncommented. Hence, I think, the lack of information, here as elsewhere, about a print's format and unconcern about discrepancies between negative or printed and projected format.

Cinemateca Uruguaya, Montevideo

Calling itself an "*[a]sociación civil*" and "a private institute of public interest", the Cinemeteca Uruguaya, founded in 1952, receives neither public nor private grants, but is supported, among others, through membership programs, its box office, and other earned income. Its presence in the Uruguayan film landscape is nevertheless prominent. It boasts Uruguay's major film archive, with over 18,000 titles; it has four auditoria for its programs of screenings.[270] Besides being an archive and a cinematheque, the institute is one of Uruguay's major distributors; it

---

[270] There is also an official national film archive, Archivo Nacional de la Imagen y la Palabra, part of the larger cultural institute SODRE. It is not included here, because its programming season runs from April through December.

organizes the annual International Film Festival of Uruguay (which *is* sponsored by national and municipal public bodies); and it runs a film school, the Escuela de Cine del Uruguay.

The Cinemateca collects and preserves all Uruguayan productions since the late nineteenth century, as well as films from all over the world. (Archivist David Francis noted that as a distributor the Cinemateca has, and exercises, the right to order negatives of the films it releases, which it duly deposits in its archive.[271]) The institute's presentations therefore have an unmistakably international orientation. Although it makes sense in a country with a relatively small film production industry to focus its activities on the broader category of film culture, the Cinemateca Uruguaya is one of the few to state this goal explicitly. Still, it does not neglect domestic productions and issues: one of the four releases it premiered in February 2014 was a Uruguayan film, while one of the retrospectives of that month was mounted in cooperation with the Movimiento Uruguay Libre to inform the public about the ecologically harmful activity of open-pit mining (and announcing a meeting on the Cinemateca's premises in that month about the initiative for a plebiscite against this activity). This thematic, politically colored type of program is not unusual in the institute's presentations (and may well be related to its independence of any institutional or corporate funding). Most other screenings in its four auditoria in February 2014, whether arranged in retrospectives or series, were of an international character.

See also: http://www.cinemateca.org.uy/index.htm

Summary of presentations:

• 4 releases

Three releases were of foreign origin (Chilean, American, Argentinian) and one a domestic production (although directed by an Argentinian filmmaker). The latter and the Argentinian production were timely screened, as both were about the carnival—they were announced to run for only a week; the other two releases ran for two weeks. All releases were premieres.

• 6 retrospectives

Un norteamericano en Londres: James Ivory (February 15-24), the only personality-based program in this format about this American director.

---

[271] Cherchi Usai, Francis, Horwath, Loebenstein (2008), p. 79.

Generación VHS (February 15-23), a nostalgic look at the films that were released at the time when VHS was introduced.

Hollywood en blanco y negro (February 15-27), about the parallel position of African Americans in both mainstream films and in American society, ranging from such dissimilar works as THE BIRTH OF A NATION (1915) to DO THE RIGHT THING (1989).

Hablemos sobre megaminería (February 24-27), activist, political program to warn against the environmental damage of open-pit mining.

Reposiciones (February 25–March 8), second chance to see recently released films.

Cantos de cisne (February 28–March 9), last films made by or featuring deceased film personalities, this month filmmaker Raoul Walsh's swan song A DISTANT TRUMPET (1964).

Remarkably, the Cinemateca's February retrospectives, like its releases, typically do not last longer than a week or two. It means they are not exhaustive and allow the institute to present an extremely varied program.

• 2 series

Trasnoches, a series of late night screenings.

Prontos, listas, YA!, is a manifestation of the well-known Best films list-mania, albeit with a wink as it intimates that it can go on forever—the film shown was listed as no. 613.

Summary of information:

The Cinemateca's four premiered releases received relatively extensive background information. Besides plot summaries of the two feature fiction films, comments took the reader as it were through the film to point out relevant matters of interest that may enhance understanding. For instance, visitor information about the Chilean film prepared the spectator against taking its visual style at mere face value. The two documentaries received factual contextualizing information: for instance, the Argentinian documentary about the carnival in Salta, in northern Argentina, traced the changes in the music played during this event back to the end of the military junta in 1983.

However, the films included in its retrospectives were all briefly introduced, albeit unevenly in terms of quality and completeness. Information about the retrospectives *Reposiciones* (Reruns) and *Cantos de cisne* (Swan songs) were brief and self-explanatory: the first one collected a

number of films that were premiered 18 months earlier, now back after an
appropriate (or legally determined) window for those who missed them at
the time; the other contained somebody's last film. Introductions to the
seemingly more ambitious, curated retrospectives, however, were not very
instructive. The one to *Un norteamericano en Londres: James Ivory* limited
itself to the mere biographical detail mentioned in its title, namely that
this director of what are considered typically British films is an American.
Even insofar as one was willing to assume that this circumstance
relevantly affected the films made, one wonders why nothing much was
made of the fact that half the films shown were based on American rather
than British novels (e.g. MR. AND MRS. BRIDGE, THE GOLDEN BOWL), or a
Japanese one (THE REMAINS OF THE DAY), nor that most of them were
produced and made in close collaboration with Ismail Merchant, who
hailed from India.

Generación VHS was copied from a homonymous Argentinian
program. It contained a small, chronological, and what the Cinemateca
called nostalgic selection of films from the 1980s and early 1990s (e.g. ONE
FROM THE HEART; PLATOON; EDWARD SCISSORHANDS). However, as it stated that
VHS only came to Uruguay in the mid-1980s, spectators *at the time*
actually had no choice but to see many of these films in continuous
sessions on the big screen. Moreover, in those early days it was certainly
not the case that theatrically released titles were all available on video after
an appropriate window, because the film industry "feared that the video
would finally destroy the cinema once and for all and it was therefore
reluctant to release its major films on video".[272] One wonders, therefore, if
the selection, if not the very program, was properly researched and
accurate. Their screening in digital formats, moreover, did not contribute
to its intention of creating an appropriately nostalgic sensation either.

The thematic program *Hollywood en blanco y negro* was essentially a
program about casting. Its introduction claimed to describe a parallel
between the roles reserved for African American performers and African
Americans' position in society generally: how the bit parts as slaves or
shoeshiners have "progressed" to the colorblind starring roles of today.
However, by focusing on casting only the text deprived itself of the
possibility to sketch a socio-political framework—beyond the mere
mention of the Civil Rights movement—against which Hollywood's output
could be measured. Still, one has to question if such a measurement was

[272] Jancovich, Faire with Stubbings (2008), p. 186.

in any way relevant, given that the number of African Americans 'behind the camera' (including screenwriting) has not significantly increased.[273] And with an African American actor starring in the British production CRY FREEEDOM, set in apartheid South Africa, the program's intentions became muddled even more.

The short program *Hablemos sobre megaminería* (February 24-27, 2014) had the most instructive introduction. A brief sketch of this theme-based program with political overtones pictured the domestic ecological impact of open-pit mining and the economic conditions under which it is profitable. The text was concise, clear, got across the urgency of the matter, and was probably written by the pressure group that co-organized this program. Brief synopses of the documentaries screened accentuated the international, particularly Latin American, dimensions of this topic, rather than their aesthetic or stylistic aspects, and set the stage for the scheduled meeting.

What becomes visible are distinct ways in which the Cinemateca Uruguaya invests in its visitor information: new releases (a business consideration) or domestic, societal causes (a political consideration) merit more attention than programs—mostly retrospectives and series— that contain materials apparently considered familiar enough to dispose of with minimal effort. Yet that approach becomes a serious shortcoming when the potentially rich political and sociological topic of African Americans' role in Hollywood lacks any substantial knowledge and is treated superficially, with the institute trusting rather on the drawing power of a few well-known titles.

Cinematek, Brussels

Cinematek is the new name for the Royal Belgian Film Archive (founded in 1938) after it moved around the corner of its old premises to a new residence, in 2009. The institute is funded both publicly (Federal Science Policy Office) and privately (National Lottery). It collects, preserves, and documents materials that reflect the technical, aesthetic, and historical aspects of cinema. It screens its programs at its own premises and at Flagey (a cultural center), while other venues—e.g. Bozar, the new name for the Palace of Fine Arts—are used incidentally. Through its distribution collection, moreover, it makes acknowledged masterpieces, both old and

---

[273] Alexander (2011), p. 155.

recent, available on 16 and 35mm prints, mostly for non-theatrical screenings; a selection of the MGM-United Artists library that the institute manages is also available for non-theatrical shows.

With the new premises and new name the institute also emphatically embraced digital technology, both in its exhibits (in which thematically arranged films and scenes, either in their entirety or excerpted, suggest the riches the institute guards in its collections) and in its film acquisition policies—in Belgium, 35mm distribution effectively ended in 2012.[274] In its new auditoria, Cinematek combines screenings of the *grande histoire* of cinema, both popular and arthouse, with works of a more experimental character. Its Asta Nielsen retrospective is among the few sizeable programs of silent films—here shown in 35mm rather than in a digital format—in the survey with live musical accompaniment (for which the 'old' Cinemathèque royale was quite renowned). Traditionally, a fairly large part of its screenings comes from its own, immense archive.

See also: http://www.cinematek.be/

Summary of presentations:

• 3 permanent exhibitions

Wunderkammer, devoted to cinema's 'pre-history', shows equipment and gadgets in display cases, although selected objects can be touched and handled.

Remix consists of eight screens hanging from the ceiling, each of which contains recombined excerpts that are arranged into thematic programs: 'Shadows and apparitions'; 'Violence and destruction'; 'Assembly and disassembly'; 'Cut up body language'; 'Sleepy towns and metropolitan frenzy'; 'Chases'; 'Duels'; and 'Machines and machineries'.

Moviola's unlocks and thematically arranges the archive's nonfiction records of life in Belgium and its colonial territories in central Africa, made between 1900 and 1970—after which date TV became the primary source for that type of image.

• 1 one-off screening

NEWS FROM HOME, restored version of this film by Belgian filmmaker Chantal Akerman; screened in DCP.

---

[274] *Rapport annuel | Jaarverslag 2013* (n.d.), p. 55.

• 2 releases

AN EPISODE IN THE LIFE OF AN IRON PICKER, the latest film by Danis Tanovic, the subject one of Cinematek's retrospectives.

TROIS JOURNÉES D'AOÛT 1914, part of the retrospective *The Great War 1: 100 years already.*

• 9 retrospectives

Orson Welles (January 1–February 26), with four films he directed and two more in which he only acted.

Martin Scorsese (January 3–February 13), a large overview of the films of this director, parallel with an exhibition about the filmmaker based on his private collections of photos, posters, storyboards, etc., as well as on the collections of people he worked with.

Hommage Eliane Dubois (January 7–February 28) honored this Belgian distributor of auteur and art cinema, who died the previous August.

Danis Tanovic (January 19–February 27), a program on the occasion of the release of this Bosnian filmmaker's latest film.

Albert Serra: avant-première + rétrospective (January 31–February 6), a program on the occasion of this Catalan filmmaker's new film HISTORIA DE LA MEVA MORT, plus *Carte blanche Albert Serra* (February 1-26) for which the director was asked to select his favorite films on religion and mysticism.

Asta Nielsen (January 3–February 20) contained a selection of this actress's films from the later years of the silent era.

Isabella Rosselini (13-28 February), organized in honor of the actress's appearance in Brussels in the stage version of her online series of short films *Green porno.*

The Great War 1: 100 years already (January 2–February 27), a retrospective on a historical theme, which showcased this month a number of renowned feature fiction films (LA GRANDE ILLUSION; PATHS OF GLORY), alongside the new film TROIS JOURNÉES D'AOÛT 1914, whose two parts premiered already on January 15 and 29, 2014 respectively, at the Flagey venue.

Cinéma de l'intime (February 4-28), a thematic retrospective on autobiographical films, on the occasion of an issue of the journal *Smala Cinéma* devoted to this topic; it was one of the few programs in the survey featuring experimental films.

• 3 series

Inédits/Onuitgegeven, showing films previously unreleased in Belgium.

Het zilveren scherm (The silver screen), screenings that not only revive once popular feature films, but also contain, if the feature's length allows, a program of shorts; titles of the latter, if any, were not provided.

Museum night fever, 7th edition of this annual event (in its everyday sense) during which a number of the city's museums stay open after hours and organize special activities. Cinematek engaged experimental artist and filmmaker Tine Guns as the event's curator.

Summary of information:

As in its mission and funding statements, Cinematek doesn't waste many words on its public information. The screening of its "new restoration" of NEWS FROM HOME got the briefest of summaries, without any comment on the restoration itself nor whether its screening in DCP implied that no new analogue print was made or not. The *Orson Welles* retrospective, continued from January, got the same perfunctory treatment, and a rather lame one at that: "Orson Welles is one of the greatest figures in the history of cinema. Director, producer, scriptwriter or performer: this Renaissance man of the cinema was all." Plot summaries were disposed of in two sentences (which is the length of the majority of them), forcing its redactor here and there into cobbling mystifying statements, as in "an absurd, baroquely labyrinthine yet therefore even more brilliant noir experiment" (about THE LADY FROM SHANGHAI). A similar statement could be found in the descriptions of one of its permanent exhibitions, *Remix*, in which the juxtaposition of its thematically organized, excerpted scenes was said to reveal "the heart of cinema".

What the longer introductions (to e.g. *Martin Scorsese*, *Asta Nielsen*, *Hommage Eliane Dubois*, *Isabella Rossellini*) brought out even more clearly was the lack of any substantial information beyond tidbits of received knowledge and anecdotes. And as most retrospectives were about personalities, no other meaningful contexts were considered apart from personal ones (such as Martin Scorsese's Catholic background). The texts were utterly devoid of any film historical expertise. The introduction to *Hommage Eliane Dubois*, the recently deceased founder of the Belgian distribution company Cinélibre/Cinéart, added indolence to ignorance by delegating the provision of visitor information to its 39-film *program* that will "speak" of her importance for Belgium's national film culture. One would have thought that the six months that had elapsed since her death were sufficient to provide a decent obituary. A ten year old radio interview "sprinkled with funny and interesting anecdotes", reproduced on Cinematek's website, didn't promise much additional substance.

Cinematek's public information is promotional rather than anything else, telling its visitors no more than they need to know to enjoy a show. Generally, introductions to its retrospectives and their plot summaries consist of truisms (as in, "Naturally, over the years World War I has been a source of inspiration for various directors"), a small set of stock superlatives ("brilliant", "unsurpassed", "unforgettable"), and trivia.

Cinémathèque de la Ville de Luxembourg

Founded in 1975 as a nonprofit association, the Cinémathèque de la Ville de Luxembourg was supported by the city of Luxemburg from 1977 onwards. This is one of a minority of film heritage institutes in the survey that has a single auditorium (although during the summer months it also organizes outdoor screenings at another venue, the Grand-Ducal Palace, in cooperation with a private sponsor). A large proportion of its screenings comes from its own collections of international cinema—which it, like the Cinemateca Uruguaya, explicitly mentions in its mission statement (and makes equal sense for an even smaller country in terms of size and population). In fact, all its screenings are archival; the Cinémathèque does not show any new films in release.[275]

Its programming makes a clear distinction between weekdays and weekends, i.e. from Sunday night through Friday afternoon and from Friday night through Sunday afternoon. The weekdays are reserved for the Cinémathèque's retrospectives, usually devoted to personalities, national cinemas, or genres. A number of series make up the weekends' film screenings. The series format, as a matter of fact, is one of the most prominent aspects of the Cinémathèque's programming style. Largely arranged according to genre, it is meant to present *"toutes les couleurs du cinéma"* in a compact way. Some colors are missing, however, as it screens feature fiction films only (except the documentaries shown in the Discovery Zone festival, of which it is merely one of the venues). It accentuates its communal responsibilities with two special series: *Tous les styles du cinéma*, a film course; and the monthly screenings of *Kino mat*

---

[275] The entirely publicly funded Centre National de l'Audiovisuel (CNA), in nearby Dudelange, does precisely the opposite: its two auditoria are almost exclusively programmed like a cinema theater with new releases.

Häerz...a mat Kaffi! (Films with a heart...and with coffee!), in cooperation with the city's Senior Citizens Service, Help/Red Cross, and Maison des Associations; repeat screenings for the benefit of disabled persons are held at the Cinémathèque's archive.

See also: http://www.vdl.lu/-p-63593.html

Summary of presentations:

• 3 retrospectives

Pedro Almodóvar: rétrospective à l'aube de son 65e anniversaire (February 3-12), continued from January 2014.

Le Broadway musical au cinéma, des années 1960 aux années 2000 (February 4-27).

In memoriam Peter O'Toole (1932-2013) (February 5-19).

• 6 series

Comedy classics; Arthouse classics; Sense & sensibility, all featuring romantic stories in different genres or types.

Midnight movies at 10, which screens cult films.

Université populaire du cinéma, a part of the film course.

Kino mat Häerz...a mat Kaffi!, aimed at a target audience of senior citizens.

• 1 festival

4th edition of *Discovery Zone-Luxembourg City Film Festival* (February 28-March 9), of which the Cinémathèque was one of the venues. Information about the festival, which included a competitive program along with documentaries, shorts, a *jeune public* section, among others, could be found in a separate brochure.[276]

Summary of information:

While the two retrospectives devoted to personalities, Pedro Almodóvar and Peter O'Toole, were occasioned by turning points in their lives (the traditional retirement age of the former, the death of the latter), its program *Le Broadway musical au cinéma, des années 1960 aux années*

---

[276] *Discovery Zone: Luxembourg city festival, 28 feb-9 mar 2014* at: http://2014.discoveryzone.lu/en/posts/display/1.

2000 remained unmotivated. In actual fact, though, none of these programs was introduced or accounted for in any meaningful way.

All the (feature fiction) films that they contained, as well as the films in all other program formats, were described in relatively lengthy paragraphs. Almost without exception these descriptions consisted of a brief, bare plot summary provided by the Cinémathèque, followed by lengthier quotes from one, but usually more published print or web sources in French, English, and/or German, mostly written by film critics. This way of compiling quotes did not really add up to a coherent whole. A clear example (as an example, that is) are the excerpts raked together about Pedro Almodóvar's film CARNE TRÉMULA: first, the director is quoted as saying that it is "fundamentally a story about men"; then, according to *Le Guide Cinéma*, the film "evokes the dark years of Francoism and celebrates the victory of democracy in Spain"; next, the *Guide des films* calls it "an hommage to Buñuel"; and *TimeOut Film Guide*, finally, sums up, "The performances are spot on, the control of pace, mood and narrative is assured, the visuals are crisp, stylish and imaginative, and the whole film has, for Almodóvar, an unprecedented weight and substance."

Visitors who felt invited to connect the dots might well have come up with very strange beasts. This type of information borders on opacity, if not mystification. For instance, referencing the work of other filmmakers or artists, whether Buñuel or—in another quote from Almodóvar's own comments—"Feydeau and the boulevard comedy", assumed a knowledge that apparently obviated the need for further explication, suggesting that the names of "Buñuel" or "Feydeau" stood for a well-defined quality visitors were unanimously familiar with. And the brief quotations of isolated stylistic and/or thematic aspects rather served as promotional material ("spot on", "stylish and imaginative") than the valorization that the institute, according to its mission statement, is committed to.

The predominantly cinephile, insider-oriented register of its public information was modified for programs that had specific target audiences. The summaries for the *Midnight movies at 10* series were written entirely by its programmers in a style that would doubtlessly have been appreciated by the buffs of *giallo*, horror, and other cult genres (particularly those penned by Jack Stevenson); information about the film in *Kino mat Häerz...a mat Kaffi!*, aimed at senior citizens, was conspicuous for focusing on plot, thereby curiously dismissing the thought that members of this audience might have been regular visitors of the Cinémathèque for decades.

Cinémathèque française-Musée du cinéma, Paris

Founded in 1936, this is one of the oldest of the modern film heritage institutes.[277] In 2005, the institute moved into its current, new premises, where it merged with the Bibliothèque du Film (commonly known as BIFI), in 2007. This merger effectuated the online launch of *Ciné ressources*, the collective, digitized catalogue of film archives and libraries, an initiative of BIFI and the Cinémathèque de Toulouse. Besides the Cinémathèque française-Musée du Cinéma (who now administers the site) and the Cinémathèque de Toulouse, today it includes the catalogues of the Institut Jean Vigo, Fiches du Cinéma, Cinémathèque de Corse-Casa di Lume, and Archives Audiovisuelles de Monaco.[278]

Noteworthy in its terse mission statement is the specificity of its presentations, notably "the programming of the great classics as well as complete retrospectives of and hommages to filmmakers, performers, producers, and technicians", as well as organizing "temporary exhibitions to show the richness of its collections and valorize the links between cinema and the other arts." This statement, particularly the notions of "classics", "filmmakers", and links with other arts, reveals how the Cinémathèque française still very much sees itself as operating in the spirit of its controversial founder, Henri Langlois, to whose "genius" and "legend" it dedicated an exhibition in the spring and summer of 2014.[279] However, this spirit has not been allowed to live on in all its activities; notably the quality of preservation and cataloguing have come up to standard. With regard to its screenings, its large retrospectives, largely of makers of feature fiction film, indeed dominate its presentations; they can easily include dozens of titles spread over a period of two to three months. Its exhibitions, too, focus largely on personalities.

---

[277] Houston (1994), pp. 49-59.

[278] '*Ciné Ressources*: Présentation', at: http://www.cineressources.net/ pages.php?id _page=presentation.

[279] 'Exposition *La musée imaginaire d'Henri Langlois*', at:
http://www.cinematheque.fr/fr/expositions-cinema/precedentes-expositions/centenaire-langlois/exposition.html.
For the controversial aspect, see: Houston (1994), pp. 54-57, 63-67. It is no surprise, given that Langlois preferred to deal with film personalities directly in programming as well as in building the Cinémathèque's collections, that his reputation is more secure in the filmmaking than in the film heritage world.

While largely subsidized by the French state, many separate activities are sponsored by corporate partners. In its three auditoria it shows an average of 40 screenings a week (except for the annual summer closure in August), and its three-level gallery space can accommodate its permanent exhibition as well as one or more simultaneous temporary exhibitions. It is one of the few institutes that has deliberately and inventively exploited digital technology in expanding its exhibition 'space' as well as enhancing its visitor information, besides the *Ciné ressources*.

See also: http://www.cinematheque.fr/

Summary of presentations:

• 1 permanent exhibition

Showcasing a large variety of objects and equipment, either originals or replicas.

• 2 temporary exhibitions

Jean Cocteau et le cinématographe (October 2, 2013-August 3, 2014), an exhibition on Cocteau as both filmmaker and critic, based on the rich collections of film-related materials at the Cinémathèque as well as on materials on loan from other collections.

Amos Gitai, architecte de la mémoire (February 26–July 6), an exhibition conceived as an imaginary trip through 40 years of this Israeli filmmaker's personal archives, presented for the first time to the public.

Each of these exhibitions came with a retrospective of its director's films. The exhibition on Amos Gitai was introduced by its curator in a 14' video (a video on Cocteau's work, a recording of 93' lecture, focused exclusively on one film, LA BELLE ET LA BÊTE—the retrospective finished in November 2013 already).

• 21 virtual exhibitions

Eleven of these are so-called *Zooms*, relatively brief, educational applications that zoom in on collection objects on the occasion of a temporary exhibition or film program (e.g. *Une affiche de* MON ONCLE, *par Pierre Étaix*; Jules et Jim, *roman de la Nouvelle Vague*; *Le robot de* METROPOLIS, *de Fritz Lang*; *Le théâtre optique d'Emile Reynaud*). The other 10 virtual exhibitions are mostly extensions of temporary exhibitions or film programs (e.g. *Brune/blonde*; *Lola Montès*; *Story-board de cinéma*). Their number changes; at the time I write this, September 2014, the Cinémathèque's website features eight of them, as a result of both deletion and replacement. The other two were introductions to retrospective programs.[280]

• 4 retrospective*s*

Érographie (December 13, 2013–February 14, 2014), featured the erotic works of three experimental filmmakers—in February 2014, those of Roland Lethem. This program constituted one of the few retrospectives, besides its own series *Cinéma de poche* (see below) and the ones at Cinematek and the Cinémathèque québécoise, devoted to experimental cinema in the survey.

Henry Hathaway (January 8–February 23), a nearly complete overview of the work of this Hollywood veteran director.

Caroline Champetier (February 5-23), extensive overview of this French director of photography who worked with many major domestic and foreign filmmakers.

Amos Gitai (February 26–April 6), Israeli director of documentary and fiction films, who lived in voluntary exile in France between 1982 and 1993.

• 4 series

Cinéma de poche 2013-2014, an amalgam of various film formats, mostly of an exprimental character, featured in February 2014 two Brazilian filmmakers, Gustavo Beck and Kleber Mendonça Filho.

Cinéma Bis 2013-2014, the Cinémathèque's cult series.

Voir-revoir le cinéma d'aujourd'hui 2013-2014 brought back to its screens a number of recent films that, according to the Cinémathèque, had disappeared too soon or merited another look. These screenings could turn into an event when the filmmaker was present.

Ciné-club Jean Douchet: Regards sur le cinéma contemporain 2013-2014, a cinephile's view of contemporary cinema

---

[280] Since writing this text in 2014-2015, the Cinémathèque française has changed the design of its website. As a result the abovementioned nomenclature of its web applications has been replaced by a categorical term on its home page, *Découvrir*. Under it all the institute's digital productions are collected, subdivided in type of (original) document (collection item, article, video, web production), which can be accessed by name, title, type of object, genre, country, etc.

• 1 event

"Tourne au son!": Evolutions et révolutions de la prise de son au cinéma (February 7), featuring sound recordist Philippe Vandendriessche who presented and talked about a selection of rare recording devices.

Summary of information:

The most distinctive aspect of Cinémathèque's visitor information are the web applications of its Online editions department. Having various names—virtual exhibition; *Zoom*; introduction (*"présentation"*)—and performing slightly different functions, most of them expand on linear presentations in the institute's gallery space and/or its auditoria. Of these three, the introductions are the most straightforward type of information. As a rule they come with the more ambitious film programs, whose film descriptions are simple, one- or two-sentence affairs. So, in order to know more about, for instance, the 37-film program devoted to director of photography Caroline Champetier and her approach to her work, visitors were almost compelled to consult the 44' video interview alternated with clips (while a two hour recording of a conversation with Champetier, organized during the retrospective, was added later). The same goes for the 55-film retrospective of American director Henry Hathaway and its equally nondescript plot summaries. But in a 15' video interview its curator explained the significance of the program, viz. where to situate Hathaway in terms of the studio system (was he an *auteur* or a studio craftsman?), and did a brief close reading of the oeuvre to identify what Hathaway's particular 'signature' is.

Both virtual exhibitions and *Zooms* are more complex in that they combine various media and discourses. Virtual exhibitions are meant to comment on all kinds of archival materials, from complete oeuvres to individual objects in the collections, while the *Zooms* focus exclusively on collection objects. The *Zoom* on Amos Gitai, for example, is actually a web documentary (the production of which was outsourced) that had its own title: DES TERRITOIRES À VENIR. When compared with other instances of *Zoom* its greater ambition and 'production value' reveal the possibilities that are being explored and the changes the format undergoes as a result. DES TERRITOIRES À VENIR, based on elements from Gitai's large personal archive that he donated to the Cinémathèque in 2007, focuses on the creative process of his films as well on excerpted, purposely recorded conversations with Gitai and three of his close and longtime collaborators. It has a text that one can scroll and read linearly, but parts of it can be hidden, while hidden footnotes can be made to pop up. Visitors can also follow their own route by skipping the visuals that expand on the text—the filmed conversations and excerpts, stills, set photos, scripts, etc.—for later viewing. This *Zoom*, then, combines the bi-modal arrangement—"*visite guidée*" and "*visite libre*"—common in other examples of this application. Its three-part structure—'*Le processus créatif*'; '*D'un film à l'autre*'; '*KIPPOUR - film-emblème*'—allows visitors to choose between progressively shorter sections, which, although perfectly understandable autonomously, nevertheless maintained thematic links with each other. Because the exploration of the entire *Zoom* might well take an hour or two, it was a source of information to return to.

The virtual exhibitions are more textual in character, with links to other sources of information (catalogue, film excerpts, other websites, etc.); many of them have their own, rather lengthy introductory texts (which, of course, one can skip). They are much enlivened whenever there is a film excerpt, interview or conversation, because what predominates is their absence of sound, particularly in the older ones that were produced by BIFI. Their topics cover a number of different histories, thereby breaking out of the dominant auteurist mold of the institute's presentations. However, the differences between virtual exhibitions and *Zooms* are not strict; the *Zoom* about the robot in the 1927 film METROPOLIS, of which the Cinémathèque had a replica built, is to a significant extent devoted to visually illustrated, lucid explanations of process photography, such as matte, superimposition, rear projection, multiple exposure and masking, rather than about its director.

Both the larger and the smaller film programs and series received comparatively brief introductions, complemented by perfunctory plot summaries. For more information one either had to watch the digital introductions (if any) or click to longer, general-purpose texts in *Ciné Ressources*. This source also provides longer resumés and credits of individual films, although they were not written with an eye to the considerations that went into a specific program. But what is an asset of the institute's visitor information is the listing with each program or individual screening of related objects and literature in its collections and library.

With its highly developed, and evolving, digital apparatus and a separate department to conceive and/or (executive) produce a variety of digital products the Cinémathèque has not only created highly enlightening visitor information. It also manifests an increasingly sophisticated balance between education and exploration, between guided and 'unguided' tour. In a real sense the Cinémathèque française-Musée du Cinéma exploits its presentations to promote *all* its collections.

Cinémathèque québécoise, Montreal

The Cinémathèque québécoise was founded in 1963 as Connaissance du cinéma, renamed Cinémathèque canadienne a year later. Only in 1971 did it get its current name to mark its focus on the promotion of Quebec cinema. In its mission statement its tasks are defined as "collecting, documenting, and preserving the Quebec audiovisual heritage". "Audiovisual" includes all moving image works: film, video, TV, and new media. (In 2006, the Quebec government mandated the responsibility of legal deposit for Quebec film and TV to the institute in a five-year renewable—and renewed—contract.) "Heritage" is defined as all the elements in their original and preserved formats as well as film-related materials that allow "the documentation of the works and their artistic, aesthetic, sociological, economic, and technical contexts." Besides, it collects, documents, and preserves international animation films—with c. 5,000 titles the largest collection in the world—as well as "significant films" from Canada and abroad. It is a mixed public (national, municipal) and privately funded institute.

The Cinémathèque has two auditoria (150 and 84 seats) and two gallery spaces, of which the Norman McLaren Hall is actually a studio-like space that is adaptable to various types of presentation; its lobby and agora spaces are used for exhibits, too, while the terrace of its bar also functions as a venue for screenings. Film is clearly the most frequently featured medium in the Cinémathèque's presentations, although its collection boasts 20,000 hours of materials on magnetic tape (much of which can be accessed in its mediatheque), while its collection of animation titles ranges from works on 35mm to HD CAM and other digital formats. The institute frequently cooperates with Quebec media organizations that specialize in video and new media (e.g. Vidéographe and VOX: Centre de l'Image contemporaine).

What is most distinctive about its presentations is the mix of categories (rather than the near-monoculture of feature fiction found in so many other institutes): documentary, animation, and experimental works abound. As well, it creates a balance between its decidedly regional orientation, both in terms of content and personality (what it calls "the core of the Cinémathèque's holdings") and an international outlook in its programming. Furthermore, the institute doesn't screen (commercial) releases, although it does sometimes preview new work within the context of a retrospective.

See also: http://www.cinematheque.qc.ca/

Summary of presentations:

• 1 permanent exhibition

Secrets et illusions–la magie des effets spéciaux (since April 10, 2013), subdivided in three "zones" devoted to the history of special effects, the joy of creation and simulation, and an ABC of techniques.

• 3 temporary exhibitions

Gros plan sur la collection (June 6, 2013-February 9, 2014), which showed a selection of prime objects—equipment, story boards, scripts, etc.—on the occasion of the Cinémathèque's 50th anniversary.

Pionniers de l'animation américaine (November 27, 2013-February 9, 2014), featured treasures from the collection that traced the development of American animation in the first half of the 20th century.

3e page après le soleil (November 27, 2013-February 2, 2014), a video installation by Theodore Ushev based on the concept of palimpsest, which reflected on creation and destruction in an era when the materiality of objects has been rendered obsolete by digital technologies.

• 1 virtual exhibition

Face à face: Gabor Szilasi photographie le cinéma, a series of portraits of filmmakers and technicians with a piece of equipment of their choice from the collections. Commissioned on the occasion of the Cinémathèque's 40th anniversary, Szilasi's portraits were exhibited in 2004; now, on its 50th anniversary, it has returned in its virtual space.

• 9 one-off screenings

A veritable mix of films made between 1950 and 2012. A few of these films returned to its screens "by popular demand" (e.g. WINTER'S BONE), while one compilation program of films by artist Michael Blum was screened in cooperation with VOX: Centre de l'Image contemporaine, on the occasion of Blum's solo exhibition at this venue. Other one-off screenings (e.g. INVASION OF THE BODY SNATCHERS [1956]; EN COMPAGNIE D'ANTONIN ARTAUD [1994]) were reminiscent of the classic cinematheque way of programming repertoire that the Cinémathèque weaves through its more focused presentations. Both LE CHANT DES ONDES: SUR LA PISTE DE MAURICE MARTINOT (19-20 February), an artistic and scientific quest of the Ondes Martinot, an early electronic musical instrument, and Fellini's INTERVISTA (19-20 February)—the latter also shown by popular demand—, had a repeat screening the following day.

• 7 retrospectives

Michel Brault: la lumière du réel. Le directeur photo (November 23, 2013–February 15, 2014), third and final part of an hommage dedicated to this key figure of Canadian direct cinema, who died in September 2013.

Robert Morin: comme d'autres sont des gars de char (January 8—February 14), on the occasion of Morin's reception of the Prix Albert-Tessier, an annual career prize awarded by the government of Quebec.

George Pal, l'expert truqueur (January 9 - March 13), an off-shoot of the permanent exhibition, spotlighted this animation filmmaker who went on to specialize in special effects in live-action films.

Fernand Bélanger, cinéaste-monteur (January 22–February 22), an overview of the majority of this editor-filmmaker's small but distinct oeuvre.

Jean Chabot–dix ans après (January 29–February 2), no information provided.

Guy L. Coté (February 5-9), select program of this director-producer and one of the Cinémathèque's founders.

Same same (mais différent): lieux de la mémoire thailandaise (February 7-8), a program outsourced to Antitube, a Quebec-based producer of film and video events, which approached laureled Thai filmmaker Apichatpong Weerasethakul to curate a brief selection of recent Thai films.

• 5 series

Coups de cœur des collègues (April 4, 2013–April 3, 2014), a carte blanche for the Cinémathèque's 63 employees on the occasion of the institute's 50th anniversary.

Secrets et illusions–la magie des effets spéciaux (September 14, 2013—October 26, 2014), film program alongside the institute's new permanent exhibition.

5 sur 5: les fictions polymorphes (January 31–June, 2014), a collaboration with Vidéographe, explores the ways in which videographic work has been used as a way of writing history. In February 2014 it featured the work of multidisciplinary artist Sylvie Laliberté.

Les essentiels (January 7, 2012-December 31, 2014), once-a-month screenings meant to valorize what are considered the Cinémathèque's prized works.

Ciné-concert, twice-monthly shows, featuring in February 2014 the films FIG LEAVES (1926) and THE WIND (1928), both accompanied live by pianist Gabriel Thibaudeau.

• 1 event

Rencontre avec Sylvie Laliberté. Lecture by the artist within the framework of the series *5 sur 5: les fictions polymorphes* (February 7).[281]

Summary of information:

Most of the Cinémathèque's online information expands on its (bi-) monthly printed program bulletins (available in PDF as well): introductions to programs are usually longer, while the website is the only place where plot descriptions and synopses, screening formats, and information about the institute's exhibitions can be found.

Generally, its major presentations receive the most extensive information. An artistic angle characterized the lengthy introductions to the comprehensive retrospectives of two unconventional Quebec filmmakers, Robert Morin (who was early in his career, in the 1980s, mainly known in festival and art circles for his video work) and editor-filmmaker Fernand Bélanger, and a more selective program on director-producer Guy L. Coté. The introductions roughly followed the chronology of their careers and pointed out the characteristics and expressiveness of their work.

A few retrospectives received decidedly less extensive introductions. The last leg of the program on Michael Brault, even though only one screening remained for the month of February, was given no longer an introduction as when it began, in November 2013. And the two-day program *Same same (mais différent): lieux de la mémoire thailandaise* received three paragraphs, none of which shone any light upon the line-up of films, while another brief retrospective, *Jean Chabot–dix ans après*, received no introduction at all. This discrepancy returned in the plot summaries and synopses: some were perfunctory, others were relatively lengthy; many were wholly or partly quoted from web or print publications (some of which were decades old), while a few were original. It made one wonder whether the sheer volume of presentations exceeded

---

[281] *5 sur 5:* 'Les fictions polymorphes. Vidéographe à la Cinémathèque: Sylvie Laliberté' (February 7, 2014).

the capacity to provide adequate and reliable information—although in the end, one would expect, this is a matter of priorities.

This is not a finding unique of the Cinémathèque québécoise, as we have seen, but the inconsistency of its visitor information is more conspicuous. On one hand, for example, it contained a knowledgeable introduction to and summaries of the films in the retrospective of Fernand Bélanger, penned by its guest curator. On the other hand, there was the relatively lengthy description of the American film WINTER'S BONE, which was copied entirely from a review in the French web magazine *Télérama*.[282] But what nobody realized apparently was that this quoted review hadn't got its background information right when claiming that the film's setting, the Ozarks, or its hillbilly population are a virtually uncharted territory for Hollywood. Quite on the contrary, filmic representations of—admittedly often geographically unspecified—hillbilly country and its people, clichéd or not, parodied or not, go back to the early 1920s, and even before Hollywood to the 1910s.[283] In fact, the film shows clear continuities with older representations: the film's depicted location's present-day illicit production of crystal meth is a strong echo of its traditional moonshining, as is its community's private way of enforcing 'law and order'. Here, as elsewhere, presentation prevailed over adequate information.

This observation applies even more to the Cinematheque's exhibitions. Its recently opened, new permanent exhibition on special effects, for instance, has a lengthy, historicizing introduction, which demarcates the exhibition as being about the use of special effects on an "ad hoc basis", not as a *dispositif* (as in video games). However, its identification of the rise of a "language" of techniques that exploits the confusion between reality and perception with a simple change from the "Cinématographe into cinema" circumvents all sorts of industrial and institutional developments. This point of view is echoed in the historical section of the exhibition, in which cinema is represented as a matter of genealogy, creating a direct lineage between Méliès, through Ptushko and Edison, all the way down to Ray Harryhausen, irrespective of their backgrounds, the

---

[282]   Compare   http://www.cinematheque.qc.ca/en/programmation/projections /film/winters-bone?pid=17025 and http://www.telerama.fr/cinema/films/winter-s-bone,422602,critique.php.

[283] Anthony Harkins, *Hillbilly: a cultural history of an American icon* (2004), pp. 57-69, 141-171, 206-210.

institutional contexts in which they worked or the techniques they used or developed. A similar view of things was found again in its introduction to the temporary exhibition *Pionniers de l'animation américaine*, which suggested that all it took to transform animation from a craft into an industry were the pioneers' enthusiasm and determination; and the introduction to the temporary exhibition *Gros plan sur la collection* highlighted two Moviola editing devices ("seated like royalty at the center of the exhibition"), yet merely linked them to specific productions and personnel. Given the apparent lack of accompanying catalogues, obvious opportunities were missed here to provide the selected works with their "sociological, economic, and technical contexts."

Cinémathèque suisse, Lausanne

Created in 1948, the Cinémathèque suisse is a private, nonprofit foundation which is financed from both public funds and private sources. Its mission is to collect, preserve, restore, and valorize films of all genres and film-related documents as well as to establish a museum and center for the study of film history. Its mission is national (although there is no legal deposit legislation for audiovisual materials in Switzerland), yet it also collects the films of foreign origin, films that dominate the Swiss market and that make up the bulk of its collections.[284] The institute has two auditoria on its own premises, while special events, previews, etc. take place at the Capitole cinema theater. This, the largest of cinema theaters (869 seats) in operation in Switzerland, is owned by the city of Lausanne and entrusted to the Cinémathèque, which will turn it into a regular venue in the near future. The institute also makes part of its film collections available in distribution prints, notably classics but also films by "contemporary auteurs" that were not picked up by commercial distributors.

The Cinémathèque has established a firmer base within the community and the region through its cooperation with a number of cultural, educational, and academic organizations and institutes in realizing an array of presentations. This cooperation, moreover, has contributed significantly to the variety of its presentations, particularly in terms of topic and genre. Insofar as it concerns exhibitions, though, this cooperation has a downside. The summary of presentations below opens

---

[284] 'Cinémathèque suisse', in: *Dictionnaire historique de la Suisse*, at: http://www.hls-dhs-dss.ch/textes/f/F10475.php.

with an exhibition, *STALKER et la Zone*, that was staged at another museum in another town, for the simple reason that the Cinémathèque suisse has no exhibition space of its own. So, on one hand it collaborates with other museums on *their* initiatives, for instance by mounting parallel film programs whenever there is an opportunity—in February 2014, besides the film program *Après l'apocalypse (histoires des survivants)* that corresponded with *STALKER et la Zone*, it also screened the retrospective *Les avant-gardes russes et le sport*, coincident with an exhibition of the same name at the Musée Olympique (while in June 2014, for instance, it screened the epic film HEAVEN'S GATE, in the presence of its director, at its Capitole venue on the occasion of the exhibition *Peindre l'Amérique* at the Lausanne-based Fondation Hermitage). On the other, it is dependent on other museums and venues for staging exhibitions that *it* has initiated, such as the traveling exhibition it co-organized with Cinematek and the Cinémathèque française on Amos Gitaï (which ran at the latter venue until July 6; its program bulletin of September-October 2014 informed visitors that this exhibition would open at the Musée de l'Elysée, in Lausanne). More importantly, the lack of an exhibition venue is apparently an obstacle to exhibiting its own film-related collections—of which I haven't seen any instances while leafing through the bulletins of the past few years.

A number of events—introductions, conversations, *vernissages*, cine concerts, master classes—at its venues have been recorded and uploaded at the Cinémathèque's website, as a rule quickly after their occurrence. Most of these records partly function as additional information sources. But the personal appearances that are the usual reason for their being made—as they are for its online 'Galerie portraits'—surely won't hurt the Cinémathèque's standing and reputation in view of the revered names of contemporary cinema that have been invited for these events.

See also: http://www.cinematheque.ch/f/

Summary of presentations:

• 1 temporary exhibition

STALKER et la Zone (September 15, 2013-March 2, 2014), occasioned by the 80th anniversary of the birthday of Russian filmmaker and director of STALKER (1979), Andrei Tarkovsky (1932-1986). The exhibition was staged at and organized by the Maison d'Ailleurs, a science fiction museum, in cooperation with the School of Business and Engineering, both in Yverdon-les-Bains, some 40km north of Lausanne. The Cinémathèque mentioned it in its program bulletin, but did not state what its role—if any—was, apart from screening a parallel program of so-called post-Apocalyptic films (see below), of which STALKER is considered a masterful example.

• 3 retrospectives

Après l'apocalypse (histoires des survivants) (January 1-February 28), this thematic program showed 22 films on the theme of post-Apocalyptic worlds, in association with the abovementioned exhibition at the Maison d'Ailleurs; the program included a "*soirée Mad Max*", screening all three parts of this film series.

Chris Marker (January 20-February 28), an overview of the films of the French writer-photographer-editor-film essayist, who died in July 2012; it shared a few films with *Après l'apocalypse*.

Les avant-gardes russes et le sport (January 28-February 22), a parallel program with the exhibition of the same name at the Lausanne-based Musée Olympique, on the occasion of and partly overlapping with the Winter Olympics in Sochi, Russia. Program notes omitted to mention whether this selection of silent films (including classics such as LES AVENTURES EXTRAORDINAIRES DE MISTER WEST [1924] and L'HOMME À LA CAMÉRA [1929]), all projected in 35mm prints, was accompanied by live or by recorded music.

• 5 series

Pour une histoire permanente du cinéma: 1964 (since 2006) offers a year-by-year selection of what the Cinémathèque considers significant films of half a century ago; in February 2014 it featured: THE WOMAN IN THE DUNES; IL DESERTO ROSSO; NIGHT OF THE IGUANA; and THE MANUSCRIPT FOUND IN SARAGOSSA.

De La 1ère à la Cinémathèque: travelling, a series screened in association with Radio 1's program *Travelling*, radio documentaries about the "*petites histoires*" of the shooting of cult films made with archival, published, and anecdotal sources as well as sound excerpts from the selected films (THE FRENCH CONNECTION [1971]; BLADE RUNNER [1982]; LOLITA [1962]; QUAI DES BRUMES [1938])

L'architecture à l'écran, in association with the architecture magazine *Tracés* and Le Silo, a collective dedicated to the study of the interrelationship between cinema and contemporary art, consists of bi-monthly screenings of programs combining a short and a feature-length film that explore the links between architecture and cinema. The February 2014 program, titled 'A flower on the asphalt', juxtaposed Brazilian filmmaker Cao Guimarães's short video BRASILIA and Iranian filmmaker Abbas Kiarostami's feature film WHERE IS THE FRIEND'S HOME?.[285]

Portraits-plans-fixes, a long-running series (since 1977) that now comprises a vast collection of filmed portraits of francophone Swiss personalities, all shot in "in black-and-white, at one location, in one day, with no retakes or cuts". The first of the two February 2014 programs contained portraits of a teacher and a geneticist, the other of two architects. With this series, of course, the Cinémathèque has *created* a heritage of films.

Trésors des archives, monthly screenings of restored films, featured in February 2014 LES ORIGINES DE LA CONFÉDÉRATION (1924), an incomplete print of a mythico-historical panorama of Swiss history centering on William Tell.

Carte blanche à Ruy Nogueira (since November 2013), monthly programs in which the former director of the Centre d'animation cinématogaphique (CAC), Geneva, present highlights of the history of cinema—in February 2014, THE FOUNTAINHEAD (1949).

The third edition of *Ciné-Concert*, a cooperation between the Cinémathèque and the composition classes of the Haute école de musique de Lausanne (HÉMU) and Cinéma de l'ECAL (Ecole cantonale d'art de Lausanne). For this particular edition the Cinémathèque provided music and film students with two films, LE LÉMAN (1937) and the Cinémathèque's recent restoration of ALICE AU PAYS ROMAND (1938), of which five different (digital) versions were made, scored, and combined into one program.[286]

Ciné-clubs UNIL-EPFL: Ouverture cycle "Parcours de vie(s)" (February 26) is a collaboration between the Cinémathèque, National Research Center LIVES, the film clubs of the University of Lausanne and the Lausanne Polytechnic. The series *Parcours de vie(s)* explores the representation of the development and vulnerabilities of real or fictional individuals through the prism of cinema. The monthly screenings will be followed by

---

[285] *'L'architecture à l'écran - 05.02.2014'*, at: http://www.cinematheque.ch/f/galeries/ videos/2014/.

[286] *'Ciné-concert ImaginaSon 2014 - 13.02.2014'*, at:
http://www.cinematheque.ch/f/galeries/videos/2014/.

debates with sociologists, psychologists, etc. This first edition featured the Belgian co-production MR. NOBODY (2009); discussants were not listed.

• 1 event

Avant-première VERLIEBTE FEINDE (February 18), preview of the new film of director Werner S. Schweizer, VERLIEBTE FEINDE, based on the book of the same title, which in its turn was based on c. 1,300 letters exchanged between a principled, unconventional couple during the late 1940s on such subjects as religion, equality, feminism, sexuality, politics, etc. The film's director, the translator of the book, and the director of the event's co-organizer, the Bureau d'égalité of the canton of Vaud, were among those who put in a personal appearance at this preview.[287]

Summary of information:

Visitor information about the more comprehensive presentations of the Cinémathèque suisse distinguished itself by sketching contexts that were often broader than what is common in the film heritage world. For example, the introduction to the retrospective *Après l'apocalypse (histoires des survivants)* provided a succinct overview of the so-called post-Apocalytic film: its conceptualization as a counterpart of the sci-fi film; its societal and historical backgrounds (nuclear arms, particularly); its dystopic and critical discourse; and its distinctive, sometimes experimental aesthetics. Similarly, the retrospective *Les avant-gardes russes et le sport*, on the occasion of the exhibition of the same name, showed that this was not a merely topical program. Its curator argued in fact that sport and the related fields of physical culture, hygiene, and living conditions played an important role in Soviet cinema in the 1920s and 1930s, particularly in documentaries, newsreels, propaganda, and pedagogical films. Sport's cinematic qualities were extremely suited to bring across ideological aspects (equality of and solidarity between classes, the sexes, etc.) in activities that were relatively easy to organize, if not 'ready-made'. None of these introductions were exhaustive, of course, but the selection of unobvious but significant aspects, interwoven with titles from the film program, provided the visitor with a useful framework. Plot summaries or synopses were separated from web information and were reserved for the institute's bulletin (in both print and PDF).

---

[287] 'Avant-première au Capitole: VERLIEBTE FEINDE de Werner S. Schweizer - 18.02.2014', at:
http://www.cinematheque.ch/f/galeries/videos/2014/.

Another distinctive element is that the Cinémathèque's partners that are wholly or partly responsible for the many film series on its program apparently have been given a latitude in writing their own program notes. Obviously, Ruy Nogueira wrote his own introductions and summaries for his *Carte blanche* program. But the organizers of *L'architecture à l'écran*, too, signed their program notes; the plot summaries were anonymous, but as they were written to fit the screening's theme they may well have come from the same source. This enhanced the quality of the information.

Nevertheless, this institute, too, resorted to quoting, partly or wholly, many other summaries and synopses from published materials, such as reviews, interviews, press kits or encyclopedias. In a few instances it enlivened the information: an excerpt reproduced from a 1924 review of the 1924 film shown in the series *Trésors des archives* introduced a whiff of history. And a director's comment can also provide a telling detail (even though quite a few of the quoted texts actually were director's statements). Curiously, in one case a quoted source was designated to deliver the 'bad news' that one of the post-Apocalyptic films was "a mere pretext to parade a number of stars and a display of trivial sentimentality". But what is often problematic in integrating such quotes is that the lack of the original context often remains noticeable. Take, for instance, the summary of Stanley Kubrick's LOLITA, which after setting the stage of the story suddenly shifted gears with a thirty-year old quote: "In New Hampshire, Humbert, a professor of French literature, rents a room for the summer in the house of a widow and her seductive daughter, Lolita... 'Who would have thought, in 1962, that Kubrick had already fathomed Kubrick? Freed from SPARTACUS [a film he directed in 1960] he expatriated to England...'."

More generally, there was not much in the quoted texts that a film heritage institute could—or should—ideally not have done better and more to the point.

Cineteca Nacional de México, Mexico City

The Cineteca Nacional, founded in 1974, is one of at least six film heritage institutes that considers the Mexican national film heritage as its remit (even though one of those six is actually, if only temporarily, located in the USA). But the Cineteca is the one that has been mandated the stewardship of cinema in Mexico. Its specific mission is to collect, preserve, restore, and disseminate both Mexican and world cinema and to strengthen the country's audiovisual culture. As a government-sponsored body (besides three other institutes that are each responsible for a sector of the country's cinema), it is administered by the Consejo Nacional para la Cultura y las

Artes (CONACULTA) under the responsibility of the Secretary of Education.

For its presentations the Cineteca boasts no less than ten auditoria and an additional open air space. With these (recently extended) spaces the Cineteca was able to realize a change in its mission and policy to enlarge its audience base and attract new, preferably younger spectators (the country's largest demographic segment by far—in 2014, 46% of the population was under 25). Releases of new or recent international art films, therefore, are the most conspicuous aspect of its presentations; in February 2014 it showed 16 released films in its theaters, seven of which were premiered that month. The increase in releases must be seen, according to a former director, as a measure to counteract the "duopoly" of the film distribution market, as a result of which most screens were filled with (American) mainstream films. For the same reason its programs regularly feature contemporary Mexican filmmakers.[288]

In order to further enrich film culture and contribute to the education of the public the Cineteca has created, in 2014, the Departamento de Extensión Académica.It began with providing courses, mostly about well-known film directors, but discussions and masterclasses will be organized in the near future. Its name notwithstanding, the activities this department plans to organize are open to the public. This can be taken as an extension of the institute's aim to allow the public at large to familiarize itself with the "quality supply" of the Cineteca's programs.

The institute plays a prominent role in the country's 'cinemascape' through a number of strategic, steady partnerships. Some of these partners featured in the Cineteca's activities during February 2014, such as Ambulante, a nonprofit organization for the promotion and support of documentary films and organizer of an annual traveling festival; Festival Internacional de Cine de la Universidad Nacional Autónoma de México (FICUNAM); Academia Mexicana de Artes y Ciencias Cinematográficas (AMACC); or the Festival Internacional de Cine Documental de la Ciudad de México (DocsDF). Others are: Riviera Maya Film Festival and the film school Centro Universitario de Estudios Cinematográficos (CUEC). These cooperations, I suspect, also help fill the Cineteca's ten screens.

---

[288] Paul Julian Smith, 'Cineteca Nacional, México', at:
http://www.cinetecanacional.net/controlador.php?opcion=noticias&id=410
(originally published in 2013 as 'Letter from Mexico').

See also: http://www.cinetecanacional.net/

Summary of presentations:

• 16 releases

Nine releases were held over from previous months—e.g. JAZMÍN AZUL (BLUE JASMINE; since December 4, 2013); DE TAL PADRE, TAL HIJO (SOSHITE CHICHI NI NARU; since January 3); DIARIO DE FRANCIA (JOURNAL DE FRANCE; since January 10); LA ESPOSA PROMETIDA (LEMALE ET HA'HALAL; since January 17); BALADA DE UN HOMBRE COMÚN (INSIDE LLEWYN DAVIS; since January 24)—, while seven premiered in February 2014—e.g. ELLA (HER; from February 1); LA VIDA DE ADÈLE (LA VIE D'ADÈLE; from February 14); 12 AÑOS ESCLAVO (12 YEARS A SLAVE; from February 21); PARAÍSO: AMOR (PARADIES: LIEBE; from February 21). Virtually all of them were arthouse films and represented, in tems of country of production, a wide, international array (Austria, Belarus, France, Germany, Greece, Israel, Japan, USA as well as, of course, Mexico).

• 6 retrospectives

Cine brasileño (January 9–March 2), a program of recent Brazilian films, recommended as a warmup for the soccer world championship—in which the Mexican team would be competing—later in the year.

World cinema project. Historias olvidadas por el cine (January 3–February 21), a selection of films preserved by the World Cinema Foundation.

Dictator's cut (February 7-13), an annual, three-month traveling program of documentaries, organized by Ambulante.

FICUNAM Retrospectiva Otar Iosseliani (February 27–March 9), as part of the Festival Internacional de Cine UNAM.

Sumario (February 2–March 2), an overview of recent Mexican documentary cinema.

Día de la Academia: los que se fueron (February 26), a brief, one-day hommage to three Mexican actors who passed away in 2013, screened around the time of the Academia Mexicana de Artes y Ciencias Cinematográficas's (AMACC) annual award ceremony.

• 1 event/retrospective

Alan Berliner en México. Retrospectiva, seminario (February 14-18), organized in cooperation AMACC, La Cátedra Ingmar Bergman, and Ambulante 2014; American filmmaker Alan Berliner was present for the entire five-day program—screenings and a seminar—to introduce and discuss his work.

Summary of presentations:

The Cineteca Nacional provides visitor information through its website and its monthly program bulletin, which is available both in print and in PDF (two clicks away from its home page). With it, the Cineteca has established a two-tier approach to attract its public. The website's brief plot summaries seem to be aimed at the more casual filmgoer, while the bulletin's more extensive information seems to appeal to the more interested or knowledgeable patron. In terms of authorship, the lengthier, more substantial pieces are for the most part written by non-employees or copied from other sources.

With regard to its releases, the brief plot summaries on its website make no distinction between premieres and films continued from the previous months; while in its bulletins premieres receive two-page, partly descriptive, partly evaluative reviews (sometimes in the shape of an interview), which are then summarized in the following months' editions. All but one of these lengthier pieces, though, were quoted (excerpts of) earlier print or web reviews. The Cineteca's only editorial contribution consists in summarizing them. The quoted texts, moreover, led to an inconsistent quality of information, as some were mere lengthy plot summaries while others were more informed. The piece on the film ELLA (HER), for instance, basically regurgitated the plot, while the one on 12 AÑOS ESCLAVO (12 YEARS A SLAVE) spent a brief paragraph summarizing the plot, while the remainder put the film in the context of its director's vision and other work.[289]

A similar inconsistency was found in the introductions to the retrospective programs, in terms of both length and quality. The shortest of these programs, the one-day retrospective *Día de la Academia* that contained three films featuring actors that had died during the past year, received a very obligatory, uninspired introduction by a member of the Mexican Academy of Motion Picture Arts and Sciences, telling the reader who wrote the scripts of the films screened and what they were about. Not a word, though, about what made the featured, deceased performers' work distinctive or memorable. The subsequent film summaries, too, focused rather on the films' plots and directors.

---

[289] For visitor information of film premieres in February 2014, see: 'Estrenos', in: *Programa mensual Cineteca Nacional de México* (February 2014), pp. 6-19.

In other cases, web or bulletin information was identical, as with the retrospective *Cine brasileño*, a program of recent Brazilian cinema, which got the briefest of obligatory introductions both at its start, in January, as well as in February, and which mainly related the program to the upcoming soccer championship in Brazil (a reason perhaps why the majority of the films were screened in the Cineteca's open air space). Their summaries and synopses didn't throw any light on contextual or other, more comprehensive considerations. The programs *Dictator's cut*, which collected very recent, international documentaries on human rights issues, and *Sumario*, which consisted of a number of very recent Mexican films, dispensed with introductions entirely. Visitor information about the small program of recently restored films by the World Cinema Foundation, *World cinema project. Historias olvidadas por el cine*, again was introduced by another obligatory text, while film descriptions merely mentioned the laboratories responsible for the restoration (mostly L'Immagine Ritrovato at the Cineteca del Comune di Bologna, which, incidentally, is also the Foundation's booking address) and the archive where original materials had been found. But with no explanation of the work involved, or even information about the screening formats, an opportunity was wasted to increase audiences' awareness of preservation work, the remit par excellence of the Cineteca Nacional, *and* of the World Cinema Foundation.

Most typically, the program about American filmmaker Alan Berliner was introduced on its website by the Cineteca itself in a short text, naming the organizations involved in setting up this event, while leaving the burden of characterizing Berliner's work to a quote, albeit incomplete, from the *New York Times*: "powerful and bittersweet, full of contradictions, innovative in their cinematic technique, unpredictable in its structures… Alan Berliner demonstrates the power of fine art to transform life." The more extensive text discussing Berliner's work somewhat more in depth in its program bulletin was written by a representative of one of the other co-organizers.

Clearly, the Cineteca Nacional de México works harder on its mission to extend its audience base than it does on providing relevant and substantial visitor information. It is not a stretch to suppose that here, as elsewhere, the volume of presentations exceeds its capacity to provide adequate and reliable information. Still, it is quite disheartening to see how little the institute itself has to say, whenever it does, and rather makes itself dependent on the opinions of others. Strengthening the country's audiovisual culture in a broad sense was, for now at least, rather a matter of quantity—filling its screens with a huge variety of films—than of quality.

Deutsches Filminstitut Filmmuseum, Frankfurt

In 2006, with the incorporation of the Deutsches Filmmuseum (founded in 1984) into the Deutsches Filminstitut (founded in 1949 as the Deutsches Institut für Filmkunde [DIF], changing its name in the meantime to Deutsches Filminstitut-DIF, in 1999) a film heritage institute emerged that includes the full range of tasks and activities: an archive of film and film-related collections, a library, a distribution department, and a museum consisting of two floors of gallery space for both permanent and simultaneous, temporary exhibitions, and a cinema theater where, besides regular programs, it also organizes or hosts film festivals. It has initiated, furthermore, filmportal.de, a database about "all German films", and administers the portal EFG1914, discussed in chapter 1. The institute is based in both Frankfurt and, c. 40 km westward, Wiesbaden (home of the film, film-related, and distribution collections as well as its restoration department). The Filminstitut Filmmuseum is financed from various public (federal, state, municipal) and private budgets (e.g. industry, TV). For larger projects additional funding is obtained.

Its permanent exhibition *Filmisches Sehen + Filmisches Erzählen* clearly is a showcase for the institute's collections, the film-related collections in particular. As a matter of fact, the Deutsches Filminstitut Filmmuseum is among a few in my set of film heritage institutes (together with the Cinemateca Portuguesa-Museu do Cinema; Cinémathèque française-Musée du Cinéma; Cinémathèque québécoise; Hong Kong Film Archive; and the National Film Center at the National Museum for Modern Art, Tokyo) where film-related objects are displayed either permanently or in regular exhibitions that highlight aspects of these collections. With the many touchable and operable objects *Filmisches Sehen + Filmisches Erzählen* shows an ambition to appeal to a large audience segment, including children. This may also betray an economic motive, what with the institute's single, small cinema theater (131 capacity—although it also makes use of a cinema theater, the 425 capacity Caligari Filmbühne, in Wiesbaden[290]). As its temporary exhibitions show, audience appeal may be a consideration, if not a requirement, for obtaining additional funding.

With its permanent and temporary exhibitions as crowd-pullers the institute is able to balance its presentations with a large variety of

---

[290] 'Deutsches Filminstitut Filmmuseum', at: *FIAF rapports annuels 2013* (2014), p. 3.

screenings, from early cinema to last year's highlights, from classics to experimental film. Of course, as not all of these programs can be expected to fill the house on a name basis it is through the series format and its additional, tailored publicity that the institute endeavors to find audiences for them. Apparently, it does not feel any pressure to show new releases, although it features one-off previews in its series *Was tut sich–im deutschen Film?* The relatively high number of screenings accompanied by personal introductions is another way in which the institute distinguishes itself from other cinema venues in the city.

See also: http://deutsches-filminstitut.de/en/

Summary of presentations:

• 1 permanent exhibition

Filmisches Sehen + Filmisches Erzählen covers both floors of the Filmmuseum and is designed as a route along thematic sections arranged under two umbrella themes, 'Filmic vision' and 'Filmic narrative'. The first is equipment-based and loosely historical, while the second is organized into formal sections, illustrated with film excerpts projected in HD. The exhibition offers the visitor, in the words of the institute, an "intensive engagement with the moving image" through a mix of screenings, objects either original or in replica—the latter are operable artifacts—, and interactive stations.

• 1 temporary exhibition

Fassbinder–Jetzt. Film und Videokunst (October 30, 2013-June 1, 2014) showed excerpts of the work of prolific German filmmaker Rainer Werner Fassbinder (1945-1982) juxtaposed with both contemporary and current video art. The exhibition was complemented with TV interviews, set photos, and other documents from the collections of the co-organizing Rainer Werner Fassbinder Foundation.

• 1 one-off

Kurzfilmprogramm (February 25), a compilation program of German animation and advertising films (by, among others, Walter Ruttmann and Julius Pinschewer), introduced by film historian Martin Loiperdinger (Trier University).

• 2 retrospectives

Fassbinder-Jetzt. Filmreihe (October 30, 2013–June 1, 2014) ran parallel with the abovementioned exhibition. Some of Fassbinder's films screened in February 2014 continued the exhibition's juxtaposition with newer work: the features ANGST ESSEN SEELE AUF (1973) and HÄNDLER DER VIER JAHRESZEITEN (1972) were both preceded by a more recent short film inspired by the first of these titles.

Kinohighlights 2013 (February 7-26) returned a selection of last year's favorite films to the screen for those who had missed them. Titles included, among others: APRÈS MAI; DIE ANDERE HEIMAT-CHRONIK EINER SEHNSUCHT; BLUE JASMINE; and GRAVITY.

• 3 series (As most of these series included in at least one of their presentations substantial personal appearances—lecture, conversation—, they are also events. However, as they are announced as series, I follow the institute's classification.)

Lecture & Film—Easier than painting: die Filme von Andy Warhol (February 6-26), an interdisciplinary series of lectures by scholars followed by screenings, in cooperation with the Frankfurt-based J.W. von Goethe University, Offenbach University of Art and Design, and Städelschule (a contemporary fine arts academy), under the umbrella of the Hessian Film- and Media Academy. The February edition of this series consisted of a lecture by Juliane Rebentisch (Offenbach University) on Andy Warhol's film INNER AND OUTER SPACE (1965), a double-screen, split screen film featuring Warhol muse Edie Segdwick and her dialogue with a video recording of herself as well with the "phantom existence of her own media trace"; the lecture was followed by said film, preceded by Warhol's SCREEN TEST #11. Each month, moreover, the institute also screens a number of films related to the lecture's theme; in February 2014 these were films on the "pop" culture of the time (PAINTERS PAINTING—THE NEW YORK ART SCENE: 1940-1970; BLOW UP; and BE KIND REWIND).

Was tut sich–im deutschen Film?: Gerhard Polt / Late Night Kultkino (February 7-22), a monthly, single screening with subsequent conversation about a current film, featuring in February 2014 writer-filmmaker-actor-satirist Gerhalt Polt and his latest film UND ÄKTSCHN! (2014), a satirical look at the worlds of high finance and the film industry. In this month, moreover, the program was expanded into a hommage, screening a selection of Polt's earlier films in the series *Late Night Kultkino*.

Klassiker & Raritäten: Ganz irdisch, ganz himmlisch–Christliche Orden im Spielfilm (February 11, 25), a four-part series of filmic representations of Christian orders, organized in cooperation with the Haus am Dom and the Institut für Stadtgeschichte. The February edition contained two feature fiction films shown on separate nights; the last screening was followed by a discussion.

Stummfilmmatinee (February 23), monthly screenings of silent films; in February STREET ANGEL (1928) was shown, albeit in a sound version, i.e. with a music track (during the transition to sound-on-film it was common for a while to distribute both sound and silent versions).

• 1 festival

Africa alive (January 30-February 6), featured a selection of recent and not so recent feature length and short films during the first week of the festival (which continued until February 23 at other venues).

Summary of information:

On its website the institute's permanent exhibition received the most lengthy description of all its presentations (as is customary with its exhibitions), detailing the sections into which the two umbrella themes were subdivided. 'Filmic vision' consisted of: 'the perception of moving images' and the various ways it was conceptualized and applied; 'curiosity' and optical illusion consists of original as well as operable, replicated equipment, such as peep-shows and kaleidoscopes; 'the generation of movement' through such devices as (operable) zoetropes, Praxinoscopes or flipbooks; 'exposure', about the technology of image retention; 'projection' is largely about the magic lantern; 'moving pictures' gives a brief overview of the equipment developed by people from such different professional backgrounds (although these differences were passed over by the institute) as Anschütz, Marey, Skladanowsky, or the Lumières—with an operable replica of the Cinématographe Lumière displayed next to an original one; 'cinema' concludes this theme with a few projected compilations of early cinema in an imitation theatrical setting. 'Filmic narrative' was arranged according to more formal, or stylistic, elements: 'performance' (costume and body language); 'sound' (particularly music, including an interactive station to find out how different musical scores affect an excerpted scene); 'editing and decoupage'; various phases and aspects of 'staging' (storyboards, sets); and 'cinematography' (camera angle, lighting, special effects, etc.). A 40' compilation brings all these aspects together in c. 100 film clips. By following the route of the exhibition, i.e. by breaking down the stylistic and material aspects of cinema and the technologies that it incorporated, its information is conceptually clear, matter-of-fact, and accessible without overloading the visitor (but while the institute publishes books and catalogues, no catalogue of this exhibition seems to be available to nuance the statements made in the exhibition or to serve the visitor who wants to know more). Blessedly, its web information avoided such misleading terms as *persistence of vision* or the teleological *pre-cinema.*

The introduction to the exhibition *Fassbinder–Jetzt. Film und Videokunst* stated its central idea of showing Fassbinder's work alongside that of video artists and, by thus highlighting thematic and aesthetic similarities and differences, the exhibition's aim to address the larger question of the influence of film on newer media. Showing Fassbinder's work beside works of younger 'film'-makers was continued in the accompanying retrospective by combining some—not all—of Fassbinder's features with short films that took inspiration from his work. However, as this was largely left unmentioned or uncommented in the program notes, which consisted of plot summaries only, the expected appeal of showing all of Fassbinder's films may well have prevailed over a more reflective or thematized approach.

Generally, information about the institute's film screenings was sparing and largely a matter of plot summaries. "Largely" here means that it was rather a matter of selectivity which programs received more and which less information. Films presumed well-known or easy to find information about, such as the ones selected for the recently released *Kinohighlights 2013* or Fassbinder's oeuvre, received mere summaries (with perhaps a one-sentence comment about one aspect or another), while titles or filmmakers presumed less known were given more extensive introductions and/or descriptions. This was the case for the ones screened in the lecture series *Easier than painting: die Filme von Andy Warhol* or the Gerhard Polt program in the series *Was tut sich–im deutschen Film?*. The fact that a number of programs was introduced or followed by a discussion may also have been a factor in deciding how much information was felt to be required. The institute, finally, is consistent in providing information about the formats of the prints screened.

Filmoteca de Catalunya, Barcelona

This film heritage institute was founded in 1981 and mandated to collect, preserve, research, and disseminate films and other audiovisual works, their related materials as well as equipment, with special emphasis on Catalan cinema (legal deposit is required for films and their publicity materials made by producers registered in Catalonia[291]). The Filmoteca is part of the Institut Català de les Empreses Culturals (ICEC), a public entity created by and accountable to the Department of Culture of the Catalan

[291] Biblioteca de Catalunya, 'Legal deposit', at:
http://www.bnc.cat/eng/Professionals/Legal-Deposit#faq1.

government. ICEC's mission is the promotion and economic and commercial development of the Catalan cultural sector as well as the dissemination of its culture. The Filmoteca's work is conceived as consisting of three basic activities: preservation and restoration (located at Terrassa, c. 20 km northwest of Barcelona); its library of books, journals, and other documentation (e.g. film-related collections, videotheque and sound archive, including those items of the collections that have been made digitally accessible); and the presentation of exhibitions and film screenings in its two auditoria (aggregate capacity 535). In addition, and an example of its task of promoting the Catalan film heritage, the Filmoteca shows parts of its programs at six other venues (Girona, Lleida, Manresa, Olot, Terrassa, and Vic) throughout the autonomous community of Catalonia.

The Filmoteca emphatically collects and shows regionally based film and film-related works—in that sense it resembles an equally self-consciously regional film heritage institute, the Cinémathèque québécoise. This may account, as in Quebec, for the more than average number of screenings featuring non-mainstream works. At the same time, it keeps an open eye, and mind, for international cinema as a context for its own cinema history.

Uncommonly many of its presentations are the fruit of cooperation with mostly local cultural or educational organizations (or, as its mission statement puts it, "civil society"), either regularly, in series, or on a one-time basis. The selection of films screened is adapted to the institute in question (e.g Museu Nacional d'Art de Catalunya, Design Museum of Barcelona or one of the city's film schools), from which the Filmoteca recruits an unusually large number of presenters and discussants. Hence, a high percentage of its screenings are bracketed by introductions, panel discussions, round tables, etc. by programmers, curators, professors or other experts as well as filmmakers and other people involved in one way or another in the work(s) in question.

See also: http://www.filmoteca.cat/web/

Summary of presentations:

• 1 temporary exhibition

Jacinto Esteva, a l'ombra de l'últim arbre (February 20-June 15), on the Catalan painter, architect, and filmmaker Jacinto Esteva Grewe (1936-1985), co-founder of the pop-art and French Nouvelle Vague-inspired Barcelona School, a network of young film directors in the early 1960s.

• 6 retrospectives

1714: història i identitats (August 10, 2013–September 11, 2014), a program about history and identity on the occasion of the tercentenary of the Siege of Barcelona (1713-1714), at the close of the Spanish Succession War (1701-1714).

Els millors films de l'any (December 6, 2013–February 28, 2014), a return to the screen of the best of the past year's films—or, because of contractual matters, commercial films released in late 2012.

Comèdia popular, un gènere a definir (December 12, 2013–March 31, 2014), an encouragement to define and reflect on the genre of the popular comedy, this month exemplified by, among others, KIND HEARTS AND CORONETS (1949), PASSPORT TO PIMLICO (1949), IL VEDOVO (1959), FOUR WEDDINGS AND A FUNERAL (1994) or LE GOÛT DES AUTRES (2000).

Orson Welles inèdit (February 12-13), on the occasion of the screening of a recently preserved film directed by Welles, TOO MUCH JOHNSON (1938), complemented by his first directed film as well as by Richard Linklater's fictional account of Welles's Mercury Theater, ME AND ORSON WELLES (2008).

Retrospectiva Jacinto Esteva (February 20-27), on the occasion of the abovementioned exhibition.

Goran Paskaljević, un gran director modest (February 21 - March 30), overview of this Serbian director's work.

• 7 series (As many of the screenings in these series are introduced by filmmakers or relevant experts, they overlap with events. However, as they are announced as series, I follow the Filmoteca's classification.) A number of its series is subsumed under a general title, 'Històries de Filmoteca'.

Clàssics d'ahir i de demà (February 19, 2012–ongoing), an examination of the phenomenon of the classic film, based on the notion of shifting values. In February 2014 the program in this series was a disguised retrospective, featuring a selection of films by Hollywood director Henry King.

Avui documental (February 23, 2012–ongoing), a series on documentary film. Its two screenings, DE OCCULTA PHILOSOPHIA (February 25) and AL FINAL DE LA VIDA (February 26), were introduced by their makers, director, scriptwriter, and critic Daniel V. Villamediana and filmmaker Carlos Benpar, respectively—the latter film coincided with the event *Carlos Benpar i THE TRIAL: 50 anys de cinema* (see below).

Disseny, càmera, acció! (October 3, 2013–June 27, 2014), a cooperation with DHUB-Museu del Disseny de Barcelona (Design Museum of Barcelona), monthly screenings of a film related to arts and industries, introduced by an expert. On February 6, the Philippine film TURUMBA (1981) was screened, on the crafts in a Philippine village and their neo-colonial exploitation, introduced by designer, teacher, and curator Uli Marchsteiner.

Educar a aprendre (October 3, 2013-ongoing), coorganized with l'Associació de Mestres Rosa Sensat (an organization for educational reform), aims to show how film has represented education. The February program consisted of two screenings of the British film IF... (1968), the first of which was introduced by educator Jaume Cela.

Per amor a l'art (October 12, 2013-ongoing), in collaboration with the Museu Nacional d'Art de Catalunya, is the sequel to *Per amor a l'art: cinema i pintura*, screenings of films that connect cinema with an artistic discipline, introduced by an expert. The February 2014 program consisted of THE PICTURE OF DORIAN GRAY (1945), introduced by film historian Rosa Gutiérrez; DIE STILLE VOR BACH (2007), introduced by its director Pere Portabella; BARRY LYNDON (1975), introduced by an employee of the Filmoteca's programming department; and THE AGONY AND THE ECSTASY (1964), introducer unknown.

L'ESCAC a la Filmo (October 31, 2013-June 26, 2014), monthly sessions of screenings and discussion in cooperation with the film school of the University of Barcelona.

Fantasmagories del desig (January 23-ongoing, but continued under the name *Cinema i psicoanàlisi*), monthly screenings on film and the subconscious and other psychoanalytic concepts. The February program consisted of two screenings of Canadian filmmaker Atom Egoyan's FELICIA'S JOURNEY, the first of which was introduced by film historian Mercè Coll.

L'Espai com a protagonista (February 20–ongoing), new series in collaboration with l'Arquinfad, an association for the promotion of interdisciplinary design in the decorative arts, screens monthly programs focusing on space as protagonist, introduced by a professional. The February program consisted of two screenings of THE MAN WHO SHOT LIBERTY VALENCE (1962), the first of which was introduced by architect Antoni de Moragas.

Aula de cinema, annual series in the shape of a film course, aimed at students of Barcelona universities and film schools as well as the general public to rediscover film history, subdivided into a number of categories and genres; the line-up of films appears to change with every new edition.

• 3 events

Dansa al cinema (February 4), special session on the occasion of the screening of COS A L'AIRE, PEUS A TERRE (BODY IN THE AIR, FEET ON THE GROUND), a new documentary by videomaker and electronic arts curator Núria Font, based on her long cooperation with the dance company Mal Pelo. Introduced and discussed by the company's founders, Pep Ramis and María Muñoz, and dancers. In cooperation with the Barcelona dance house Mercat de les Flors and l'Associació NU2's, Font's nonprofit organization to promote the use of digital media in dance works.

Special session *Homenatge a Joan Colom* (February 11), two films on the occasion of a retrospective exhibition *Jo faig el carrer. Joan Colom, fotografies 1957-2010* (I do the street. Joan Colom, photos 1957-2010) of this Catalan photographer at the Museu Nacional d'Art de Catalunya, introduced by the exhibition's commissioner David Balsells.

Cineastas en Acción (February 21), special session comprising three films by participants in Cineastas en Acción, an NGO that promotes cultural exchange between Africa and Europe through cinema in awareness campaigns in Spain and educational projects in Africa.

Session especial: Carlos Benpar i THE TRIAL: 50 anys de cinema (February 26), where this Catalan filmmaker discussed his fascination with Orson Welles's THE TRIAL (1962), about which he made the documentary AL FINAL DE LA VIDA (screened under the flag of the series *Avui documental*; see above); it was shown alongside Welles's film.

• 1 festival

Future shorts (February 7-8), a regular, trimonthly 'pop up' film festival with a selection of short films, including shorts culled from various festivals of the preceding months.

Summary of information:

Overall, it is difficult not to sense a lightness, sometimes even a hint of nonchalance, with regard to the visitor information the Filmoteca Catalunya provides. Most strikingly, its notes to the exhibition *Jacinto Esteva, a l'ombra de l'últim arbre* didn't even tell prospective visitors what the show contained. Similarly, though less glaringly nonchalant was the information to its retrospective *1714: història i identitats*, a program, begun in the summer of 2013, which commemorated and led up to the tercentenary of the end of the Siege of Barcelona (1713-1714)—ever since celebrated as the National Day of Catalonia (September 11). As the Filmoteca reports, at the basis of the program laid the question, "What happened in the world when the troops of Philip V besieged Barcelona between the summers of 1713 and 1714?" The result was a yearlong program of films old and new, set in both recent history (e.g. the creation of the state of Israel, in 1948; the military coup in Chile, 1973) and in more distant times, which presented a variety of reflections on the notion of identity. It was an unmistakably original, potentially rich idea. But what was problematic was that in its enthusiasm, certainly in its tolerance of so many manifestations of identity, the Filmoteca allowed the program to drift away from its sociopolitical moorings and the considerations it was born of. Its very lack of definition was self-defeating; it would have needed another term—for example, occupation, coercion, resistance or nationalism—to keep it within bounds. Throughout the series, films about Catalan history or colonialism made intuitive sense, because they connected identity with societal and political issues. Surely among the screenings in February 2014, THE JAZZ SINGER made sense, as one can imagine that the context of the program 'weighted' its racial theme at the expense of its family drama's generational conflict. But the screening of ÉS QUAN DORMO QUE HI VEIG CLAR (IT IS WHILE ASLEEP THAT I SEE CLEARLY), about the work and personality of Catalan poet J.V. Foix (the film's title is taken from one of his poems), seemed less pertinent.

In other instances, however, the program notes' lightness may rather be seen as a refusal to take up a superior stance. This attitude was most prominent in its information about the retrospective *Comèdia popular, un gènere a definir*. Even though the Filmoteca suggested a number of sensible—not necessarily concurrent—characteristics of the popular comedy, such as its collective protagonist, its ability to portray an era or a generation, in the end it undercut these worthwhile suggestions by stating that "popular comedy is comedy", and what matters most is that it makes you laugh. And with the facetious phrase that the exercise of the zygomatic muscles will improve neuronal connections it suggested that the spectator should laugh and reflect—and, by implication, draw his own conclusions. Sympathetic, and self-evident, as this may seem, one continues to wonder what the Filmoteca's own idea and intention were in mounting this program.

As many screenings, particularly those that are part of a series, would be contextualized by presenters, the Filmoteca usually refrained from interpretative angles in its plot summaries and simply listed the main story events and an anecdotal detail or two (or relied, in some cases, on quoted excerpts from other texts). Indeed, the odd attempt at a more evaluative comment, as in describing Orson Welles's "magnificence" as a matter of "memorable long takes", "expressionist angles", "expressive close-ups", got stuck in unexpressive terminology and was not very illuminating.

Finally, when program notes did not state the format in which films are shown (many are shown in one digital format or another), one may infer that 16 or 35mm prints were screened.

Fondazione Centro Sperimentale di Cinematografia-Cineteca Nazionale, Rome

Established by law in 1949, the Centro Sperimentale di Cinematografia consists of two branches: a film heritage institute consisting of the Cineteca Nazionale, in Rome, and, since 2005, the Archivio Nazionale del Cinema d'Impresa (ANCI), in Ivrea, where its collections of industrial and advertising films have found a home; the other branch is a film school, the Scuola Nazionale del Cinema, which has locations in four regions. Another part, CSC Production, was founded to support these film schools' students and graduates and monitor new audiovisual projects.

Thanks to the establishment of legal deposit the Cineteca Nazionale is one of the largest national film archives. In 2004, the 1949 legal deposit act was extended to include written and printed film-related matters.[292] It is therefore no surprise—confirmed by a quick scan of the overview on the Cineteca's website of programs screened since 2009—to find that Italian films prevail in its one auditorium, Cinema Trevi. Or more precisely, Italian feature fiction films prevail, often screened in (commemorative) retrospectives of directors or performers. What is striking about these programs is their compactness. This seems to be the result of the theater's custom of three daily, coherent screenings. It is no exception, therefore, to come across retrospectives that last only a day or two; the longest program in February 2014, the thematic retrospective *Italia '77: ultimo atto?*, lasted only nine days, yet contained no less than 24 films (the theater is closed on Mondays).

The theater's custom conduces to the blurring, mentioned earlier, of the formats of event and retrospective. Whenever there is a discussion or conversation, the three daily screenings that surround it are all devoted to the topic in question (see the events mentioned below). But when no personal appearance accompanies a day's screenings of films on the same

---

[292] Arianna Turci, 'Archivio Nazionale Cinema d'Impresa collections: an overview', in: Florin, de Klerk, Vonderau (2016), pp. 289, 296 n.1

topic, it seems to have become, if only in default of another format name, a (mini)-retrospective. This is the case, for instance, for a brief program of three films titled (*In)visibile italiano: fuori dal '77*, shown on February 14, which was announced as an antithesis to the retrospective program *Italia '77: ultimo atto?*, a week before the latter program began.

Besides the small Cinema Trevi (just 91 seats) the Cineteca has a colossal distribution collection for screenings elsewhere; its online catalogue contains a long list of fiction films made between the 1910s and the 2000s. What, of course, is harder to replicate at other venues are the contextualizations the institute provides through its characteristic events. Indeed, many are the meetings and discussions it organizes with filmmakers, performers, critics, academics, and other experts on the occasion of its presentations. However, a selection of these events has been recorded and uploaded on its YouTube channel to serve as an additional source of information (those of February 2014 are referenced below). Furthermore, a separate web channel has been launched, Cinemaimpresa.TV, which contains digitized materials from ANCI, featuring a fast-growing number of commercials and industrials made for Italian companies (e.g. Birra Peroni, FIAT, Olivetti, Piaggio).[293] The Cinema Trevi venue also hosts festivals and traveling programs; as a rule it does not show newly released films.

Two final, brief remarks. First of all, a number of the Cineteca's screenings are free of charge, and often indirectly sponsored by commercial parties, notably distributors and production companies. Secondly, credits and information on print formats and sources are virtually absent, even though it is safe to assume that many of its films come from the institute's vaults and may well be screened in their original exhibition formats.

See also:
http://www.fondazionecsc.it/ct_home.jsp?ID_LINK=7&area=6

Summary of presentations:

• 5 retrospectives

Omaggio ad Ashgar Farhadi (February 1-2), a touring program, organized by the Cineteca de Bologna, of films by this Iranian filmmaker.

---

[293] '*Cinemaimpresa.TV*', at: https://www.youtube.com/user/cinemaimpre satv.

Fratelli nel cinema (February 8-9), program of Italian sibling-filmmakers, this month featuring the brothers Camerini (Mario and Augusto) and Risi (Dino and Nelo).

In ricordo di Emidio Greco (February 11-13), commemorating this Italian film and television director, who died in December 2012.

Italia '77: ultimo atto? (February 20-28), announced as the first leg of a program of Italian films made at the time of the rise of the Movimento del '77, an agglomeration of extra-parliamentary leftist and feminist movements that opposed the institutionalized political parties and trade unions and were committed to more spontaneous direct action. Riots and clashes with police resulting in casualties radicalized factions of the movement into taking up arms, setting off a spiral of violence over the next few years. The films, made in various registers, are complemented by a few made decades later that reflect on these turbulent times. Various events with invited filmmakers, performers, screenwriters, and academics who discussed the films and the contemporary political climate they represent.[294]

(In)visibile italiano: fuori dal '77 (February 14), preceding the aforementioned retrospective, the Cineteca showed a brief program of three Italian films also made in 1977 that eschewed the then current political climate and set their stories in history.

• 4 series

Cinema e psicoanalisi: le forme della violenza (February 15), monthly screenings organized with the Società Psicoanalitica Italiana, which during this season focused on the theme of violence. Three screenings, of which PADRE PADRONE (1977) is probably the most well-known title, framed by a conversation with psychoanalyst Fabrizio Rocchetto.

Cineteca Classic. Dalla Polonia con amore (February 16), part of an ongoing series in which a number of Polish filmmakers, among other topics, were featured. In February 2014, two films by Jerzy Skolimowski were screened, even though both were made outside Poland during his exile —in the UK (MOONLIGHTING, 1982) and the US (THE LIGHTSHIP, 1985), respectively.

---

[294] See: '*Italia '77: ultimo atto?*, *Cinema Trevi, 20 febbraio 2014*', at: https://www.youtube.com/watch?v=B24hq8_rwsU&list=UUAaQOi9Mi9lrG6RHVex kbjQ.

L'infanzia dei generi (February 16), a series of nine silent genre films with live musical accompaniment, featuring in February 2014 THE LODGER (1926).

Incontro con il cinema Sardo a Roma (February 18-19), series of screenings of and talks about Sardinian cinema, which focused this month on two personalities, actress Marisa Solinas and director Salvatore Mereu.[295] This brief program included two events featuring each of these personalities, where they talked with other filmmakers, performers, critics, etc. Incidentally, the event featuring actress Marisa Solinas within the series was rather puzzling insofar as her presence didn't make much sense within the context of the program, except for the fact that her father was Sardinian. As far as her career was concerned, she had appeared only in foreign and mainland Italian productions, while none of the films screened had anything to do with Sardinia; indeed, one was shot in Barcelona, the other in Rome.

• 4 events

L'effetto del jazz. Lo Swing Club di Torino (February 4), meeting on the occasion of the publication of actor Toni Bertorelli's book *L'effeto del jazz*, with screenings of three Italian films about the Italian jazz scene.

Sergio Leone. Il cinema come favola politica (February 5), presentation of the book *Sergio Leone. Il cinema come favola politica* by film scholar Christian Uva (also curator of the program *Italia '77: ultimo atto?*), preceded by Leone's last western, GIÙ LA TESTA (1971); no information was provided about the short drama that followed the book launch, MARION, ARTISTA DI CAFFÈ-CONCERTO (1920), particularly with regard to its connection, if any, with the topic of Sergio Leone.

La voce e il cinema: Arnoldo Foà attore cinematografico (February 6), in memory of actor Arnoldo Foà, who died in January 2014, a conversation with relatives and critic Alessandro Ticozzi, as well as the presentation of his book *La voce e il cinema: Arnoldo Foà attore cinematografico*; screening of three films featuring Foà.

Carlo Rambaldi, il mago (February 7), a conversation with cineaste Victor Rambaldi in memory of his father, special effects "magician" and three-

---

[295] See: '*Incontro con Salvatore Mereu, Cinema Trevi, 19 febbraio 2014*', at: https://www.youtube.com/watch?v=AV3Ef88ca-U&list=UUAaQOi9Mi9lrG6RHVexkbjQ.

time Academy Award winner Carlo Rambaldi, who died in August 2012, bracketed by three American films on which Rambaldi, Sr. worked, viz. KING KONG 2 (1986)—even though Rambaldi won a Special Achievement Academy Award for the same director's KING KONG of 1976; E.T., THE EXRA-TERRESTRIAL (1982), for which he designed the Oscar-winning title character; and DUNE (1984).

Summary of information:

Typically, the introductions to its programs on the Cineteca Nazionale's website, although uneven in quality, are consistently compact. It shows a preference for communicating the most basic idea underlying the program in question. For example: "in his films, the pace of modernity in Iran is disrupted and slowed down by traditions that refuse to cede their place" (*Omaggio ad Ashgar Farhadi*); or "a cinema that is only apparently remote from reality and the present, because in truth it is a cinema that interrogates itself and appropriates the doubts of modern man, confronted with the restrictions of a society that has lost the values he believed in" (*In ricordo di Emidio Greco*). Occasionally such a summary way of providing visitor information led to stating the obvious, as in: "the aggressive aspects of our personality (...) are considered fundamental by psychoanalysts for our instincts and our unconscious" (*Cinema e psicoanalisi: le forme della violenza*). There is a sympathetic aspect to this insofar as it allows spectators to 'test' the films against such statements. But it also an approach that is removed from the actual works; it lacks, moreover, even the merest hint of an archival dimension.

In fact, the latter point suggests a more general issue, as one gets the sense that the Cineteca's public information doesn't seem to fully engage with what it presents. Apart from readymade information quoted from websites or reviews incorporated in both its introductions and plot summaries; and apart even from the fortunate circumstance that it could quote from the very books that were launched during one of its events—all of which constituted ever so many opportunities waived, as we have seen more often, to promote its own ideas or considerations at some length—, visitor information for the Cineteca's own curated programs somehow seemed disconnected from what it actually showed. Coming back once more to the retrospective *Fratelli nel cinema*, its brief introduction stated that the many films made by siblings is indicative of Italy's "artisanal cinema", but in the plot summaries quoted from other sources nothing suggesting that notion returned. The statement, therefore, left one wondering whether one could actually tell this artisanal quality from the films screened, as they were all produced in an industrial context, some made by established studios (e.g. Lux, Cines). The curator's concluding remark that this program would allow one "to better understand the importance of human relations, personal and familial, for the development and quality of [Italian] cinema"—another instance of a basic, underlying idea—didn't really answer that question.

It is clear, however, that the Cineteca attaches more importance to the conversations and round tables (and their uploaded recordings) for informing its public. These events often drew on promoted publications, which, in fact, must have been planned in tandem with a program. For instance, at one event during *Italia '77: ultimo atto?*, a special issue was presented of the Italian interdisciplinary journal *Cinema e Storia*, titled 'Italia 1977: crocevia di un cambiamento' ('Italy '77: crossroads of change'), entirely devoted to the topic of the Movimento del '77. However, as none of the contributors to the special issue, except the program's curator, was quoted in its public information, one may conclude that only a fraction of the knowledge that went into the producing the issue was reflected in the texts on the Cineteca's website.

Hong Kong Film Archive

The Hong Kong Film Archive was established in 1993 as a Planning Office, by the then Urban Council, to preserve films and film-related materials and organizing publications and presentations. After the Council's dissolution, in December 1999 (as part of the reorganization of Hong Kong's administration after the transfer of sovereignty from Britain to China, in 1997), the Film Archive became a subsidiary of the Leisure and Cultural Services Department (LCSD) of the Government of the Hong Kong Special Administrative Region (SAR). Besides the Film Archive, the LCSD manages seven museums.

Since the transition the major tasks of the archive's mandate are to acquire, preserve, catalogue and document Hong Kong films and related materials; in accordance with this mandate the Hong Kong Film Archive publishes an astonishing amount of books, catalogues, and DVDs. Yet film programs and exhibitions continue to play a prominent role in its activities. This is reflected in the five-storey building into which it moved in 2001, where its archival and public functions have been equally divided over the 7,200m^2 floor area: state-of-the-art storage space on one side, office and public access functions (i.e. cinema theater, exhibition space, resource center) on the other.

The Hong Kong Film Archive's exhibitions (free of admission whenever there is one) and its cinema (125 capacity) are open to the public six days a week. Its presentations reflect the stupendous heritage of the Hong Kong film industry, given the size of the territory—just over 1,100km²—and its population—now close to 7.5 million; its collections are largely the result of donations and voluntary deposits. As a result of mainland China's occupation by Japan, Hong Kong's film industry soared during the 1930s, most particularly with the rise of the Cantonese-spoken genre of the martial arts film. And even though foreign imports still exceed local production, most of the Film Archive's screenings are devoted to the genre films made by Hong Kong companies and to films about Hong Kong by foreign filmmakers. It is mainly in its series *Restored treasures* that, besides restorations by its own archive, a significant number of foreign films is being shown.

Whereas some program notes often explicitly state a commitment to film as an art form, in much of its information the Film Archive emphasizes the relevance of societal considerations, too. In fact, the introductory text on its homepage clearly states that it sees its task as "[promoting] the preservation of Hong Kong cinematic culture. Film is not only a medium of mass entertainment but also a witness to societal changes. On the film strip are myriad faces of our society such as our history, economic environment, people's lifestyle, social trends and political events." Not many film heritage institutes formulate their remit in such a wide sense.

See also:
http://www.lcsd.gov.hk/CE/CulturalService/HKFA/en_US/web/hkfa/aboutus/intro.html

Summary of presentations:

• 1 temporary exhibition

Down Memory Lane: movie theatres of the olden days (December 6, 2013–March 2, 2014) transformed the institute's exhibition space into a composite cinema lobby of bygone days, showcasing a mix of objects to be found in lobbies between the 1930s and 1960s.

• 3 retrospectives

Transcending space and time: early cinematic experience of Hong Kong (January 4-March 23), comprising four groups of films: 'Cityscape in early moving images', with screenings of HKFA's most valuable treasures; 'Pioneer filmmaker Hou Yao', a retrospective on this versatile, mainland

Chinese filmmaker, who moved to Hong Kong in the 1930s; 'Rediscovering pioneering females in early Chinese cinema', commemorating forgotten female filmmakers from the early years; and 'Grandview's cross-border productions', featuring films produced by Hong Kong's Grandview Film Company when it shifted production to the United States from 1939 to 1948. The silent films of the program were accompanied with live music.

Double happiness comes galloping in (January 25–February 14), four Lunar New Year films, a staple of Hong Kong cinema, that reflected shifting societal and family values between 1959 and 1986.

A myriad of charm: in commemoration of Hung Sin Nui (February 15–March 23), commemorating Cantonese Opera artist Hung Sin Nui (1927-2013).

• 3 series

100 must-see Hong Kong movies (since October 2011–ongoing), multiple screenings of films made throughout the 20th century in or about Hong Kong, at the Film Archive's premises as well as at Broadway Cinematheque, in the Yau Tsim Mong District of Hong Kong, a venue recently included for this particular program in order to broaden the institute's audience base, younger people in particular.

Morning matinee (since June 4, 2010-ongoing), this month featuring *Yu Lai-zhen, queen of the art of Dan* (January 3-February 28), commemorating the tenth anniversary of the death of Yu Lai-zhen, star of opera, martial arts films as well as of contemporary dramas.

Restored treasures (since April 2, 2010-ongoing), featuring *Digitally restored gems from China* (February 2–April 6), showing international films restored at the Hong Kong Film Archive as well as at other film heritage institutes and companies (e.g. Criterion) worldwide. The films in this program partly overlapped with the programs *Transcending time and space* and *100 must-see Hong Kong movies* "in order to inspire further dialogues between Mainland China and Hong Kong". The program included events in the shape of post-screening talks

• 2 events

Seminar Hou Yao and his films, free seminar on the occasion of the screenings in the retrospective program *Transcending space and time: early cinematic experience of Hong Kong*. The seminar was conducted in Cantonese; other events occasioned by this program were either in English or bi-lingual.

Seminar 'Digital restoration strategies of China Film Archive', on the occasion of the program *Digitally restored gems from China*.

Summary of information:

Judging from its rather brief description, *Down Memory Lane: movie theatres of the olden days* was in fact the only exhibition in the survey in which original film-related objects or their replicas (photos, handbills, souvenir programs, movie tickets, seating plans, a ticket-operated weighing machine, etc.) were displayed in an environment—a decor of a theater lobby—for which they had been meant. Extensive descriptions (or labeling), therefore, would have been superfluous, since this was above all an experience, an opportunity for visitors to "immerse themselves in nostalgia", with familiar objects from the 1930s to the 1960s.[296] It made sense, then, that visitors were informed specifically about one of the exhibition's highlights: six huge, redrawn movie posters, for which the institute asked a distinguished poster artist to come temporarily out of retirement. However, in contrast to the institute's website, its press release also announced that the exhibition provided information about "the development of Hong Kong theatres, various cinema circuits and the alliances of film distributors and production companies." As no catalogue or other publication was mentioned on the Film Archive's website, one is left to wonder how this information was communicated in the exhibition.

Visitor information about most of its retrospectives was concise. The program 'Pioneer filmmaker Hou Yao', for instance, as part of *Transcending space and time: early cinematic experience of Hong Kong*, was introduced with a biographical sketch connecting Hou's life to contemporary, turbulent political circumstances (notably Japan's invasion of China, in the early 1930s) as well as his own brief political career, how he moved from being a playwright to a film director, in the 1920s, and his eventual relocation to Hong Kong (and, later, Singapore), in the 1930s. The descriptions of the program's four films mixed the most important plot elements with information about style, memorable moments in a performance to watch out for, source materials (and in what ways they differ from the films), or the films' relevance for today's spectators. In other words, its information touched many bases, thereby efficiently

---

[296] Additional information about objects displayed and the time period the exhibition covers, as well as the quotation, come from the Hong Kong Film Archive's press release: '"Movie theaters of the olden days" exhibition opens at HK Film Archive', (December 6, 2013).

setting up an interpretative framework that went beyond the films as projected. In *Double happiness comes galloping in*, descriptions focused rather on how each of the four Lunar New Year films, made over a period of almost three decades, "reflects the difference in societal and family values across generations."

Its series *100 must-see Hong Kong movies*, begun in the fall of 2011, is representative of the transparency that characterizes much (certainly not all, given Hong Kong's precarious political situation) of the Film Archive's information. The series covers Hong Kong's film heritage of the 20th century. The decision to place the series' cut-off point at the turn of the century, the institute says, had several reasons: it "provides some historical distance to the selection process. Also, movies are the dominant art form of the last century and Hong Kong films in this century have experienced a development very different from that of the last." Although covering the entire century, the main impetus for the series was to change a "misguided perception" about the films made before the so-called "Golden Age of the 1980s". While "historical significance" (albeit unspecified) played a role in the selection of films for the series, artistic considerations prevailed: "[c]inema, despite its ready capacity for entertainment, is an art form. (...) It is therefore paramount that the people of Hong Kong should have a better understanding and appreciation of our cinema's amazing accomplishments." The series' visitor information also listed the "panel of experts" on the series' selection committee.

The institute's consideration of matters archival was explicitly evident in the series *Restored treasures*, internationally oriented in its selection of films and their various ways of restoring them to life, but also in the attention to details, particularly the consistency with which it provided information about print formats and sources.

Irish Film Institute, Dublin

Established in 1945, the Irish Film Institute (IFI) is a company limited by guarantee with a charitable status that is partly funded from public money through the country's Arts Council. According to the figures for 2014 published on its website, this subsidy of €750,000 covers 25% of its annual costs—c. €3,000,000—to deliver the institute's core activities. Additional income is generated "by IFI Commercial [IFI Café Bar and IFI Film Shop].... and through cultural partners and sponsors."[297]

The IFI sees its core business as consisting of preservation, education, and exhibition. Being Ireland's national institute for cinema it collects and preserves historically, socially, and culturally relevant materials that reflect the country's visual record, most particularly its domestic moving image production in all known genres, many of which are educational and information films produced by the National Film Institute, IFI's forerunner. Digitized film-related materials from its collections of documents, posters, and stills are selectively uploaded at its online exhibitions. Its educational programs are largely aimed at schools, both at its own premises and through touring programs. Its on-site film screenings consist of a mix of "the best of international and Irish film culture"; international cinema comes to the IFI mostly through releases and festivals.

IFI also operates internationally by providing contextualized programs of Irish cinema abroad; in order to achieve this, Culture Ireland, an organization for the promotion of Irish arts abroad through funding and other means, is an important cultural partner.

In its current form, the institute was opened in 1992. Its premises reflect, on one hand, its national mandate, with storage and research facilities. On the other, it is also an arthouse cinema in whose three auditoria (aggregate capacity 422) materials from its film collection as well as new releases and retrospectives are being shown, together with the festivals that it organizes or hosts at regular intervals.

See also: http://www.ifi.ie

Summary of presentations:

• 13 releases

IFI's releases came in a number of distinctive, mainly publicity-led variations. There were 'ordinary' releases—12 YEARS A SLAVE (January 10-February 6); AUGUST: OSAGE COUNTY (January 24-February 20); INSIDE LLEWYN DAVIS (January 24-February 20); JOURNAL DE FRANCE (January 31-February 6); OUT OF THE FURNACE (January 31-February 13); DALLAS BUYERS CLUB (February 7-27); STRANGER BY THE LAKE (L'INCONNU DU LAC) (February 21-27); HER (14-27

---

[297] Irish Film Institute, 'Financial statement for the year ended 31 December 2014' (May 9, 2015), p. 6.

February), screenings of which were preceded by the IFB-funded short, ON DEPARTURE, by Eoin Duffy; while ONLY LOVERS LEFT ALIVE (February 14, 21-28), was included in a special Valentine's Day screening. BASTARDS (LES SALAUDS) was announced as being screened "exclusively" at the IFI (February 14-20), with a French Film Club screening on February 19. And there were IFI Classic releases, also exclusive: LIFT TO THE SCAFFOLD (ASCENSEUR POUR L'ÉCHAFAUD) (February 7-13), THE GODFATHER PART II (February 21-23, 26), and FUNNY FACE (from February 28). Finally, a one-time back-to-back screening on the premiere night of NYMPH()MANIAC, VOLUME I & VOLUME II (from February 28). All releases had a predetermined run.

• 2 retrospectives

Sex&drugs&rock&roll (February 1-27), second leg of a three-part retrospective on excess, with February's program focusing on drugs, largely made up of Americans films; the program included among others THE MAN WITH THE GOLDEN ARM (1955), THE CONNECTION (1962), UP IN SMOKE (1978) as well as the German-made CHRISTIANE F. (1981).

William Klein (February 14-20), small retrospective, co-organized by IFI and the 2014 edition of the Jameson Dublin International Film Festival (JDIFF), of the widely divergent film oeuvre of this famous photographer. The program also featured an event on February 20, when Klein appeared for a Q&A. Because IFI was one of the venues of the festival, only three of William Klein's films were screened at its premises, while three other films screened elsewhere.

• 8 series

Arrive at lunchtime: Double bill (throughout February), featuring two programs of free, usually short (i.e. under 30') lunchtime screenings of films from the IFI's collections. The two were shown back-to-back on Saturdays, while each program was screened separately on Mondays and Wednesdays. Program 1 consisted of a 1974 documentary about pre-marriage courses from IFI's huge Radharc collection (*Radharc*—Gaelic for "view", "vision" or "panorama"—is the title of a documentary series broadcast by Irish television between 1962 and 1996); program 2 had a sports theme and consisted of an Oscar-nominated romantic short set in the world of hurling and camogie (two variants, for men and women, respectively, of an Irish sport, a cross between field hockey and lacrosse) and a short documentary on trapeze artists.

Ireland on Sunday, IFI's monthly showcase for new Irish films, featuring this month BABYGIRL, the second feature from writer-director Macdara

Vallely and winner of Best Irish Feature at Jameson Dublin International Film Festival 2013.

From the vaults, another archival program (though not necessarily programmed from IFI's own vaults). In February it screened I WAS HAPPY HERE, the second feature in the trilogy of writer Edna O'Brien's works directed by Desmond Davis.

IFI & Experimental Film Club, with a screening of Pip Chodorov's feature-length documentary FREE RADICALS—A HISTORY OF EXPERIMENTAL FILMS, about avant-garde cinema, including interviews with Stan Brakhage, Jonas Mekas, Peter Kubelka, and others, and film excerpts. [event]: Introduced and discussed by the filmmaker.

IFI Family, monthly screenings of films for the entire family, children in particular, featuring this month THE RETURN OF THE PINK PANTHER.

Feast your eyes, a monthly "gastronomic feature", which screened in February the Czech avantgarde classic DAISIES (1966), preceded by the short recipe film WINTER PIZZA, from www.forkful.tv. The screening was followed by a meal (menu published on the website) at the IFI Café Bar.

Wild strawberries (February 26, 28), IFI's bi-monthly film club for over 55s screened Gus Van Sant's PROMISED LAND, announced as a "thought-provoking drama" of corporations attempting to buy up land cheaply for fracking, and recommended as being relevant for communities all over Ireland.

Evening course 'Heroic gestures' (February 4–March 11), a six-week evening course on the hero in film, which included screenings of MANDELA: LONG WALK TO FREEDOM (2013); MALCOLM X (1992); BERNADETTE: NOTES ON A POLITICAL JOURNEY (2011; on Bernadette Devlin-McAliskey, former Ulster republican political activist); BROTHER (BRAT, 2013; on Russian cosmonaut Yuri Gagarin); and PINK FLAMINGOS (1972). Each film was introduced by another speaker.

• 1 event

preview NYMPH()MANIAC, VOLUME I & VOLUME II (February 22), a "[o]ne night stand" screening marking the British release of this film, bracketed with a live transmission from the Curzon Chelsea cinema in London where members of the cast Stellan Skarsgård, Stacey Martin, and Sophie Kennedy-Clark introduced each of the two volumes, followed by a post-screening Q&A.

• 1 festival

Reel Art (February 18-19), two screenings, both world premeries, of the festival Reel Art, an Arts Council scheme (showcased by IFI and JDIFF) that provides film artists the "opportunity to make highly creative, imaginative and experimental documentaries on an artistic theme." Films shown were THE DEVIL'S POOLS: MADNESS, MELANCHOLIA AND THE ARTIST (February 18) and A VISION: A LIFE OF W.B. YEATS (February 19).

Summary of information:

For an institute that has to generate a turnover of more than €3 million to cover operating costs, which includes 60 employees, it makes economic sense to structure its program largely by means of releases—of both new films and classics—and series that target niche audiences of very different feathers (e.g. lovers of experimental film, families with children, over-55s). Other ways to draw audiences were its special Valentine's Day package, consisting of a preview of a future release followed by a two-course dinner in the institute's cafe (when copying this information in early February this occasion was already sold out); its monthly combined screening and dinner in the gastronomic film series *Feast your eyes;* or the hook-up with the Curzon Chelsea for the 'borrowed event' of the British premiere of the widely publicized film NYMPH()MANIAC, the only opportunity to see the films' two "volumes" back-to-back.

With regard to its releases, IFI stated that these films "would not otherwise have a theatrical release", or even "would not otherwise be seen in Ireland". The quoted phrase implicitly refers to the eleven distribution companies that operate in Ireland and suggests that they do not adequately service the country's theatrical audiences. Indeed, seven of these are subsidiaries of American majors, while three of the four independent companies largely distribute British and American films; only one focuses quite prominently on Irish films.[298] IFI's releases, then, do fulfill a complementary function, with four French titles and one European co-production in February alone. The popularity of and publicity for such films as 12 YEARS A SLAVE, INSIDE LLEWYN DAVIS or ONLY LOVERS LEFT ALIVE, the last two made by established star directors of the arthouse circuit, would be expected to draw large numbers of spectators from a certain audience segment. No wonder, then, that among its 13

[298] Irish Film Board, 'Irish distributors', at:
http://www.irishfilmboard.ie/festivals_and_distribution/distributors/.

releases the abovementioned films were scheduled for a much longer period—three to four weeks—than the French (re-)releases, which all played for a single week (although one would think that two of their directors, Louis Malle and Claire Denis, were not unknown in those circles either). Since August 2014, spurred, perhaps, by ending the run of 12 YEARS A SLAVE before it won an Oscar for Best Film at the Academy Awards, IFI has added "a greater degree of flexibility" by announcing the screening of its new releases and IFI Classics on a weekly basis rather than for a predetermined period.

IFI's visitor information about its releases was of a kind with the commercial considerations that determines its programming schedule to a large extent. Most of it was promotional (epitomized by copying print and web reviews' star-ratings), foregrounding plot summaries followed by brief comments on cast, performance, direction or source material, which were more often than not non-committal fillers (as in "the cast [...] more than do the material justice" [AUGUST: OSAGE COUNTY]; "[Depardon's] work is celebrated as brilliant and vital" [JOURNAL DE FRANCE]; "HER might just be Spike Jonze's finest film to date"—apparently the jury was still out on this one). As a matter of fact, this way of informing its audiences characterized all its programs, regardless whether the material came from its archive or not. Here and there, the information appeared to underestimate even specific target audiences, as when it stated in its introduction to the screening in the series *IFI & Experimental Film Club* that the featured documentary is an "introduction to one of the most important, yet perpetually marginalised, realms of filmmaking: avant-garde cinema". Hopefully, visitors with a more than average interest may learn more at the regular, free, and open-to-all film club meetings IFI frequently organizes under the name *The Critical Take*.

Film historically speaking, its information did certainly not match the institute's stature in the country and its mission "to provide opportunities for audiences (...) to learn and critically engage with film." In the introduction to its mission's most explicit elaboration, the course *Heroic gestures*, the reader was taken in a mere three sentences from Greece to Shakespeare to the bank robbers and cowboys of early cinema, and, "later", the blockbuster's action hero. As a 'historical overview' this was futile stuff, as no films from the era of early cinema were shown nor did the featured films consist of genuine blockbusters, MALCOLM X excepted perhaps. And while the speakers who introduced these films would no doubt have provided the opportunities to learn and engage, the website's visitor information offered no inkling whatsoever of what the course would be about.

Its retrospective *Sex&drugs&rock&roll* was announced as "three months of seasons dedicated to excess, presenting examples of how cinema has taken on sex, drugs and rock`n'roll". However, the central term "excess" was not really developed. In its February program, on drugs, the summary for SCARFACE (1983) rather mentioned its "ruthless use of *extreme violence*" (my italics). Again, this film program turned out a to be a popular success,[299] but the triviality of its information was another missed opportunity. And with respect to Ireland's own filmmaking history, not all its programs could be said to be accompanied sufficiently by "historically, socially, and culturally relevant" contextualizations. *Arrive at lunchtime* series, which specifically featured films from its collections, got the briefest of synopses or summaries with no substantial or relevant additional information. However, IFI's FIAF 2013 report tells us that screenings in its other archival series, *From the vaults*, are introduced "by IFI staff, filmmakers, academics and other informed commentators".[300] Finally, IFI provides minimal credits, while print formats are mentioned inconsistently.

Jerusalem Cinematheque-Israel Film Archive

The Jerusalem Cinematheque-Israel Film Archive was founded in 1981, the outcome of the combined private initiatives of the Jerusalem Foundation, the Ostrovsky Family Foundation, and the Van Leer Group Foundation. It is funded from national (Ministry of Science, Culture & Sport) and municipal (the city of Jerusalem) budgets as well as by private sponsoring; of its total budget, the equivalent of c. US$ 750,000, some 40% comes from earned income (2014 figures).

The institute's Israeli Film Archive is the officially designated repository of Israeli cinema; the 1999 Cinema Law requires that of every film supported by an Israeli fund a copy must be deposited at the archive. However, the archive also collects, preserves, and catalogues international cinema. This policy may well support, if not express, the institute's humanist mission: promoting "the universal language of cinema" in the "education and quest for tolerance, peace, and freedom" and a commitment "to maintain openness and pluralism". It is certainly reflected in the wide variety of films in its programs. Nevertheless, it leans

---

[299] Irish Film Institute (May 29, 2015), p. 3.

[300] 'Irish Film Archive 2013', at: *FIAF rapports annuels 2013* (2014), p. [3].

rather heavily one way, as a significant part of its screenings consists of both domestic and international cinema and TV productions about Jewish history, particularly the 20th-century diaspora and the state of Israel.

The institute's Jerusalem Film Festival, established in 1984, amplifies its mission by combining Israeli and international features and documentaries alongside such sections as 'The Jewish experience', dealing with questions of Jewish identity, and 'In the Spirit of Freedom' (after which the festival's award has been named), concerned with questions of freedom and human rights.[301] The Cinematheque also hosts the Jerusalem Jewish Film Festival, which was established in 1999. This festival collects an international lineup of films of all genres that "explore themes of Jewish faith and practice, history, culture, music, the Holocaust, contemporary life in Israel and the Jewish Diaspora, the relationship between Judaism and other world religions and the role of Jewish identity in the State of Israel. (...) A special sub-theme on the Holocaust, which springs from the work of the Joan Sourasky-Constantiner Holocaust Multimedia Reaserch Center, is a key part of the Festival's program."[302] This research center, a privately funded initiative of Leon Constantiner, of a Mexican Jewish family of philanthropists and crusaders for Jewish causes, is devoted to the "research, acquisition, cataloguing and preservation of films and film material related to the Holocaust" and has actually been made part of the institute.

The Cinematheque's four auditoria (aggregate capacity 796) make for a busy schedule of screenings with an enormous amount of films, predominantly shown in a few short-term formats—mostly one-off screenings, relatively brief releases—and monthly screenings within its many series. The archive, finally, also serves other cinematheques in the country for their programs.

See also: http://jer-cin.org.il/Default.aspx?Lang=En

Summary of presentations (films marked * are treated here as releases; although they were announced as being part of the retrospectives *New Films* and *New Cinema*, the retrospective format for new films seems self-contradictory.)

---

[301] 'About the festival', at:
http://www.jff.org.il/?CategoryID= 361&ArticleID=163&sng=1.

[302] 'The Jerusalem Jewish Film Festival', at:
http://www.jer-cin.org.il/Cinematheque/The%20Jewish%20Film%20Festival.aspx.

• 21 one-off screenings, including preview screenings of theatrical releases as well as of TV premieres some time from the following month onwards: parts one and two of GENERATION WAR (UNSERE MÜTTER, UNSERE VÄTER; shown back-to-back on February 5, 8, 13, 15, 20, 22, 27); the first two episodes, on February 10 and 13, respectively, of THE CURSED, a four-part docudrama series on Israeli cultural heroes (by the creator of the international hit series IN TREATMENT); the three-part Czech mini-series for HBO, BURNING BUSH (HOŘÍCÍ KER), about Czech student Jan Palach's self-immolation, in January 1969, in protest against the Soviet invasion of his country. Not surprisingly, the remainder of the one-off screenings contained a relatively large number of works, whether domestically produced or not, that dealt with Jewish history and/or the state of Israel. Examples are: THE ESCAPE (HA'BRICHA), an Israeli 'road documentary' that follows eight young Israelis of all stripes who retrace, against the backdrop of today's Europe, the illegal journeys that were organized by the underground Bricha Movement to lead Jewish survivors from postwar Europe's Displaced Persons camps to Palestine; GISI, an international co-production relating the story of Gisi Fleischmann, who saved thousands from the Holocaust, but not herself; preview screening of OPERATION SUNFLOWER (MIVTZA HAMANIYA), Israeli historical drama that reconstructs the country's development of the "nuclear option", in the 1960s, in order to keep up with Iran; JACQUES FAITLOVICH AND THE LOST TRIBES, documentary about Faitlovich's fascination with the Ethiopian Jews; THE LAST OF THE UNJUST (LE DERNIER DES INJUSTES), Claude Lanzmann's conversations with Benjamin Murmelstein, the last president of the Jewish Council of Theresienstadt.

What was surprising was the variety of single screenings (and for no obvious or stated reason, such as a commemorative occasion): RICHARD PRYOR IN CONCERT, first recording of Pryor's 1979 live stand-up comedy show; PLAY MISTY FOR ME, Clint Eastwood's 1971 directorial debut; TOUS LES MATINS DU MONDE, Alain Corneau's 1991 reenactment of the life of baroque musician Marin Marais; LA CHINOISE (PORTRAITS DE PARIS), Godard's 1967 attack on capitalism; ROOM SERVICE, the 1938 Marx Brothers farce; LEGEND OF THE TAIRA CLAN (SHIN HEIKE MONOGATARI), Mizoguchi's 1955 epic of power struggles in 12th-century war-torn Japan; and PICNIC AT HANGING ROCK, 1975 Australian drama about the mysterious disappearance of three girls and their teacher.

• 20 releases

Here, too, a relatively large number of productions, for both cinema and TV, about Europe's Jewish population during World War II and/or the state of Israel: e.g. BETHLEHEM*, Israeli drama tracing the complex relationship between an Israeli Secret Service officer and his teenage Palestinian informant; OMAR*, Palestinian love drama that gets entangled in the larger political stand-off; SWEETS* (SUKARYOT), story of an Arab Israeli's candy store that becomes a pawn in a political, cultural, and business conflict; special screening of PRESENT CONTINUOUS, Israeli family drama set during the Second Intifada; special screening of FAREWELL HERR SCHWARZ, Israeli-German co-production that constructs (and de-constructs) a family myth set in immediate postwar Poland. The other releases were made up of a domestic and international array of mostly arthouse films, e.g. BLUE IS THE WARMEST COLOR* (LA VIE D'ADÈLE); LIKE FATHER, LIKE SON* (SOSHITE CHICHI NI NARU), Japanese filmmaker Koreeda Hirokazu's drama of a life-changing choice; special screening of IN ENVELOPES, "an intimate inside look into the process of creating the dance and musical performance *Envelopes*"; preview screening and release of THE BEST OFFER*, Giuseppe Tornatore's first English-spoken film; THE ACT OF KILLING, European co-produced 2012 documentary in which participants in the 1965 military coup in Indonesia reenact their own atrocities; AUGUST: OSAGE COUNTRY*; special screening of PARADISE: LOVE (PARADIES: LIEBE); OUT OF THE FURNACE*.

• 4 retrospectives

Joseph Pitchhadze retrospective (February 1-28), organized on the occasion of the release of the new film SWEETS (see above) of this Israeli director.

Could've, would've, should've (February 4-25), a program of films on the occasion of the upcoming Academy Awards, collecting a number of films that missed out on an Oscar.

Tribute to Fred Kelemen (February 20-27), program of this German director and cinematographer (who was director of photography of Joseph Pitchhadze's film SWEETS)

The Hitchcock 9 (February 21-March 20), traveling program of the earliest surviving films that Alfred Hitchcock directed between 1925 and 1929, restored by the BFI-NFTVA; the three films shown in February were all accompanied with live music.

• 12 series, most consisting of monthly screenings.

"Out of the mouth of babes and sucklings hast thou ordained" (since October 6, 2013), a quote from Psalm 8:2, featured a screening of PIXOTE (February 24), about "abandoned children in the streets of Brazil's impoverished neighborhoods." Whether or not this was actually a children's program was unclear.

Architecture in cinema (October 15, 2013–March 3, 2014), screening SLUMDOG MILLIONAIRE.

Preview club 2013-2014 (since October 18, 2013), screening PHILOMENA.

Orthodox—a look from within (October 23, 2013–April 23, 2014), screening THE WONDERS, a "journey into the very heart of darkness of Jerusalem."

Around the world—Northern lights (October 27, 2013–April 6, 2014), screening Finnish film LE HAVRE (February 2) and the European co-production with Danish and Swedish participation MELANCOLIA (February 16).

Stop making sense—Rock'n roll at the Cinematheque (January 16-February 13), screening LOU REED'S BERLIN (February 13).

Concerto 2013-2014, featuring the American 1975 film HESTER STREET (February 1), named after one of the main streets of the Lower East Side of Manhattan, the biggest Jewish ghetto in the world at the turn of the 20th century, with an introduction and a concert of songs of Jewish immigration and early American klezmer music; and the UK 2012 documentary IN SEARCH OF HAYDN (February 15), with an introduction and a concert of Haydn's *Piano sonata in C minor, Piano sonata in E minor, Piano variations in F minor*, and *Trio in G major* (*"Gypsy Trio"*) for piano, violin and cello.

Part of the Met: live in HD 2013-2014, a series of performance transmissions from New York's Metropolitan Opera to movie theaters worldwide, featuring Dvořák's *Rusalka* (February 8).

Wacky film club, screening the French comedy LE DINER DE CONS (February 15) and the US comedy THE PRODUCERS (February 22).

Course: Man changes the world (October 24, 2013–March 20, 2014), screening Wim Wenders's PINA (February 20), about German choreographer Pina Bausch; no mention of a lecturer.

Under the radar, screening Alain Resnais' YOU AIN 'T SEEN NOTHIN' YET (VOUS N'AVEZ ENCORE RIEN VU), with an introduction by film critic Meir Schnitzer.

The critics' society, organized in cooperation with the Film Critics Forum. Once a month two film critics will discuss and analyze a film. In February 2014 the series featured GRAVITY (February 18, 21-22), chosen by the Forum as best film of the year.

Cinema and human rights, in cooperation with the Hebrew University, Jerusalem, screening Israeli film THE OPTIMIST AND THE BUDDHIST (February 27).

• 1 event

The good, the bad, and the ugly (February 20), actor and comedian Idan Barkai and friends in a show that combines standup comedy and video footage.

Summary of information:

Given the mission of the Jerusalem Cinematheque-Israeli Film Archive, a number of programs were oriented to film heritage per se. Although it aims to present the best of national and international cinema, many of its presentations were actually screened less for cinematic and film historical reasons than for societal and moral ones. As a matter of fact, here and there the institute tended to plug a film's moral. See, for instance, the concluding statement in its information for THE ESCAPE: "For the young people, the journey, both physical and emotional, is made up of moments of laughter and tears, at the end of which they have a better sense of themselves and of the society in which they live"; or for SWEETS: "Under the guise of a business struggle the story reveals moral dilemmas and cultural differences. Salah's Russian wife, his French brother-in-law, his German partner and the French lover of the German partner manifest the fact that the struggle does not take place in a vacuum but in a complex multinational reality."

Fuller background information beyond mere plot summaries was largely absent. And whenever there was a comment about filmic qualities it was largely formulaic, as in "Stunning cinematography, meticulous cinematic style, and fantastic performances" (about the Italian drama MIELE); "With an intense script and a sensational cast", about OUT OF THE FURNACE; or "Baroque music, period imagery, and special lighting are present in every frame; combine this with the terrific acting and the result is one of aesthetic perfection and tremendous emotion" (about TOUS LES MATINS DU MONDE).

Exceptional was the programming of the series *Concerto 2013-2014*. The two films it featured were both framed by an introductory lecture and live performances of relevant music. Generally, though, information for programs that were of a more explicitly cinematic character was not very generous and didn't make one much wiser. The introduction to the Fred Kelemen retrospective was strictly biographical—his training, his teaching—, but nothing was said about his direction or cinematography.

The program *Could've, would've, should've*, on the occasion of the upcoming Academy Awards, was a rather expedient collection that brought together films that had been passed over for "truly bizarre reasons", but are "still most worthy of your attention". In other words, the program was basically a number of one-off screenings strung together by the flimsiest of justifications: *not* receiving the Oscar. Parenthetically, even if one had had inside information about the decision-making process of the Academy, it is doubtful that a program of screenings was the appropriate way to get that knowledge across. The introduction to the *Hitchcock 9* program largely copied a speech by the director of the British Council's Israel office—an occasion, of course, of a highly promotional and ritual character. One did learn that the restorations were based on a number of the earliest surviving copies of these silent films held by BFI-NFTVA, combined with materials from other archives, but with no further elaborations on the work done. The statement that the new prints— "crisper and fresher than ever"—"uncover new layers of meaning, encouraging a deeper appreciation of the precocious genius at work" was again more promotional than anything else. Finally, one wonders why a film heritage institute would screen a series of live transmissions from the Metropolitan Opera in New York.

National Film Center at the National Museum for Modern Art, Tokyo

The National Film Center (NFC) began its life as a film library at the National Museum for Modern Art in 1952. From these modest beginnings it gradually extended and moved house until it settled in its current location, in 1995, where it now commands over 40% of the institute's budget. It has a full range of film heritage activities, from collecting, preservation, research, publication, and presentation. In its gallery space and two auditoria, with a capacity of 310 and 151 seats, much attention is given to Japan's own cinema history. Over the past two years many of its presentations centered on Japanese film personalities (e.g. retrospectives of Imai, Kinoshita, Shimizu, Yamada, Masumura; exhibitions on Ozu), a retrospective of an important studio, Nikkatsu (which also traveled internationally), as well as temporary exhibitions on ephemera (e.g. souvenir movie programs) and other film-related objects (e.g. stills, posters). It also regularly updates its public with recurrent programs of films that have become available again through NFC's preservation work through two series, one called *The little known Japanese cinema*, of which seven editions have been programmed since 2011, and another *Lost and found*, showcasing "valuable films newly collected and restored by NFC", of which the 9th edition was shown in 2014. A permanent exhibition is also devoted to Japan's film history.

Presentations featuring foreign films or film-related materials, then, are a minority. In February 2014, only the program on the Technicolor process contained foreign films. Over the past year NFC has mounted a few presentations on foreign topics: an exhibition of Czech film posters, a program of Portuguese cinema, as well as film programs based on the collections of foreign film heritage institutes (MoMA-Film Department, New York; Filmarchiv Austria, Vienna), while in 2014 it organized the 12th edition of the *EU Film Days*, "a series showcasing films from the member states of the European Union".

See also: http://www.momat.go.jp/english/nfc/index.html

Summary of presentations:

• 1 permanent exhibition

Nihon Eiga: the history of Japanese film. From the NFC non-film collection, featuring a range of film-related and personal objects.

• 1 temporary exhibition

Iconography of Yasujiro Ozu films (December 12, 2013-March 30, 2014).

• 1 retrospective

Selected films printed by Technicolor I. B. process from the National Film Center Collection (January 23—February 12).

• 1 series

vol.7: NFC's newly acquired collection from major film studios (February 19—March 16)

Summary of information:

NFC's visitor information is not only sparse (on its English as well as, it seems, on its Japanese website), but it doesn't really tell much. I therefore simply quote it here in the same order as above:

(*Nihon Eiga*) "Japanese cinema has already had a history of over one century with two golden ages. Targeted towards diverse generations of viewers ranging from elementary school students to adults, this exhibition will survey the history through posters, still photographs, devices and equipments for filmmaking, and the personal items that belonged to noted film personalities, among others from the NFC collection."

(*Iconography of Yasujiro Ozu films*) "Commemorating the 110th anniversary of the birth of the late Yasujiro Ozu (1903–1963) as well as the 50th anniversary of his death, this exhibition will pay attention to various kinds of iconography such as paintings, designs, lettering and so on, which appeared in Ozu films, and shed light on the unique aesthetic sensibility of Ozu through new perspectives."

(*Technicolor I.B. process*) "This program will showcase carefully selected foreign films with Japanese subtitles from the NFC collection. These valuable films will be shown on the big screen of NFC."

(*NFC's newly acquired collection from major film studios*) "This is the 7th installment of the series that showcases films of newly acquired collection provided under special project expenses for film preservation in supplemental budgets of 2009 fiscal year. The curatorial focus will be given on those films that have become available for film screenings once again thanks to the preservation work NFC has conducted on the original film materials. This program features the films of Shochiku."

Ngā Taonga Sound & Vision, Wellington/Auckland/Christchurch

On August 1, 2014, after a two-year process of integrating the New Zealand Film Archive and the Sound Archives Ngā Taonga Kōrero (including the transfer of the sound archives, in 2013, from Radio New Zealand), and with the transfer of Television New Zealand Archive from government-owned Television New Zealand (TVNZ) to the Ministry for Culture and Heritage, a new, amalgamated organization was launched: Ngā Taonga Sound & Vision (or New Zealand Archive of Film, Television and Sound). The merger is the result of a government decision—the new organization's website mentions the usual argument of synergy, but not much more. This independent, bi-cultural, non-profit organization is funded by the abovementioned ministry and by the Lottery Grants Board.[303-304]

---

[303] New Zealand Film Archive Ngā Kaitiaki O Ngā Taonga Whitiāhua – Sound Archives Ngā Taonga Kōrero, *Annual report 2013-2014*, at: http://www.ngataonga.org.nz/about/corporate-information, pp. 3-4.

[304] Manatū Taonga Ministry for Culture & Heritage, 'Agencies we fund. Ngā Taonga Sound & Vision', at: http://www.mch.govt.nz/funding-nz-culture/agencies-we-fund/heritage/NgaTaongaSoundVision.

The institute's film archive, apart from boasting the famous Alan Roberts Collection of internationally produced early cinema, has a strong national focus: its 160,000 titles consist predominantly of domestic productions in all genres, including c. 15,000 "personal records" (i.e. home and privately made movies), dating back to 1895. Its national focus is perhaps even stronger reflected in its presentations, not just in February 2014 when all but a few of its screenings were foreign productions, but throughout its recent seasons. And the initiative, started in 2012, to hire annual curators-at-large for a number of temporary exhibitions based on their explorations of the archive, has widened and deepened the screening of the national film heritage. With the merging of three institutes available materials will range even wider, from 1895 up to "yesterday's news", both radio and TV.

Its focus is also national in the sense that the archive has branches in Wellington, Auckland (which houses the recorded speech collections), and Christchurch (which houses the recorded sound and sound-related collections).[305] In terms of public spaces the Wellington branch has a cinema and a gallery space, called the Media Gallery, while it also organizes traveling film shows; the Auckland branch has a gallery space and film viewing facilities. Admission to all the institute's screenings and exhibitions, as well as the research libraries in Wellington and Auckland, is free. For online access the institute has provided 17 medianet viewing sites at partner organizations, such as galleries and museums, throughout the country. The institute does not present the usual retrospectives of international cinema nor does it distribute or screen new releases, foreign or domestic. It does screen selected films and video works from various New Zealand festivals, such as the New Zealand International Film Festival and Pollywood, "a showcase of Pasifika [i.e. the Pacific islands] stories and ideas on screen", as well as from international venues.

Finally, the institute's philosophy, or *kaupapa*, of establishing and preserving continuity is expressed in both its collection policies and its presentations. Virtually all its exhibitions and screenings show a comprehensive concern for connecting past and present, in terms of both the environment and the country's various peoples, particularly between

---

[305] "[T]he Sound Archives are still recovering from the effects of the earthquakes of 2011 and 2012 and a major part of the Film Archive's immediate task is assistance with that recovery", the institute wrote in its 2013 annual report to FIAF, the link of which is now defunct; but see: John Kelcher, 'SANTK staff on life post-earthquakes', on the institute's weblog *Gauge* (February 21, 2014).

Māori and the descendants of European settlers. The latter concern is also expressed in the institute's consistent bilingualism and the requirement that its employees embrace Māori perspectives.

See also: http://www.ngataonga.org.nz

Summary of presentations:

• 3 temporary exhibitions

THE DAM (O) (November 29-December 20, 2013 and January 13-February 8, 2014), New Zealand artist Gavin Hipkins's short fiction film THE DAM (O) incorporated naturalist and abstracted footage of Auckland's five dams built during the 1920s. At the Wellington venue.

Rangahaua (December 3-20, 2013 and January 13-February 21, 2014), moving image exhibition by New Zealand artist Dawson Clutterbuck that explored the processes of traditional kite fishing and flying, historical forms of communication and measurement, as ways to connect the past and present. At the Auckland venue.

Pet (February 14–April 12), a moving image exhibition by the institute's 2014 curator-at-large Gareth Watkins about New Zealanders and their pets, one of four exhibitions Watkins curated across 2014. This exhibition drew upon many parts of the Film Archive's collection—silent features, shorts, the newly merged Sound Archives Ngā Taonga Kōrero catalogue and the Personal Records collection. At the Wellington venue.

• 5 one-off screenings (all except the first at the Wellington venue)

Christchurch modernist architecture on film (February 1), traveling film show by the institute combined with a screening of FOUR HOUSES FROM FOUR DECADES (2008) by the New Zealand Historic Places Trust, at the Pallet Pavillion, Christchurch.

Pollywood (February 1), a compilation of recent short films and multimedia works from the 2013 Pollywood festival in Auckland.

Assemblé: the Royal New Zealand Ballet at sixty (February 12), program on the occasion of the 60th anniversary of the Royal New Zealand Ballet (founded in 1953), compiled of materials held at the Film Archive; screened in conjunction with the exhibition of photographic and other materials of the ballet company held at the Turnbull Gallery,.

My pet Valentine (February 13), compilation program to mark the opening of the *Pet* moving image exhibition (see above).

Turbulence: the ocean as cinematic space (February 22), double bill presented by the Adam Art Gallery, Wellington, in conjunction with their *Cinema & painting* exhibition, curated in cooperation with Philippe-Alain Michaud of the Centre Georges Pompidou, Paris, featuring Nathaniel Dorsky's ALAYA (1976-1987) and Heinrich Hauser's WINDJAMMER UND JANMAATEN. DIE LETZTE SEGELSCHIFFE (1930), with live music accompaniment.

• 2 releases

GARDENING WITH SOUL (February 5, 7-8, 15, 19-21), premiered at the New Zealand International Film Festival in July 2013, is a portrait of Sister Loyola, the nonagenarian main gardener at Our Lady's Home of Compassion, at Island Bay, Wellington, a religious institution "to meet the needs of the oppressed and powerless in their communities".

SOUL IN THE SEA (February 26–March 1, 6-8), which also premiered at the 2013 edition of the New Zealand International Film Festival, is a documentary about the attempt to break "through the invisible wall between people and animals" and befriend a wild dolphin. The screening was preceded by a 1959 composite newsreel from the film archive "on two of New Zealand's other beloved dolphins", combining footage made in 1910 and 1956.

Both films had already been released in New Zealand cinemas in September and July 2013, respectively.

Summary of information:

With the exception of the program *Turbulence: the ocean as cinematic space* most visitor information about the institute's presentations rather uniquely downplayed formal or even archival considerations (although *Turbulence*, in fact, was rather summarily treated). The two temporary gallery shows in particular, THE DAM (0) and *Rangahaua*, in Wellington and Auckland, respectively, got lengthy descriptive texts, partly quoted from dialogues or interviews, interwoven with matters of environmental, societal or cultural import: a reflection on invasive choices made in the New Zealand landscape (THE DAM (0)) and "an ongoing dialogue between traditional knowledge and new ideas and innovations" in an area, Hokianga, that is considered the birthplace of the nation, as many Māori trace their origin, and that of the nation, to its discovery and settlement (*Rangahaua*). Information about the third temporary exhibition, *Pet*, by the institute's 2014 curator-at-large, offered a 'Home movies 101' in its introduction, as much of this exhibition comes from the film archive's large collection of "personal records". Parenthetically, the information for this exhibition signalled that the long process of merging the New Zealand

Film Archive and Sound Archives Ngā Taonga Kōrero had already been effected in this presentation, as it "draws upon many parts of the Film Archive's collection" and "the newly merged Sound Archives Ngā Taonga Kōrero catalogue". Probably, the appointment of the exhibition's curator-at-large Gareth Watkins was part of this process: besides a photographer, he is an award-winning maker of radio documentaries.

Another way of creating continuity was the compilation program titled *Christchurch modernist architecture on film*, shown at Christchurch's Pallet Pavillion, a makeshift cultural center made of 3,000 blue wooden pallets, a part of the community-initiated project Gap Filler, that arose after the two devastating earthquakes that hit the city in 2011 and 2012. This was a combined program of the New Zealand Historic Places Trust, which presented the film FOUR HOUSES FROM FOUR DECADES: CHRISTCHURCH POST-WAR DOMESTIC ARCHITECTURE (a repeat of its 2008 screening there), and a traveling program of the Film Archive on the city's modernist architecture, "now partially or fully demolished."

The two releases also received relatively lengthy introductions, partly quoted from print or broadcast reviews. Again, nothing much was said about the filmic quality of the films. Instead, GARDENING WITH SOUL evoked the philosophy of the Home of Compassion's founder, Sister Suzanne Aubert, through the work of one of its aged nuns, while information about SOUL IN THE SEA zoomed in on the impact an animal had on the lives of humans. The spirit of harmony that permeates these films prevailed in all the presentations and information of Ngā Taonga Sound & Vision, bolstered no doubt by the almost exclusive focus on domestic productions.

Österreichisches Filmmuseum, Vienna

This is one of Austria's two national film heritage institutes. Ever since its establishment, in 1964, the Österreichisches Filmmuseum (ÖFM) has had a strong, though not exclusive, international orientation.[306] The aim for

---

[306] The other institute, Filmarchiv Austria, was not eligible for inclusion in the survey, because its cinema was under reconstruction and reopened in September 2014. Although both institutes are subsidized by the Austrian government, Filmarchiv Austria has a mandate of collecting materials related to Austria's national film production, specifically films supported by the Österreichisches Filminstitut; see: http://filmarchiv.at/sammlungen/depot-legal/.

high quality in all its activities was one of the institute's founding principles and has remained unchanged to this day. And while the ÖFM undertakes the full range of a film heritage institute's tasks, this aim is most particularly expressed in its preservations and in its screenings. Nevertheless, the majority of its screenings feature materials from outside the institute, which leaves one somewhat nonplussed about its preservation ambitions that are formulated as "film itself—as artefact and as an event, in our archival and exhibition activities—takes priority over film's derivatives and facsimiles. Thus, the preservation of films always also implies the preservation of their specific technical and spatial forms of exhibition; in other words, the preservation of the visibility and comprehensibility of film in its analogue cinematographic exhibition mode."

Still, the material aspect of artifacts and their achievement as a performing art are not only central to its mission, they also position the Filmmuseum as, indeed, a museum.[307] It occasionally does premiere nights, but it does not release films or show newly released films in a prolonged way. Yet its one, black-walled auditorium (163 seats) is less a reminder of the cinemas of yesterday than an instrument to increase concentration on the performance of the materials projected and the experience they provide. In that sense, the Filmmuseum's 'black box' is the equivalent of the art museum's white wall.

ÖFM's collection policies are based on the representativeness of film as both art and document, yet it emphasizes a number of particular foci for archiving that have strongly resonated within the country and in the archive: international independent avant-garde cinema; Austrian avant-garde and independent film since 1950; the transnational film oeuvre of Central- and East-European émigrés; and Soviet cinema made between 1918 and 1945. The focus on experimental cinema is reflected in regular screenings of the work of national and international makers of such works. In general, the institute stresses the democratic nature of being a (publicly mandated) museum and archive, where the promotion of a tolerant cultural climate is pursued.

The Filmmuseum is funded from federal and municipal public budgets as well by private donations and earned income from ticket and book sales, membership programs, and its cafe.

---

[307] An approach that shaped in no small measure the discussion about and definition of curatorship in: Cherchi Usai, Francis, Horwath, Loebenstein (2008).

See also: http://www.filmmuseum.at/

Summary of presentations:

• 2 retrospectives

Mizoguchi Kenji (February 7–March 5), overview of the multifaceted work of this Japanese filmmaker, spanning the largest part of his career, between 1936 and 1956.

Tanaka Kinuyo (February 7–March 5), small yet complete retrospective of the six films this actress directed between 1953 and 1962, after separating both professionally and privately from Mizoguchi Kenji.

• 2 series

Die Utopie Film, a series subdivided into multiple monthly "chapters" consisting of weekly screenings that are made to cohere in various ways. February 2014's chapter 76 extended into March, with the war films THE LIFE AND DEATH OF COLONEL BLIMP (1943); BALLADA O SOLDATE (BALLAD OF A SOLDIER; 1959), preceded by the Soviet Ministry of Information's short SALUTE TO THE RED ARMY (1943); THE THIN RED LINE (1998); and IDI I SMOTRI (COME AND SEE; 1985).

Was Ist Film, a cyclical series of 63 weekly programs that "define (...) film as an autonomous art form, as a tool that provides new ways of thinking", assembled by the museum's former director and co-founder Peter Kubelka. In February, programs 5, 6, and 7 were screened: Soviet classic ZEMLJA (EARTH; 1930); Jack Smith's FLAMING CREATURES (1963) in combination with Leni Riefensthal's TRIUMPH DES WILLENS (1935); and a compilation program of innovations and experiments from the silent era, made within both commercial and avantgarde contexts, from Georges Méliès to Man Ray.

Summary of information:

The Filmmuseum's visitor information, in both its (bi)monthly program bulletin and on its website, has two aspects. On one hand, particularly with regard to its retrospectives, it is plentiful and perceptive, yet at the same time it leaves room for the spectator's own ideas and experiences. To take the retrospective of the work of Mizoguchi as an example, its introduction stresses how, in the West, the critical reception of his oeuvre has evolved "in the changing light of history", favoring at various times formalist, feminist or humanist readings (besides the reputation of expediency that has clung to the filmmaker, an effect of his easy adaptation to Japan's shifting political circumstances between the 1920s and 1950s). However, the text takes no position, but provides 'tools' for understanding. What is particularly unusual is that the individual films are hardly ever summarized; rather, the comments seem to continue the introduction by providing additional information about Mizoguchi's life and work and by picking up the various critical positions, now emphasizing one characteristic or important element, then another. The description of ZANGIKU MONOGATARI (THE STORY OF THE LAST CHRYSANTHEMUM), for example, focuses entirely on one, seven-and-a-half minute sequence shot—the element of foremost importance to formalists—and its significance, while the one of WAGA KOI WA MOENU (FLAME OF MY LOVE), a biopic about one of Japan's pioneering feminists, provides an occasion to focus on the country's patriarchal society and the many women's lives it has wasted, a constant theme in Mizoguchi's work.

On the other hand, especially with regard to its series, information is withheld in favor of allowing the programs to create their own context. This, of course, is a risk, because only insofar as spectators are willing or able to see a significant number of a program's films does this leave room for their own interpretations. For instance, the 76th chapter of the series *Die Utopie Film* obviously featured films set during times of war, but spectators were invited, if they so chose, to establish connections that transcended the individual screenings. Nevertheless, generally speaking the Filmmuseum's approach is to a large extent predicated on the intelligence of its public and apparently feels no need or pressure to attract the largest crowds possible (indicated, too, by the absence of new, commercial releases). It assumes a willingness to act and contribute to the formation of meaning and understanding—an element that one might call essential, if not conditional, for its mission of accessing knowledge.

Finally, the reference, in the introduction to the Mizoguchi retrospective, to screenings of his films that featured actress Tanaka Kinuyo in an earlier program, *Acteur: Auteur*, as well as the fact that BALLADA O SOLDATE, now screened in the series *Die Utopie Film*, had been screened two years before in its program on the so-called thaw period in Soviet cinema, supported the restraint that characterizes the museum's visitor information by refusing to impose one interpretation.[308] Both

---

[308] As a matter of fact, the entire series *Die Utopie Film* was conceived for just that reason, "as an invitation to reassemble under changed circumstances"; see: 'Die Utopie Film. Leben und Kino: 100 Vorschläge', in: *Mitteilungen des Österreichischen Filmmuseum* (September-October, 2012), p. 3.

instances illustrated its general philosophy that each screening is a unique event, taking place within changing contexts with shifting meanings.

Its positioning as a museum is also expressed in its consistent listing of the screening formats of the presented films (recently, this information has also been included in its cinema attendants' announcements).

UCLA Film & Television Archive, Los Angeles

This University of California-based institute was established in 1976, the outcome of a merger between UCLA's Film Department's Film Archive and ATAS/UCLA Television Library ("ATAS" stands for Academy of Television Arts and Sciences). One of the largest archives in the United States (with over 200,000 film titles alone), it boasts, among others, the Paramount Pictures Nitrate Print Library (containing most of that studio's sound films made between 1930 and 1950) as well as acquisitions from other major and minor studios: Warner Bros., Columbia, 20th Century-Fox, Republic, Hearst-Metrotone News as well as the SabuCat collection of nitrate trailers, the Sundance collection of independent films, and the Outfest UCLA Legacy Project for LGBT Film Preservation. In its Billy Wilder Theater (capacity 294) the institute can screen its materials in all original formats.

Its important collections of American cinema notwithstanding the institute's presentations have a strong international flavor. In recent years there were retrospectives, either curated in-house or traveling programs, devoted to new or recent films from, among others, the Czech Republic, Kazakhstan, and Slovenia; general overviews of Chinese, Iranian, and—in February 2014—Taiwanese cinema; and more genre-specific programs, e.g. Austrian experimental cinema or contemporary Brazilian documentaries. As well it showed retrospectives dedicated to foreign personalities of the past and the present—Chilean director Patricio Guzmán, Soviet filmmaker Dziga Vertov or French ethnographic filmmaker Jean Rouch, among others. In fact, the retrospective is its favored format regardless of the subject—most often personality, genre or geography. It is one of two institutes in my set, along with National Film Center at the National Museum for Modern Art, Tokyo, that pays systematic attention in its presentations to restoration: in its UCLA Festival of Preservation, "when the Archive presents films preserved by its world-renowned preservation department", and *Out of the archive: recent work from MIAS*, a "showcase of student achievement" featuring preservations by students and recent graduates of UCLA's the Moving Image Archive Studies program.

The institute receives stable, albeit proportionally shrinking funding from the public university system which is the University of California and from the State of California. Additional funding comes from sales, services, and fundraising programs. Substantial private gifts have made possible its Billy Wilder Theater and its state-of-the-art storage facilities.

See also: https://www.cinema.ucla.edu/

Summary of presentations:

• 4 retrospectives

Columbia in the 1930s: recent restorations (January 3-February 14), a selection of recent restorations by Sony Pictures Entertainment of films made by this studio between 1931 and 1933.

This strange passion: Arturo de Córdova (January 10-March 9), featuring the work since the 1930s through the 1950s of this Mexican movie star in a selection of both his Mexican and Hollywood films.

Dark city, open country: the films of Anthony Mann (January 31-March 20), program inspired by the 2013 book *The crime films of Anthony Mann* by Max Alvarez, showing Hollywood director Mann's 1940s film noirs alongside his 1950s westerns.

What time is it there? Taiwan as crossroads (February 15-March 19), an "eclectic selection" of new and classic films from this country.

• 2 series

Outfest/UCLA Legacy Project (since 2005), bimonthly screenings from the LGBT archive, featuring in February 2014 the "landmark queer hit" TRICK (1999).

Family flicks, presentations, in cooperation with UCLA's Armand Hammer Museum of Art and Culture Center (where its Billy Wilder Theater is located), of free monthly matinee screenings, showing in February 2014 THE ADVENTURES OF ROBIN HOOD (1938).

Summary of information:

All the films in its presentations received brief plot summaries, while background information was provided in brief introductions to some of the programs. These introductions' succinctness was meant to point out the program's most salient aspects. The retrospective of Mexican actor Arturo de Córdova, for instance, focused on his "flair for portraying fractured, ambivalent, ironic and inscrutable human beings [that] flew in the face of his leading man beauty, and was certainly an affront to traditional machismo". However, it didn't account for his swashbuckling roles nor for a supporting role in which he is shown "to great advantage", whatever that meant.

By contrast, the introduction to the small program *Columbia in the 1930s: recent restorations* lists the company's rise in the 1930s, the range of its genres, the tightness of its budgets, and the quality of the films nevertheless, thanks to the talent the company was able to attract (notably two directors who won it Academy Awards). However, these elements only tangentially addressed the program's lineup of *lesser*-known films made between 1931 and 1933. Here, in other words, the introduction served as publicity, rather than as a meaningful framework, to make these works palatable. Moreover, in spite of this retrospective's title nothing much was said about the prints' restorations. The institute's links to an article on film critic Leonard Maltin's weblog 'Movie Crazy' and to *LA Times* reporter Susan King's online news article did not really expand on its own information. The latter seemed to have been basically assembled from a press kit, while Maltin, a self-confessed film buff, essentially addressed his peers. But there was nothing on preservation as such. (Surprisingly, given the institute's attention for matters relating to preservation, the same paucity of information characterizes its more specialized programs. For instance, visitor information on its website for all retrievable editions of its *UCLA festival of preservation* contains relatively extensive summaries complemented with comments on style, performance, careers, source materials or other aspects considered relevant. But as far as preservation is concerned they do not as a rule go beyond mentioning what original material was input for the new print, as in, say "preserved from multiple 35mm nitrate prints" or "from 35mm nitrate and acetate materials". One hopes that such information was disclosed in introductory talks or Q&As.)

The information's succinctness, however, can also become counterproductive when too much and/or too complicated information had to be pressed within the same mold. The introduction to the program *What time is it there? Taiwan as crossroads* stated that its selection of films was meant to correspond "with paradigm shifts in scholarly thought about the reality and image of Taiwan in the world". What these shifts and thoughts were was unclear, unless these were represented by the "visions" of the country "not only as an origin or a destination, but as a relay point or hub through which people, art, investment, technology and social change pass, undergoing creative adaptations and transformations." And that "vision" [sic], in its turn, would provide "a rewarding insight". I wonder.

Evaluation

The following evaluation of the above survey is largely determined by the importance I attach to public accountability that comes with funding from public budgets. It therefore focuses on a few general yet important and salient aspects of the performance of film heritage institutes as described in the survey. Of course, each of these aspects does not equally apply to all institutes, as will have become clear from my comments. As well I will not expand much on my words of praise for or criticism of (linear) exhibitions, because my limitation to web-based information prevented me from consulting the texts that may have been included within the exhibitions or on their audio guides, if any. All in all, however, I think the data do suggest that film heritage institutes deal with a number of issues in similar ways. Further research, research that exceeds the goals set for the present study, is needed to establish whether this is indicative of the political, economic, and technological factors that affect their modus operandi nowadays and the measures taken to accommodate them. For now, I have subdivided my evaluative conclusions according to the elements of the definition of curatorship quoted in chapter 2: history, technology, and aesthetics.

History

The volume of presentations that film heritage institutes commonly, and distinctively, offer—film shows—is enormous. During the month of February 2014 the Cinemateca Portuguesa-Museu do Cinema screened 101 titles; Cinémathèque française-Musée du Cinéma: 89; Jerusalem Cinematheque-Israel Film Archive: 77; Cinematek: 76; Fondazione Centro Sperimentale di Cinematografia-Cineteca Nazionale: 74; British Film Institute-National Film & Television Archive: 72; Cinémathèque québécoise and Filmoteca de Catalunya: 70—to name just the biggest guns. In the aggregate the 24 institutes screened c. 1,170 titles.[309] A more interesting figure emerges when these screenings are broken down by decade: 306 titles screened, or over 25%, were made during the current

---

[309] The number is actually higher: not included are the screenings of the National Film Center at the National Museum for Modern Art, Tokyo, whose website didn't specify the titles of its film programs, nor of the films screened at some institutes' subsidiary venues, as these could not all be retrieved.

decade, i.e. between 2010 and early 2014. And when the figures for the last decade and a half are combined, its proportion rises to 489 titles screened, or almost 43%.

These are staggering figures for institutes, even a limited set of them, devoted to film heritage,[310] all the more so when one sees that between them they showed a mere seven films—just over 0.5%—that were made during the first two decades of film history (which I conveniently date from 1895 onwards). In fact, "between them" is hardly an appropriate turn of phrase, since six of these seven films were screened at one institute during a single evening's program. I will not dwell on further breakdowns of these numbers. For one thing, this month's outlier can be next month's laggard (in my survey, for instance, the 1970s ranked as the third highest in terms of number of titles; this was largely due to one comprehensive, thematic retrospective). But the absence of early cinema, at one end, and the large share of recent and new films, at the other, are no anomalies. A cursory glance at other months' presentations over the past year and a half, as well as a smaller trial survey I did in June 2013, convinced me that this is systematic.[311]

The very absence of early cinema makes attributing an explanation difficult. What is nonetheless clear is that these films do not handily fit the two-hour slots into which film heritage institutes commonly program their screenings. As I heard an institute's programmer once say, they have

---

[310] Apparently, in administrative and industrial circles this notion of heritage is a given. In a recent report for the Council of Europe it is argued that "a cinematographic work is part of the heritage 10 years after its original theatrical release as it is expected to have completed a first commercial cycle through the various distribution channels (theatrical release, TV, home video)." This notion of *heritage* comprises classic, cult as well as back catalogue films; see: Gilles Fontaine, Patrizia Simone, *The exploitation of film heritage works in the digital era* (n.d. [September 20, 2016]), p. 13. Their report, note, is not restricted to releases by or in film heritage institutes, but is concerned with the (European) market—cinema releases, TV (on demand), and (subscription) video-on-demand—for film heritage works as defined above. Not surprisingly, this market concern weights works of more recent date.

[311] Despite the lack of statistical representativeness due to the circumstances mentioned above, it was clear from regular inspections of the websites of institutes *outside* my set that their film programs generally agreed with those included in the survey in terms of the time frame within which the screened films were produced, i.e. overwhelmingly between the 1920s and today.

an "inconvenient length", which I understood to mean as being far below that of the standard length that began to assert itself on commercial film programs near the end of the 1910s. Had films produced before that time been made to fit these slots, it would have involved more work—or to be precise, more curatorship—to realize, through compilation or the reconstruction of the program format, for instance. Another reason may be that screenings of early cinema programs are more costly, as they require live music accompaniment (although digital screening formats with a music track have created a trend to screen silent films as if they are sound films). The few cine concerts presented by the institutes in my set favored feature-length films from the 1920s. So, notwithstanding the partly tandem developments in early cinema scholarship and restoration technologies over the past three decades,[312] film heritage institutes present their national publics with a skewed idea of film history and of their collections. As a matter of fact, they reserve the display of their early cinema holdings for—and shift the burden of expenditure to—archival festivals, notably Le Giornate del Cinema Muto, in Pordenone, and Il Cinema Ritrovato, in Bologna, events that are predominantly frequented by an international interpretive community of archivists, technicians, scholars, students, and critics.[313]

Although not information in a strict sense, I nevertheless regard the lack of a proportional presence of early cinema as an instance of insufficient provision of information. This incommunicativeness hinders a significant aspect, in terms of both volume and importance, of cinema history and, by implication, a number of institutes' collections—some sizeable—from becoming more widely and thoroughly known. This is all the more unfortunate, as early cinema's specific *dispositifs* (e.g. with musical accompaniment, magic lantern slides, sing-alongs, and/or spoken narrative) and combinatory presentation formats (e.g. amid a sequence of various live acts) not only provide potentially distinctive, perhaps even competitive attractions, but also compelling opportunities

---

[312] Bregtje Lameris, *Opnieuw belicht: de pas de deux tussen filmmuseale praktijk en filmhistorische debatten** (2007), pp. 109-110; 147-151.
**Re-exposed: on theories and practices of film museums and film historiography*

[313] These archival festivals as well as screenings in the archival sections of prominent international film festivals, such as the Berlinale or the Festival International du Film de Cannes, gain a film heritage institute prestige; this is another symptom of the institutes' tendency to break out of the urban cultural domain, as described in Crane (1994).

for sharing an institute's expertise.[314] This happens to be one of the recommendations of the report for the Council of Europe quoted above, even though its suggestions are rather lamely restricted to undisputed classics and well worn promotional occasions.[315] Yet distinctive and well-considered screenings need not even be limited to early cinema: as the Jerusalem Cinematheque showed in its series *Concerto 2013-2014*, the screening of the 1975 feature fiction film HESTER STREET, set in the Jewish ghetto of Manhattan's Lower East Side at the turn of the 20th century, was contextualized by a pre-screening lecture followed by period klezmer performances of tenement songs; a comparable approach was used for the presentation of the 2012 feature-length documentary IN SEARCH OF HAYDN. Obviously, I cannot comment on the shows' substantive and performative qualities, but what is clear is that a simple idea was all it took.

What caused the volume of recent and new films—of convenient length—is self-evident from the survey: retrospectives of living or recently deceased film personalities, not seldom occasioned by the release of a new or last work; overviews of recent developments in national cinemas (often put together and toured by embassies or national cultural associations); festivals; and commercial distribution. In the survey this presence was augmented by a few 'best of 2013' or 'return-to-our-screens'-programs of films shown in the recent past. Quite a number of these films, then, had a commercial release; and of those, most were *new* premieres, as opposed to the handful of restored and rereleased vintage titles, such as THE GENERAL, PATHS OF GLORY or ASCENSEUR POUR L'ÉCHAFAUD.

---

[314] A similar argument could be made for various performative—or expanded—film screenings initiated in avantgarde circles since the 1960s, such as the London Filmmakers' Co-op or Amsterdam's Electric Cinema.

[315] Fontaine, Simone (n.d. [September 20, 2016]), pp. 49-50. Of course, this report takes the marketing challenges and opportunities of what it defines as film heritage works as its starting point, not their curatorial potential or their resonance, a term literary historian Stephen Greenblatt defined as "the power of the (...) object to reach out beyond its formal boundaries to a larger world, to evoke (...) the complex, dynamic cultural forces from which it has emerged"; see his: 'Resonance and wonder', in: Ivan Karp, Steven D.Lavine (eds.), *Exhibiting cultures: the poetics and politics of museum display* (1991), p. 42.

The commercial distribution of new films in particular has changed the face of a considerable number of film heritage institutes.[316] By including premieres and releases in their presentations they have become even less distinct from the theatrical setting of commercial and arthouse venues discussed earlier. And whereas the films shown in other presentation formats are commonly screened no more than three times, often less, releases commonly require much more repeat screenings. While this makes them easy to program—they potentially fill a screen for weeks or more without requiring any curatorial effort or imagination—, a minimum number of shows per day and a minimum number of play-weeks by distributor demand do compromise programming autonomy.[317] However, as the Irish Film Institute explicitly argues, the new films it premieres "would not otherwise have a theatrical release".[318] Understandably, with this country's apparently negligent film trade, the IFI acts on its commitment to provide "audiences throughout Ireland with access to the finest independent, Irish and international cinema", as its mission statement says. But substituting for commercial distributors is at odds with another of its missions, viz. the preservation and promotion of "Ireland's moving image heritage". In other words, it weights the country's film heritage by the *institute*'s history. In more general terms, instead of a steward or custodian an institute becomes a stakeholder in shaping a country's film culture and its memory. This issue is even more fraught when an institute releases films under its own label; it thereby creates

---

[316] Besides nine institutes in my set—BFI-NFTVA; Cinemateca Boliviana; Cinemateca Brasileira; Cinemateca Uruguaya; Cinematek; Cinémathèque suisse; Cineteca Nacional de México; Irish Film Institute; Jerusalem Cinematheque-Israel Film Archive—other film heritage institutes with a similarly national or regional function that regularly screen distribution titles are: Australian Centre for the Moving Image, Melbourne; Centre National de l'Audiovisuel, Dudelange; Cinémathèque de Tanger; Cineteca del Comune di Bologna; Cineteca Nacional de Chile, Santiago; Cineteca Nueva Leon, Monterrey; Det Danske Filminstitut, Copenhagen; Eye, Amsterdam; Filmoteca Canaria, Santa Cruz de Tenerife – Las Palmas de Gran Canaria; National Film and Sound Archive, Canberra.

[317] The abovementioned, geography-based programs of films packaged and distributed by embassies and cultural associations are another instance of relinquishing programming autonomy, as these programs were not commissioned; an institute was simply asked to sign up. Countries in need of an image boost can thus make a convenience of film heritage institutes.

[318] Irish Film Institute, at: http://ifi.ie/about/.

what I would call instant heritage: from the screen the films go directly into its vaults.

Distribution is certainly a way of making the institutes' work more widely known, but at the same time it gives a slant to what their work actually is. In the survey the ubiquity of such popular titles as 12 YEARS A SLAVE, BLUE JASMINE, INSIDE LLEWYN DAVIS or LA VIE D'ADÈLE, titles that found audiences in regular theatrical venues all the same, shows that the heritage aspect runs the risk of getting lost along the way. Programming commercially distributed titles accentuates that a number of institutes are deliberately angling in the same pond as regular distributors and exhibitors. One is therefore entitled to ask why, for instance, they do not play up their archival wealth or distribute their and sister institutes' preserved or restored films more frequently; now that number is negligible. Or, if release they must as they say they do, why not focus on other types and genres, such as documentary or experimental films that also "would not otherwise have a theatrical release". As well, programs of short films of any genre, of any decade, either in a stand-alone compilation or preceding a feature, constitute a tiny minority and would benefit from greater exposure. The argument, in other words, does not really hold up. And besides, theatrical distributors have always 'neglected' films; certainly today they cannot keep pace with the increasingly wide range of moving image fare available for both theatrical and home consumption.

For future research of wider scope than this study it might be fruitful to formulate a hypothesis that film heritage institutes' widespread, unmistakable trend of commercial distribution has been reinforced by changing views of public investment—even though this is a consideration not found on the institutes' websites. With this hypothesis one may properly suppose that where public funding has been diminished or made conditional on matching funds, visitor targets, etc., it is perhaps inevitable that this type of public programming's estimated drawing power will be weighed against archival screenings. After all, showing new releases goes a long way toward paying the rent. One may, therefore, also properly ask why public bodies have allowed the institutes' mandates to be thus adulterated.

What is more, it is not unimaginable that these mandates will be under further pressure in the face of digital developments in film production and distribution. First of all, what is increasingly and rapidly becoming a reality is that film artifacts (or 'artifacts') will not be deposited at an archive, but remain at their creator's or owner's. Individuals as well as production and distribution companies can now easily store their digital and/or digitized moving image and related files in house and with no extra cost (here space, rather than time, is money).[319] Yet when proprietors need to make decisions about, for instance, long-term preservation or migration it may well be that in the near future a film heritage institute will be called upon, not as custodian, but as a consultant (and perhaps even made to tender in competition with private consultants). Whether film heritage institutes should answer that call is another matter, because such commissions are aleatory, i.e. not self-initiated, rather than based on systematic collection policies. And they may only be found worthwhile when a sufficient amount of prestige and/or financial reward is involved. These changing circumstances will bring sharply into focus to what extent film heritage institutes' public and independent, cultural role will remain safeguarded, by themselves and their mandators.

Secondly, as a consequence of the transfer to digital file projection the traditional, protective limitations on screening vintage or archival prints at non-archival venues may increasingly become immaterial. So, if there is any culturally and societally relevant way for film heritage institutes to carve a niche for themselves as expert institutes, it is through emphasizing their archival and museum function and become a repository where film archivists and curators research, create knowledge about, and meaningful access to, the collections and that knowledge. In its turn, that may prove to be the basis for the enrichment of an institute's curatorial function and the development of presentations more firmly rooted in both.

Technology

Not unrelated to the latter point is the fact that in this day and age films are shot, processed, and, insofar as it concerns archival materials, restored

---

[319] Archivist Arianna Turci reports that with regard to promotional and industrial materials this has already been going on since the 1980s: "Because of the original formats of these films—video or, today, digital—companies assume they can properly store those kinds of materials on their own premises."; see: Turci (2016), p 296 n. 6. The internet and its concomitant user expectations of maximal access have also stimulated distributors and broadcasters to (re-)disseminate their holdings themselves (e.g. by streaming), albeit in often more competitive surroundings; see e.g.: Rosemary Bergeron, 'Archiving moving-image and audio-cultural works in Canada', in: *Archivaria* (Spring 2007), pp. 56-57; 62-63.

in various and variously combined analogue and digital formats, and subsequently made available for theatrical projection in both or either analogue and digital (server or satellite-based) versions. Although exhibitors in many countries still have a choice, that window is rapidly closing where it concerns new productions—in Belgium, Luxemburg, the Netherlands, and Norway, for instance, the film trade has already made a complete transition.[320] The least one would expect film heritage institutes to do, therefore, is distinguish themselves by accounting for their motivated decisions about the projection formats of their choice, in view of the efforts invested in preservation and restoration, if not simply of being the appointed keepers of heritage objects. But this does not seem to be the case. And that is a circumstance that can only partly be attributed to relinquishing programming autonomy.

Very few institutes have published presentation policy statements on their websites. One of the exceptions is the Österreichisches Filmmuseum, which is explicitly committed to "exhibit the medium of film in all its dimensions and historical forms".[321] In order to realize that goal it goes to great lengths to show films in their original exhibition format, which, as noted, is duly listed for each programmed title. Even then, though, the quality of the print, its generation, the elements that went into its restoration, invasive measures applied, etc. are as a rule left unmentioned.[322] Incidentally, there may well be other institutes that show films in their original exhibition format, albeit implicitly and as a matter of fact. For instance, the Fondazione Centro Sperimentale di Cinematografia-Cineteca Nazionale largely shows domestic productions which, thanks to legal deposit, are likely screened in their first (yet unlisted) exhibition formats.

On the other hand, BFI-NFTVA, the other exception, gives an account of its strategic priority "to digitise and make accessible to the public all of

---

[320] *DCinema Today* (June 27, 2011); Cinematek (n.d.), p. 55; Lenk (Fall 2014).

[321] 'Mission statement', at: http://www.filmmuseum.at/jart/prj3/filmmuseum/main .jart?reserve-mode=active&rel=en&content-id=1215680369205.

[322] Of course, the term "original" is in many cases and for many reasons an approximation. For example, as the exhibition of nitrate prints, the common material for 35mm prints before the mid-1950s, is forbidden, they first need to be transferred to acetate-based, so-called safety prints. And even if an institute has an original safety print, it may be advisable to make a copy as a protective measure; that copy's stock and its properties, however, are likely to differ from those they are copied from.

our screen heritage", both theatrically and online. This laudable measure has been taken in response to the increasing lack of visibility of the country's film heritage: "as the cinema industry completes the transition to digital, a significant part of this heritage will become ever more inaccessible, stranded in the analogue domain."[323] In other words, this is less about its own premises than about venues nationwide. (Parenthetically, while BFI-NFTVA is working on digitizing the British cinema heritage, of which it administers a very significant part, to date, however, the Hong Kong Film Archive, without providing a general account, is the most consistent of all institutes in my set in screening its programs in non-original, subsequent formats such as DCP or Digital Beta—even though its website states that its facilities can handle all analogue formats, too.)

The two quoted policy statements reflect the antithetical considerations that recent technologies have amplified. This antithesis, note, is not simply a matter of purism v. compromise, or conservatism v. cutting edge, because the respective motivations are determined by different priorities. ÖFM, in its archival practices, has included digital restoration technology, but regards it as a means to museological ends,[324] while BFI-NFTVA's priorities are less concerned with considerations of authenticity than with facilitating wide access. However, its screenings, in February 2014, of THE GENERAL and THE GODFATHER, PART II in Digital 4K on its own premises and "2K elsewhere" reflect the apparent state of facilities throughout the United Kingdom. Unwittingly the transition to digital formats has created a situation reminiscent of the difference between film shows in metropolitan and provincial venues during the silent era. BFI-NFTVA's webpage on strategic priorities, however, papers over this difference and how it will be overcome.

Not listing screening formats in an institute's visitor information, then, cannot nowadays be unequivocally taken as a sign of one or another default option. A mixture of screening original and subsequent formats is the rule rather than the exception. As a result, even within individual programs there is a fluidity with regard to projection formats. A few institutes in particular—Australian Cinematheque, BFI-NFTVA, and

---

[323] 'Strategic priority three', at: http://www.bfi.org.uk/about-bfi/policy-strategy/film-forever/strategic-priority-three.

[324] 'Digital film restoration policy/ Österreichisches Filmmuseum' (September 20, 2011).

Cinemateca Uruguaya—prominently combined original analogue and non-original, digital projection formats in their retrospectives and series. But such mixtures show how easy this can lead a lowering of standards, if not indifference, in the sense that some institutes are not above showing films in formats that are considered substandard by the interpretive community. The Australian Cinematheque, as noted, showed black-and-white reduction prints of silent films of which restored 35mm color prints were available. Filmoteca de Catalunya's brief retrospective of Orson Welles' films resorted to broadcast formats such as Digital Betacam and HDcam, while it showed the 2008 feature ME AND ORSON WELLES in a consumer market format, Blu-ray, even though this particular feature had been 'traditionally' released in 35mm; as well some of the films in its program devoted to Jacinto Esteva and the Barcelona School were shown in broadcast and home cinema formats. And it, along with Cinémathèque française and Irish Film Institute, also screened a few films on DVD of which higher grade formats must logically have been available.

Regardless of an institute's preference, such technical and material aspects and the decisions about them are by and large left unexplained, save the differently motivated policy statements mentioned above. Consequently, and particularly with regard to substandard formats, it appears to be less sinful to screen than to draw attention to them. In general, reasons for screening DCP and other digital formats rather than analogue gauges, as well as the provision of full information about preservations, restorations, and/or digitizations, about the state of the prints screened, their sources (i.e. from which archives or other repositories prints have come), about possible or recorded measures that have led to material changes (e.g. reduction prints or blowups, black-and-white instead of color) or of content (e.g. excisions, permutations), either by the institute itself or by others (e.g. censorship boards, exhibitors, collectors), are overwhelmingly missing. Insofar as screening formats do get listed at all, the odd comment—"new restoration", "4K"—rather functions as a promotional flare that leaves potential visitors none the wiser. No substantial attempts were made to increase visitors' awareness of and knowledge about such matters. Given the current state of material and technological flux, this lack of both informativeness and sharing of expertise is a serious flaw.

Aesthetics

The implicitness of material and technical considerations notwithstanding, the miscellany of gauges and formats or the resort to substandard projections is not just a matter of the unavailability of original formats. And if it were, the argument to drop a particular title doesn't seem to have carried much weight. A few explicit pointers suggest another, more overriding consideration. One is contained in the Cinémathèque française's mission statement that it wants to present "complete retrospectives of and hommages to filmmakers, performers, producers, and technicians". Another is the Cinemateca Portuguesa's annual report for 2013 to FIAF, which mentions in its program overview "full" retrospectives of a number of filmmakers.[325] And, finally, a curator's introduction to a retrospective at the Cinémathèque québécoise emphasized the importance of screening the films together, "since only seeing the totality (...) will permit spectators to explore an oeuvre that is little known until this day."

Despite their small number the quoted statements are nonetheless representative for the sense of completeness that emanates from many film heritage presentations. This is particularly true for the retrospective format, and a fortiori for retrospectives centered on personalities—mostly performers and directors—, of which I counted 45, more than all other instances of this format put together.[326] But regardless of its topic, this was the format used most widely in the survey: all but three institutes in my set programmed one or more retrospectives. These presentations, moreover, suggest that the retrospective is considered the most important format in terms of realizing the institutes' ambitions of promoting film as an aesthetic object.

---

[325] 'Lisbon annual report 2013' (2014), p. 4.

[326] In addition to personality-based retrospective programs I distinguished programs based on—in order of magnitude—non-filmic themes (e.g. World War I) (14), specific film historical topics (e.g. Technicolor) (9), geography (6), genre (5), and overviews of various scope (e.g. *Kinohighlights 2013*) (4). Five programs, among which *Dominica en documental*, a program of documentaries on topics related to the Dominican Republic, and *Dictator's cut*, a program of documentaries on human rights and freedom of speech issues, were counted twice (as genre and geography-based and genre and theme-based programs, respectively); this didn't significantly affect the ratio between the types of retrospective distinguished.

The high number of personality-based programs is therefore not surprising, since they commonly, and conveniently, have a greater measure of coherence. They are more self-contained than ones based on, say, genre or non-filmic themes, topics where one title or another might be less noticeably missed. And, of course, they are more familiar, because personalities commonly are, and were, the focus of publicity. Given the conception of film as an aesthetic object that governs most public activities of film heritage institutes, personality-based programs are its most concrete manifestation. But they also bring out more clearly the problems inherent in this type of program.

Compare them to retrospective exhibitions in art museums. Even though art shows commonly last longer and consist of more works, their duration and size match: the investments in mounting these exhibitions, often with works on loan from other museums or private collections, require time to prepare, recoup their high costs (transport, insurance) and, if publicity has done its job, accommodate the number of expected visitors. Recently, for instance, huge crowds queued up daily for the exhibition of Mark Rothko's paintings at the Hague Gemeentemuseum. It was the first show in Holland of this artist in 40 years (the museum's website played up this unique aspect with pride and a hint of tease: "this exhibition will be held only in The Hague and nowhere else"[327]). Lasting for over five months, the exhibition covered the painter's entire career through more than 60 works, many from the National Gallery of Art, Washington, D.C.

This is the model for film heritage retrospective programming: a single focus, with a 'natural' narrative that traces an artist's development through as many works as can be assembled. Its cinematic counterparts, however, are at a disadvantage. At a practical level, they usually run for a shorter period of time; programs of more than three months are exceptional. And, although they hardly ever consist of 60 works, their size and temporal compactness are usually at odds and do not in any practical sense "permit spectators to explore an oeuvre". Half or even a third of that number would already make too big a demand on most people's leisure time. The art show, on the other hand, when it is too beautiful, too big or too busy for one visit, or when most of the works will for all practical purposes be locally unavailable forever after it closes, lends itself more

---

[327] 'First Rothko exhibition in 40 years at Gemeentemuseum Den Haag', at: http://www.gemeentemuseum.nl/en/exhibitions/mark-rothko.

easily to a second look. And practical matters, finally, contribute to the relatively small time frame within which film retrospectives need to be shown and watched: an agreed maximum number of projections for archival materials; print traffic (no repeated deliveries; scheduled bookings elsewhere); or other events in an institute's own auditoria. Surely digitized formats have rendered the limited number of projections obsolete from a material point of view (although rights issues still put a cap on screenings), yet in those institutes that have no principled objection to digital projection the preference for the retrospective and its intension of completeness has not appreciably lessened.

A more basic disadvantage, besides the practices particular to the film heritage world, is the notion of completeness itself: it stands in the way of realizing the very claims that are made with retrospectives, because it is the sort of format in which the works constitute each other's context, yet only at intervals of repeat visits. Whether it is "an opportunity to revisit some of the genre's most popular titles, and to discover other films that investigate and reinvigorate these narrative genres on the big screen" (Australian Cinematheque's genre-based *Fairytales and fables*); "[t]wenty films (or 'cine essays') that trace the career of a prolific documentarist and fine observer of his time" (Cinémathèque suisse's *Rétrospective Chris Marker*); or "work from the various genres and periods of de Córdova's oeuvre, pointing up his versatility and depth" (UCLA Film & Television Archive's actor's retrospective *This strange passion: Arturo de Córdova*), the majority of potentially interested spectators will commonly go and see a couple of films at best. Only those who seem to have no other pressing needs, such as devotees or cinephiles, will try and follow an entire retrospective program. In such a state of affairs, visitor information becomes of crucial importance in sketching relevant contexts that allow less single-minded visitors to make a reasoned and feasible selection (the Rothko show, incidentally, allowed alternative routings: visitors could either follow the artist's career chronologically from one room to the next, or take the "emotional" shortcut to some of the abstract works only[328]). However, most institutes make no distinctions between a retrospective's films. With all films being presented as equally valuable, they effectively address their publicity at small, dedicated audiences.

---

[328] Walter van Teeffelen, 'De grote Mark Rothko tentoonstelling in het Gemeentemuseum'*, at: *Den Haag Direct* (September 21, 2014).
**The great Mark Rothko exhibition at the Gemeentemuseum*

Archival consultant David Bearman has written:

The actions taken by archivists and curators to their holdings (...)
have an impact upon the meaning of the records as evidence.
Weeding collections, publishing about them or from them,
exhibiting items from a collection in conjunction (or juxtaposition)
to other materials, all effect our future understanding and
interpretation of the materials. Therefore we need to keep records of
archival actions not just for the administrative purposes of tracking
work and improving our methods (...), but for the reason that the
intellectual content of records is affected by processing.[329]

Although meant as a comment on the archival activities of arrangement and description, the connection Bearman makes here between evidentiary and information values is instructive. First of all, it points up, by contrast, the missed opportunity of informing visitors about the interrelations between technology, history, and aesthetics, particularly where it concerns activities undertaken by film heritage institutes themselves (e.g. elucidating the reasons why one object, and not another, has been collected, preserved and/or restored, which considerations were weighed against each other in making restorations, and their consequences for the object on display). But it also opens up the notion of context and all the possible ways it shapes "the intellectual content" of collection items, particularly in the activities central to my argument, "publishing"—which I take here as public or visitor information—and "exhibiting".

What has become abundantly clear from the survey is a tendency (and its few exceptions) of film heritage institutes to rather monotonously frame the intellectual content of cinema as an art. This is reinforced by their theatrical settings, by molding public information in a largely 'textual', aesthetic discourse, either self-produced or, more commonly, through quotations picked from a continuous sushi belt of opinions in print and web reviews, catalogues, online databases, press kits, etc. Such discourse, as was noted earlier, may be the convenient consequence of

---

[329] Bearman (1989), chapter III: 'Arrangement and description'.

processing a large volume of presentations. Certain is that state-of-the-art research and knowledge formation, either initiated in house or drawn from authoritative sources, are conspicuously and sorely missing.

Most astounding, nevertheless, is that the aesthetics underlying film heritage programs is by and large left implicit, and—to recall Roger Kelly's terminology—its intellectual connotation is low. With precious few exceptions there was no solid argumentation regarding the surveyed institutes' presentations. It was rather a matter of an "unformalized aesthetic", that is to say, the result of "workaday choices",[330] a routine of 'factettes', unquestioned terms and undisputed reputations. Overlooking the survey, combined with my impressions from other website visits for the duration of more than a year, this seems to have led to a conformist tendency, most poignantly exemplified by an itinerant repertoire of personalities and titles. In fact, this repertoire only could be itinerant because its elements are assumed to mean the same everywhere, blithely irrespective of voluntary and involuntary changes for foreign destinations, of measures of appropriation, either material (invasive measures on the print) or contextual (e.g. marketing, publicity), and of local modes of reception. Visitor information essentializes rather than tells about the specifically local and historical ways in which films, their modes of screening, their stars and directors, and their ancillary products were presented and promoted. Fundamentally, film heritage institutes have set their aesthetics in the key of a universal language.

But that, of course, is not what recent film historiography has demonstrated. For instance, the changing perceptions of French multinational Pathé in the American market during the first fifteen years of the 20th century; or the ways German feature films starring Asta Nielsen were marketed by their foreign distributors in the early 1910s; or the three, differently censored German versions of the 1925 Soviet silent film BATTLESHIP POTEMKIN released in 1926, 1928, and 1930,[331] the latter of which, moreover, was a sound version with synchronized German

---

[330] The quoted phrases come from: Becker (1984), p. 132.

[331] While, interestingly, the third edition of the 1926 German-language novelization *Panzerkreuzer Potemkin. Der Matrosenaufstand von Odessa 1905*, published as a so-called *"Filmroman"* with five "original" photographs and ten reproduced film frames, was cleverly advertised by its publisher as the only available uncensored version: *"Der Film—verboten! Das Buch—ins Fenster!"*; see: Lange (2010), pp. 133, 184.

dialogue, music, and sound effects recorded on gramophone records; the 'variant editions' of Roberto Rossellini's 1950s films with Ingrid Bergman; the reception of Western-made films in Dutch-controlled New-Guinea in the late 1950s; the fate of the first series of broadcasted cinema verite films by Robert Drew and his associates in the early 1960s; and the wide array of experiences collected in the essays of the volume *Hollywood abroad: audiences and cultural exchange* referenced above, these are just a handful from a number of studies and reports about the various histories of and ways in which films, in the shape of specific (appropriated) prints and their specific (appropriated) accompanying discourses were perceived and received both inside and outside their country or culture of origin.[332] As I wrote in the concluding paragraph to chapter 2, "artifacts (...) allow all sorts of aesthetic considerations". Yet, one cannot but conclude that in the public activities of film heritage institutes aesthetic considerations are only tenuously related to artifacts. By definition this undercuts both the informativeness and the professed expertise of these activities. And as long as these institutes profess to see their missions in terms of the heritage they administer, their relevance diminishes in proportion to the public activities that deviate from that mandate.

---

[332] See, respectively: Abel (1999 and 2006); Loiperdinger, Jung (2013); Thomas Tode, 'The soul of a century: PANZERKREUZER POTEMKIN und seine Filmmusik im Spiegel der zeitgenössische deutschen Presse' and Martin Reinhart, '131 Minuten Meisel', in: *Maske und Kothurn: Internationale Beiträge zur Theater-, Film- und Medienwissenschaft* (2015), pp. 11-28, 55-66, respectively; Geoffrey Nowell-Smith, '*Le varianti trasparenti: i film con Ingrid Bergman di Roberto Rossellini* by Elena Dagrada', in: *Senses of cinema* (February 2006) [review article]; *Papoea en film: verslag van een filmenquête gehouden door het Kantoor voor Bevolkingszaken. Rapport no. 81** (Hollandia: Gouvernement van Nederlands Nieuw-Guinea, 1956), discussed in: De Klerk (2004a and 2004b); P.J. O'Connell, *Robert Drew and the development of cinema verite in America* (1992); Stokes, Maltby (2004).
**Papua and film: report of a survey conducted by the Office of Population Affairs. Report #81.*

Chapter 4
A programmatic conclusion

The findings of the survey confirmed my statement that on the whole film heritage institutes' public activities have failed to fully exploit the materials they manage and promulgate the knowledge they are expected to possess about their signifying contexts. And although my focus throughout has been on the underuse of their collections, I acknowledge the consideration to inform their publics about international or otherwise more widely framed concepts of film history. But whether it concerned an institute's own materials or those obtained from external archival sources, or whether it concerned the cinema history of its own country or region or of a foreign one, in my view it made no difference to their performance of public accountability. To put it generally and succinctly, transferring full knowledge, in word and image, is not a major concern in the public activities of film heritage institutes. Moreover, the survey's snapshot of these institutes' production of culture captured them in a process of transition towards what sociologist Diana Crane called the peripheral cultural domain: many have expanded their public spaces, volume of presentations, audience base, and/or range of products (notably museum stores, catering, facilities rental) with an attendant, more mainstream-oriented repertoire of presentations. Specific materials, those regarding early cinema in particular, and specialist knowledge, both historical and methodological, were largely reserved for their network of interpretive communities.

One may object that this is inconsistent with the good business some institutes do according to available attendance figures submitted in their 2013 annual reports to FIAF. But with not all variables known, particularly seating capacity and number of screenings per day per auditorium, they are not straightforwardly comparable: some stressed occupancy rate, and others totals (where occupancy rate may be low); one also counted visitors to its exhibitions, the rest only screenings.[333] On the whole, numbers play a prominent role in these reports, whether it concerns the volume of acquisitions of materials of all sorts, restorations and digitizations, loans or sales of archival materials (mostly moving image materials), book and DVD publications, enquiries or researchers visiting the premises, etc. This quantitative focus, most emphatically the range of film materials collected, underlines these reports' ritual character, as the reported acquisitions over the past few years of home movies and other amateur films, agricultural and industrial documentaries, trailers, commercials, newsreels, animation, and avantgarde works do not appear to have had any noticeable effect on an institute's publicly propagated concept of film heritage. Insofar as this concept is perceived as what their publics appreciate, or their governments actually encourage, it suggests a collective, convenient amnesia of what their mandated tasks require.

The abovementioned transition described by Diana Crane is a tendency that did not occur in the film heritage world alone. In recent times, diminished public funding, whether for ideological, economic or expedient reasons, has forced many cultural heritage institutes to seek alternative income by developing activities theretofore not pursued— reasons, apparently, that factored out the potential drawing power of

---

[333] Cinemateca Portuguesa-Museu do Cinema reported to have had over 52,000 visitors for its 1,361 screenings—no figures were given for its exhibitions; Cinémathèque suisse counted 68,000 visitors for its 960 film shows in its three venues; Cineteca Nacional de México, with four new auditoria in 2013 (making a total of ten), had a staggering 823,000 visitors; Deutsches Filminstitut Filmmuseum welcomed a hefty 200,000 visitors in its museum and its one onsite cinema; Filmoteca de Catalunya received over 140,000 spectators for 1,423 screenings in its two cinemas (aggregate capacity 535), resulting in an occupancy rate of 101 spectators per screening; the National Film Center, Tokyo, received almost 90,000 spectators in its two cinemas (aggregate capacity 461), attaining an occupancy rate of 131; Österreichisches Filmmuseum's 709 screenings attracted over 52,000 spectators in its one cinema (capacity 163); Jerusalem Cinematheque-Israel Film Archive, on the other hand, reported a general number of c. 2,000 screenings "annually" for c. 400,000 visitors in its four auditoria (aggregate capacity 796). See the following annual reports to FIAF: 'Lisbon annual report 2013' (2014), p. 3; 'Cinémathèque suisse: rapport d'activités pour l'année 2013' (2014), p. 10; 'Informe Cineteca Nacional de México 2013' (2014), [pp. 4-5]; 'Deutsches Filminstitut Filmmuseum' (2014), p. 3; 'Filmoteca de Catalunya' (2014), [p. 4]; 'National Film Center-the National Museum of Modern Art, Tokyo (Japan): activities report for 2013' (2014), p. 2; 'Österreichisches Filmmuseum/Wien: FIAF annual report 2013' (2014), p. 2; 'Israeli Film Archive – annual report 2013' (2014), [p. 2].

knowledgeable, imaginative curatorship. This effectively has allowed them to stretch their mandates and core tasks. Nevertheless, I don't intend to just shift the blame; after all, one can do one thing without necessarily renouncing another. Moreover, also in recent years a number of institutes within (and without) my set have received generous financial support, from both public and private sources, for the realization of new or reconstructed premises. The expansion of exhibition space, auditoria, and/or seating capacity has in turn put more pressure on attracting visitors in greater numbers to finance the increased rent and upkeep of these accommodations, a calculated risk entirely these institutes' responsibility. But whether or not diminished operational funding and expanded venues can actually be seen as two facets of the same set of conditions—a pressure on increased self-earned income, on attracting larger audiences, and other quantifiable indicators—, it is clear they have conduced to a trend of resorting, if not retreating, to time-tested yet uninformed and unimaginative methods and an overwhelmingly mainstream repertoire.

Other heritage institutes also have renovated, expanded, relocated, or were subjected to the pressures of reduced public funding, yet there are also differences. The most obvious and publicized one is the challenge to, even attack on, the authority of many museums over the past few decades with regard to materials—or their absence—of or about minority and marginalized communities. Whether it concerned issues of participatory activities, acquisition, appraisal, presentation or repatriation, such public engagements with and debates about the heritage that they administer have particularly affected ethnographic and (living) history museums as well as Halls of Fame and museums of specific, contested subjects (e.g. archaeology, the military, the marine, labor and industry[334]), forcing these

---

[334] See the section 'The new history and the new museum' in: Warren Leon, Roy Rosenzweig (eds.), *History museums in the United States: a critical assessment* (1989), pp. 183-320; see also Kwame Anthony Appiah's 'Whose culture is it, anyway?', in his: *Cosmopolitanism: ethics in a world of strangers* (2007 [2006]), pp. 115-135.

institutes to review their long and unquestioned "power to represent" and the ideologies underlying it.[335]

While it is my conviction that the foundation of a museum's or archive's power to represent is a matter of deep understanding of the materials and their histories under its remit, reflected in its curated public presentations and information, a society's pluralism is a challenging and potentially important context for film heritage institutes, too—and another argument against blindly assigning a universal meaning to the topics of their presentations. Yet it is not widely identified as such, let alone acted upon.[336] The only institute in my set that has integrated the notion of pluralism most deliberately and consistently is New Zealand's

---

[335] For the notion of the "power to represent" see: Ivan Karp, 'Introduction. Museums and communities: the politics of public culture', in: Karp, Kreamer, Lavine (1992), pp. 1-2; see also: Edmund Barry Gaither, '"Hey! That's mine": thoughts on pluralism and American museums', in the same volume, pp. 56-64; Katie Shilton, Ramesh Srinivasan, 'Participatory appraisal and arrangement for multicultural archival collections', in: *Archivaria* (Spring 2007), pp. 87-101; James Clifford, 'Museums as contact zones', in: *Routes: travel and translation in the late twentieth century* (1997), pp. 188-219, which proposes the notion of "moral relationship", specifically between "museums-as-collections" and indigenous, marginalized communities—as is implied in the term "contact zone", which has been defined as a situation "in which peoples geographically and historically separated come into contact with each other and establish ongoing relations, usually involving conditions of coercion, radical inequality, and intractable conflict"; see: Mary Louise Pratt: *Imperial eyes: travel writing and transculturation* (1995 [1992]), p. 6.

Although more about the power to represent per se than about a marginalized community, the case study of the exhibition *The last act: the atomic bomb and the end of World War II* at the Smithsonian National Air and Space Museum, Washington D.C. is instructive. Meant to commemorate the 50th anniversary of Japan's capitulation, but eviscerated for the politicized controversy that arose around the idea to display the *Enola Gay*, the aircraft that dropped the first atomic bomb, it shows how such controversies can become affairs of national moment through the publicity they—often wittingly—generate; see: Mike Wallace, 'The battle of the *Enola Gay*', in: *Mickey Mouse history and other essays on American memory* (1996), pp. 269-318.

[336] For instance, salvaging business papers, posters and other publicity materials from the now practically defunct Dutch videotheque market, which included a number of ethnic niches, is already a missed opportunity. See also: '90 procent minder videotheken'* (January 18, 2016), at:
http://www.cultuurindex.nl/nieuws/90-procent-minder-videotheken.
* '90 percent less videotheques'

Ngā Taonga Sound & Vision, whose presentations are of predominantly domestic significance, while its visitor information and corporate philosophy emphasize a spirit of inclusivity. On the other hand, the Jerusalem Cinematheque-Israel Film Archive, an institute of national stature in a deeply contested area, is to a certain extent exclusivist (contrary to its mission statement's commitment to pluralism) in that it favors Jewish topics and personalities in its presentations and festivals. The Cinémathèque québécoise and Filmoteca de Catalunya, institutes of regional stature in other, albeit less violently contested areas, favor regional personalities and topics, yet their mission is dedicated to safeguard their particular region's heritage rather than exclude other ones. Their very existence, one might say, is a measure to strengthen their position as cultural minorities. But while many countries, particularly in Europe, that were largely monoethnic until the era of decolonization now have increasingly diverse populations, film heritage institutes overall still seem to operate in a more 'monochrome' niche. It has been suggested that this might be a matter of the type of public activity film heritage institutes generally offer, viz. a focus on "visual experience", as in the art museum, rather than on "narrative content".[337] But I rather think it is the ways in which visual experience and narrative content have been accounted for that are symptomatic of the marginal intellectual position in the public sphere that most film heritage institutes have allowed to put themselves in. And this reflects the lack of authority and reliability they have as an expert system, despite the good business they do.

Safeguarding

One of the challenges of the archival profession is "to assure the use of cultural evidence in the continuing construction of the culture."[338] Cultural evidence is not just about the significance of the past, i.e. about custodianship, but also about its pertinence for the present, i.e. about curatorship. And thus it is about the activation of heritage— notwithstanding the quoted statement's author's skepticism regarding the management and preservation of the ever-increasing archival record. The

---

[337] Karp (1992), p. 2.

[338] Bearman (1989); the quotation can be found in the section 'Introduction: the archival endeavor'.

public activities that I surveyed, however, hardly reflect on visual cultural evidence specifically (partly a result, I suspect, of their self-imposed knowledge gap referred to earlier). It is, in fact, only since a few decades, roughly since the late 1970s, early 1980s, that some film heritage institutes have pushed themselves to the forefront in the field of film preservation. In cooperation with technicians of various private and academic organizations (e.g. film laboratories, notably Haghefilm in Amsterdam, and research institutes, notably the Image Permanence Institute in Rochester, NY) they have gone beyond the mere duplication of image and sound information. (In actual fact, having commonly transferred their 35mm materials to smaller gauges—so-called reduction prints—not even that had been widely accomplished.) By experimentally developing and innovating restoration and reconstruction technologies, first analogue, now digital, as well as a concomitant ethics that also took into account material and expressive elements (e.g. gauge, projection speed, aspect ratio, color system), preservation activities began to attain museological standards by reflectively conceptualizing a distinctive notion of *original* and by "interpretation and opinions, (...) taste and editorial decisions."[339]

Hence the museum world was the first benchmark for film heritage institutes to gain a certain measure of standing in the heritage world and in the public sphere. This orientation has served to increase awareness of the particular importance of film heritage artifacts as perishable dimensional objects, time-based performances, as well as sources of historical information—even though that information was quite specific or doctored,[340] a point not pressed in successfully convincing administrations of the need for financial support in safeguarding the moving image heritage. Such 'consciousness-raising' happened none too late, as it coincided with the onset of an era in which the artifactual, analogue basis of film, practically as well as attitudinally, was beginning to feel the impact of machine-readable (instead of wholly or partly machine-*dependent*) formats. And with it the venue for, or rather the mode of, watching moving images has increasingly become a matter of choice. (For instance, besides the mainstream theatrical, communal, and to a certain

---

[339] Paul Read, Mark-Paul Meyer (eds.), *Restoration of motion picture film* (2000), pp. 3; 69-70.

[340] This ranges from the way filmed subjects' demeanors and locations are adapted in accordance with the technical requirements of cinematic equipment to the harnessing of film's essentially concrete images to issues of wider or general scope (e.g. propaganda, publicity).

extent immersive experience film scholar Nicole Brenez has designated the distinct mode of machine-readable, un-theatrical viewing, as on laptops for instance, as "consultative".[341] As archives and museums, then, film heritage institutes needed to retain, preserve, and research the artifacts (prints, equipment) as well as the records that have constituted and supported film as a performative phenomenon for over a century— including recent digital technologies that have become included in these manifestations, partly in order to *re*-constitute them.[342] In other words, by keeping its artifacts in working order a film heritage institute qua museum distinguished itself by its ability to continue presenting and updating the technological, performative, aesthetic, and—to a certain extent and insofar as its venues allowed—social configurations of the history of cinema.[343]

It may seem incongruous in this light that the museum world itself has recently extended its remit in what could be seen as the opposite direction, away from its artifactual basis. The International Council of Museums' current definition of *museum* runs as follows:

A museum is a non-profit, permanent institution in the service of

society and its development, open to the public, which acquires,

conserves, researches, communicates and exhibits the tangible and

---

[341] Quoted in: 'Das Unsichtbare Kino: Film, Kunst, Geschichte und das Museum', in: *Mitteilungen des Österreichischen Filmmuseum* (October-November 2014), p. 59.

[342] Cherchi Usai, Francis, Horwath, Loebenstein (2008), pp. 49; 60-66; 83-95.

[343] With regard to technology, the George Eastman Museum, in Rochester, NY, announced in a press release that "its conservation department has reverse-engineered and replicated the making of early motion picture film (...) that reflects the processes used by Eastman Kodak Company and other makers of motion picture film stock in the early years of cinema." The museum's director was quoted as saying that "'[b]y making motion pictures film in a way similar to when it was first invented, we are improving our understanding of cinematic history and laying the foundation to ensure the survival of filmmaking with 35mm stock for artists of this and future generation' and that it is the museum's objective 'to help preserve the history, technology, and art of film.'" Of course, current legal restrictions on the use of nitrate film affected the replication to the extent that the reverse-engineered emulsion was coated on a "polyester film base"—polyester was only introduced in 1941. See: 'George Eastman Museum makes 35mm motion picture film from early cinema period' (May 19, 2016).

intangible heritage of humanity and its environment for the

purposes of education, study and enjoyment.[344]

This definition, adopted at ICOM's 21st general conference in 2007, differs in an important way—its extension to "intangible heritage"—from the one it replaced, which was adopted over thirty years earlier, in 1974, when its remit was conceived of as being "the material evidence of man and his environment".[345] While the 1974 definition already cast its nets wide, the enlarged 2007 definition was meant to include "the living expressions like the traditions that many groups and communities worldwide have been passed down by their ancestors and will continue to pass on to their descendants", traditions that ICOM wants to protect "by means of recordings and transcriptions."[346] As a trend meant to support UNESCO's 2003 Convention for the Safeguarding of the Intangible Cultural Heritage and to protect cultural diversity in the face of globalization this salvage museology implies more than a difference in terms of remit. First of all, it means that artifacts have become less defining, as their distinctiveness from records appears to be less urgent.[347] Secondly, this definition implies that a museum can also become a creator of collection items.

Even though the expansion of ICOM's definition seems particularly relevant for ethnographic and (living) history museums, a fairly recent example, involving the letters of Vincent van Gogh, may here serve as an illustration. I give this example not only to introduce a different museum environment, but even more to emphasize the potential productiveness of the blurring of terms that has come with the extended definition, which in the end neutralizes the incongruity hinted at above. The Van Gogh Museum, in Amsterdam, holds the majority—over 800 of 902—of the

---

[344] 'Museum definition', at: http://icom.museum/the-vision/museum-definition/.

[345] Quoted in: Stephen E. Weil, 'Fighting off some dry rot, woodworm, and damp', in: *Rethinking museums and other meditations* (1997 [1990]), p. 23 (orig. publ. in 1985).

[346] 'Intangible heritage', at: http://icom.museum/programmes/intangible-heritage/.

[347] "Artifact is often used to distinguish man-made items from physical specimens. Even though documents and other two-dimensional objects are artifacts because of their physical nature, 'artifact' is often used to distinguish three-dimensional materials from two-dimensional materials."; Pearce-Moses (2005), p. 36.

known letters van Gogh wrote to his brother Theo and other relatives as well as to fellow artists, among others. According to current definitions these letters would be readily classified as archival *records*, since they were clearly "created (...) in the course of individual (...) activity", "used as an extension of human memory", and contain detailed and continuous evidentiary information about the painter's everyday life and his thoughts.[348] Because of their uniqueness, age, and associational qualities, in short their intrinsic value, these letters obviously do not easily lend themselves to being exhibited (apart even from overriding their status as private matter). They are, therefore, treated as circumspectly as *artifacts* are: they need to be shielded against touch and certain levels of humidity and light intensity. Moreover, their handwriting is sometimes hard to decipher, even outside a display case, because of fading ink, stains, tears or overwrites, while within it double sided letters would obstruct perusal in an arbitrary way. Other than in printed form they are hard to comprehend. And that is precisely what the museum provided. In 2009, it presented the results of its Van Gogh Letters Project in new, annotated, and modernized print as well as digital editions of all known correspondence, both from and to Van Gogh. While this seemed to emphasize their status as records, the publication was also occasion for the museum to actually exhibit a selection of the letters. Interestingly, this selection was displayed in combination with the paintings of which the letters contained sketches (either as work-in-progress or as aides-mémoire of finished canvases), thereby highlighting their pictorial, i.e. more traditionally museum–like, rather than their writerly aspects.[349] In other words, the Van Gogh Museum created a public presentation by turning 'typical' records into 'typical' artifacts. Most importantly, of course, it succeeded in enriching both exhibited types of object by recreating the nearness of painting and letter the way it might have been at the moment a letter was being written.

---

[348] Pearce-Moses (2005), p. 326.

[349] http://www.vangoghmuseum.nl/vgm/index.jsp?page=161662&lang=nl; http://www.vangoghletters.org/vg/.
The Van Gogh Museum has withstood the temptation to wholeheartedly embrace the opinion of "some people who were in a position to know" to elevate the letters to the status of "world literature". On its website it diplomatically skirts the issue ("qualifications like this are in part personal"), while simultaneously avoiding the risk of enshrining these materials and maintaining the liberty to bring out their qualities from various angles and in various ways; see:
http://vangoghletters.org/vg/letter_writer_1.html.

The 'intangible turn' of the museum world as a whole seems at first sight to have rendered museums less helpful as a reference for film heritage institutes to emulate. Yet it actually brings out a practice common to both. Working with artifacts as well as records is, one might say, standard operational procedure for those film heritage institutes that have film collections and actively preserve them by making new objects: new prints or digital files (while of course the preservation of, for instance, film posters has followed 'traditional' museological procedures by safeguarding or restoring the artifact itself). These new objects clearly are copies of other artifacts—so-called originals—, yet also have record status in that they contain "[d]ata or information that has been fixed on some medium; that has content, context, and structure", where "content" is defined as "the text, data, symbols, numerals, images, sound, graphics, and other information that make up the substance of the record", while "its ability to fix information so that it can be repeated, recited, or recalled at a later date functions as an extension of memory and is at the heart of the concept of record. A record may be created specifically to preserve information over time or to prevent future misinterpretation of that information, although a record cannot be presumed to be reliable without authentication."[350] The latter part of this definition also meets the museological requirement of reversibility—or in the case of film restoration, "repeatability".[351]

The creation of new artifacts, then, is not a matter of mere duplication. It is also a record determined by historical, contextual information: whether one intends to make a restoration—"[t]he process of compensation for degradation by returning an image or artefact to close to its original content"—or a reconstruction—"[t]he editorial procedure of reassembling a version of a film production to an authoritative original version")[352]—or whether one wants to simulate a print's characteristics or

---

[350] *Structure* refers to a record's physical characteristics and internal organization of the contents", while "[c]*ontext* is the organizational, functional, and operational circumstances surrounding a record's creation, receipt, storage or use." See: Pearce-Moses (2005), pp. 326-328.

[351] Read, Meyer (2000), pp. 69-70.

[352] Read, Meyer (2000), pp. 335; 334. These two definitions also reflect the prevailing two meanings of the term *original,* one referring to the reconstruction of a "film element exposed in the camera, the first generation of image" (Read, Meyer (2000), p. 332), while the other reproduces as much as possible the qualities and properties of the element that was input for the restoration, regardless of its generation.

repeat as closely as possible a film's production method (e.g. the applied color techniques of the silent era, monaural sound or the very use of a film strip) and/or exhibition sensation,[353] each requires preliminary research into both historical circumstances (e.g. of technology, trade practices, aesthetic conventions) and current technological possibilities, purposes and/or audience experience. So, besides the definitional overlap of artifact and record, both also potentially inform each other. This, of course, makes even more sense when film and film-related items are being connected, not just in relational databases, but also in public activities or publications.

The research, however, that went into recovering historical contexts for preservation and restoration cannot be said to have been widely reflected in film heritage institutes' public information, nor are the principles that inform these activities clarified in their public presentations, not even in the online presence that a number of institutes have created for their collections. One ambitious example of such open source access is the abovementioned Cinemaimpresa.TV, the YouTube channel for the commercials, promotional, and industrial films held by the Archivio Nazionale del Cinema d'Impresa (ANCI), in Ivrea, a division of the Fondazione Centro Sperimentale di Cinematografia-Cineteca Nazionale. Given the almost exclusive focus on feature fiction films in the Centro's theatrical venue, in Rome, ANCI's digital venue is a way to present this other significant part of the institute's collections. In that sense you might say that Cinemaimpresa.TV is the digital counterpart of the institute's film theater. In fact, the resemblance is even stronger than one would like, as ANCI's metadata are just as poor as those for the institute's screenings: Cinemaimpresa.TV commonly provides only a director's name (if any), the company who sponsored the film or video, and a brief synopsis of its topic. Surely this meagre provision of information will reflect priorities and/or the allocation of limited funds or staffing. So one must conclude that the channel has been made to get the archive's stuff 'out there'. (This is a common consideration, a provisional prioritizing with the promise,

---

[353] Paul Read, 'New technologies for archive film restoration and access: film images', in: GAMMA Group (ed.), *The use of new technologies applied to film restoration: technical and ethical problems* ([1996]), pp. 37-38. For the notion of simulation see: Giovanna Fossati, 'Coloured images today: how to live with simulated colours (and be happy)', in: Daan Hertogs, Nico de Klerk (eds.), *'Disorderly order': colours in silent film. The 1995 Amsterdam Workshop* (1996), pp. 83-89.

usually implicit and frequently unfulfilled, of a more professional follow-up). Still, it does so without taking advantage of the opportunities a digital venue offers. For instance, in contrast to standard expectations of projected screenings, the channel's contents show a wide range of—and a tolerance for—variations in visual quality. Some uploaded materials begin and end properly, while others show the film leader countdown; again others have been copied from a video with a plainly visible time code track, or have been recorded straight off TV; and some have clearly been restored, while others have not.[354] Users of YouTube—both 'uploaders' and 'downloaders'—are well accustomed to such qualitative variety (with no explanation or excuse given either, certainly when materials have been ripped from copyright-protected sources). A digital venue, therefore, seems a way to show materials that would otherwise be considered substandard and of minor historical significance. And if this is the only recourse taken, the opportunity missed is of informing a user, whether professional or layman, about the material and archival qualities and particularities of the films or videos presented, about their gauge; their assembly (if any); their provenance; what version or variant (a highly relevant consideration for commercials); or to what extent their current conditions, if restoration has been done, differ from former conditions. Without all this, access means no more than being allowed to watch semblances of inconsistent quality.

What is more, one can distinguish a self-propelling tendency that fogs museological considerations in restoration and reconstruction practices. It is doubtful, for instance, if the ever-expanding, reconstructed versions of METROPOLIS or NAPOLÉON VU PAR ABEL GANCE—iconic (silent) titles in the history of film preservation—presented over the past three decades or so can still be called authoritative, what with their inclusion of scenes and fragments from multiple takes, discrepant print generations, different language versions, etc. Even if the resulting version happens to be more complete in terms of storyline (or even of any known *released* version), it

[354] See, for instance, the differences between the uploaded materials of: LA PATTUGLIA DEL PASSO S. GIACOMO (https://www.youtube.com/watch?v= zYOdy_TCoVg); UNO SU TRE (https://www.youtube.com/watch?v =ZsY_Zri49U0); INCONTRO CON LA OLIVETTI (https://www.youtube.com/ watch?v=iobjKjjiJy4&index=6&list =PL15B-32H5GlJej0W8WIOhGiOuS_ 9h6eC3); *UNO MATTINA* ALLA FERRANIA (https://www.youtube.com/ watch?v=yQMcz04OfmU); [MARTINI VERMOUTH, REALIZZATO PER EXPO 1911] (https://www.youtube.com/watch?v=wLyWLBRrKHY&list =PL15B-32H5GlJej0W8WIOhGiOuS_9h6eC3).

pushes the envelope of the film heritage world's own notions of *original*. For example, after the discovery of the most complete extant version of METROPOLIS, in 2007, at the Museo del Cine Pablo Ducrós Hicken, Buenos Aires, film archivist Martin Koerber wrote, "[O]ne can now see the *director's cut* of METROPOLIS, 80 years after we all believed the *original version* was destroyed" (my italics). No doubt in his enthusiasm Koerber here equated Fritz Lang's lengthy box-office failure in Germany with a 16mm duplicate negative struck from a deteriorating—and now lost—35mm Spanish-language distribution print for Argentina that, while bought before production company Ufa withdrew and shortened the film for a German rerelease, still was at a considerable remove.[355] Watching such reconstructions in theatrical settings with musical accompaniment one feels expected not to notice how the storyline vies for attention with the various 'texts' and, by implication, the technological, aesthetic, historical and/or local contexts from which their components have been lifted. Emblematic of this implied, unfocused perception are the sound-on-film fragments from later prints of NAPOLÉON cut in but screened with the sound off. These reconstructions, or rather these palimpsests, cannot be said to either simulate or emulate. As a result of their implied advancement ("the most complete") and consequent 'irreversibility' they rather flaunt their assemblage and heterogeneity.

No less foggy is the other extreme, not uncommon either, made up by the many preserved films that do not even tell us on which elements their preservation or restoration was based and in what aspects and to what extent original and new prints correspond. Neither, moreover, are these contextual matters commonly communicated in presentations,[356] nor in the liner notes to an institute's or archival festival's DVD editions, most of

[355] Martin Koerber, 'The METROPOLIS of Buenos Aires' (July 4, 2008); see also: Anke Wilkening, 'METROPOLIS 2010: a new effort to recapture the lost METROPOLIS', in: Kerstin Parth, Oliver Hanley, Thomas Ballhausen (eds.), *Works in progress: digital film restoration within archives* (2013), pp. 134-147.
In her introduction, at the 2011 Flaherty Seminar, to a program of Argentinian films from the abovementioned Museo del Cine its director Paula Félix-Didier put the METROPOLIS case in proportion with her throwaway remark, "*Not our greatest find.*"

[356] A few film heritage institutes—notably Cinematek and Cinémathèque française-Musée du Cinéma—systematically notify audiences about the preservation they are going to see with a brief text preceding the film proper (yet part of the print) stating that new print's source(s). This allows visitors to learn whether its gauge, the presence or absence of color, etc. match or not.

which I assume are targeted to a niche market not uninterested in such information. And it should be said that notwithstanding the campaigns in the 1980s and 1990s (e.g. 'Nitrate can't wait') aimed at convincing national or supra-national legislators of the significance of the moving image heritage—and which led to increased appropriation of funds for film archives and museums (and, in its wake, for film archival training) as well as an acceleration in preservation and presentation activities—, these efforts have not resulted in a widely shared, *practically* implemented set of standards. The film heritage world, therefore, may well be in need of a new reflective boost from another neighboring discipline: archival science.

Future scenarios

An appeal to archival science, though, is not meant to make life necessarily easier. First of all, one would expect that because of its generic name it is a discipline that has much to say about film heritage practices. It potentially has, but actually it did not. The reason surely is that it is rooted in, and has concerned itself largely with, theories of and their application to documents of administrative transactions of public and corporate organizations, most commonly paper and electronic records. And while some of its practitioners claim flexibility when it comes to the meaning of *document, text,* or *writing,* they differ in their assessment of how these statements relate to the types of artifact that film archives ordinarily have in their care, such as film prints, handbills, posters, and other items of publicity, let alone recording and projection equipment.[357]

Of course, a gap can only exist between two sides, so it should be pointed out that, in its turn, film archival practice (its cataloguing and library departments often excepted) is rarely appreciably informed by activities and concepts developed within archival science. For instance,

---

[357] See e.g.: Lorraine O'Donnell, 'Towards total archives: the form and meaning of photographic records', in: *Archivaria* (Fall 1994); Michael K. Buckland, 'What is a "document"?', in: *Journal of the American Society for Information Science* (September 1997), pp. 804-808; Lisa Darms, 'Study in documents. The archival object: a memoir of disintegration', in: *Archivaria* (Spring 2009), p. 144. A more radical approach is one that criticizes the textual bias of archival science's vocabulary and methods; see: Joan M. Schwartz, 'Coming to terms with photographs: descriptive standards, linguistic "othering", and the margins of archivy', in: *Archivaria* (Fall 2002), pp. 142-171.

the abovementioned lack of proper information regarding the materials that were input for restorations or reconstructions clashes with the principle that "[a]ll descriptions and arrangements begin with the record, defined as context, structure and content. This combination describes the circumstances of creation and use of the record (its context), the physical, or extrinsic, qualities and formulaic layout (structure), and the information contained within the record or its intrinsic qualities (content)".[358] And even when film archival practice is informed by notions of archival science, film heritage institutes are often faced with a recalcitrant reality. Not a few of them began as places where collectors stored salvaged materials, film prints in particular. Perhaps romantic accounts short on detail of those pioneering days have stuck in the popular mind, or else because of the mere constraints on disposing of large quantities of film materials, it is not uncommon for donors to confront an institute with impossible terms to decide about acquiring materials they want to rid themselves of (the related papers can be, and usually have been, cleared up in standard ways). That is one reason why appraisal and selection may only begin long after materials were precipitately deposited, rather than before.[359]

Furthermore, film heritage institutes usually hold a mixture of what (non-film) archivists call *archival fonds* and *(artificial) collections*. The first term is defined by one glossary as "[t]he entire body of records of an organization, family, or individual that have been created and accumulated as the result of an organic process reflecting the functions of the creator", while the second is used for "[a] group of materials with some unifying characteristic" and assembled by a person, organization, or

---

[358] Nordland (2004), p. 154; see also: Pearce-Moses (2005), pp. 326-328.

[359] Sam Kula, *Appraising moving images: assessing the archival and monetary value of film and video records* (2003), p. 2; Helen P. Harrison (ed. & comp.), *Audiovisual archives: a practical reader* (1997), pp. 126-128; see also: De Klerk (2016), pp. 131; 140.

repository from a variety of sources".[360] In this view, the minutes of the Colonial Institute's board meetings, for instance, constitute a fonds, while an archive's film prints acquired through legal deposit (assuming they have come from various production or distribution companies) is a collection, or an aggregate of collections (one reason perhaps, besides their specific missions, why institutes that collect such materials are called *collecting institutions*[361]). So, even though archival science glossaries, manuals, and other instructive publications do contain entries or chapters on moving image-related topics,[362] debates about and efforts to accommodate visual (and other non-textual) collections within the conceptual frameworks of archival science, let alone pleas for the necessity of reviewing the frameworks, have been isolated (a notable exception is the discussion of the concept of *total archives*[363]).

Of major importance is the fact that during the past decades the archival world has operated in, and adapted to, a turbulent field of forces. Besides the debates over the abovementioned power to represent, examples are the sharp increase in volume of documents produced by the traditional creators of archival records; the transition from paper to electronic documents; the consequent, increasing dependence on developments outside of (and commonly unconcerned with) the discipline, such as computer engineering and information technology; the blurring of traditional distinctions between types of repository, media, and

---

[360] Pearce-Moses (2005), pp. 173, 76 resp. However, the terminology is elastic: a gloss on the entry 'Collection' states that "it should be emphasised that both these classes of aggregates (the fonds and the artificial collection) are 'collections' in the more general sense in which the term is used here." (p. 76). See also: Proctor, Cook (2012), for whom provenance is not essential either when defining fonds, or group, as "the largest entity of organizationally related records established on the basis of provenance" and collection as "an artificial gathering (...) from diverse sources, which are to be treated as a group." (p. 14).

[361] Blouin, Jr., Rosenberg, (2013), pp. 4-5; 32-33; 156-158. Another term, emphasizing rather the remit of an institute's collecting policy, is *special-subject repository*.

[362] Proctor, Cook (2012), pp. 216-225; Pearce-Moses (2005); Kula (2003); Harrison (1997); a volume devoted entirely to broadcast news is: Richard Lochead (ed.), *Beyond the printed word: the evolution of Canada's broadcast heritage news/Au-delà de l'écrit: le patrimoine de la radio-télédiffusion des nouvelles au Canada* (1991).

[363] Laura Millar, 'Discharging our debt: the evolution of the total archives concept in English Canada', in: *Archivaria* (Fall 1998), pp. 103-146.

record-management responsibilities in digital environments (in the case of the latter that has meant a shift from records creator to electronic record systems); concern about the reliability of digital access and storage; as well as the proposals for different appraisal procedures and collection policies, in terms of both media (and combinations thereof) and focus.[364] But it is precisely this turbulence and the self-reflective stance that has come with it that makes an archival science perspective apposite.

It would seem urgent, therefore, that the two related but unparallel disciplines of archival science and film heritage work align themselves more closely. If nothing else, the digital convergence and the challenges digital technologies entailed have brought them closer than each may have been aware of or willing to acknowledge. Moreover, separation of media is noncurrent in another way: in a number of cases the creation of publicly funded, mandated film heritage institutes can retrospectively be understood as a mere pragmatic measure, a form of outsourcing that obviated "contradictory policies, priorities and methodologies" within one general archival institute.[365] Surely, in terms of their materiality analogue moving images require distinct storage conditions and methods of preservation. But the different approaches to appraisal, description or access they have received as collections need not have been—and partly are not—so different. Particularly the notion of intellectual control and curatorship, or "the capacity and competence of the institution to create 'stories' and draw knowledge out of that repository, to produce cultural history",[366] is a reference, if not a precondition, for regaining relevance in film heritage institute's presentations. (Archival science, in its turn, may

---

[364] For a recent overview of the changes introduced by the digital turn, see: Blouin, Jr., Rosenberg (2013), ch. 10, pp. 183-206; see also: Bauer (2013). For selection and acquisition policies see: Cook (2009); Bearman (1989), ch. I.

[365] Eric Ketelaar, 'Exploitation of new archival materials', in: *The archival image: collected essays* (1997), p. 78 (orig. publ. in 1988). An exception was the (then-named) Public Archives of Canada, founded in 1912, whose "legislated mandate was to acquire archival material in its various forms"; see: Millar (1998); O'Donnell (Fall 1994) p. 106.
Certainly not all of these archives were newly created. Quite a number of film archives that began as private collectors' initiatives were transformed, sometimes after intense lobbying, into public archives or museums; see for a general overview: Houston (1994); see for detailed case studies: Kumar (2016); Lameris (2007), pp. 6-7, 27-47.

[366] Cherchi Usai, Francis, Horwath, Loebenstein (2008), p. 96.

benefit from film archival expertise in working with artifacts the former, at least some of its guiding lights, unproblematically conceived of as being of evidentiary value only.[367]) In other words, if public film heritage institutes are mere extensions of the mandate of general archives, the conceptual gap should be closed lest practical circumstances continue to overshadow common principles.

Finally, modern archival science's public administrative bias foregrounds its activities and concerns as being inherently part of the democratic process: at the deepest level they are rooted in the idea that public governance and the activities public institutes have been mandated to fulfill, through funding, should be as open and accountable as possible, enabling the public to learn about their own society and its histories. This has not, by the way, always been the case: these notions had to be promoted and argued, if not pleaded. An important advocate was archivist Gerald F. Ham, who criticized the profession for its "politicization" in focusing on "unrepresentative indicators", by which he meant, among other things, an overrepresentation of governmental and other official records, a condition that constituted an obstacle to the idea that "history should help people to understand the world they live in."[368] And as we know all too well, in less democratically inclined administrations these goals continue to get twisted by overmuch politics or underbudgeted funding. But that should not keep the film heritage world from taking their eyes off these core principles.

One of archival science's relevant contributions was already discussed in the concluding paragraph of chapter 2: the notion of *functional context*. This I conceived of as all the signifying contexts of the film heritage in a given geographic region and historical era. Its most direct implications would involve research into the entire range of an institute's collection items. For this, of course, film heritage institutes can profitably turn to academic film historiography, particularly when it would imply research done outside their own archives, as signifying contexts will lead every which way. But they might also want to set an agenda of their own (and for other parties in their interpretive communities to follow), based on in-

---

[367] Terry Cook 'The tyranny of the medium: a comment on "total archives"', in: *Archivaria* (Winter 1979-1980), pp. 141-149; for a critique of Cook's concept of evidentiary value see: O'Donnell (Fall 1994).

[368] The terms Ham used were quoted from historians Gould P. Colman and Carl Becker, respectively; see: Ham (1975), pp. 6; 5.

house initiated research of 'uncharted' materials or matters specific to a historical period in their country or region. As such it is a precondition for public activities that are meant to reflect the array of a national cinema's manifestations—"national" meaning here emphatically not merely a country's film production, but also its distribution, exhibition, and viewing.[369] At the same time, research of functional contexts, whatever its sources, may well increase an institute's standing within the academic world.[370]

One type of these public activities would greatly benefit from the digital turn and the ideas developed within archival science on appraisal. In chapter 3 I briefly sketched a possible future scenario for film heritage institutes in a digital environment from the point of view of preservation, in which creators or owners of artifacts and records would have no urgent need to hand over their materials to film heritage institutes for safe storage: their moving images and most of their company 'papers' could remain comfortably on their own computers (and no one else would make money off of their work, as a popular, though misinformed argument among copyright holders against archival deposit goes). Now consider an alternative, possibly even parallel, scenario from the point of view of access and presentation. For those creators or owners who want to have a prominent online presence it could actually be advantageous to make their artifacts and/or records available through a film heritage institute. This could either be for a specified time, similar to works on loan for art exhibitions, or it could be open-ended, as in a permanent exhibition (leaving proprietary matters aside for now). The motives creators and owners might have in considering this are: it saves time and effort; it entrusts the presentation to professionals with archival and curatorial expertise; and it relies on an institute's reputation and prominence (either or both of the latter two considerations, of course, are additional reasons to call this section *future* scenarios). While linear presentations, particularly screenings, reconstruct an experience, typically on the basis of a few items at most, such online presentations can much easier retain the

---

[369] De Klerk (2004b).

[370] It is noteworthy in this connection that to date membership of Domitor, the association for the study of early cinema, among film heritage institutes' staff as well as their presence at its conferences and in its published papers has been minimal. Equally noteworthy is that one of the most stimulating, recent initiatives in the field of film heritage, the Orphan Film Symposium, has come from within the academe.

principle of provenance and allow one to see coherence and connections between larger amounts of items. And because, as noted, bulk and prominence are two concerns that often go together, collection items from one donor or lender might even be meaningfully contextualized and enriched by those of another collection, either in house or from another institute, domestic or foreign.

An example from past practices that I once suggested for contextualization is that of the papers of the aforementioned Dutch exhibitor-cum-distributor Jean Desmet. This collection contains, besides papers concerning his private life and his later involvement in the real estate business, a vast amount of various materials—letters and telegrams, invoices, cash-books, ledgers, tenders and contracts, minutes and statutes, handbills, posters, program synopses, agendas, periodicals, etc.— that concern a range of cinema-related business activities, notably his fairground career, the acquisition, distribution, and sale of films and film-related objects as well as correspondence concerning personnel. Particularly the comprehensive correspondence of Desmet's office with exhibitors, distributors, production companies, agencies, and a host of manufacturers and service providers clearly shows how Desmet's theatrical and distribution activities were part of a network of businesses and organizations both domestic and foreign. The digitization of the paper collection, notably the domestic and international correspondence, could also be the occasion to induce European archives—both public and private—to jointly develop a database with which it would be possible to show how the film industry and all its related enterprises were interwoven. Bit by bit, additions could be made: Edison, Ernemann, Messter, Nordisk, Pathé, etc. For the Netherlands, the Desmet papers are a unique and uniquely rich collection of documents, but within the context of the European film entertainment business it is just another link, the significance of which is only partly—locally—visible. The context of an international industry—including matters such as patents and other rights, ownership, technical and organizational developments (patent exchange, vertical integration, marketing) and institutionalization— makes us appreciate its importance for a small production country such as the Netherlands more fully and clearly.

And that, of course, just concerns the film business. Because the papers also provide a spyhole on various aspects of Dutch society during the first two decades of the twentieth century. The correspondence and transactions provide information about, among others, salaries and rates (of cinema theater staff, but also of plumbers, carpenters, printers, piano tuners, lawyers, window washers, etc.), prices (of programmes and films, but also real estate, printed matter, coal, water, electricity, etc.); the organization of the entertainment business (the changing relationships between itinerant and theatrical film shows; copyright; taxes; advertising; legislation; etc.); the communication infrastructure (postal and telegraph services; trains; shipping between Holland and its colonies; etc.); welfare: health care, education (letters of application in particular reveal the dramatic effects of sickness and hardship; each postal item tells something about the command of written language and its social implications); or the effects of World War I.

These considerations together could lead to the development of a multi-faceted, multi-linked digital database in which the Desmet papers are combined with data sources about contemporary Dutch society as well as with similar collections in other film heritage institutes. The basic idea is that every archival item is a metonym: individual cases—a contract, letter of application, invoice, program handbill, etc.—can be linked to information about, say, contemporary legislation, labor statistics, domestic and foreign business partners, etc. etc. Such a database has a dual purpose. It shows, first of all, how Desmet's activities were linked up with all kinds of social situations and bodies, the possibilities they offered as well as the limits they imposed upon his business (such as a new Act concerning games of chance, in 1904, which affected his exploitation of the wheel of fortune on Dutch fairgrounds).

Secondly, it allows one to reconstruct various activities involving film at the beginning of the twentieth century and give a sense of both cinema's enormous popularity and international interconnectedness: buying, selling, and renting; the fitting out of cinema theatres; the performance of traveling film shows; the printing of admission tickets, handbills (5,000 a week in 1910, 7,000 in 1915 for Desmet's Parisien Theater), posters or stationery; the placement of advertisements (not just in newspapers, but also in football or military magazines, illuminated advertising on Dam Square, etc.); or the payment of copyrights for musicians.[371] Instead of a short-term project, the updating and maintenance of which would cease the moment the funding runs out, this is conceived as an open-ended, modular workflow, the assembly of which can be gradually expanded, unhindered by narrow time constraints during which individual institutes' procedures are disrupted or priorities

---

[371] Nico de Klerk, 'What the papers say: the case of the film-related papers of Jean Desmet', in: *KINtop*, no. 14-15 (2006), pp. 113-121

disregarded. Here, advancement depends rather on such matters as cooperation, compatibility, and authorization (notably copyrights).

Given current technological developments, film heritage institutes, as archives, may be expected to perform two distinct types of activity in the very near future. One is keeping their analogue materials and equipment in working order as an enabling condition to make public, museological presentations of cinema manifestations and experiences that will largely disappear—or already have—in the world of film industry and business practices (and these experiences, of course, can be enhanced by digitized related materials). I will not discuss this type of presentations further here, as it constituted the majority of the activities surveyed and evaluated in chapter 3 (see also the referenced publication *Film curatorship: archives, museums, and the digital marketplace*). Nor do I consider it my place to sketch a model of presentations for materials I am not familiar with.

The other type of activity exploits the possibilities and opportunities presented by digital technological developments for online presentations. The scenario and examples sketched above take into account, first of all, that in a digital environment artifact and record, technologically speaking, are not intrinsically different. Secondly, web-based presentations, whether open-source, geo-filtered, in-house, etc. (according to the legal circumstances that obtain), have no necessary time limits. Rather, they enable users to consult a site at their own leisure. Think in this connection, for instance, of the erstwhile Zooms at the Cinémathèque française, produced on the occasion of a linear program or exhibition, yet available through the institute's website long afterwards.

Above, I used the word "gradual" advisedly, because this type of curatorial work is not merely a matter of bulk and its concomitant notion of having as many materials as possible a mere mouse click away. To recall my earlier example, when EFG claims that its portal "gives quick access to hundreds of thousands of film historical documents as preserved in European film archives and cinémathèques", it is in fact throwing sand in our eyes. To such a vast amount of materials one simply cannot have "quick access", not, that is, if one wants to make sense of it. There is a suggestion of a democratic environment here, and suggestion it remains. Democracy, I prefer to think, is about enabling people to make well-considered choices and decisions. And curatorship is an elaboration of that, as it implies organizing, programming, and communicating the materials and knowledge at one's command in archivally and historically meaningful and understandable ways. "Gradual", then, stands for an unhurried yet informed and considerate accretion of presentations of digitized artifacts and records to anyone interested. Its curatorial success may in fact accelerate the dynamics of cooperation and extension of such databases.

"Web-based information sources have no institutional home at all." That, indeed, is one of the major changes, and in some cases accomplishments, of contemporary databases. But, as the same authors say, such resources are also "released from the institutional authorities that once assured their validity."[372] Without implying that there is anything inherently disadvantageous to being non-institutional (after all, the success of Wikipedia was a poke in the eye of the traditional, corporate model of knowledge production), this actually leaves a large stretch of the field for film heritage institutes to occupy in a distinctive way. There is no point for film heritage institutes, most of which are bureaucratically organized, in emulating the wikis of this world. Yet the cutting edge, I would suggest, is up for grabs, because Wikipedia stipulates—as any encyclopedia would—that original research and its results cannot be accepted, because "the topic of an article must have already been the subject of publication in reliable sources such as books published by major publishing houses, newspapers, magazines, peer-reviewed scholarly journals and websites that meet the same requirements as reputable print-based sources."[373] Moreover, what one commentator called the "larger cultural trends" that transcend Wikipedia's narrow focus on hard facts and on countries and topics of the West signals its problem of a shrinking and less diversified corps of editors, if not enthusiasm for crowdsourcing tout court.[374] So, rather than sharing their poverty, film heritage institutes may well succeed in creating cutting edge, online presentations in terms of the organization and navigation of their wealth of 'content'. At the same time they might even manage to make a step towards reconciling scholarship and public orientation, the two conflicting approaches to the presentation policies of art museums that Victoria Alexander observed in her research about their shifting sources of financial support.[375] Finally, in insisting on democracy and accountability,

---

[372] Blouin, Jr., Rosenberg (2013), p. 203.

[373] 'Contributing to Wikipedia', at: http://en.wikipedia.org/wiki/Wikipedia: Contributing_to_Wikipedia.

[374] Simonite (2013); see also: Rosenzweig (2011), pp. 70-78.

[375] Alexander (1996).

the performance of which I see as an element of the reciprocal relation between film heritage institutes as an expert system and the public, as a return in kind for the trust and funding conferred upon them, I second the views of some of archival science's prominent practitioners.[376]

Back to the present from my future scenarios, however, it is clear that many film heritage institutes overall have not exploited their opportunities and realized their potential. The retreat to a relatively restricted repertoire of materials and topics has obstructed the dissemination of full accounts of a country's or region's film heritage to a wider public. Or, to recall Anthony Giddens's term, it has inhibited reflexivity by withholding new information from feeding into opinion formation and other social practices. But in today's world, of course, published, reflective considerations importantly shape people's working knowledge about and conception of any aspect of that world and our lives in it. Surely, such considerations do not necessarily come from academic sources alone; they are also offered through educational settings or popularizations in the media, and in all sorts of discourses—lessons, lectures, consults; treatises, reviews, and essays; news reports, editorials, columns, and talk shows; propaganda, advertising, and commercials—to percolate down through plain, everyday conversations. It is only because most people have at least a basic, internalized knowledge of the law, of health hazards or of any other issues that matter in their daily lives that such expert systems can gain in importance. And as there is no clincher, no "ultimate authority to turn to"[377] in a modern world, the best bet for film heritage institutes to distinguish themselves is to play the heritage card and base their avowed expertise on their collections. Here, then, in the production and dissemination of informed, reflective information, is located their responsibility to provide and circulate state-of-the-art knowledge. Here, more specifically, is located the opportunity, the main gate through which their film heritage materials and their signifying historical contexts are returned to society.

Judging from the most salient conclusions that my survey allowed, however, that gatekeeping function is in an important sense outbalanced by received knowledge, emblematized by an auteurist tradition that over the years has been watered down to mere biography as well as by an interpretive, essentializing discourse that has become virtually

---

[376] See e.g.: Blouin, Jr., Rosenberg (2013); Cook (1992 and 2009); Ham (1975).

[377] Giddens, Pierson (1998), p. 111.

indistinguishable from film reviewing (and film reviewing, in its turn, basically approaches film heritage programs—whenever they do—in the same way as releases). Film heritage institutes' main occupation can therefore be described as "the reinterpretation and clarification of tradition", in other words as unmodern.[378] By neglecting to seize the opportunity to promote their specificity and wealth, for all practical purposes they forbear to advance reflexivity. And where there is no reflexivity there is no reasoned change, i.e. change based on new or up-to-date, published and percolated research and insights. In a world and a culture that is often called visual this is something the institutes should worry about. Stated bluntly, this is a public disservice.

Naturally, I am aware of the differences between the performance of accountability of individual institutes as well as of the significance of film culture between countries—the Netherlands, for sure, is quite unlike France (Roland Barthes was once quoted as saying that he didn't go much to the cinema, only twice a week; "twice" is, and always has been, more than the Dutch average *annual* cinema attendance). Nevertheless, I see the two points discussed above—the development of curatorial expertise, particularly within the context of the opportunities provided by digital technologies, and the notions of democracy and accountability—as signposts to the improvement of the film heritage gatekeeper function. As the institutes take up a middle position between the main providers of film-related knowledge—on the one hand, a popular, largely biographical discourse (centered on name directors and stars) in the mass media and, on the other, an academic discourse that serves a limited readership—, film heritage institutes are potentially equipped to stake out their own claim to authority between both. Obviously, not only can they tell their opinion, they can show it, too. That is to say, they can make distinctive (and preferably attractive and imaginative) programs, linear and online, based on the wealth of their vaults (as well as their access to sister organizations elsewhere), in terms of both film and film-related sources and their historical contexts. And by either capitalizing on the names known from the media whenever it is expedient or by filtering academic knowledge, they can supplement both by information that is uniquely local and material. After all, not all film scholars, let alone reviewers, are troubled over such notions as print history, appropriation or functional context.

---

[378] Giddens (2013), p. 37.

Political developments are too volatile and technological developments too quick and their applications too manifold to provide surefire guarantees. But anything is better than a lack of intellectual relevance and a loss of trust. Film heritage institutes may well claim that they are "followed" and "liked" by thousands or more, but whatever that signifies it is probably even more volatile, certainly more trivial and flimsy, than politics and technology. Sadly, such statistics merely serve to make funders and communication departments happy. Gaining, or regaining, a trusted, publicly meaningful position and power to represent requires more steadfastness, proficiency, and imagination than we see now.

References

Archives

DA (Desmet Archief), Eye, Amsterdam

KIT (Koninklijk Instituut voor de Tropen [Royal Tropical Institute]), Amsterdam

NA (Nationaal Archief), The Hague

Print

['City Film advertisement for LES CLANDESTINS']
    Nieuw Weekblad voor de Cinematografie, vol. 22 no. 32 (May 7, 1948)

['List of censored films']
    Nieuw Weekblad voor de Cinematografie, vol. 22 no. 44 (July 30, 1948)

A people and a nation: a history of the United States, vol. 2: since 1865
    by Mary Beth Norton, David M. Katzman, David W. Blight et al., 6th edn.
    Boston–New York: Houghton Mifflin, 2001 [1982]

'Das Unsichtbare Kino: Film, Kunst, Geschichte und das Museum'
    Mitteilungen des Österreichischen Filmmuseum, no. 7 (October-November 2014), pp. 56-60

'Die Utopie Film. Leben und Kino: 100 Vorschläge'
    Mitteilungen des Österreichischen Filmmuseum, no. 6 (September-October 2012), pp. 3-46

Papoea en film: verslag van een filmenquête gehouden door het Kantoor voor Bevolkingszaken. Rapport no. 81
    Hollandia: Gouvernement van Nederlands Nieuw-Guinea, 1956

Richard Abel, *The red rooster scare: making cinema American, 1900-1910*
    Berkeley–Los Angeles–London: University of California Press, 1999
    - *Americanizing the movies and "movie-mad" audiences, 1910-1914*
    Berkeley–Los Angeles–London: University of California Press, 2006

Victoria D. Alexander, *Museums and money: the impact of funding on exhibitions, scholarship, and management*
Bloomington–Indianapolis: Indiana University Press, 1996
- *Sociology of the arts: exploring fine and popular forms*
Malden, MA–Oxford–Carlton: Blackwell, 2011 [2003]

Robert Allen, *Vaudeville and film 1895-1915: a study in media interaction*
New York: Arno Press, 1980

Emilie Altenloh, *Zur Soziologie des Kino, die Kino-Unternehmung und die sozialen Schichten Ihrer Besucher*
Jena: Eugen Diederichs, 1914

Rick Altman, *Silent film sound*
New York - Chichester: Columbia University Press, 2004

Paula Amad, *Counter-archive: film, the everyday, and Albert Kahn's Archives de la Planète*
New York: Columbia University Press, 2010

Charles Ambler, 'Popular films and colonial audiences in Central Africa'
in: Melvyn Stokes, Richard Maltby (eds.), *Hollywood abroad: audiences and cultural exchange*
London: British Film Institute, 2004, pp. 133-157

Vincent Amiel, Pascal Couté, *Formes et obsessions du cinéma américain contemporain (1980-2002)*
Paris: Klincksieck, 2003

Joseph Anderson, Barbara Anderson, 'The myth of persistence of vision revisited'
Journal of Film and Video, vol. 45 no. 1 (Spring 1993), pp. 3-12

Arjun Appadurai, Carol A. Breckenridge, 'Museums are good to think: heritage on view in India'
in: Ivan Karp, Christine Mullen Kreamer, Steven D. Lavine (eds.), *Museums and communities: the politics of public culture*
Washington–London: Smithsonian Institution Press, 1992, pp. 34-55

Kwame Anthony Appiah, 'Whose culture is it, anyway?'
in: *Cosmopolitanism: ethics in a world of strangers*
New York: W.W. Norton & Company, 2007 [2006], pp. 115-135

Philippe Azoury, 'L'invitation à l'art'
    in: Michel Marie, Laurent Le Forestier (eds.), *La firme Pathé Frères, 1896-1914*
    Paris: AFRHC, 2004, pp. 85-94

Tino Balio, 'Surviving the Great Depression'
    in: Tino Balio, *Grand design: Hollywood as a modern business enterprise, 1930-1939*
    New York: Charles Scribner's Sons, 1993, pp. 13-36

Elke Bauer, 'Bildarchive im digitalen Wandel: Chancen und Herausforderungen'
    in: Irene Seehe, Ulrich Hägele (eds.), *Fotografie und Film im Archiv: sammeln, bewahren, erforschen*
    Münster: Waxmann, 2013, pp. 27-38

Jeanne Beausoleil, Pascal Ory (eds.), *Albert Kahn 1860-1940: réalités d'une utopie*
    Boulogne: Musée Albert-Kahn, 1995

Howard S. Becker, *Art worlds*
    Berkeley–Los Angeles–London: University of California Press, 1984 [1982]

Colin Bennett, *The handbook of kinematography: the history, theory, and practice of motion picture photography and projection*
    London: The Kinematograph Weekly, 1911

Sacvan Bercovich, *The American jeremiad*
    Madison: University of Wisconsin Press, 1978

Giorgio Bertellini, 'Shipwrecked spectators: Italy's immigrants at the movies in New York, 1906-1916'
    The Velvet Light Trap, no. 44 (1999), pp. 39-53

Wiebe E. Bijker, *Of bicycles, Bakelites, and bulbs: toward a theory of sociotechnical change*
    Cambridge, MA–London: MIT Press, 2002 [1995]

Ernst Bloch, 'Die Melodie im Kino oder immanente und transzendentale Musik'
    in: Fritz Güttinger (ed.), *Kein Tag ohne Kino. Schriftsteller über den Stummfilm*
    Frankfurt: Deutsches Filmmuseum Frankfurt, 1984, pp. 313-319
    (orig. publ. in 1914)

Ivo Blom, *Jean Desmet and the early Dutch film trade*
Amsterdam: Amsterdam University Press, 2003

Francis X. Blouin, Jr., William G. Rosenberg, *Processing the past: contesting authority in history and the archives*
New York: Oxford University Press, 2013 [2011]

Henri Bousquet, *Catalogue Pathé des années 1896 à 1914: 1907-1908-1909*
n.p. [Bures-sur-Yvette]: Henri Bousquet, 1993

Eileen Bowser, *The transformation of cinema: 1907-1915*
New York: Charles Scribner's Sons, 1990

Richard Brown, 'New Century Pictures: regional enterprise in early British film exhibition'
in: Vanessa Toulmin, Patrick Russell, Simon Popple (eds.), *The lost world of Mitchell and Kenyon: Edwardian Britain on film*
London: British Film Institute, 2004, pp. 69-82

Richard Brown, Barry Anthony, *A Victorian enterprise: the history of the British Mutoscope and Biograph Company, 1897-1915*
Trowbridge: Flicks Books, 1999

Ian Buruma, *Year zero: a history of 1945*
London: Atlantic Books, 2013

Paolo Cherchi Usai, David Francis, Alexander Horwath, Michael Loebenstein (eds.), *Film curatorship: archives, museums, and the digital marketplace*
Vienna: Österreichisches Filmmuseum–Synema, 2008

Ian Christie, '"Excuse me, this is where I came in..."'
in: Maša Peče, Koen van Daele (eds.), *Films you wouldn't want to see anywhere else than in a movie theatre*
Ljubljana: Javni zavod Kinodvor, 2014, pp. 63-65

James Clifford, 'Museums as contact zones'
in: *Routes: travel and translation in the late twentieth century*
Cambridge, MA–London: Harvard University Press, 1997, pp. 188-219

Terry Cook, 'Mind over matter: towards a new theory of archival appraisal'
in: Barbara L. Craig (ed.), *The archival imagination: essays in honour of Hugh A. Taylor*
Ottawa: Association of Canadian Archivists, 1992, pp. 38-71
- 'Remembering the future: appraisal of records and the role of archives in constructing social memory'
in: Francis X. Blouin, Jr., William G. Rosenberg (eds.), *Archives, documentation and institutions of social memory: essays from the Sawyer Seminar*
Ann Arbor: University of Michigan Press, 2009 [2006], pp. 169-181

Donald Crafton, *The talkies: American cinema's transition to sound 1926-1931*
Berkeley–Los Angeles–London: University of California Press, 1999 [1997]

Diana Crane, *The production of culture: media and the urban arts*
Newbury Park–London–New Delhi: Sage Publications, 1994 [1992]

Suzan Crommelin, 'Filmografie'
in: Janneke van Dijk, Jaap de Jonge, Nico de Klerk, *J.C. Lamster, een vroege filmmaker in Nederlands-Indië* Amsterdam: KIT Publishers, 2010, pp. 118-121

Hans Daalder, *Vier jaar nachtmerrie: de Indonesische kwestie. Willem Drees 1886-1988*
Amsterdam: Balans, 2004

Karel Dibbets, 'Op zoek naar een digitale conservator'
in: Mieke Lauwers, Bert Hogenkamp (eds.), *Audiovisueel: van emancipatie tot professionalisering. Jaarboek 2005*
The Hague: Stichting Archiefpublicaties, 2006, pp. 189-197

Janneke van Dijk, Jaap de Jonge, 'Johann Christian Lamster (1872-1954)'
in: Janneke van Dijk, Jaap de Jonge, Nico de Klerk, *J.C. Lamster, een vroege filmmaker in Nederlands-Indië* Amsterdam: KIT Publishers, 2010, pp. 11-77

Ine van Dooren, Peter Krämer, 'The politics of direct address'
in: Karel Dibbets, Bert Hogenkamp (eds.), *Film and the First World War*
Amsterdam: Amsterdam University Press, 1995, pp. 97-107

Willem Drees, *Zestig jaar levenservaring*
Amsterdam: Arbeiderspers, 1962

Allen Eyles, 'Goldwyn, RKO, and the war: Garson Kanin'
    Focus on film, no. 17 (1974), pp. 39-49

Scott Eyman, *The speed of sound: Hollywood and the talkie revolution
    1926-1930*
    Baltimore: Johns Hopkins University Press, 1999 [1997]

Rychard Fink, 'Introduction: Horatio Alger as a social philosopher'
    in: Horatio Alger, Jr., *Ragged Dick* and *Mark, the match boy*
    New York: Collier Books, 1962, pp. 5-31

Stanley Fish, 'Introduction, or How I learned to stop worrying and learned
    to love interpretation'
    in: *Is there a text in this class?: the authority of interpretive
    communities*
    Cambridge, MA–London: Harvard University Press, 1980, pp. 1-17

Gilles Fontaine, Patrizia Simone, *The exploitation of film heritage works in
    the digital era*
    Strasbourg: Observatoire européen de l'audiovisuel, [September 20,
    2016]

Giovanna Fossati, 'Coloured images today: how to live with simulated
    colours (and be happy)'
    in: Daan Hertogs, Nico de Klerk (eds.), *'Disorderly order': colours in
    silent film. The 1995 Amsterdam Workshop*, pp. 83-89
    Amsterdam: Nederlands Filmmuseum, 1996

Eliot Freidson, *Professional powers: a study of the institutionalization of
    formal knowledge*
    Chicago–London: University of Chicago Press, 1988 [1986]

Edmund Barry Gaither, '"Hey! That's mine": thoughts on pluralism and
    American museums'
    in: Ivan Karp, Christine Mullen Kreamer, Steven D. Lavine (eds.),
    Museums and communities: the politics of public culture (1992)
    Washington–London: Smithsonian Institution Press, 1992, pp. 56-
    64

Harold Garfinkel, 'What is ethnomethodology?'
    in: *Studies in ethnomethodology*
    Cambridge: Polity Press, 1984 [1967], pp. 1-34

John A. Garraty, 'The Great Depression and the New Deal'
in: William E. Leuchtenburg, *The FDR years: on Roosevelt and his legacy*
New York–Chichester: Columbia University Press, 1995, pp. 209-235
(orig. publ. in 1970)

André Gaudreault, 'Showing and telling: image and word in early cinema'
in: Thomas Elsaesser with Adam Barker (eds.), *Early cinema: space, frame, narrative*
London: British Film Institute, 1992 [1990], pp. 274-281

Gérard Genette, *Seuils*
Paris: Seuil, 2002 [1987]

Anthony Giddens, *The constitution of society: outline of the theory of structuration*
Cambridge–Malden, MA: Polity Press, 2014 [1984]
- *The consequences of modernity*
Cambridge–Malden, MA: Polity Press, 2013 [1990]

Anthony Giddens, Christopher Pierson, *Conversations with Anthony Giddens: making sense of modernity*
Cambridge: Polity Press, 1998

Erving Goffman, *Frame analysis: an essay on the organization of experience*
Boston: Northeastern University Press, 1986 [1974]

Douglas Gomery, *The Hollywood studio system*
Basingstoke: Macmillan, 1986

Rémy de Gourmont, 'Epilogues: cinématographe'
in: Richard Abel (ed.), *French film theory and criticism 1907-1939, vol. 1: 1907-1929*
Princeton: Princeton University Press, 1988, pp. 47-50 (orig. published in 1907)

Stephen Greenblatt, 'Resonance and wonder'
in: Ivan Karp, Steven D.Lavine (eds.), *Exhibiting cultures: the poetics and politics of museum display*
Washington - London: Smithsonian Institution Press, 1991, pp. 42-57

Tom Gunning, *D.W. Griffith and the origins of American narrative film: the early years at Biograph*
Urbana - Chicago: University of Illinois Press, 1991

Michael Hammond, '"A great American sensation": Thomas Ince's
    CIVILIZATION at the Palladium, Southampton, 1917'
    in: Melvyn Stokes, Richard Maltby (eds.), *Hollywood abroad:
    audiences and cultural exchange*
    London: British Film Institute, 2004, pp. 35-50

Anthony Harkins, *Hillbilly: a cultural history of an American icon*
    New York: Oxford University Press, 2004

Daan Hertogs, Nico de Klerk (eds.), *Nonfiction from the teens: the 1994
    Amsterdam Workshop*
    Amsterdam: Nederlands Filmmuseum, 1994

Robert V. Hine, John Mack Faragher, *The American West: a new interpretive
    history*
    New Haven–London: Yale University Press, 2000

Bert Hogenkamp, *De documentaire film 1945-1965: de bloei van een
    filmgenre in Nederland*
    Rotterdam: 010, 2003

Penelope Houston, *Keepers of the frame: the film archives*
    London: British Film Institute, 1994

Nancy Huggett, Kate Bowles, 'Cowboys, Jaffas and pies: researching
    cinemagoing in the Illawarra'
    in: Melvyn Stokes, Richard Maltby (eds.), *Hollywood abroad:
    audiences and cultural exchange*
    London: British Film Institute, 2004, pp. 64-77

Pierre-Emmanuel Jacques, 'Asta Nielsen in the cinema theatres of
    Lausanne, 1911-1913'
    in: Martin Loiperdinger, Uli Jung (eds.), *Importing Asta Nielsen: the
    international film star in the making 1910-1914*
    New Barnet: John Libbey, 2013, pp. 169-177

Mark Jancovich, Lucy Faire, with Sarah Stubbings, *The place of the
    audience: cultural geographies of film consumption*
    London: British Film Institute–Palgrave Macmillan, 2008 [2003]

Loe de Jong, *Het Koninkrijk der Nederlanden in de Tweede Wereldoorlog.*
  10a: Het laatste jaar I, eerste helft
  The Hague: Staatsuitgeverij, 1980
  - *Het Koninkrijk der Nederlanden in de Tweede Wereldoorlog. 10b:*
  Het laatste jaar II, eerste helft
  The Hague: Staatsuitgeverij, 1981
  - *Het Koninkrijk der Nederlanden in de Tweede Wereldoorlog. 10b:*
  Het laatste jaar II, tweede helft
  The Hague: Staatsuitgeverij, 1982

Tony Judt, *Postwar: a history of Europe since 1945*
  London: Vintage, 2010 [2005]

Ivan Karp, 'Introduction. Museums and communities: the politics of
  public culture'
  in: Ivan Karp, Christine Mullen Kreamer, Steven D. Lavine (eds.),
  Museums and communities: the politics of public culture
  Washington–London: Smithsonian Institution Press, 1992, pp. 1-17

Lisa Kernan, *Coming attractions: reading American movie trailers*
  Austin: University of Texas Press, 2004

Eric Ketelaar, 'Exploitation of new archival materials'
  in: *The archival image: collected essays*
  Hilversum: Verloren, 1997, pp. 67-80 (orig. publ. in 1988)

Nico de Klerk, 'A few remaining hours: news films and the interest in
  technology in Amsterdam film shows, 1896-1910'
  Film History, vol. 11 no. 1 (1999), pp. 5-17 (orig. publ. in 1998 as
  'Nur noch wenige Stunden: Nachrichtenfilm und Technikinteresse
  in Amsterdamer Filmvorführungen zwischen 1896 und 1910')
  - 'Programme of programmes: the Palace Theatre of Varieties'
  Griffithiana, no. 66-70 (1999-2000), pp. 241-247
  - '"Pictures to be shewn": programming the American Biograph'
  in: Simon Popple, Vanessa Toulmin (eds.), *Visual delights: essays on
  the popular and projected image in the 19th century*
  Trowbridge: Flicks Books, 2000, pp. 204-223
  - 'Das Programmformat. Bruchstücke einer Geschichte'
  KINtop, no. 11 (2002), pp. 15-19
  - '"Volgt het voorbeeld van John Wayne": over onze grenzeloze
  nationale cinema'
  in: Rommy Albers, Jan Baeke, Rob Zeeman (eds.), *Film in
  Nederland*
  Gent–Amsterdam: Ludion–Nederlands Filmmuseum, 2004b, pp.

414-421
- 'Program formats'
in: Richard Abel (ed.), *Encyclopaedia of early cinema*
New York: Routledge, 2005, pp. 533-535
- 'What the papers say: the case of the film-related papers of Jean Desmet'
KINtop, no. 14-15 (2006), pp. 113-121
- 'The transport of audiences: making cinema national'
in: Richard Abel, Giorgio Bertellini, Rob King (eds.), *Early cinema and the 'national'*
New Barnet: John Libbey, 2008, pp. 101-108
- 'Een onmogelijke opdracht: J.C. Lamsters filmopnamen voor het Koloniaal Instituut'
in: Janneke van Dijk, Jaap de Jonge, Nico de Klerk, *J.C. Lamster, een vroege filmmaker in Nederlands-Indië* Amsterdam: KIT Publishers, 2010, pp. 79-114
- '100 years of image control: the case of J.C. Lamster's films for the Dutch Colonial Institute'
Early Popular Visual Culture, vol. 11 no. 4 (November 2013), pp. 312-321
- 'Dream-work: Pan Am's *New Horizons* in Holland'
in: Bo Florin, Nico de Klerk, Patrick Vonderau (eds.), *Films that sell: moving pictures and advertising*
London: BFI-Palgrave, 2016, pp. 131-144

Esben Krohn, 'The first film archive'
in: Thomas C. Christensen, Esben Krohn (eds.), *Det første filmarkiv/The first film archive*
Copenhagen: Det Danske Filminstitut, 2002, pp. 11-15

Sam Kula, *Appraising moving images: assessing the archival and monetary value of film and video records*
Lanham, MD–Oxford: Scarecrow Press, 2003

Eric de Kuyper, 'Le cinéma de la seconde époque: le muet des années dix (I)'
Cinémathèque, no. 1 (May 1992), pp. 28-35

Bregtje Lameris, *Opnieuw belicht: de pas de deux tussen filmmuseale praktijk en filmhistorische debatten*
doctoral thesis, Utrecht University, 2007

Jasmin Lange, *Der deutsche Buchhandel und der Siegeszug der Kinematographie 1895-1933*
Wiesbaden: Harrassowitz, 2010

Laurent Le Forestier, *Aux sources de l'industrie du cinéma: le modèle Pathé, 1905-1908*
Paris: L'Harmattan, 2006

Elfriede Ledig (with Gerhard Ullmann), 'Rot wie Feuer, Leidenschaft, Genie und Wahnsinn. Zu einigen Aspekten der Farbe im Stummfilm'
in: Elfriede Ledig (ed.), *Der Stummfilm. Konstruktion und Rekonstruktion*
München: Schaudig/Bauer/Ledig, 1988, pp. 89-116

Robert D. Leighninger, Jr., *Long-range public investment: the forgotten legacy of the New Deal*
Columbia: University of South Carolina Press, 2007

Sabine Lenk, 'Archives and their film collection in a digital world, or: What futures for the analog print?'
The Moving Image, vol. 14 no. 2 (Fall 2014), pp. 100-110

Warren Leon, Roy Rosenzweig (eds.), *History museums in the United States: a critical assessment*
Urbana–Chicago: University of Illinois Press, 1989

Carina Lesky, '"Der Nordbahnhof in Wien ist seit 4 Uhr morgens ein Bild lebhafter Bewegung." Szenen und Gestalten des Alltäglichen am Wiener Nordbahnhof zwischen 1914 und 1918'
paper presented at *Kriegsschauplatz Wien. Transit, Verwaltung, Konsum. Internationales Kolloquium des Clusters Geschichte der Ludwig Boltzmann Gesellschaft*, Vienna, April 21-22, 2016

William E. Leuchtenburg, 'The achievement of the New Deal'
in: *The FDR years: on Roosevelt and his legacy*
New York–Chichester: Columbia University Press, 1995, pp. 236-282
(orig. publ. in 1985)

Trevor Livelton, *Archival theory, records, and the public*
Lanham, MD–Oxford: Society of American Archivists–Scarecrow Press, 2003 [1996]

Richard Lochead (ed.), *Beyond the printed word: the evolution of Canada's broadcast heritage news/Au-delà de l'écrit: le patrimoine de la radio-télédiffusion des nouvelles au Canada*
Kingston, ON–Clayton, NY: Quarry Press, 1991

Martin Loiperdinger, 'Kaiserbilder. Wilhelm II. als Filmstar'
in: Uli Jung, Martin Loiperdinger (eds.), *Kaiserreich 1895-1918*
Stuttgart: Philipp Reclam, 2005, pp. 253-268
- 'DES PFARRERS TÖCHTERLEIN: ein Schlüsselfilm für die Karriere von Henny Porten'
KINtop, no. 14-15 (2006), pp. 206-220

Martin Loiperdinger, Uli Jung (eds.), *Importing Asta Nielsen: the international film star in the making 1910-1914*
New Barnet: John Libbey, 2013

Robert S. Lynd, Helen M. Lynd, *Middletown: a study in American culture*
New York: Harcourt, Brace and Company, 1929
- *Middletown in transition: a study in cultural conflict*
New York: Harcourt, Brace and Company, n.d. [orig. publ. in 1937]

George F. MacDonald, 'Change and challenge: museums in the information society'
in: Ivan Karp, Christine Mullen Kreamer, Steven D. Lavine (eds.), *Museums and communities: the politics of public culture* (1992)
Washington–London, Smithsonian Institution Press, 1992, pp. 158-181

John M. MacKenzie, *Museums and empire: natural history, human cultures and colonial identities*
Manchester–New York: Manchester University Press, 2010 [2009]

Richard Maltby, 'Introduction: "the Americanisation of the world"'
in: Melvyn Stokes, Richard Maltby (eds.), *Hollywood abroad: audiences and cultural exchange*
London: British Film Institute, 2004, pp. 1-20
- 'Why boys go wrong: gangsters, hoodlums, and the natural history of delinquent careers'
in: Lee Grieveson, Esther Sonnet, Peter Stanfield (eds.), *Mob culture: hidden histories of the American gangster film*
Oxford: Berg, 2005, pp. 41-66

Bolesław Matuszewski, *A new source of history*
Warsaw: Filmoteka Narodowa, 1999 (orig. publ. in 1898 as *Une nouvelle source de l'histoire*)

Theodor Heinrich Mayer, 'Lebende Photographien'
    in: Fritz Güttinger (ed.), *Kein Tag ohne Kino. Schriftsteller über den Stummfilm*
    Frankfurt: Deutsches Filmmuseum Frankfurt, 1984, pp. 119-130
    (orig. publ. in 1914)

Robert S. McElvaine, *The Great Depression: America, 1929-1941*
    New York: Three Rivers Press, 1993 [1984]

Carla Mereu Keating, '"As time goes by". You must *not* remember this'
    in: Johannes Roschlau (ed.), *Kunst unter Kontrolle. Filmzensur in Europa*
    München: edition text + kritik, 2014, pp. 109.121

Jean-Jacques Meusy, 'La stratégie des sociétés concessionaires Pathé et la location des films en France (1907-1908)'
    in: Michel Marie, Laurent Le Forestier (eds.), *La firme Pathé Frères, 1896-1914*
    Paris: AFRHC, 2004, pp. 21-48

Verena Moritz, 'Amerika'
    in: Verena Moritz, Karin Moser, Hannes Leidinger, *Kampfzone Kino. Film in Österreich 1918-1938*
    Wien: Verlag Filmarchiv Austria, 2008, pp. 108-127

Gerard Mulder, Paul Koedijk, *H.M. van Randwijk: een biografie*
    Amsterdam: Nijgh & van Ditmar–Raamgracht, 1988

Corinna Müller, *Frühe deutsche Kinematografie: formale, wirtschaftliche und kulturelle Entwicklungen*
    Stuttgart - Weimar: J.B. Metzler, 1994

Charles Musser, *The emergence of cinema: the American screen to 1907*
    New York: Charles Scribner's Sons, 1990
    - 'Early advertising and promotional films, 1893-1900: Edison Motion Pictures as a case study'
    in: Bo Florin, Nico de Klerk, Patrick Vonderau (eds.), *Films that sell: moving pictures and advertising*
    London: BFI-Palgrave, 2016, pp. 83-90

Charles Musser with Caroline Nelson, *High-class moving pictures: Lyman H. Howe and the forgotten era of traveling exhibition*
    Princeton: Princeton University Press, 1991

Kemp R. Niver (ed.) *Biograph Bulletins 1896-1908*
    Los Angeles: Locare Research Group, 1971

Martha C. Nussbaum, *Not for profit: why democracy needs the humanities*
    Princeton - Oxford: Princeton University Press, 2012 [2010]

P.J. O'Connell, *Robert Drew and the development of cinema verite in
    America*
    Carbondale–Edwardsville: Southern Illinois University Press, 1992

Constance Perin, 'The communicative circle: museums as communities'
    in: Ivan Karp, Christine Mullen Kreamer, Steven D. Lavine (eds.),
    Museums and communities: the politics of public culture
    Washington–London, Smithsonian Institution Press, 1992, pp. 181-
    220

Jennifer Lynn Peterson, *Education in the school of dreams: travelogues and
    early nonfiction film*
    Durham–London: Duke University Press, 2013

Richard A. Peterson, 'From impresario to arts administrator: formal
    accountability in nonprofit cultural organizations'
    in: Paul J. DiMaggio (ed.), *Nonprofit enterprise in the arts: studies in
    mission and constraint*
    New York–Oxford: Oxford University Press, 1986, pp. 161-183

C.F. Plaisier, C. van Katwijk, K. Schoenmaker (eds.), *Bedrijfsvoering in
    musea*
    The Hague: VUGA, 1992

Mary Louise Pratt, *Imperial eyes: travel writing and transculturation*
    London - New York: Routledge, 1995 [1992])

Margaret Proctor, Michael Cook, *Manual of archival description*, 3rd edn.
    Farnham–Burlington, VT: Ashgate, 2012 [2000])

Paul Read, 'New technologies for archive film restoration and access: film
    images'
    in: GAMMA Group (ed.), *The use of new technologies applied to film
    restoration: technical and ethical problems*
    Bologna: GAMMA Group, n.d. [1996], pp. 37-50

Paul Read, Mark-Paul Meyer (eds.), *Restoration of motion picture film*
    Oxford–Woburn, MA: Butterworth-Heinemann, 2000

Martin Reinhart, '131 Minuten Meisel'
    in: *Maske und Kothurn: Internationale Beiträge zur Theater-, Film-
    und Medienwissenschaft*, vol. 61 no. 1 (2015), pp. 55-66

Graham Roberts, *Forward Soviet: history and non-fiction film in the USSR*
London: I.B. Tauris, 1999

Roy Rosenzweig, 'Wikipedia: can history be open source?'
in: *Clio wired: the future of the past in the digital age*
New York: Columbia University Press, 2011, pp. 51-82 (orig. publ. in
2006)

Roy Rosenzweig, David Thelen, *The presence of the past: popular uses of
history in American life*
New York: Columbia University Press, 1998

Corey Ross, *Media and the making of modern Germany: mass
communications, society, and politics from the Empire to the Third
Reich*
Oxford: Oxford University Press, 2008

Deac Rossell, *Living pictures: the origins of the movies*
Albany: State University of New York Press, 1998

Elias Savada, *The American Film Institute catalogue of motion pictures
produced in the United States: film beginnings 1893-1910*
Metuchen, NJ: Scarecrow Press, 1995

Kees Schuyt, Ed Taverne, *1950: prosperity and welfare*
Basingstoke–New York/Assen: Palgrave Macmillan/Royal Van
Gorcum, 2004 (orig. publ. in 2000 as *1950: welvaart in zwart-wit*)

Richard Slotkin, *The fatal environment: the myth of the frontier in the age
of industrialization, 1800-1890*
Norman: University of Oklahoma Press, 1998a [1985]
- *Gunfighter nation: the myth of the American frontier in twentieth-
century America*
Norman: University of Oklahoma Press, 1998b [1992]

Jan A. Somers, *Nederlandsch-Indië: staatkundige ontwikkelingen binnen
een koloniale relatie*
Zutphen: Walburg Pers, 2005

Janet Staiger, 'The Hollywood mode of production, 1930-1960'
  in: David Bordwell, Janet Staiger, Kristin Thompson, *The classical
  Hollywood cinema: film style & mode of production to 1960*
  London–Melbourne–Henley: Routledge & Kegan Paul, 1985, pp.
  309-337
  - 'Combination and litigation: structures of US film distribution,
  1896-1917'
  in: Thomas Elsaesser with Adam Barker (eds.), *Early cinema: space,
  frame, narrative*
  London: British Film Institute, 1992 [1990], pp. 189-210
  - *Media reception studies*
  New York–London: New York University Press, 2005

Melvyn Stokes, Richard Maltby (eds.), *Hollywood abroad: audiences and
  cultural exchange*
  London: British Film Institute, 2004

Warren I. Susman, 'Culture and commitment'
  in: *Culture as history: the transformation of American society in the
  twentieth century*
  New York: Pantheon Books, 1985, pp. 184-210 (orig. publ. in 1973)

Brian Taves, 'The B-film: Hollywood's other half'
  in: Tino Balio, *Grand design: Hollywood as a modern business
  enterprise, 1930-1939*
  New York: Charles Scribner's Sons, 1993, pp. 313-350

Richard Taylor, Ian Christie (eds.), *The film factory: Russian and Soviet
  cinema in documents 1896-1939*
  Cambridge, MA: Harvard University Press, 1988

Mark van den Tempel, 'Making them move again: preserving Mutoscope
  and Biograph'
  Griffithiana, no. 66-70 (1999-2000), pp. 225-239

Studs Terkel, *Hard times: an oral history of the Great Depression*
  New York: Pantheon, 1986 [1970]

Thomas Tode, 'The soul of a century: PANZERKREUZER POTEMKIN und seine
  Filmmusik im Spiegel der zeitgenössische deutschen Presse'
  *Maske und Kothurn: Internationale Beiträge zur Theater-, Film-
  und Medienwissenschaft*, vol. 61 no. 1 (2015), pp. 11-28

Vanessa Toulmin, *Electric Edwardians: the story of the Mitchell & Kenyon
  collection*
  London: British Film Institute, 2006

Yuri Tsivian, 'Notes historiques en marge de l'expérience de Koulechov'
    Iris, vol. 4 no. 1 (1986), pp. 49-59
    - *Early cinema in Russia and its cultural reception*
    Chicago–London: University of Chicago Press, 1998 [1994]

Arianna Turci, 'Archivio Nazionale del Cinema d'Impresa collections: an
    overview'
    in: Bo Florin, Nico de Klerk, Patrick Vonderau (eds.), *Films that sell:
    moving pictures and advertising*
    London: British Film Institute-Palgrave, 2016, pp. 289-297

William Uricchio, 'Media-specificity and its discontents: a televisual
    provocation'
    in: Nicolas Dulac, André Gaudreault (eds.), *From media to post-
    media: continuities and ruptures*
    Paris: L'Âge d'Homme (forthcoming)
    - 'Selling the motion picture to the *fin-de-siècle* American public'
    in: Bo Florin, Nico de Klerk, Patrick Vonderau (eds.), *Films that sell:
    moving pictures and advertising*
    London: BFI-Palgrave, 2016, pp. 71-82

William Uricchio, Roberta E. Pearson, *Reframing culture: the case of the
    Vitagraph quality films*
    Princeton: Princeton University Press, 1993

Michael Ventura, 'The Great Wall of Hollywood'
    in: *Shadow dancing in the USA*
    Los Angeles: Jeremy P. Tarcher, 1985, pp. 163-176

Mike Wallace, 'The battle of the *Enola Gay*'
    in: *Mickey Mouse history and other essays on American memory*
    Philadelphia: Temple University Press, 1996, pp. 269-318

Gregory Waller, *Main Street amusements: movies and commercial
    entertainment in a southern city, 1896-1930*
    Washington - London: Smithsonian Institution Press, 1995

Stephen E. Weil, 'Fighting off some dry rot, woodworm, and damp'
    in: *Rethinking museums and other meditations*
    Washington - London: Smithsonian Institution Press, 1997 [1990]
    (orig. publ. in 1985).

Anke Wilkening, 'METROPOLIS 2010: a new effort to recapture the lost
    METROPOLIS'
    in: Kerstin Parth, Oliver Hanley, Thomas Ballhausen (eds.), *Works in
    progress: digital film restoration within archives*
    Vienna: Synema, 2013, pp. 134-147

Ian E. Wilson, '"The gift of one generation to another": the real thing for
    the Pepsi generation'
    in: Francis X. Blouin, Jr., William G. Rosenberg (eds.), *Archives,
    documentation and institutions of social memory: essays from the
    Sawyer Seminar*
    Ann Arbor: University of Michigan Press, 2009 [2006], pp. 333-342

Herman de Wit, *Film in Utrecht van 1895-1915*
    graduate thesis, Utrecht University, 1986

Gordon S. Wood, 'The American revolutionary tradition, or Why America
    wants to spread democracy around the world'
    in: *The idea of America: reflections on the birth of the United States*
    New York: Penguin Press, 2011, pp. 319-335

Digital

'5 sur 5: Les fictions polymorphes. Vidéographe à la Cinémathèque: Sylvie
    Laliberté, February 7, 2014'
    Cinémathèque québécoise
    https://www.youtube.com/watch?v=w8rLXRyuE7s

'90 procent minder videotheken'
    Cultuurindex Nederland
    http://www.cultuurindex.nl/nieuws/90-procent-minder-
    videotheken

'A matter of rights: a talk with Lee Tsiantis'
    http://selfstyledsiren.blogspot.nl/2010/02/matter-of-rights-talk-
    with-lee-tsiantis.html (February 18, 2007)

'About the festival'
    Jerusalem Film Festival
    http://www.jff.org.il/?CategoryID=361&ArticleID=163&sng=1

'Agencies we fund. Ngā Taonga Sound & Vision'
    Manatū Taonga Ministry for Culture & Heritage
    http://www.mch.govt.nz/funding-nz-culture/agencies-we-
    fund/heritage/NgaTaongaSoundVision

'Agenda'
Haagsche Courant (May 21, 1948), p. 2 (PDF)

'American Biograph'
Haagsche Courant, no. 4922 (March 20, 1899), p. 1
http://www.delpher.nl/nl/kranten/view?coll=ddd&query=%28PRE
SIDENT+MAC+KINLEY%29&facets%5Bperiode%5D%5B%5D=0%7
C19e_eeuw%7C&facets%5Btype%5D%5B%5D=artikel&facets%5Bs
patialCreation%5D%5B%5D=%27sGravenhage&identifier=MMKB0
4%3A000126563%3Ampeg21%3Aa0087&resultsidentifier=MMKB04
%3A000126563%3Ampeg21%3Aa0087

Annual report 2013-2014
New Zealand Film Archive Ngā Kaitiaki O Ngā Taonga Whitiāhua–
Sound Archives Ngā Taonga Kōrero
http://www.ngataonga.org.nz/about/corporate-information

'Article creation and notability'
Wikipedia
https://en.wikipedia.org/wiki/Wikipedia:Contributing_to_Wikiped
ia#Article_creation_and_notability

'Avant-première au Capitole: VERLIEBTE FEINDE de Werner S. Schweizer–
18.02.2014'
Cinémathèque suisse
http://www.cinematheque.ch/f/galeries/videos/2014/

'BFI IMAX faq'
British Film Institute-National Film & Television Archive
http://www.bfi.org.uk/about-bfi/help-faq/bfi-imax

'CASABLANCA in "massakrierter Fassung"'
Deutsches Filminstitut Filmmuseum
http://deutsches-filminstitut.de/blog/casablanca-in-
massakrierter-fassung/

'Centenaire de la Grande Guerre au cinéma. Présentation par Laurent
Véray'
Cinémathèque française-Musée du Cinéma
http://www.dailymotion.com/video/x1ihbrg_centenaire-de-la-
grande-guerre-au-cinema-presentation-par-laurent-
veray_shortfilms

'Ciné-concert ImaginaSon 2014–13.02.2014'
Cinémathèque suisse
http://www.cinematheque.ch/f/galeries/videos/2014/

'*Ciné Ressources*: Présentation'
  http://www.cineressources.net/pages.php?id_page=presentation

Cinema Context. Film in Nederland vanaf 1896: een encyclopedie van de
  filmcultuur
  http://www.cinemacontext.nl

'Cinemaimpresa.TV'
  Fondazione Centro Sperimentale del Cinematografia-Cineteca
  Nazionale
  https://www.youtube.com/user/cinemaimpresatv

'Cinémathèque suisse'
  Dictionnaire historique de la Suisse
  http://www.hls-dhs-dss.ch/textes/f/F10475.php

'Cinémathèque suisse: rapport d'activités pour l'année 2013'
  FIAF rapports annuels 2013 (2014)
  https://web.archive.org/web/20151018030352/http://www.fiafnet.
  org/pdf/AR2013/2013_Lausanne.pdf

'Colonial film: moving images of the British Empire'
  http://www.colonialfilm.org.uk/

'Contributing to Wikipedia'
  Wikipedia
  http://en.wikipedia.org/wiki/Wikipedia:Contributing_to_Wikipedi
  a

'Contributor zone'
  International Movie Database (IMDb)
  http://www.imdb.com/czone/?ref_=nv_cm_cz_2

'Corporate information'
  Ngā Taonga Sound & Vision
  http://www.ngataonga.org.nz/about/corporate-information

'Digital cinemas lead to increased attendance'
  DCinema Today (June 27, 2011)
  http://www.dcinematoday.com/dc/PR.aspx?newsID=2392

'DEN HVIDE SLAVEHANDEL'
  IMDb
  http://www.imdb.com/title/tt0001258/?ref_=fn_tt_tt_1

'Deutsches Filminstitut Filmmuseum'
    FIAF rapports annuels 2013 (2014)
    https://web.archive.org/web/20151018233227/http://www.fiafnet.
    org/pdf/AR2013/2013_Frankfurt.pdf

'Digital film restoration policy/Österreichisches Filmmuseum'
    Österreichisches Filmmuseum
    http://www.filmmuseum.at/jart/prj3/filmmuseum/data/uploads/
    Digital%20Film%20Restoration%20Policy.pdf

'Discover Arab Cinema: from November 2013'
    British Film Institute-National Film & Television Archive
    http://www.zenithfoundation.com/film-festival/discover-arab-
    cinema-bfi/

Discovery zone: Luxembourg city festival, 28 feb–9 mar 2014
    http://2014.discoveryzone.lu/en/posts/display/1

'Estrenos'
    Programa mensual Cineteca Nacional de México, no. 364 (February
    2014), pp. 6-19
    http://issuu.com/cinetecanacional/docs/pmfebrero2014__2_

European Film Gateway 1914
    http://project.efg1914.eu/

Europeana
    http://www.europeana.eu/

'Exposition "La musée imaginaire d'Henri Langlois"'
    Cinémathèque française-Musée du Cinéma
    http://www.cinematheque.fr/fr/expositions-cinema/precedentes-
    expositions/centenaire-langlois/exposition.html

'Filmoteca de Catalunya'
    FIAF: Rapports annuels 2013 (2014)
    https://web.archive.org/web/20151018022404/http://www.fiafnet.
    org/pdf/AR2013/2013_Barcelona.pdf

'Films over Oost-Indië'
  Nieuwe Rotterdamsche Courant, vol. 72 no. 112 (April 22, 1915)
  morning edn. B, p. 2
  http://www.delpher.nl/nl/kranten/view?coll=ddd&query=%28film
  s+over+oost-indie%29&cql%5B%5D=%28date+_gte_+%2222-04-
  1915%22%29&cql%5B%5D=%28date+_lte_+%2222-04-
  1915%22%29&cql%5B%5D=ppn+any+%28832495182%29&facets%
  5Btype%5D%5B%5D=artikel&identifier=ddd%3A010034111%3Am
  peg21%3Ap002&resultsidentifier=ddd%3A010034111%3Ampeg21%
  3Aa0028&pres%5Bmaxperpage%5D=36

'Films van deze week'
  Haagsche Courant (May 22, 1948), p. 6 (PDF)

'Financial statement for the year ended 31 December 2014'
  n.p. [Dublin], Irish Film Institute, May 29, 2015
  http://www.ifi.ie/wp-content/uploads/2011/09/2014-
  Accounts.pdf

'First Rothko exhibition in 40 years at Gemeentemuseum Den Haag'
  Gemeentemuseum Den Haag
  http://www.gemeentemuseum.nl/en/exhibitions/mark-rothko

'Fratelli nel cinema'
  Fondazione Centro Sperimentale del Cinematografia-Cineteca
  Nazionale
  http://www.fondazionecsc.it/events_detail.jsp?IDAREA=85&ID_EV
  ENT=999&GTEMPLATE=newsletter_mailing_ctTrevi.jsp

'Fundación Cinemateca Boliviana, proyecto "Imágenes de Bolivia, fase 1".
  Convocatoria al primer censo nacional de cineastas, videastas y
  productores'
  Bolpress (May 29, 2012)
  http://www.bolpress.com/?Cod=2012052908

'George Eastman Museum makes 35mm motion picture film from early
  cinema period'
  George Eastman Museum, Rochester, NY, May 19, 2016 (PDF)
  https://eastman.org/george-eastman-museum-makes-35mm-
  motion-picture-film-early-cinema-period

Historic photos (Library of Congress Flickr pilot project)
  Flickr
  https://www.flickr.com/photos/library_of_congress/collections/72
  157601355524315/

'IFI Irish Film Archive 2013'
    FIAF: Rapports annuels 2013 (2014)
    https://web.archive.org/web/20151018022348/http://www.fiafnet.
    org/pdf/AR2013/2013_Dublin.pdf

Irish Film Institute
    http://ifi.ie/about/

INCONTRO CON LA OLIVETTI
    Archivio Nazionale del Cinema d'Impresa
    https://www.youtube.com/watch?v=iobjKjjiJy4&index=6&list=PL1
    5B-32H5GlJej0W8WIOhGiOuS_9h6eC3

'Incontro con Salvatore Mereu, Cinema Trevi, 19 febbraio 2014'
    Fondazione Centro Sperimentale del Cinematografia-Cineteca
    Nazionale
    https://www.youtube.com/watch?v=AV3Ef88ca-
    U&list=UUAaQOi9Mi9lrG6RHVexkbjQ

'Informe Cineteca Nacional de México 2013'
    FIAF: Rapports annuels 2013 (2014)
    https://web.archive.org/web/20151018030335/http://www.fiafnet.
    org/pdf/AR2013/2013_Mexico%20CN.pdf

'Intangible heritage'
    International Council of Museums (ICOM)
    http://icom.museum/programmes/intangible-heritage/

'Introducing new audiovisual archive, Ngā Taonga Sound & Vision'
    Ngā Taonga Sound & Vision
    http://www.ngataonga.org.nz/about-nga-taonga-sound-and-
    vision/news/introducing-new-audiovisual-archive-nga-taonga-
    sound-and-vision-2/

'Irish distributors'
    Irish Film Board
    http://www.irishfilmboard.ie/festivals_and_distribution/distributo
    rs/

'Is het Circus-Carré 's avonds de verzamelplaats...'
   Nieuws van den Dag, no. 8906 (January 27, 1899), 3rd section, p. 9
   http://www.delpher.nl/nl/kranten/view?coll=ddd&query=Carre&c
   ql%5B%5D=%28date+_gte_+%2227-01-
   1899%22%29&cql%5B%5D=%28date+_lte_+%2227-01-
   1899%22%29&cql%5B%5D=ppn+any+%2883249562X%29&identifi
   er=ddd%3A010126134%3Ampeg21%3Ap009&resultsidentifier=ddd
   %3A010126134%3Ampeg21%3Aa0137&pres%5Bmaxperpage%5D=
   36

'Israeli Film Archive–annual report 2013'
   FIAF: Rapports annuels 2013 (2014)
   https://web.archive.org/web/20151018234940/http://www.fiafnet.
   org/pdf/AR2013/2013_Jerusalem.pdf

'Italia '77: ultimo atto?, Cinema Trevi, 20 febbraio 2014'
   Fondazione Centro Sperimentale del Cinematografia-Cineteca
   Nazionale
   https://www.youtube.com/watch?v=B24hq8_rwsU&list=UUAaQOi
   9Mi9lrG6RHVexkbjQ

'Kinematografisch archief'
   Sumatra Post, vol. 13 no. 219 (September 20, 1911), p. 2
   http://kranten.delpher.nl/nl/view/index?query=matuszewski&coll
   =ddd&image=ddd%3A010323495%3Ampeg21%3Aa0056&page=1&
   maxperpage=10&cql%5B0%5D=%28date+_gte_+01-01
   1900%29&cql%5B1%5D=%28date+_lte_+31-12-
   1914%29&cql%5B2%5D=%28content+all+matuszewski%29

'KINO-KRIEGSSCHAU NO. 14'
   European Film Gateway
   http://www.europeanfilmgateway.eu/node/33/detail/KinoKriegssc
   hau+Nr+14/video:ZDA5NzZlMTYtZDFkMy00MmQ5LWIzMTQtZD
   g5YmVkY2VmM2NjX1VtVndiM05wZEc5eWVWTmxjblpwWTJWU1
   pYTnZkWEpqWlhNdlVtVndiM05wZEc5eWVWTmxjblpwWTJWU1p
   YTnZkWEpqWlZSNWNHVT06OmF2Q3JlYXRpb24uRElGL0RJRl9hd
   kNyZWF0aW9uXzRFNzMzQkQxN0Q1RDQ4NkU5QTVBQUQwOTA
   4QzUyMTgy/paging:dmlkZW8tMS00LWltYWdlLTEtNC1zb3VuZC0x
   LTQtcGVyc29uLTEtNC10ZXh0LTEtNA==

'KOPICZINCE'
European Film Gateway
http://www.europeanfilmgateway.eu/node/33/detail/Kopiczince/
video:NGIyYWY5MWYtZGViNC00NmUzLTgwYmYtM2YxMTUxYTV
kNDVkX1VtVndiM05wZEc5eWVWTmxjblpwWTJWU1pYTnZkWEp
qWlhNdlVtVndiM05wZEc5eWVWTmxjblpwWTJWU1pYTnZkWEpq
WlZSNWNNHVT06OmF2Q3JlYXRpb24xOTE0TGtZ20bv21vdGdlYy5subC
9FWUVfYXZDcmVhdGlvbl9jYXQzNjI2OQ==/paging:dmlkZW8tMS
00LWltYWdlLTEtNC1zb3VuZC0xLTQtcGVyc29uLTEtNC10ZXh0LTEt
NA==

'L'architecture à l'écran– 05.02.2014'
Cinémathèque Suisse
http://www.cinematheque.ch/f/galeries/videos/2014/

'L'effetto del jazz. Lo Swing Club di Torino'
Fondazione Centro Sperimentale del Cinematografia-Cineteca
Nazionale
http://www.fondazionecsc.it/events_detail.jsp?IDAREA=16&ID_EV
ENT=991&GTEMPLATE=ct_home.jsp

LA PATTUGLIA DEL PASSO S. GIACOMO
Archivio Nazionale del Cinema d'Impresa
https://www.youtube.com/watch?v=zYOdy_TCoVg);

'Legal deposit'
Biblioteca de Catalunya
http://www.bnc.cat/eng/Professionals/Legal-Deposit#faq1

'Lisbon annual report 2013'
FIAF Rapports annuels 2013 (2014)
https://web.archive.org/web/20151018020440/http://www.fiafnet.
org/pdf/AR2013/2013_Lisboa.pdf

'Major BFI projects announced to mark First World War centenary'
British Film Institute-National Film & Television Archive
http://www.bfi.org.uk/news-opinion/news-bfi/features/major-
projects-announced-mark-first-world-war-centenary

[MARTINI VERMOUTH, REALIZZATO PER EXPO 1911]
Archivio Nazionale del Cinema d'Impresa
https://www.youtube.com/watch?v=wLyWLBRrKHY&list=PL15B-
32H5GlJej0W8WIOhGiOuS_9h6eC3

'Mission statement'
    Österreichisches Filmmuseum
    http://www.filmmuseum.at/jart/prj3/filmmuseum/main.jart?reser
    ve-mode=active&rel=en&content-id=1215680369205

'"Movie theaters of the olden days" exhibition opens at HK Film Archive'
    Hong Kong Film Archive, press release, December 6, 2013
    http://www.info.gov.hk/gia/general/201312/06/P201312060312.ht
    m

'Museum definition'
    International Council of Museums (ICOM)
    http://icom.museum/the-vision/museum-definition/

'National Film Center-the National Museum of Modern Art, Tokyo (Japan):
    activities report for 2013'
    FIAF: Rapports annuels 2013 (2014)
    https://web.archive.org/web/20151018024224/http://www.fiafnet.
    org/pdf/AR2013/2013_Tokyo.pdf

'Österreichisches Filmmuseum/Wien: FIAF annual report 2013'
    FIAF: Rapports annuels 2013 (2014)
    https://web.archive.org/web/20151018023746/http://www.fiafnet.
    org/pdf/AR2013/2013_Vienna%20Filmmuseum.pdf

'Policies and guidelines'
    Wikipedia
    http://en.wikipedia.org/wiki/Wikipedia:Policies_and_guidelines

'Projections itinérantes'
    Bophana Centre de Ressources Audiovisuelles
    http://bophana.org/event/mobile-screenings

Queensland Art Gallery Board of Trustees annual report 2014-2015
    Brisbane: The Queensland Art Gallery | Gallery of Modern Art,
    September 18, 2015
    http://www.parliament.qld.gov.au/documents/tableOffice/Tabled
    Papers/2015/5515T1154.pdf

'Queer pagan punk: Derek Jarman at BFI Southbank. BFI press release'
    BFI-NFTVA
    http://www.bfi.org.uk/sites/bfi.org.uk/files/downloads/bfi-press-
    release-jarman-2014-12-19_0.pdf

Rapport annuel | Jaarverslag 2013
    n.p. [Brussels] Cinematek, n.d.
    http://www.cinematek.be/dbfiles/mfile/222400/222465/RA2013_n
    l_web.pdf

Rapport annuel 2013-2014
    Montreal: Cinémathèque québécoise, n.d. [2014]
    https://web.archive.org/web/20161203155043/http://www.cinema
    theque.qc.ca/sites/default/files/files/reports/lf_150dpi_complet_r
    appannuel_cq1409_0.pdf

Relatório anual 2009
    Saõ Paolo: Cinemateca Brasileira, March 2010, p. 55
    http://bases.cinemateca.gov.br/content/docs/relatorio_anual_cb_
    2009.pdf

Relatório anual 2012
    Saõ Paolo: Cinemateca Brasileira, March 2013, pp. 64-65
    http://cinemateca.gov.br/sites/default/files/relatorio_anual_cb_20
    12.pdf

'Rijkspensioen voor verzetsslachtoffers'
    Medisch Contact, vol. 3 no. 21 (May 26, 1948), pp. 478-479 (PDF)

'Sala dos Carvalhos'
    Cinemateca Portuguesa-Museu do Cinema
    http://www.cinemateca.pt/CinematecaSite/media/Documentos/L
    ivro-carvalhos.pdf

'Sammlungen'
    Filmarchiv Austria
    http://filmarchiv.at/sammlungen/depot-legal/

'SARA de Saïd Naciri'
    YallaCiné
    http://www.yallacine.com/sara-de-said-naciri/

'The Jerusalem Jewish Film Festival'
    Jerusalem Cinematheque-Israel Film Archive
    http://www.jer-
    cin.org.il/Cinematheque/The%20Jewish%20Film%20Festival.aspx

'Trasnoches'
    Boletín Cinemateca Uruguaya, no. 473 (February-March 2014), p.
    22.
    http://www.cinemateca.org.uy/PDF/473.pdf

'Turner Classic Movies plays sleuth, discovers six previously lost RKO
        classics'
        TCM press release (October 18, 2006) (PDF)
        http://www.prnewswire.com/news-releases/turner-classic-
        movies-plays-sleuth-discovers-six-previously-lost-rko-classics-
        56560792.html

UNO MATTINA ALLA FERRANIA
        Archivio Nazionale del Cinema d'Impresa
        https://www.youtube.com/watch?v=yQMcz04OfmU

UNO SU TRE
        Archivio Nazionale del Cinema d'Impresa
        https://www.youtube.com/watch?v=ZsY_Zri49U0

'Van Gogh as a letter-writer'
        Van Gogh Museum
        http://vangoghletters.org/vg/letter_writer_1.html

'Van Goghs brieven'
        Van Gogh Museum
        http://www.vangoghmuseum.nl/vgm/index.jsp?page=161662&lan
        g=nl; http://www.vangoghletters.org/vg/

'WINTER'S BONE'
        Cinémathèque québécoise
        http://www.cinematheque.qc.ca/en/programmation/projections/f
        ilm/winters-bone?pid=17025

Philip N. Alexander, Helen W. Samuels, 'The roots of 128: a hypothetical
        documentation strategy'
        The American Archivist, no. 50 (Fall 1987), pp. 518-531 (PDF)
        http://americanarchivist.org/doi/pdf/10.17723/aarc.50.4.v889q118
        2r11p36u

Jonathan Auerbach, 'McKinley at home: how early American cinema made
        news'
        American Quarterly, vol. 51 no. 4 (December 1999), pp. 797-832
        (PDF)

David Bearman, 'Archival methods: Archives and Museum Informatics
        technical report #9'
        Archives & Museum Informatics (Pittsburgh, 1989)
        http://www.archimuse.com/publishing/archival_methods/

Rosemary Bergeron, 'Archiving moving-image and audio-cultural works in
    Canada'
    Archivaria, no. 63 (Spring 2007), pp. 55-74 (PDF)
    http://archivaria.ca/archivar/index.php/archivaria/article/view/1
    3127/14367

Hans Booms, 'Society and the formation of a documentary heritage: issues
    in the appraisal of archival sources'
    Archivaria, no. 24 (Summer 1987), pp. 69-107 (PDF) (orig. publ. in
    1972 as 'Gesellschaftsordnung und Überlieferungsbildung: zur
    Problematik archivarischer Quellenbewertung')
    http://archivaria.ca/index.php/archivaria/article/view/11415/123
    57

Stephen Bottomore, *Filming, faking and propaganda: the origins of the
    war film, 1897-1902*
    doctoral thesis, Utrecht University, 2007
    http://igitur-archive.library.uu.nl/dissertations/2007-0905-
    204358/index.htm

Michael K. Buckland, 'What is a "document"?'
    Journal of the American Society for Information Science, vol. 48 no. 9
    (September 1997), pp. 804-808
    http://www.columbia.edu/cu/libraries/inside/units/bibcontrol/os
    mc/bucklandwhat.pdf

Edward A. Chappell, 'Social responsibility and the American history
    museum'
    Winterthur Portfolio, vol. 24 no. 4 (Winter 1989), pp. 247-265 (PDF)

Terry Cook, 'The tyranny of the medium: a comment on "total archives"'
    Archivaria, no. 9 (Winter 1979-1990), pp. 141-149 (PDF)
    http://archivaria.ca/index.php/archivaria/article/view/12566/137
    24
    - 'Many are called but few are chosen: appraisal guidelines for
    sampling and selecting case files'
    Archivaria, no. 32 (Summer 1991), pp. 25-50 (PDF)
    http://archivaria.ca/index.php/archivaria/article/view/11759/127
    09

Lisa Darms, 'Study in documents. The archival object: a memoir of
    disintegration'
    Archivaria, no. 67 (Spring 2009), pp. 143-155 (PDF)

Samuel Douhaire, 'WINTER'S BONE'
    Télérama
    http://www.telerama.fr/cinema/films/winter-s-
    bone,422602,critique.php

John Fiske, 'Manifest destiny'
    Harper's New Monthly Magazine (March 1885), pp. 578-590
    http://www.unz.org/Pub/Harpers-1885mar-00578

Philippe Gauthier, *Histoire(s) et historiographie du cinéma en France:*
    1896-1953
    doctoral thesis, Université de Montréal - Université de Lausanne,
    2013 (PDF)
    https://papyrus.bib.umontreal.ca/xmlui/bitstream/handle/1866/1
    0797/Gauthier_Philippe_2013_these.pdf?sequence=2&isAllowed=y

Karen F. Gracy, 'Moving image preservation and cultural capital'
    Library Trends, vol. 56 no. 1 (Summer 2007), pp. 183-197 (PDF)
    http://hdl.handle.net/2142/3776

Gerald F. Ham, 'The archival edge'
    The American Archivist, vol. 38 no. 1 (January 1975), pp. 5-13 (orig.
    presented in October 1974 at the 38th annual meeting of the Society
    of American Archivists [SAA]) (PDF)
    http://americanarchivist.org/doi/pdf/10.17723/aarc.38.1.7400r864
    81128424

Helen P. Harrison (ed. & comp.), *Audiovisual archives: a practical reader*
    Paris: UNESCO, 1997 (PDF)
    http://unesdoc.unesco.org/images/0010/001096/109612eo.pdf

Carolyn Heald, 'Are we collecting the "right stuff"?'
    Archivaria, no. 40 (Fall 1995), pp. 182-188 PDF)
    http://archivaria.ca/index.php/archivaria/article/view/12104/130
    97

Vinzenz Hediger, *Verführung zum Film: der amerikanische Kinotrailer seit*
    1912
    Marburg: Schüren, 2001 (PDF)

Olaf Helmer, Nicholas Rescher, *On the epistemology of the inexact sciences*
    Santa Monica: RAND Corporation, October 13, 1958 (PDF)
    https://www.rand.org/content/dam/rand/pubs/papers/2005/P15
    13.pdf

Paul M. Hirsch, 'Processing fads and fashions: an organization-set analysis
of cultural industry systems'
in: Simon Frith, Andrew Goodwin (eds.), *On record: rock, pop, and
the written word*, (1990), pp. 127-139 (orig. publ. in 1972) (PDF)

David S. Hulfish, *Motion-picture work: a general treatise on picture taking,
picture making, photo plays, and theater management and
operation*
Chicago: American School of Correspondence, 1913
https://archive.org/stream/motionpicturewor00amer#page/n7/m
ode/2up

John Kelcher, 'SANTK staff on life post-earthquakes'
Gauge (February 21, 2014)
http://www.ngataonga.org.nz/blog/archiving-practice/santk-staff-
on-life-post-earthquakes/

Susan King, 'Back in the RKO fold'
Los Angeles Times (April 1, 2007), p. E24 (PDF)

Martin Koerber, 'The METROPOLIS of Buenos Aires'
http://orphanfilmsymposium.blogspot.nl/2008/07/metropolis-of-
buenos-aires.html (July 4, 2008)

Ramesh Kumar, *National archives: policies, practices, and histories. A study
of the National Film Archive of India, Eye Film Institute
Netherlands, and the National Film and Sound Archive, Australia*
doctoral thesis, New York University, 2016 (PDF)

F. Paul Liesegang, *Handbuch der praktischen Kinematographie*, 2nd edn.
Leipzig: Liesegang's Verlag, M. Eger, 1911 [1907]
http://www.gutenberg.org/files/41367/41367-h/41367-h.htm

Laura Millar, 'Discharging our debt: the evolution of the total archives
concept in English Canada'
Archivaria, no. 46 (Fall 1998), pp. 103-146 (PDF)
http://archivaria.ca/index.php/archivaria/article/view/12677/138
46

Tom Nesmith, 'Still fuzzy, but more accurate: some thoughts on the
"ghosts" of archival theory' [review article]
Archivaria, no. 47 (Spring 1999), pp. 136-150 (PDF)
http://archivaria.ca/index.php/archivaria/article/view/12701/138
75

Lori Podolsky Nordland, 'The concept of "secondary provenance": re-
interpreting Ac co mok ki's map as evolving text'
Archivaria, no. 58 (2004), pp. 147-159 (PDF)
http://archivaria.ca/index.php/archivaria/article/view/12481/135
96

Geoffrey Nowell-Smith, '*Le varianti trasparenti: i film con Ingrid Bergman
di Roberto Rossellini* by Elena Dagrada'
Senses of cinema, no. 38 (February 2006)
http://sensesofcinema.com/2006/book-
reviews/varianti_trasparenti

Frank S. Nugent, 'A memorable film is A MAN TO REMEMBER, now at the
Rivoli'
New York Times (November 7, 1938), p. 23 (PDF)

Lorraine O'Donnell, 'Towards total archives: the form and meaning of
photographic records'
Archivaria, no. 38 (Fall 1994) pp. 105-118 (PDF)
http://archivaria.ca/index.php/archivaria/article/view/12028/129
99

Richard Pearce-Moses, *A glossary of archival and records terminology*
Chicago: Society of American Archivists, 2005 (PDF)
http://files.archivists.org/pubs/free/SAA-Glossary-2005.pdf

H.M. van Randwijk, 'Omdat ik Nederlander ben'
Vrij Nederland, vol. 7 no. 48 (July 26, 1947), pp. 1, 5
http://blogs.vn.nl/boeken/wp-
content/uploads/vn28_26071947_preview.jpg

Franklin D. Roosevelt, 'Inaugural address, March 4, 1933'
John T. Woolley, Gerhard Peters (eds.), *The American Presidency
Project*
http://www.presidency.ucsb.edu/ws/?pid=14473

Joan M. Schwartz, 'Coming to terms with photographs: descriptive
standards, linguistic "othering", and the margins of archivy'
Archivaria, no. 54 (Fall 2002), pp. 142-171 (PDF)
http://archivaria.ca/index.php/archivaria/article/view/12861/140
92

Katie Shilton, Ramesh Srinivasan, 'Participatory appraisal and
    arrangement for multicultural archival collections'
    Archivaria, no. 63 (Spring 2007), pp. 87-101 (PDF)
    http://archivaria.ca/index.php/archivaria/article/view/13129/143
    71

Tom Simonite, 'The decline of Wikipedia'
    MIT Technology Review (October 22, 2013)
    https://www.technologyreview.com/s/520446/the-decline-of-
    wikipedia/

Paul Julian Smith, 'Cineteca Nacional, México'
    Cineteca Nacional de México
    http://www.cinetecanacional.net/controlador.php?opcion=noticia
    s&id=410 (orig. publ. in 2013 as 'Letter from Mexico City')

Teresa Soleau, 'Preventing digital decay'
    The Iris (October 20, 2014)
    http://blogs.getty.edu/iris/preventing-digital-
    decay/?sthash.byZesavU.mjjo

Walter van Teeffelen, 'De grote Mark Rothko tentoonstelling in het
    Gemeentemuseum'
    Den Haag Direct (September 21, 2014)
    http://www.denhaagdirect.nl/de-grote-mark-rothko-
    tentoonstelling-in-het-gemeentemuseum/

Walter D. Welford, Henry Sturmey (comps. & eds.), *The indispensable
    handbook to the optical lantern: a complete cyclopaedia on the
    subject of optical lanterns, slides and accessory apparatus*
    London: Iliffe & Son, 1888
    https://archive.org/stream/indispensableha00unkngoog#page/n6
    /mode/2up

Index

1

12 AÑOS ESCLAVO
(2013), 180, *See* 12 YEARS A SLAVE
12 YEARS A SLAVE
(2013), 202, 205, 231
100 must-see Hong Kong movies,
199, 201
1714: història i identitats, 188,
190

2

20th Century-Fox, 223

3

3e page après le soleil, 168

5

5 sur 5: les fictions polymorphes,
169

7

7 CAJAS
(2012), 142
7th BFI Future Film festival, 136,
139

A

À BOUT DE SOUFFLE

(1960), 149
A FAREWELL TO ARMS
(1932), 22
A MAN TO REMEMBER
(1938), 72, 73, 75, 79, 85, 86, 88, 90
A myriad of charm: in
commemoration of Hung Sin
Nui, 199
A night at the cinema in 1914, 23
À NOS AMOURS
(1983), 150
A serious man, a modern world:
Buster Keaton and the cinema
of today, part 2, 135, 138
A VISION: A LIFE OF W.B. YEATS
(2013), 205
Abbas Kiarostami, 175
Africa alive, 185
Akira Kurosawa, 143
Al Pacino, 136, 139
Alain Corneau, 209
Alan Berliner, 179, 181
Alan Berliner en México.
Retrospectiva, seminario, 179
Alan Roberts Collection, 216
Albert Serra: avant-première +
rétrospective, 157
Alexander. *See* Victoria
Alexander
Alfred Hitchcock, 210
ALICE AU PAYS ROMAND
(1938), 175
ALL QUIET ON THE WESTERN FRONT
(1930), 23, 143
American Mutoscope &
Biograph Company, 37
Amiel. *See* Vincent Amiel

Amos Gitai, 165, 173
   (program), 164
   architecte de la mémoire, 163
AN EPISODE IN THE LIFE OF AN IRON
   PICKER
   (2013), 157
ANCI
   Ivrea. *See* Archivio Nazionale del
      Cinema d'Impresa (ANCI)
Andrei Tarkovsky, 173
Andy Warhol, 184
ANGST ESSEN SEELE AUF
   (1973), 184
Ante-estreias, 149, 151
Anthony Giddens, 11, 13, 32, 266
Antoni de Moragas, 189
Apichatpong Weerasethakul, 169
appropriation, 99, 110, 267
   (definition), 98
*Après l'apocalypse (histoires des
   survivants)*, 173, 174, 176
APRÈS MAI
   (2012), 184
Architecture in cinema, 211
Archivio Nazionale del Cinema
   d'Impresa (ANCI)
   (Ivrea), 253
   Ivrea, 192
ARIA
   (1987), 136
Arnoldo Foà, 195
*Around the world—Northern
   lights*, 211
Arrive at lunchtime, 203
Arturo de Córdova, 224
ASCENSEUR POUR L'ÉCHAFAUD
   (1958), 229
*Assemblé: the Royal New
   Zealand Ballet at sixty*, 217
Association of Moving Image
   Archivists
   (AMIA), 75
Asta Nielsen

   (program), 157
Atom Egoyan, 189
AUGUST: OSAGE COUNTY
   (2013), 202, 206, 210
Aula de cinema, 189
Australian Centre for the Moving
   Image
   (Melbourne), 230
Australian Cinematheque,
   Brisbane, 23, 120, 128–31, 234,
   238
AUTOTOCHT DOOR BANDOENG
   (1912/1913), 62
Avant-première VERLIEBTE FEINDE,
   176
AVIATIKEREN OG JOURNALISTENS
   HUSTRU
   (1911), 56
Avui documental, 188

B

*BAFTA masterclass:
   cinematography with Anthony
   Dod Mantle*, 136
BALADA DE UN HOMBRE COMÚN
   (2013). *See* INSIDE LLEWYN DAVIS
BALLAD OF A SOLDIER
   (1959), 221
BALLADA O SOLDATE
   (1959), 221, *See* BALLAD OF A
      SOLDIER
BARRY LYNDON
   (1975), 189
BASTARDS
   (2013). *See* LES SALAUDS
BATIK
   (1912/1913). *See* HET BATIK
BATTLESHIP POTEMKIN, 240
BE KIND REWIND
   (2008), 184
Becker. *Zie* Howard Becker
Before the war

(program series), 23
Béla Balász, 92
Benjamin Murmelstein, 209
BERNADETTE: NOTES ON A POLITICAL
  JOURNEY
  (2011), 204
Berne Convention
  (1908), 52
BETHLEHEM
  (2013), 209
BFI-NFTVA
  (London), 123, 210, 213, 233, *See*
    British Film Institute-National
    Film & Television Archive
  London, 23
BLADE RUNNER
  (1982), 174
BLOW UP
  (1966), 184
BLUE IS THE WARMEST COLOR
  (2013). *See* LA VIE D'ADÈLE
BLUE IS THE WARMEST COLOUR
  (2013), 135
BLUE JASMINE
  (2013), 142, 184, 231
Bolesław Matuszewski, 42
Bophana Centre de Ressources
  Audiovisuelles, Phnom Penh,
  119, 122, 123, 131–34
BRASILIA
  (2011), 175
BRAT
  (2013), 204
British Film Institute-National
  Film & Television Archive,
  London, 22, 134–40, 226
British M&B, 40, *See* British
  Mutoscope & Biograph
  Company
British Mutoscope & Biograph
  Company, 38
BROTHER
  (2013). *See* BRAT
Brune/blonde, 163

BUG 41, 135
BURNING BUSH
  (2013). *See* HORÍCÍ KER

C

Caligari and his sideshows:
  mental and representational
  instability, 131
Cantos de cisne, 153
Cao Guimarães, 175
CAR RIDE THROUGH BANDUNG
  (1912/1913). *See* AUTOTOCHT DOOR
    BANDOENG
CARAVAGGIO
  (1986), 136
Carlo Rambaldi, 196
  il mago, 195
Carlos Benpar i THE TRIAL: 50 anys
  de cinema, 190
CARNE TRÉMULA
  (1997), 161
Caroline Champetier, 165
  (program), 164
Carte blanche à Ruy Nogueira,
  175
Carte blanche Albert Serra, 157
CASABLANCA
  (1942/1947), 90
  (1942/1952), 90
Centenaire de la Grande Guerre
  au cinéma, 24
Centre cinématographique
  marocain, Rabat, 123, 140–41
Centre National de l'Audiovisuel
  (Dudelange), 230
Centro Sperimentale di
  Cinematografia-Cineteca
  Nazionale
  (Rome), 126
Chantal Akerman, 156
Chris Marker
  (program), 174

Christchurch modernist architecture on film, 217, 219
CHRISTIANE F. (1981), 203
Ciclo 100 años Primera Guerra Mundial, 143
Ciclo Historias compartidas: raices comunes. Mes de la herencia afroamericana, 143
Cine brasileño, 179, 181
Ciné Club, 133
Ciné samedi, 133
Cineastas en Acción, 190
Ciné-club Jean Douchet, 164
Ciné-clubs UNIL-EPFL: Ouverture cycle "Parcours de vie(s)", 175
Ciné-Concert, 170, 175
Cinema and human rights, 212
Cinema Context (website), 95
Cinéma de l'intime, 157
Cinéma de poche, 164
Cinema e psicoanalisi: le forme della violenza, 194, 196
Cinema Trevi, 192, 193
Cinemaimpresa.TV, 193, 253
Cinemateca Boliviana, La Paz, 22, 115, 118, 119, 141–44
Cinemateca Brasileira, São Paolo, 122, 144–45
Cinemateca Dominicana, Santo Domingo, 119, 123, 146–47
Cinemateca Portuguesa (Lisbon). *See* Cinemateca Portuguesa-Museu do Cinema
Cinemateca Portuguesa-Museu do Cinema, Lisbon, 27, 115, 125, 147–51, 182, 244
Cinemateca Uruguaya, Montevideo, 118, 126, 151–55, 235

Cinematek, Brussels, 22, 126, 155–59, 226
Cinémathèque de la Ville de Luxembourg, 159–61
Cinémathèque de Tanger, 230
Cinémathèque de Toulouse, 23
Cinémathèque française (Paris), 236, 264, *See* Cinémathèque française-Musée du Cinéma)
Cinémathèque française-Musée du Cinéma, Paris, 23, 115, 123, 162–66, 182, 226
Cinémathèque Québécoise, Montreal, 115, 116, 122, 123, 167–72, 182, 226, 236, 247
Cinémathèque Suisse, Lausanne, 115, 123, 172–77, 238, 244
Cines, 197
Cineteca Classic. Dalla Polonia con amore, 194
Cineteca del Comune di Bologna, 230
Cineteca Nacional de Chile (Santiago), 230
Cineteca Nacional de México, Mexico City, 177–81, 244
Cineteca Nueva Leon (Monterrey), 230
CIRCLE OF IRON (1978), 142
City Film (The Hague), 94, 96, 98, 99
CIVILIZATION (1916), 29
Claire Denis, 206
Clàssics d'ahir i de demà, 188
Claude Lanzmann, 209
Clint Eastwood, 209
COLLISION (2011), 141

COLONEL ROOSEVELT'S ROUGH
   RIDERS
   (1898), 39
Colonial film: moving images of
   the British Empire
   (website), 28
Colonial Institute
   (Amsterdam), 60, 64, 65, 69, 70,
   107, 108, 109, 114, 258
Columbia, 223
Columbia in the 1930s: recent
   restorations, 224, 225
COME AND SEE
   (1985), 221
Comèdia popular, un gènere a
   definir, 188, 191
COMMON
   (2014), 135
Concerto 2013-2014, 212, 229
Cooper. See Merian C. Cooper
COS A L'AIRE, PEUS A TERRE
   (2013), 190
Cosmopolitan Studios, 85
Could've, would've, should've,
   210, 213
Council of Europe, 227, 229
Coups de cœur des collègues, 169
Course: Man changes the world,
   211
Couté. See Pascal Couté
COWPOX VACCINATION IN THE
   VILLAGE
   (1912). See KOEPOK-INENTING IN DE
   DESA
Crane. See Diana Crane
CRUISING
   (1980), 139
cultural domain. See cultural
   domains
cultural domains, 24
curatorship, 109, 110, 114, 115,
   128, 226, 228, 245, 247, 259,
   264

(definition), 105

D

DAISIES
   (1966), 204
DALLAS BUYERS CLUB
   (2013), 202
Dalton Trumbo, 73, 85
Danis Tanovic, 157
   (program), 157
Dansa al cinema, 190
Dark city, open country: the films
   of Anthony Mann, 224
DARK GIRLS
   (2011), 143
David Balsells, 190
David Robinson, 136
Dawson Clutterbuck, 217
De La 1ère à la Cinémathèque:
   travelling, 174
DE PLATTELANDSDOKTER
   (1938), 90, See A MAN TO REMEMBER
DE TAL PADRE, TAL HIJO
   (2013). See SHOSHITE CHICHI NI-
   NARU
DEN HVIDE SLAVEHANDEL
   (1910), 55
Derek Jarman: strange magick,
   134
Derek Jarman's sketchbooks
   (lecture), 136
DES PFARRERS TÖCHTERLEIN, 47
DES TERRITOIRES À VENIR
   (2014), 165
Desmet, 55, 56, 57, 58, 263, See
   Jean Desmet
Desmond Davis, 204
Det Danske Filminstitut
   (Copenhagen), 230
Deutsches Filminstitut
   Filmmuseum, Frankfurt, 20,
   22, 115, 182–86, 244

Deutsches Filminstitut Filmmuseum,Frankfurt, 18

Dexter Fletcher, 136

Día de la Academia. See Día de la Academia: los que se fueron

Día de la Academia: los que se fueron, 179

Diana Crane, 24, 243, 244

DIARIO DE FRANCIA (2012). *See* JOURNAL DE FRANCE

Dictator's cut, 179, 181

DIE ANDERE HEIMAT-CHRONIK EINER SEHNSUCHT (2013), 184

DIE STAND DER DINGE (1982), 149

DIE STILLE VOR BACH (2007), 189

Die Utopie Film, 221, 222

Discover Arab cinema, 136, 139

Discovery Zone-Luxembourg City Film Festival, 160

Disseny, càmera, acció!, 188

DO THE RIGHT THING (1989), 153

DOG DAY AFTERNOON (1975), 139

Dominica en documental, 146, 147

Domitor, 25

Don Boyd, 136

Double happiness comes galloping in, 199

Down Memory Lane: movie theatres of the olden days, 198, 200

Drees, 101, 104, *See* Willem Drees

Dziga Vertov, 223

E

E.T., THE EXRA-TERRESTRIAL (1982), 196

EARTH (1930), 221

Easier than painting: die Filme von Andy Warhol, 186

Edie Segdwick, 184

Edison Company, 45

Edmund Hubert, 18, 19

Educar a aprendre, 189

Edward Ellis, 74

EDWARD SCISSORHANDS (1990), 154

Edwardian drama on the small screen, 23

EFG Project (2008-2011), 22

EFG1914, 18, 20, 21, 22, 182, *See* European Film Gateway 1914

EL PODER DEL JEFE (1991-1996), 147

Electro Bioscope (Middelburg), 56

ELLA (2013), 180, *See* HER

Els millors films de l'any, 188

EN COMPAGNIE D'ANTONIN ARTAUD (1994), 168

EN DIRIGEABLE SUR LES CHAMPS DE BATAILLE (1918), 23

epitext, 64, 65, 99

épitextes (definition). *See* epitext

Ernest L. Scanlon, 73

Érographie, 164

EROTIKON (1920), 149

ÉS QUAN DORMO QUE HI VEIG CLAR (1989), 191

Essor Cinématographique Française, 98

EU Film Days, 214
European Film Gateway 1914, 17
Europeana network, 17, 20
Evening course 'Heroic gestures',
   204
EVERYONE SAYS I LOVE YOU
   (1996), 149
evidentiary value, 260
   (definition), 112
expert system, 32
   definition, 13
Eye
   (Amsterdam), 18, 23, 230

F

Face à face: Gabor Szilasi
   photographie le cinéma, 168
Fairytales and fables, 129, 130,
   238
Family flicks, 224
FAREWELL HERR SCHWARZ
   (2014), 210
Fassbinder
   -Jetzt. Film und Videokunst, 183,
      186
   -Jetzt. Filmreihe, 183
Fassbinder:. *See* Rainer Werner
   Fassbinder
Feast your eyes, 204, 205
Fédération Internationale des
   Archives du Film
   (FIAF), 24, 118
FELICIA'S JOURNEY
   (1999), 189
Feng Xiaogang, 136
   spectacular China, 136
*Fernand Bélanger, cinéaste-
   monteur*, 169
*Festival internacional de
   documental de República
   Dominicana y el Caribe*, 146

FIAF, 25, *See* Fédération
   internationale des Archives du
   Film (FIAF)
*FICUNAM Retrospectiva Otar
   Iosseliani*, 179
FIG LEAVES
   (1926), 170
FilmAffinity, 143
Filmarchiv Austria
   (Vienna), 22
*Filmisches Sehen + Filmisches
   Erzählen*, 182, 183
Filmmuseum
   (Munich), 22, 23
Filmoteca Canaria, Santa Cruz
   de Tenerife – Las Palmas de
   Gran Canaria, 230
Filmoteca de Catalunya
   (Barcelona), 22, 115, 122, 123,
      186–92, 226, 235, 244, 247
Filmoteca Española
   (Madrid), 22
Fish. *See* Stanley Fish
FLAME OF MY LOVE
   (1949), 222
FLAMING CREATURES
   (1963), 221
Fondazione Centro
   Sperimentale di
   Cinematografia-Cineteca
   Nazionale, Rome, 28, 115, 123,
   192–97, 226, 233, 253
FOUR HOUSES FROM FOUR DECADES:
   CHRISTCHURCH POST-WAR
   DOMESTIC ARCHITECTURE
   (2008), 219
FOUR WEDDINGS AND A FUNERAL
   (1994), 188
Franco Zeffirelli, 143
Frank Capra, 83, 92
Frank Nugent, 72
Fratelli nel cinema, 28, 194, 196
Fred Kelemen, 212

FREE RADICALS—A HISTORY OF
    EXPERIMENTAL FILMS
    (2011), 204
Fritz Lang, 255
From the vaults, 204
functional context, 260, 267
    (definition), 110
FUNERAL OF PRESIDENT MCKINLEY
    note 61, 39
FUNNY FACE
    (1957), 135, 137
Future shorts, 190

G

GABRIEL OVER THE WHITE HOUSE
    (1933), 84
Gabriel Thibaudeau, 170
GALLIPOLI
    (1981), 143
GARDENING WITH SOUL
    (2013), 218, 219
Gareth Watkins, 217, 219
Garson Kanin, 72, 75
gatekeeper function, 113, 267
    definition, 12
gatekeepers. *See* gatekeeper
    function
    gatekeeper function, 33
gatekeeping function, 266
Gavin Hipkins, 217
Gemeentemuseum
    (The Hague), 237
Generación VHS, 153, 154
GENERALYA LINNIA
    (1929), 149
GENERATION WAR
    (2013). *See* UNSERE MÜTTER, UNSERE
    VÄTER
Genette, 71, *See* Gérard Genette
George Eastman Museum
    (Rochester, NY), 249

George Pal, l'expert truqueur,
    169
Gérard Genette, 63
Gerhalt Polt, 184
Giddens. *Zie* Anthony Giddens
GISI
    (2014), 209
Gitai. *See* Amos Gitai
GIÙ LA TESTA
    (1971), 195
Giuseppe Tornatore, 210
GOLD DIGGERS OF 1933
    (1933), 78
GONE WITH THE WIND
    (1939), 149, 150
*Goran Paskaljević, un gran
    director modest*, 188
*Grandes directores y
    Shakespeare*, 142, 143
GRAVITY
    (2013), 135, 184, 211
Green porno, 157
Gros plan sur la collection, 168,
    172
Gustavo Beck, 164
Guy L. Coté, 170
    (program), 169

H

H.M. van Randwijk, 97
HA'BRICHA
    (2013), 209
Hablemos sobre megaminería,
    153, 155
Hammond, 29, *See* Michael
    Hammond
HÄNDLER DER VIER JAHRESZEITEN
    (1972), 184
Hearst-Metrotone News, 223
HEAVEN'S GATE
    (1980), 173

Heinrich Hauser, 218
Helen M. Lynd
  note 164, 81
Henny Porten, 47
Henri Langlois, 162
Henry Hathaway, 165
  (program), 164
HER
  (2013), 179, 202, 206
HEROES FOR SALE
  (1933), 83
Heroic gestures. See Evening
  course 'Heroic gestures'
HESTER STREET
  (1975), 211, 229
HET BATIK
  (1912/1913), 62
HET LEVEN VAN DEN INLANDER IN DE
  DESA
  (1912/1913), 61
Het zilveren scherm (The silver
  screen), 158
Hitchcock 9, 213
Hollywood en blanco y negro,
  153, 154
HOLY MOTORS
  (2012), 149
Homenatge a Joan Colom, 190
Hommage Eliane Dubois, 157,
  158
Hong Kong Film Archive, 122,
  182, 197–201, 234
Horatio Alger. *See* Horatio Alger,
  Jr.
Horatio Alger, Jr., 81
HORÍCÍ KER
  (2013), 209
HOTEL DES AMÉRIQUES
  (1981), 149
Hou Yao, 200
Howard Becker, 11, 25, 26, 109

I

I WAS HAPPY HERE
  (1966), 204
ICOM. *See* International Council
  of Museums (ICOM)
*Iconography of Yasujiro Ozu
  films*, 214
Idan Barkai, 212
IDI I SMOTRI
  (1985). *See* COME AND SEE
Ieu Pannakar, 131
IF…
  (1968), 189
IFI
  & *Experimental Film Club*, 204,
    206
  (Dublin), 204, 205, 206, 230, *See*
    Irish Film Institute (Dublin)
  Family, 204
Il Cinema Ritrovato
  Bologna, 228
IL DESERTO ROSSO
  (1964), 174
IL VEDOVO
  (1959), 188
*Imágenes de Bolivia: propuesta
  de catastro, rescate y
  conservación de la memoria
  histórica del audiovisual, FASE
  1*, 141
IMDb, 17, *See* Internet Movie
  Databaxse (IMDb)
IN ENVELOPES
  (2013), 210
In memoriam Peter O'Toole, 160
In ricordo di Emidio Greco, 194,
  196
IN SEARCH OF HAYDN
  (2012), 211, 229
*In the tradition of magick: the
  cinema of Derek Jarman*
  (lecture), 136

Incontro con il cinema Sardo a Roma, 195
Inédits/Onuitgegeven, 158
inemateca Portuguesa-Museu do Cinema, 226
informational value (definition), 112
Ingrid Bergman, 241
INNER AND OUTER SPACE (1965), 184
INSIDE LLEWYN DAVIS (2013), 202, 205, 231
International Council of Museums (ICOM), 249
Internet Movie Database (IMDb), 17
interpretive community, 26 (definition), 25
INTERVISTA (1987), 168
INVASION OF THE BODY SNATCHERS (1956), 168
(In)visibile italiano: fuori dal '77, 194
Ireland on Sunday, 203
Irish Film Institute, Dublin, 115, 122, 201–7, 230, 235
Isabella Rosselini (program), 157
Italia '77: ultimo atto?, 194, 197

J

J.C. Lamster, 59, 71
J.V. Snow, 51
Jacinto Esteva Grewe, 187
Jacinto Esteva, a l'ombra de l'últim arbre, 187, 190
JACK RYAN SHADOW RECRUIT (2014), 135

Jack Smith, 221
Jack Stevenson, 161
JACQUES FAITLOVICH AND THE LOST TRIBES (2012), 209
Jameson Dublin International Film Festival (JDIFF), 203
Jarman on the Thames (lecture), 136
Jaume Cela, 189
JDIFF. *See* Jameson Dublin International Film Festival (JDIFF)
Jean Chabot – dix ans après, 169
Jean Cocteau et le cinématographe, 163
Jean Desmet, 47, 262
Jean Rouch, 223
Jenny Runacre, 136
JERUSALEM (2013), 135
Jerusalem Cinematheque. *See* Jerusalem Cinematheque-Israel Film Archive
Jerusalem Cinematheque-Israel Film Archive, 115, 125, 207–13, 226, 244, 247
Jerusalem Jewish Film Festival, 208
John Ford, 92
John L. O'Sullivan, 87
John L. Stoddard, 67
Jon Jost, 150 (program), 149
Jornada Brasileiro de cinema silencioso, 144
Jorng Nam, 132
Joseph Pitchhadze, 210 retrospective, 210
JOURNAL DE FRANCE (2012), 202, 206
JOURNEY WILLIAM I-YOGYAKARTA (1912). *See* REIS WILLEM I-DJOCJA

JUBILEE
   (1978), 136
Jules et Jim, *roman de la Nouvelle Vague*, 163
Juliane Rebentisch, 184
Julius Pinschewer, 183

K

Kenneth Branagh, 143
KIND HEARTS AND CORONETS
   (1949), 188
KING KONG
   (1933), 73
   (1976), 196
KING KONG 2
   (1986), 196
Kino mat Häerz...a mat Kaffi!, 160, 161
Kinohighlights 2013, 184, 186
KINO-KRIEGSSCHAU NO. 14
   (1914), 18
Klassiker & Raritäten: Ganz irdisch, ganz himmlisch – Christliche Orden im Spielfilm, 184
Kleber Mendonça Filho, 164
KOEPOK-INENTING IN DE DESA
   (1912), 108
Koloniaal Instituut
   (Amsterdam). *See* Colonial Institute
KOPICZINCE
   [1916], 18
Koreeda Hirokazu, 210
Kurzfilmprogramm, 183

L

L'architecture à l'écran, 174, 177
L'effeto del jazz
   (book), 126, 195

L'effetto del jazz. Lo Swing Club di Torino
   (program), 195
L'ESCAC a la Filmo, 189
L'Espai com a protagonista, 189
L'INCONNU DU LAC
   (2013), 202
L'infanzia dei generi, 195
LA BELLE ET LA BÊTE
   (1946), 163
LA CHINOISE (PORTRAITS DE PARIS)
   (1967), 209
LA ESPOSA PROMETIDA
   (2012). *See* lemale et ha'halal
LA GRANDE ILLUSION
   (1937), 157
LA PASSION DE JEANNE D'ARC
   (1928), 149
LA TARE
   (1911), 56
LA VIDA DE ADÈLE
   (2013). *See* LA VIE D'ADÈLE
LA VIE D'ADÈLE
   (2013), 231
La voce e il cinema: Arnoldo Foà attore cinematografico, 195
LADY FOR A DAY
   (1933), 83
Lamster, 69, 108, *See* J.C. Lamster
Late Night Kultkino, 184
Le Broadway musical au cinéma, des années 1960 aux années 2000, 160
LE CHANT DES ONDES: SUR LA PISTE DE MAURICE MARTINOT
   (2012), 168
LE DERNIER DES INJUSTES
   (2013), 209
LE DINER DE CONS
   (1998), 211
Le Giornate del Cinema Muto Pordenone, 228

LE GOÛT DES AUTRES
  (2000), 188
LE LÉMAN
  (1937), 175
Le robot de METROPOLIS, de Fritz
  Lang, 163
Le théâtre optique d'Emile
  Reynaud, 163
Lecture & Film—Easier than
  painting: die Filme von Andy
  Warhol, 184
LEGEND OF THE TAIRA CLAN
  (1955). See SHIN HEIKE MONOGATARI
LEMALE ET HA'HALAL
  (2012), 179
Leni Riefensthal, 221
LEON'S FLIRT
  (1913), 53, 58, See LÉONCE FLIRTE
LÉONCE FLIRTE, 47
Les avant-gardes russes et le
  sport, 174, 176
LES AVENTURES EXTRAORDINAIRES DE
  MISTER WEST
  (1924), 174
LES CLANDESTINS
  (1946), 94, 95, 96, 98, 100, 103, 104
Les essentiels, 169
LES ORIGINES DE LA CONFÉDÉRATION
  (1924), 175
LES SALAUDS
  (2013), 203
L'HOMME À LA CAMÉRA
  (1929), 174
LIFE OF MOSES
  (1909-1910), 53
LIFT TO THE SCAFFOLD
  (1958), 137, 203
  1958. See ASCENSEUR POUR
  L'ÉCHAFAUD
LIKE FATHER, LIKE SON
  (2013). See SHOSHITE CHICHI NI-
  NARU
Lino Brocka, 129
LITTLE CAESAR

  (1931), 82
LIVING ON LOVE, 73
Lola Montès, 163
LOLITA
  (1962), 174, 177
LONE STAR
  (1996), 93
Lord of the Rings, 134
  trilogy-all nighter, 135
Lost and found, 213
LOU REED'S BERLIN
  (2007), 211
Louis Malle, 206
Lux, 197

M

MACBETH
  (1971), 143
MALCOLM X
  (1992), 204, 206
MANDELA: LONG WALK TO FREEDOM
  (2013), 204
MANILA IN THE CLAWS OF LIGHT
  (1975), 129
María Muñoz, 190
MARION, ARTISTA DI CAFFÈ-
  CONCERTO
  (1920), 195
Mark Rothko, 237
Martin Loiperdinger, 183
Martin Scorsese, 158
  (program), 157
Marx Brothers, 209
Matuszewski, 43, 44, See
  Bolesław Matuszewski
MAUDITE SOIT LA GUERRE
  (1913), 23
Maurice Pialat, 150
McKinley, 38, See William
  McKinley
MCKINLEY AT HOME, CANTON, OHIO
  (1896), 37

ME AND ORSON WELLES
   (2008), 188, 235
MELANCOLIA
   (2011), 211
Mercè Coll, 189
Merian C. Cooper, 73
METROPOLIS
   (1927), 254
Michael Blum, 168
Michael Hammond, 29
*Michel Brault: la lumière du réel.
   Le directeur photo*, 169
Midnight movies at 10, 160, 161
MIELE
   (2013), 212
Mitchell & Kenyon, 45
MIVTZA HAMANIYA
   (2014), 209
Mizoguchi, 221, 222, *See*
   Mizoguchi Kenji
Mizoguchi Kenji, 221
   (program), 221
Morning matinee, 199
*Mostra Cinema e direitos
   humanos na América do Sul*,
   144
Mostra Mundo Árabe de Cinema,
   145
Moviola's, 22
MR. AND MRS. BRIDGE
   (1990), 154
MR. DEEDS GOES TO TOWN
   (1936), 83
MR. NOBODY
   (2009), 176
MR. SMITH GOES TO WASHINGTON
   (1939), 83
Museo del Cine Pablo Ducrós
   Hicken
   (Buenos Aires), 255
Museum night fever, 158
Museum of Modern Art-Film
   Department

(New York), 22
My pet Valentine, 217

N

NAPOLÉON VU PAR ABEL GANCE
   (1927), 254
National Film and Sound
   Archive
   (Canberra), 230
National Film Center
   (Tokyo). *See* National Film Center
   at the National Museum for
   Modern Art
National Film Center at the
   National Museum for Modern
   Art, Tokyo, 122, 182, 213–15,
   223, 226
National Film Preservation
   Board, 118
NATIVE VILLAGE LIFE
   (1912/1913), 62, *See* HET LEVEN VAN
   DEN INLANDER IN DE DESA
NEBRASKA
   (2013), 135
NEWS FROM HOME
   (1976), 156, 158
*NFC's newly acquired collection
   from major film studios. See*
   vol. 7: NFC's newly acquired
   collection from major film
   studios
Ngā Taonga Sound & Vision,
   Wellington/Auckland/Christc
   hurch, 123, 124, 215–19, 247
NIGHT OF THE HUNTER
   (1955), 135, 137
NIGHT OF THE IGUANA
   (1964), 174
Nihon Eiga. See Nihon Eiga: the
   history of Japanese filnm.
   From the NFC non-film
   collection

Nihon Eiga: the history of Japanese film. From the NFC non-film collection, 214

Norodom Sihanouk, 133

NOTHING BUT A MAN
   (1964), 93

NYMPH()MANIAC
   (2013). *See* NYMPH()MANIAC,
      VOLUME I & VOLUME II

NYMPH()MANIAC, VOLUME I &
   VOLUME II
   (2013), 203, 204

O

ÖFM
   (Vienna). *See* Österreichisches
      Filmmuseum

OKRAINA
   (1933), 23

Omaggio ad Ashgar Farhadi,
   193, 196

OMAR
   (2013), 210

On the eve of war: around the world in 80 films, 23

ONE FROM THE HEART
   (1981), 154

ONE MAN'S JOURNEY, 73

ONLY LOVERS LEFT ALIVE
   (2013), 135, 203, 205

OPERATION SUNFLOWER
   (2014). *See* MIVTZA HAMANIYA

Orson Welles, 190, 191
   (program), 157, 158

Orson Welles inèdit, 188

Orthodox—a look from within, 211

Österreichisches Filmmuseum,
   Vienna, 23, 219–23, 233, 244

OTTO E MEZZO
   (1963), 149

OUR DAILY BREAD

   (1934), 80

Out of the archive: recent work from MIAS, 223

OUT OF THE FURNACE
   (2013), 202, 210, 212

"Out of the mouth of babes and sucklings hast thou ordained", 210

Outfest/UCLA Legacy Project, 224

P

PAINTERS PAINTING—THE NEW YORK
   ART SCENE: 1940-1970
   (1973), 184

PAISÀ
   (1946/1948), 104

Palace Theatre, 40, *See* Palace
   Theatre of Varieties (London)

Palace Theatre of Varieties
   (London), 38

PARADISE: LOVE
   (2012). *See* PARADIES: LIEBE

PARAÍSO: AMOR
   (2012). *See* PARADIES: LIEBE

paratext, 65, 69
   (in film shows), 67, 71

paratexts
   (definition). *See* patatext

Parisien
   (theater), 47, 48, 54, 57, 58, 263

Part of the Met: live in HD 2013-2014, 211

Pascal Couté, 91

PASSION PLAY. *See* Passion Play
   screenings

Passion Play film. *See* Passion
   Play screenings

Passion Play screenings, 50

PASSPORT TO PIMLICO
   (1949), 188

Pathé Frères, 60, 63, 72, 111

PATHS OF GLORY

(1957), 22, 143, 157, 229
Patricio Guzmán, 223
Pedro Almodóvar, 160
*Pedro Almodóvar: rétrospective à
l'aube de son 65e anniversaire,*
160
Pep Ramis, 190
Per amor a l'art, 189
Pere Portabella, 189
peripheral cultural domain. *See*
cultural domains
peritext, 64
(in magic lantern shows), 65, 66
péritextes
(definition). *See* peritext
Pet, 217, 218
Peter Greenaway, 143
Peter Kubelka, 221
Peter O'Toole, 160
Philippe Vandendriessche, 165
Philippe-Alain Michaud, 218
PHILOMENA
(2013), 135, 211
PICNIC AT HANGING ROCK
(1975), 209
PINA
(2011), 211
PINK FLAMINGOS
(1972), 204
*Pionniers de l'animation
américaine,* 168, 172
Pip Chodorov, 204
PIXOTE
(1981), 210
PLATOON
(1986), 154
PLAY MISTY FOR ME
(1971), 209
Pollywood, 217
Portraits-plans-fixes, 175
*Pour une histoire permanente du
cinéma: 1964,* 174
POWWOW HIGHWAY

(1989), 93
PRESENT CONTINUOUS
(2012), 210
PRESIDENT MCKINLEY AND HIS
SECRETARY DISCUSSING TERMS OF
PEACE (IN THE GARDEN OF HIS
VILLA IN CANTON)
(1899). *See* MCKINLEY AT HOME,
CANTON, OHIO (1896)
Preview club 2013-2014, 211
Prontos, listas, YA!, 153
provenance
(definition), 112

Q

QUAI DES BRUMES
(1938), 174
*Queer pagan punk: Derek
Jarman part 1: Jarman and the
occult,* 136, 138

R

R. W. Paul, 43
Radharc collection, 203
RAFTER ROMANCE, 73
Rainer Werner Fassbinder, 183
RAN
(1985), 143
Rangahaua, 217, 218
reconstruction
(definition), 252
Reel Art, 205
reflexivity, 266, 267
(definition), 33
REIS WILLEM I-DJOCJA
(1912), 70
Remix, 158
Rencontre avec Sylvie Laliberté,
170
Reposiciones, 153

Republic, 223
restoration
  (definition), 252
Restored treasures, 198, 199, 201
Retrospectiva Jacinto Esteva, 188
Rétrospective Chris Marker, 238
Richard Linklater, 188
RICHARD PRYOR IN CONCERT
  (1979), 209
Richard Slotkin, 76
Rithy Panh, 131
RKO, 72, 73
Robert Drew, 241
Robert Morin, 170
*Robert Morin: comme d'autres
  sont des gars de char*, 169
Robert S. Lynd
  note 164, 81
Roberto Rossellini, 241
Roland Lethem, 164
ROMA, CITTÀ APERTA
  (1945), 103
Roman Polanski, 143
ROOM SERVICE
  (1938), 209
Rosa Gutiérrez, 189
ROSE O'SALEM-TOWN
  (1910), 55
Ruy Nogueira, 177

S

SabuCat, 223
SALUTE TO THE RED ARMY
  (1943), 221
*Same same (mais différent):
  lieux de la mémoire
  thailandaise*, 169, 170
SARA
  (2013), 141
Sascha Film, 18
SCAGL

(Société cinématographique des
  auteurs et gens de lettres), 53
SCARFACE
  (1932), 82
  (1983), 207
SCREEN TEST #11
  (1964-1966), 184
secondary provenance
  (definition), 113
*Secrets et illusions–la magie des
  effets spéciaux*, 168, 169
*Selected films printed by
  Technicolor I. B. process from
  the National Film Center
  Collection*, 214
*Seminar 'Digital restoration
  strategies of China Film
  Archive'*, 200
Seminar Hou Yao and his films,
  199
Sergio Leone, 195
*Sergio Leone. Il cinema come
  favola politica*, 195
Sex&drugs&rock&roll, 203, 207
Shochiku, 215
SKIRT DANCE BY ANNABELLE
  (1896), 40, 41, 49
Slotkin, 87, *See* Richard Slotkin
SLUMDOG MILLIONAIRE
  (2008), 211
Sophie Kennedy-Clark, 204
SOSHITE CHICHI NI NARU
  (2013), 210
SOUL IN THE SEA
  (2013), 218, 219
SPARTACUS
  (1960), 177
Stacey Martin, 204
STALKER
  (1979), 173
STALKER et la Zone, 173
Stanley Fish, 25
Stanley Kubrick, 177

Stellan Skarsgård, 204
Stop making sense—Rock'n roll at the Cinematheque, 211
Story-board de cinéma, 163
STRANGER BY THE LAKE
  (2013). *See* L'INCONNU DU LAC
STREET ANGEL
  (1928), 185
Stummfilmmatinee, 185
SUKARYOT
  (2013), 210
Sumario, 179, 181
Suzanne Grandais, 47
SWEET CHARITY
  (1969), 149
SWEETS
  (2013), 210, 212, *See* SUKARYOT
Sylvie Laliberté, 169

T

Tanaka Kinuyo, 222
  (program), 221
TCM, 75, *See* Turner Classic Movies
TEENAGE
  (2014), 135
TEUFELSAUGE
  (1914), 57
THE ACT OF KILLING
  (2012), 210
THE AGONY AND THE ECSTASY
  (1964), 189
THE AVIATOR AND THE JOURNALIST'S WIFE
  (1911), 56, *See* AVIATIKEREN OG JOURNALISTENS HUSTRU
THE BEST OFFER
  (2013), 210
THE BIRTH OF A NATION
  (1915), 153
The centenary of The little tramp, 136

THE CONNECTION
  (1962), 203
The Critical Take, 206
The critics' society, 211
THE CURSED
  (2014), 209
THE DAM (O), 217, 218
THE DEFECT
  (1911), 56, *See* LA TARE
The Derek Jarman archive
  (lecture), 136
THE DEVIL WEARS PRADA
  (2006), 138
THE DEVIL'S EYE
  (1914). *See* TEUFELSAUGE
THE DEVIL'S POOLS: MADNESS, MELANCHOLIA AND THE ARTIST
  (2014), 205
THE ESCAPE
  (2013), 212, *See* HA'BRICHA
THE FOUNTAINHEAD
  (1949), 175
THE FRENCH CONNECTION
  (1971), 174
THE GANGSTER SQUAD
  (2013), 93
THE GENERAL
  (1926), 135, 229, 234
THE GHOST AND MRS. MUIR
  (1947), 149
THE GODFATHER PART II
  (1974), 203, 234
THE GOLDEN BOWL
  (2000), 154
The good, the bad, and the ugly, 212
THE GRAND BUDAPEST HOTEL
  (2014), 135
The Great War 1: 100 years already, 157
THE HELP
  (2011), 143
The Hitchcock 9, 210

THE HOBBIT: THE DESOLATION OF
  SMAUG
  (2013), 142
THE LAST OF THE UNJUST
  (2013). *See* LE DERNIER DES INJUSTES
THE LIFE AND DEATH OF COLONEL
  BLIMP
  (1943), 221
*The little known Japanese
  cinema*, 213
THE LOVING STORY
  (2011), 143
THE MAN WHO SHOT LIBERTY
  VALENCE
  (1962), 189
THE MAN WITH THE GOLDEN ARM
  (1955), 203
THE MANUSCRIPT FOUND IN
  SARAGOSSA
  (1964), 174
THE PASTOR'S DAUGHTER
  (1913), 47, 53, *See* DES PFARRERS
    TÖCHTERLEIN
THE PICTURE OF DORIAN GRAY
  (1945), 189
THE PUBLIC ENEMY
  (1931), 82
THE REMAINS OF THE DAY
  (1993), 154
THE RETURN OF THE PINK PANTHER
  (1975), 204
THE ROBE
  (1953), 149
THE SECRET LIFE OF WALTER MITTY
  (2013), 142
THE STORY OF THE LAST
  CHRYSANTHEMUM
  (1939), 222
THE TEMPEST
  (1979), 136
THE THIN RED LINE
  (1998), 221
THE TRIAL
  (1962), 190

THE WILD BUNCH
  (1969), 149
THE WIND
  (1928), 170
THE WOMAN IN THE DUNES
  (1964), 174
*This strange passion: Arturo de
  Córdova*, 224, 238
Thomas H. Ince, 29
Toni Bertorelli, 126, 195
TOO MUCH JOHNSON
  (1938), 188
*"Tourne au son!": Evolutions et
  révolutions de la prise de son
  au cinema*, 165
TOUS LES MATINS DU MONDE
  (1991), 209, 212
Toyah Willcox, 136
*Transcending space and time:
  early cinematic experience of
  Hong Kong*, 198, 199, 200
Trasnoches, 126, 153
Trésors des archives, 175, 177
Tribute to Fred Kelemen, 210
TRIUMPH DES WILLENS
  (1935), 221
TROIS JOURNÉES D'AOÛT 1914
  (2013), 22, 157
Trumbo. *See* Dalton Trumbo
*Turbulence: the ocean as
  cinematic space*, 218
Turner Classic Movies, 73
TURUMBA
  (1981), 189

U

UCLA festival of preservation,
  225
UCLA Film & Television Archive,
  Los Angeles, 115, 122, 223–25,
  238

Ufa, 255
UGLY BETTY
   (2006), 138
ULEE'S GOLD
   (1997), 93
Uli Marchsteiner, 189
*Un norteamericano en Londres:
   James Ivory*, 152, 154
UND ÄKTSCHN!
   (2014), 184
Under the radar, 211
Une affiche de MON ONCLE, *par
   Pierre Étaix*, 163
Université populaire du cinéma,
   160
UNSERE MÜTTER, UNSERE VÄTER
   (2013), 209
UP IN SMOKE
   (1978), 203

V

Van Randwijk, 100, 102, 104, *See*
   H.M. van Randwijk
Verão de clássicos, 144, 145
VERDUN
   VISIONS D'HISTOIRE
   (1928), 23
VERLIEBTE FEINDE
   (2013), 176
Victoria Alexander, 120, 265
Vincent Amiel, 91
Vitagraph, 53
*Voir-revoir le cinéma
   d'aujourd'hui 2013-2014*, 164
*vol.7: NFC's newly acquired
   collection from major film
   studios*, 214
VOUS N'AVEZ ENCORE RIEN VU
   (2012), 211

W

Wacky film club, 211
WAGA KOI WA MOENU
   (1949). *See* FLAME OF MY LOVE
WALKING WITH DINOSAURS
   (2013), 142
Walter Ruttmann, 183
Walter Wanger, 85
Warner Bros., 78, 223
Was Ist Film, 221
*Was tut sich – im deutschen
   Film?*, 183, 186
   Gerhard Polt, 184
Welles. *See* Orson Welles
WESTFRONT 1918: VIER VON DER
   INFANTERIE
   (1930), 23
*What time is it there? Taiwan as
   crossroads*, 224
WHERE IS THE FRIEND'S HOME?
   (1987), 175
WHITE SLAVERY
   (1910). *See* DEN HVIDE
   SLAVENHANDEL
Wikipedia, 17, 265
WILD BOYS OF THE ROAD
   (1933), 84
Wild strawberries, 204
Willem Drees, 97
William Hearst, 85
William Klein, 203
   (program), 203
William McKinley, 37
WILLIAM MCKINLEY, AT HOME,
   CANTON, OHIO, U.S.A.
   (1896). *See* McKinley at home,
   Canton, Ohio (1896)
WINDJAMMER UND JANMAATEN. DIE
   LETZTE SEGELSCHIFFE
   (1930), 218
WINTER PIZZA
   [2013], 204

WINTER'S BONE
(2010), 93, 168, 171
World Cinema Foundation, 129,
179, 181
*World cinema project. Historias
olvidadas por el cine*, 179, 181
Wunderkammer, 156

Y

Yasujiro Ozu, 215
YI YI
(2000), 149
YOU AIN'T SEEN NOTHIN' YET
(2012). *See* vous n'avez encore
rien vu

YOU CAN'T TAKE IT WITH YOU
(1938), 83
YouTube, 17, 254
YVY MARAEY-TIERRA SIN MAL
(2013), 142

Z

ZANGIKU MONOGATARI
(1939). *See* THE STORY OF THE LAST
CHRYSANTHEMUM
ZEMLJA
(1930). *See* EARTH
Zooms, 163, 165

www.ingramcontent.com/pod-product-compliance
Lightning Source LLC
Chambersburg PA
CBHW070555270326
41926CB00013B/2327